Emot
Intelli

6 Books in 1:

Emotional intelligence for
Leadership + Dark
Psychology Secrets + Anger
Management + Empath
Healing + Memory
Improvement + Narcissist
Nightmare

By: Adam Goleman

1

Disclaimer Notice.

Please note the information contained within this document is for educational and entertainment purposes only. This book not intended to be a substitute for medical advice. Please consult your health care provider for medical advice and treatment.

Table of Contents

Emotional Intelligence for Leadership

A Practical Guide to Growing Up Your Ability to Leading Others and Manage People

By: Adam Goleman

INTRODUCTION

Over the past ten years there has been an enormous increase in the confirmation that emotional intelligence is an imperative issue in management. Several studies have revealed a constructive association between emotionally intelligent leadership and worker happiness, preservation, and presentation. As organizations become more conscious of this, they are looking for ways to employ and endorse from within people that are sturdy in emotional intelligence. It has been usually seen that great leaders stir us. They set fire to our fervor and inspire the best in us. When we attempt to make clear why they are so effectual, we speak of policy, dream, or influential ideas. But the truth is much more original: Great management works from side to side the emotions. No issue what leaders set out to do, whether it's creating about the approach or mobilizing teams to feat their achievement depends on how they do it. Even if they get the whole thing else just right, if leaders fail in this primitive task of motivating emotions in the right direction, naught they do will work as well as it might or be supposed to.

How to find a leader in you

Here are some reasons that are central for emotionally intelligent leadership:

1. Self-awareness for Success

When influential people are grounded, they are able to be well-organized and purposeful in staying on task, and being adjusted to those around them.

Leaders who have the ability to manage their mind and emotion help to direct those around them to enlarge their own self-knowledge and achievement. Learning to be conscious of yourself isn't always simple, but mastering this ability can help you turn out to be a much more effective leader.

A.   Have Open Mind

When you have the aptitude to control your own emotional world, you can be familiar with the emotions of others. To be a victorious leader, you have to be inquisitive about new people and all they have to offer. This shows that you can be a team player, and don't require being No. 1. The more open you are to others, the more artistic you become.

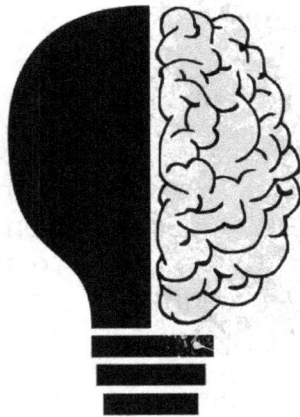

B.   Be mindful of your weaknesses

Self-aware persons know their own emotions and weaknesses and are able to work from that space.

Being aware of this means that you know when to arrive at out for aid, and when you are good on your own.

C.   Keep yourself Focused

Making relations with those around you is very significant as a leader. But you cannot make those relations if you are unfocused. Coach yourself to focus for periods of time without getting sucked into societal issues, emails and other little distractions.

D.   Create boundaries

A leader desires to have strong restrictions in place. Be temperate toward others, but say no when you require saying no. Be solemn about your job and your dreams, and keep your limits firmly to uphold the honesty of your goals and the effort you put into them.

E.   Know your emotional triggers

Self-aware persons are enough talented at recognizing their emotions as they are happening. Don't suppress your emotions or refute their causes; instead, be clever to twist and flex with them, and completely process them before communicating with others.

F.   Embrace your intuition

Triumphant people belief their gut instinct and take risks linked with them. Your instinct is based on the endurance of the fittest and the need to be successful. They tell us what to do next. Learn to trust these and make use of them.

G.   Practice Daily self-discipline

Excellent leaders are inclined to be disciplined at work and in each area of their life. It is a personality trait that provides them with the lasting focus essential for strong management.

But true leaders can be found everywhere in society, and many of them do not have a big title, a fancy office or any kind of obvious throne; they are everyday people who even sometimes have had to take up leadership positions; without being told to be one. Within organizations today, many employees get assigned more and more tasks and responsibilities without that big promotion to go with it.

This book has been written for these kinds of leaders. Every chapter is designed with the intention of guiding those of you who need leadership skills at work, who have to redefine your own roles and don't know how to get started. It is made for those encountering ever-changing expectations and having to learn how to adapt to them on your own. It is for those who have to lead now; having no clear compass or a lifetime of experience to draw from.

With that said, just about anybody would still benefit from this book because contrary to popular belief, leadership does not only belong in the workplace but is useful almost anywhere else, be it in your personal life, at home or in your locality. It doesn't matter if you're a CEO or a stay-at-home mom; leadership is a skill you should know about and learn how to use.

Chapter 1: The Benefits of Emotional Intelligence

Emotional intelligence has been pinpointed as a key leadership trait. While it is not EQ that is considered as the basis for recognition or promotion in most business organizations, it is actually a critical component in exemplary performance. It is actually high EQ that kicks up the technical skills and allows executives to think of more creative solutions. Assuming that you and the other executives have the same set of technical skills and knowledge, you can sprint ahead of the pack when you have high emotional intelligence. Various studies have linked high emotional intelligence to the financial success of many companies around the world. Similarly, case studies have illustrated the EI-leadership connection at work in a number of organizations. Even the US Air Force has been listed as an example of how using EI diagnostics in its recruitment process has increased its annual savings and considerably improved its success rate. Sales organizations had also observed significant increases in their annual performance figures when they adopted an EI-focused approach. Sanofi and L'Oreal are just two of the global brands that have included emotional competencies as part of their selection criteria. These two companies reported that sales agents who had emotional intelligence skills consistently outsold those who did not have the same skills. The value of high emotional intelligence is also seen both in jobs of medium complexity and in executive positions. EI has been proven to improve productivity and retention rates. In fact, one study cited that the main reasons for executive resignations are mostly due to issues that have to do with the lack of certain EI skills.

Top-level executives with high EI were found to stay in the position longer, usually even exceeding their annual targets.

Teamwork

A leader impacts the performance of the group and individual participants through his or her actions. Why is control needed? A group works together best when everybody is heading in the same course. If a plan is to be correctly carried out, someone must lead the effort, this comes down to you the leader.

The workplace is the best situation where the importance of EQ over IQ is most apparent. EQ is a trait that many companies will look for in a potential leader first, not the IQ. This is because a leader's primary job would be to **lead** the people around them. They need to inspire others, get their teams working well together in a cohesive and unified manner, and manage conflict when it arises. All of these skills require the leader to gauge the emotions and read people around them. Having high EQ is what helps leaders distinguish and identify what an employee's strengths and weaknesses are, not IQ.

Having high EQ is what will enable leaders to get along well with diverse groups of individuals, not IQ. To possess great social and communication skills to help you excel in business and with the clients, you need a high EQ, not IQ.

Leadership Skill

Working on developing your EQ is something that is going to benefit you in the long run. Not only does it improve your leadership skills, but it enhances your ability to negotiate, manage disagreements, collaborate effectively and even be an agent of positive change in any setting that you find yourself in. Humans are social creatures, and much of our success is highly dependent on how well we can interact with others, even though we may not give much thought to it. According to Goleman, EQ is not that much different from IQ. The quality that distinguishes these two traits is that EQ is focused on **how smart** you are in the way that you interact with your own emotions and with other people. It is not merely about interacting with the people around you, but **how effectively** you interact with them that sets you apart from someone with low EQ. Although both EQ and IQ are equally important traits and ideally should be used to maximize your strengths, EQ is without a doubt the trait that is much more important to succeed both in life and the workplace. So much of success depends on how well you manage the challenges that you are faced with, and without being aware of your emotions and the emotions of others, without regulating the way that you respond with high EQ, without effective social skills, without the determination and motivation, and empathy, you will always find yourself falling short no matter how hard you may try.

Conversation Skills

There are many who have studied language, communication, and listening to fully express the importance and the necessity of listening. The more we come to understand how humans communicate and how ideas are spread, the more important listening becomes to us. Listening is more than an action. It's a cognitive process of dissecting, digesting, comprehending, and establishing thoughts and events as valid or invalid in our lives. Only by listening can our lives open up to newer and more wonderful possibilities than we originally had. In truth, listening is the core of all communication. So you've learned why listening in communication is important, some steps to start listening better, and how it can improve your relationships and your career, so start employing what you've learned. Hopefully you already have. You'll be able to see the changes in your relationships because people will treat you differently when you listen more than you speak. They will feel like they're in the presence of someone smart, wise, and sage. They will seek your opinions, your thoughts, your responses, and your viewpoints on matters. Listening is how you grow in wisdom and intelligence and you'll be surprised at your own effects on your life. Now, before we part ways, here are some last tips. First of all, take baby steps. Sure, some people are going to drone on about things that feel meaningless and in the end, it probably is. But remember that everyone shares something for a reason. By listening, you can probably discern the reason for their discontent or interest in what happened. Secondly, be aware of how much you're speaking or where your mind is. Remember that distractions are the enemy and that sometimes we're our own worst enemies. If you feel like you're dominating the conversation, step back and listen to them. Start asking them questions to encourage them to talk more.

Remember that the way to keep you from talking too much is to ask more questions. People love answering them and sharing them. Thirdly, unplug. Seriously, if you ask anyone who has done it and they'll tell you how vastly their life has increased and grown in richer quality. It's not a conspiracy. You'll feel happier, find focusing easier, and realize that you have more time to invest in others if you unplug. Take some baby steps or go full-on cold turkey; whatever you need to do, but cut back in some form. It will make your conversations deeper, richer, and listening will be so much easier.

Human Emotions

Every basic emotion has three major parts. The first one is a subjective component. It refers to how you are subjectively experiencing the feeling in question. The second part is the physiological component, which details how your body reacts to every emotion. Finally, there is the expressive component, which refers to how you behave in response to the emotion in question. Each individual feeling has a different trajectory, and there are hundreds of emotions that can make you react and act in a different way. Whereas anger can cause you to lash out at a co-worker or employee, anxiety can cause you to make wrong decisions or panic. That is not something you want to do as a leader. At their core, however, every human reaction stems from eight basic emotions. They are like primary colors building into all those other shades. Everything starts with these feelings.

1. **Anticipation**
From the get-go, you have anticipation. It is generally a positively geared emotion that entails looking forward to a specific action or thing.

Anticipation is everywhere. You can see it, for instance, when you are in the grocery line to buy yourself chocolate milk. You anticipate owning and drinking that bottle of chocolate milk. At the same time, when you sit in an exam hall, worried about the questions, you tend to look forward to the questions that you will face. This, in turn, means that the emotion can be both positive and negative, although it does tend to tilt towards the former, especially when the individual is healthy and neutral.

What do we need to know about anticipation as a leader?

Well, for one, anticipation, if used right, can lay out a road map of exactly how you need to behave in order to get people to react the way you want them to. Remember, anticipation is not about reaction; it is a precursor to a reaction. It is similar to a crystal ball that shows you a bunch of possible actions that lead to specific reactions, and all you need to do is pick the reaction you want and act accordingly.

2. Fear

Fear is a negatively charged emotion that is often considered as one of the most powerful emotional forces there is. Not only does it behave in a more controlling and overwhelming manner, but the emotion is also inherently reactive. It is different from anticipation in which the emotion is easier to guide and control.

What do we need to know about fear as a leader?

You need to keep in mind that fear is more than just an emotion. It is almost like a disease that impacts the present and leads you to change how you react in the future. Because this emotion induces panic, it also takes away your ability to think clearly.

Meaning, once you feel fear, it is hard to get away from it. It does not simply exist; it breeds hatred, envy or both. Thus, any good leader must know how to be fearless in the face of everything.

3. Disgust

Another common negatively charged emotion that we encounter more often than we realize is disgust. Referring to a tendency to reject or feel revulsion towards something that one considers distasteful or offensive, disgust tends to influence your morals and all those prejudices that you may have not known you have. It starts from racial prejudices to sexual preferences, which seem to arise inexplicably even though there is no scientific reasoning to assume that one is better than the other. As a matter of fact, these moral judgments that we regularly make tend to be among the main causes behind our snap moral judgments. Back in prehistoric times, these generally stemmed from lack of knowledge and kept people from eating poisonous berries and food, making disgust an essential safety tool. However, it became redundant in modern times, considering the emotion not only reflects on food and safety anymore but also on thoughts, morals, and beliefs.

4. Joy

Coming back to positive emotions, joy is commonly used to refer to how human beings feel when there are positive things happening around them and they sense an impending gain, be it monetary or otherwise. Joy itself is a very buoyant emotion. It is usually triggered by success or some sort of happy event, such as the birth of a child. It is the equivalent of a golden star from our limbic system, telling us that we are doing all the right things. Joy can also be a form of encouragement so that we continue to do everything.

5. Sadness

Joy is often directly contrasted with the emotion called sadness, which is the most known negative feeling. While the former stems from a sensation of gain, the latter is closely related to the concept of loss, be it material (when you lose your favorite necklace), emotional (a bad breakup or a loss of a loved one), social (loss of fame or social accolades), or even professional (a demotion or a pay cut). The resulting feeling that tends to overpower the mind is a deep sorrow that connects with the need to seek refuge and comfort, as well as protection of the mind and soul from the loss in question. Generally, sadness acts as a base or supplementary emotion for many other common feelings that we deal with, particularly disappointment, pity, and anger.

6. Anger

Another extremely strong negative emotion is anger. Although it is considered as a secondary feeling, recent studies have shown that the feeling of anger is more dominant than we realize.[3] The emotion tends to arise from a sense of urgency, generally directed at some form of action or injustice that the individual in question believes requires rectification. Anger indicates that the immediate reaction to a situation is the need for some change and can manifest in many ways, starting from irritation to indignation or even, in extreme cases, rage, or fury. A typical misconception regarding anger is that violent outbursts, which are simply known as 'venting,' are good for the individual and a healthy way to rid oneself of rage or anger. In reality, venting is like putting a bandage on the emotional condition; it does nothing to solve the problem. The best way to approach anger is with logic. Figure out what causes it and why, how this emotion can be dealt with, etc.

7. **Surprise**

This brings us to the feeling of surprise, which is a sense of amazement or wonder that develops or arises from a sudden or unexpected occurrence. Surprise can be both negatively and positively charged. The former can come from the expectation of something that we have projected to take place but still has not, while the latter can stem from a positive circumstance that we have not even anticipated happening. Interestingly, 'surprise' is one of the most important emotions as well, regardless of whether it is positive or negative. The reason is that surprise brings in dopamine and acts as a shot of stimulus to the human mind. Aside from giving our brains an energy boost, it also helps us focus.

8. **Trust**

The final primary emotion we deal with another positive emotion, which is known as trust. It refers to your ability to rely on another person or the confidence to depend on someone else or an institution outside of oneself with any sort of positive expectation. Here's the thing, though: we know that trust is a feeling, but is it really an emotion, too?

Well, as it turns out, yes! Trust is not just an emotion; it is also an emotional feeder that acts as a base for other emotions, such as interest or rage. Most secondary emotions stem from the existence of trust itself.

Chapter 2: Leadership

A certain paradox exists where a person can be the smartest person in the room and yet still manage to be the dumbest as well. Yes, this sounds like a contradiction, and to answer that prodding question in your gut, yes, it is possible. The real question, however, is how? How can a person be smart and yet dumb at the same time? This dichotomy comes into play when a person possesses a high or significantly admirable IQ but unfortunately possesses a rather low EQ. When this is the case, it really doesn't matter if you're a phenomenally intellectual leader because with a low EQ. You may not be phenomenal or a leader for long.

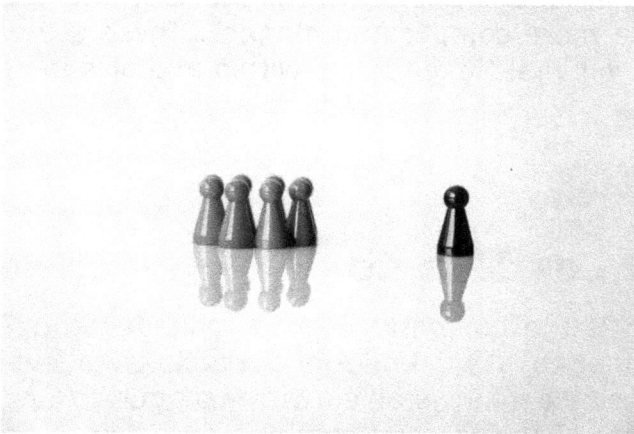

EQ means emotional quotient, mostly referred to as emotional intelligence, which we have been discussing all along in this book. Many people will argue that a high IQ (intelligence quotient) is more favorable to a person especially in leadership, but this belief or notion only holds water for a little while.

In the long run, studies and meticulous observations have revealed that a person possessing a high IQ without a high EQ to match will eventually burn out. Your ability to manage your emotions regardless of the situation, problem, or challenge defines who a true leader is. Humans are critical beings who have been conditioned to be superior since the dawn of time. This superiority emanates from beliefs theorized and to an extent proven that we function on a more complex level than any other animal. Now, this complex functionality comes at a price as it is both a blessing and a burden. Being complex beings, we are faced daily with the task of processing complex thoughts, analyzing complex behavioral patterns, and so on. The kinds of emotions we want to focus on are not just emotions of love or hate—no, these are basic human emotions at the very least. What we want to talk about is emotions cut out from the aforementioned but exist in a more complicated manner. These are emotions a leader will first have to deal within and also in others.

What Leaders do

Planning is the hallmark of good management. Planning is essential to avoid knee-jerk reactions to events and situations. Planning enables the manager to understand the nature of the job and communicate that to the team, and have a forward vision of the project. Here are some important elements of planning that a good manager must ensure.

Goal-setting.

The manager must set a clear goal for which the planning exercise is being done. There may be more than one goal ahead, but it better to plan one goal at a time, so as not to confuse goals and staff assigned to them. These may be termed "short-term" goals and "long-term goals." Short-term goals are generally those that have to be implemented in a couple of months, while long-term goals are those that have later deadlines.

Deadlines.

Set clear deadlines for each goal. The deadline setting must take into account whether the deadline is realistic or not. That is, whether the goal can be achieved within the deadline. The assessment of a deadline as realistic and achievable is based on many factors; such as timely availability of raw materials, weather conditions of rain or snow, uninterrupted power supply, holiday seasons, and so on. If a deadline is not realistic, corrective measures need to follow. Either more staff have to be assigned to the job, or the client has to be informed that a modification in the deadline is required. Staff is generally trained to work under pressure, but it is unfair to expect them to meet sudden deadlines on a regular basis. Such a situation shows up the manager in poor light; it shows that the manager is not doing his own homework in goal-setting with his superiors.

Break up the goal.

Discussing a goal at the macro level sounds daunting to everyone. An announcement in the month of June for releasing a film in December is likely to shoot up everyone's blood pressure. But the same goal broken up into smaller goals, with fortnightly or monthly deadlines, makes everyone relax. The macro announcement is likely to be met with cynicism, even fear; but the second one breaking up the main goal into smaller targets, infuses enthusiasm among the staff for the project.

Announcement of a big goal causes no one to own it; but planning for smaller goals allows the staff assigned to that goal to take ownership of it.

Resource allocation.

Good planning takes into consideration who is going to do what, and how. This involves the allocation of knowhow, labor, and equipment. For a particular goal, it may happen that the existing staff in the section may not be fully competent to handle the job; in this case the manager has to requisition suitable staff from another section, from outside, or even outsource that particular job. Whatever it is, the idea is that the right people for the job must be allocated to the job. Similarly with physical resources. Good planning includes making a list of all the equipment and accessories required to execute the project; it often happens that midway through the project, resources dry up, and everyone sits around twiddling their thumb until the resources become available again. This is a most undesirable situation for the company since it results in unnecessary cost escalation. This situation is often observed in public works, where a project comes to an abrupt end due to the sudden halt of resources.

Anticipate bottlenecks.

A mark of good management is anticipating bottlenecks and making adequate provisions for their eventuality, rather than trying to remove them as and when they occur. No project runs like clockwork; it will always experience bottlenecks. A good manager, through dint of his own experience, and that of his staff, will be able to anticipate many of these, and make suitable provisions. However, despite your best efforts at anticipating bottlenecks, there will be some that no one could have anticipated, such as a cyclone or a fire in the warehouse.

34

Leadership CheckList

What separates the two are the trust and respect and esteem of the team for the leader. Here are the actions one needs to display to earn the trust of a team:

1. Lead by example

You cannot request someone to do something that you wouldn't or couldn't do yourself. For example, if you were being taught a programming language by a tutor you knew full well could not programme, would you learn from them or even respect them.

2. Transparency

Transparency builds trust.

True leaders are honest and direct. They communicate all the time. Minimal information creates assumptions that are usually wrong. This can disrupt a team's motivation and their output. Remedy this by over-communicating, this then leads to transparency. This is especially critical in times of reorganization or layoffs. Always be transparent. Every now and then, however, there are situations outside your control that might come into force. In this case your team will understand, as long as you display to them that you keep your promises consistently. This will carry you all as a team through unsettling times.

3. Trust your team

Be the best and they will trust you to oversee. Trust is a two-way street.

If you struggle to trust your team, they struggle to trust you. Remember. Take the blame, but give away the praise. Acknowledge people for their assistance. And when something drops out of line, acknowledge the fact that the mistake was made under your leadership and don't over analyses your team.

Leadership Style

Balance: Everywhere you go and in anything you do, there must be a balance. What a high EQ does is that it transforms a leader into a master who can easily parade himself or herself as the master of both worlds. By worlds, we're referring to joggling between being serious and having a sense of humor which means being able to switch from the excessively formal to the person who lightens the mood with a joke or a dose of relatable sarcasm at will. You cannot do this if you do not possess a tangible amount of EQ. As a leader, your subordinates should be able to tell you apart from a robot or a machine or even worse, a dictator. Remember we are talking about balance, and hence being too carefree is also a sign of having a faulty EQ. The only way to avoid this is by possessing a sufficient emotional quotient.

Confidence: There's an almost unexplainable air of confidence a leader with a high EQ possesses. The ingenious ability to analyze and respond appropriately to themselves first and then to others boosts their confidence and self-esteem as a leader. When in crisis, for example, a leader with a high EQ will not fret even if the situation, condition, or predicament may warrant them to become so uncomfortable that they act out.

This is not because the leader isn't naturally faced with an emotion intended to overwhelm him or her, but because he or she chooses to analyze and process the emotion and decides not to be fazed by it.

Be Motivational and Positive

An emotionally intelligent leader understands how emotions work, how they can be affected by it and how it affects others. Such a leader is capable of choosing an outcome that is less conflicting in difficult situations.

Passion: Without passion, most things will die or fizzle out, however, passion can be revived when it wanes. Emotional intelligence is necessary to foster productivity, commitment, and dedication, especially in the workplace when and if passion starts to dwindle. So, when people forget why they're in the career they've chosen or why they're involved in the business that they currently operate, a leader can revive the passion by helping them filter distractions and keep their eyes on the prize.

What Make a Good Leader

With basic analysis, you are following the lead of your target. This means that you are a follower in the conversation. While this can hold great success in turning results, you can gain even more success in becoming the leader of the conversation. This essentially means that you use analysis to identify which personality profile your target has, and then you use that knowledge to generate a map of how you intend to manipulate them.

Even though you are in the lead, however, you are still going to look for specific cues and refine your strategy if necessary to get your desired results.

The biggest benefit of this type of analysis, though, is that you get to manufacture organic connections. You can predict which type of stories people will most relate to and appreciate, and be the first one to share them. This gets your target saying "me too" and feeling excited that they have generated a connection with someone who understands them. Then, because they feel like you are similar to them on a deep level, the person you are targeting will be more likely to agree with you and want to go along with anything you say or do. This is how you can become the leader and encourage them to follow you right to the finish line, where you get exactly what you want from them.

Chapter 3: The EQ Model

As we open the door to the notion of emotional intelligence, we find that, as a leader, we are forced not only to deal with a diverse group of people daily but also continuously confront the same questions. How do we make the right decision? How do we motivate our team? How do we do things better?

The core of everything, however, is the same: a willingness to changes and adapt to suit the needs of the workforce and the company. We will soon learn that if we can properly balance and redirect the way we lead.

Once you begin to understand the importance of emotion and emotional intelligence, you will automatically realize that you are in need of a solid theoretical base from which you can work forward – this theoretical base is henceforth provided in the form of the three most important models of emotional intelligence produced by modern research. These three models once properly understood and instilled can and will act as the gravitational center of all your leadership decisions, and will act as an anchor and a tool to help you simplify and tackle any upcoming and current problem. It is, in other words, your light at the end of the tunnel, not just a beacon of hope, but also a guide to lead you forward.

Now, are you ready to brush up on your theory?

Emotional Intelligence Ability

The ability model is an EQ model developed by Yale's Peter Salovey and the University of New Hampshire's John Mayer. It is based on four individually standing yet interconnected emotion-related abilities. when combined, they can basically measure the level of emotional intelligence that an individual has. These four abilities have been identified and are discussed in detail below.

- **Emotional Perception**

    The first and most basic ability is perception. In order to accurately master and apply emotions and emotional intelligence, one must first be able to not only understand the verbal emotional cues provided but also accurately identify the non-verbal cues that workers and peers use in their regular interactions. Non-verbal cues include body language, facial expression, tone, vocabulary, and even contextual behavior or omission of an act.

40

To become a good leader, you need to pick up these cues and identify them masterfully.

- **Use of Emotion**

The second most important ability according to the ability model is the capacity to control and use one's own emotions, as well as the emotions of other people, to your advantage. It is an undisputed fact that feelings play a major role in the decision-making process. We have already highlighted how emotions can even influence logical decisions and lead to emotion-based ideas and logical fallacies. However, what we haven't really touched upon is the truth that, despite all this, every decision not taken by a robot or AI is still influenced by some degree of emotion. As such, it is critical for a leader to know how to mold and manipulate their feelings to achieve their desired ends. This is particularly vital when a leader is dealing with an issue that needs to be resolved at once.

- **Understanding Emotions**

Another important part of EQ is the ability to properly comprehend the depth and implications of emotion. Now, unlike what most people seem to think, identifying an emotion is not always enough. Furthermore, it is hard to navigate through it without understanding its roots and effects first. For instance, if you were dealing with an individual who happened to be angry, your first question as a leader should be "Why?" By unmasking the reasoning that the individual is using, whether or not you agree with it, you are also giving yourself insight into the possible future actions that he or she may take.

41

When it comes to anger, after all, a possible future action can be seeking revenge, attacking, or retreating fearfully. As a leader, you need to have that insight into all of your employees and other people you interact with. Remember, knowledge is power, and EQ is emotional knowledge at its peak.

- **Managing Emotions**

   This brings us to the final emotional competency measured by the ability model: the management of emotions. Managing emotions deals with three main factors - is the person in question being able to adequately take into account the emotions that they are perceiving? If they are, then are they comprehensively using those emotions to control the root cause and reactive elements in question.

Mixed Model Intelligence

The good news is, unlike IQ, which is mostly built-in and fixated after our teen years, our EQ is learned and can be learned at any age. In fact, there are five specific components of emotional intelligence that help buoy your ability to function with better emotional stability, which is covered in the David Goleman model of EQ, a.k.a. the Mixed Model.

- **Self-Awareness**

   The development of self-awareness as a business leader is critical. As a business leader, after all, you need to be aware of your own moods and emotions so that you can also follow and anticipate how they will impact others. It is also important because self-awareness allows you to understand what motivates you as an individual.

The more in tune you are with your personal strengths, weaknesses, interests, and disinterests, the better you will be able to control and influence your own actions. Self-awareness allows a person to have a strong sense of self-worth as well. This is super important as it lets you identify your own strengths and teaches you how to accept criticism, which is a critical part of human development. Such a need intensifies when you become a business leader because the more you develop self-awareness, the more your organization can grow under your leadership.

- **Self-Control**

Self-control is another extremely important competency. Unlike self-awareness that focuses on the understanding of the self, self-control concentrates on the ability to conform and redirect actions or reactions. This way, the things that we do are not impulsive. Self-control works to actively increase the process of rational thinking under pressure and is meant to encourage and boost productive actions.

- **Motivation**

It is extremely important to keep in mind that one's ability and will to work do not merely depend on the logical factors that generally govern work-life balance, such as monetary gain or professional advancement. There are many times in which a person's desire to work comes from something more basic like their passion or determination to do well and succeed in life. And these factors, when combined together, are what we often call as motivation. The thing is, it is more than just drive. It is the force that allows someone to easily overcome the obstacles that they will undoubtedly face as they continue to pursue their goals. That is exactly why any good leader needs to have a strong grasp of what motivates their employees and how to increase those motivational levels best.

Why?

While being aware of how you impact your employees is great, so is being able to control your own emotions. Nevertheless, what's genuinely important is having the ability to handle your employee's emotions, which is basically what motivation does.

- **Empathy**

Empathy is also very important, particularly for business leaders. It allows a good leader to feel what other people - more importantly, what their co-workers or employees - feel. Even in cases wherein a leader is unable to completely understand others' emotions, the mere establishment of the intent to reach out, understand, and work through these problems is a core skill for any mentor. Especially for people in diverse work cultures, that is such an integral part of today's business world.

44

Social Skill

Finally, we find ourselves dealing with social skills. Despite being able to empathize, understand, and even control our own emotions, it is impossible to be a good business leader if one cannot demonstrate strong and consistent ability to deal with conflict situations and manage mutually beneficial relationships. This skill to be whoever their consumers and employees need them to be is always common in every great leader. A person manages to do that by obtaining and maintaining a high degree of emotional intelligence, of course!

Emotional Intelligence Trait Model

This specific model does not merely test one's perception of their own emotions, but it does so in a manner that allows self-assessment to help build the EQ framework. It has often been criticized for its vulnerability to result in manipulation. For instance, if a person decides to answer dishonestly, their EQ would theoretically be scored incorrectly; however, the model itself has been known to reject such implications. A basic Trait Model EQ test imposed on an adult would consist of the measure of 15 major points.

- **Adaptability**
  Adaptability is an individual's emotional intelligence trait that is considered to indicate his or her flexibility. It refers to how rigid they are in their own thought pattern, as well as how capable they are of adapting to newfound situations or conditions. Adaptability is a key component of emotional intelligence, considering the only way to bolster teamwork is by putting together a cohesive team and showing a willingness to change their

ways, which is something that any good leader should be on the lookout for.

- **Assertiveness**
  Next up is assertiveness. It is a sociability trait that determines the individual's ability to stand up for the rights that they have inherited or gained, as well as communicate their feelings or opinions in a frank and forthright way. The higher the assertiveness of an individual is, the more emotionally intelligent they are considered to be. After all, the trait is indicative of clarity and consistency of mind.

Emotional Expression

Emotional expression is a similarly important trait. Unlike assertiveness, however, emotional expression is an emotionality trait that determines how capable a person is at communicating their thoughts and feelings to other people. The higher a person scores on their emotional expression, the more in tune they are with their emotionality and personal views. This serves as an indicator of high emotional intelligence.

Emotional Management

Another sociability trait is emotional management. This is thought to measure how well an individual can use their other sociability skills, such as assertiveness, to control and influence other people, especially their thoughts and feelings. The more adept a person is at managing or controlling others' emotions, the higher their emotional intelligence score is, considering the entire objective of emotional intelligence is to be able to exert some sort of control over other people through emotional manipulation.

Emotional Perception

Unlike emotional management, though, emotional perception centers more around the emotionality factor and is used to check how comprehensive one's understanding is of their own feelings, as well as the others'. It is another extremely important factor since most actions are undertaken due to the individuals' understanding of the emotional state of the other person or even themselves.

Emotional Regulation

Emotional regulation, on the other hand, falls under the category of self-control and is a trait that assesses how capable the individual is when it comes to not only influencing but completely controlling and regulating how people feel regularly. The better a person is at handling their own emotions, the better and more balanced their decisions will be, and the more likely it is for these decisions to be good. As such, emotional regulation is another key factor measured.

- **Impulsiveness**
  Another self-control variety that trait models measure is the scale of impulsiveness that is displayed by individuals. Unlike the other sectors in this book, the lower the impulsiveness levels a person shows, the higher their emotional intelligence is deemed to be. The reason is that being impulsive is the exact opposite of acting with emotional intelligence. In truth, it has a tendency to destabilize any decision because it is usually a not-well-thought-out reaction.

- **Relationships**

  Another emotionality-based trait is relationships. A critical part of measuring emotional intelligence is weighing a subject's ability to not only perceive or act on but also fully function in an emotionally balanced manner to maintain personal relationships that are meaningful and fulfilling. Think of Sheldon Cooper's ability to keep friendships and relationships as opposed to a normal person - that is what you're trying to avoid. Sheldon from the first season of Big Bang Theory is not very high on the EQ scale, and maintaining personal relationships is challenging for him. His other friends like Penny may not have a high IQ level, but they are quite capable in terms of EQ maintenance.

- **Self-Esteem**

  How a person views himself or herself is also an important part of emotional intelligence. You should keep in mind, however, that the trait test is not a simple case of high means good or low equates bad in terms of its scoring. On the contrary, each score is contextually based. As it involves self-assessment, it is based more on the perceptions that someone has of himself or herself instead of the actual measure of competencies or skills that the individuals hold. Nevertheless, positive well-being is determined by higher levels of self-esteem, among other factors.

- **Self-Motivation**

  Self-motivation is one of the auxiliary facets of the test that is used to assess how driven an individual perceives themselves to be and how likely they are to either succeed or persist in their attempts to achieve a goal despite the situation at hand.

In other words, it seeks to measure how much drive an individual has when it comes to how they approach issues daily.

- **Self-Awareness**
  Interestingly, self-awareness, which is a sociability factor, differs from self-esteem and self-motivation, in the sense that it does not measure any positive view that one may have or think they have about themselves. Instead, it seems single-mindedly focused on identifying how accomplished a person is in terms of how they perceive their own social skills and subsequent networking abilities. It matters to keep in mind that awareness does not depend on how good one is about their skills but how well they can realize whatever abilities they have.

Stress Management

Emotional or stress management is another sociability factor and the last of the three used to measure trait EQ. An individual's perception of their ability to withstand and work under stress, as well as their perceived ability to regulate or control the stress levels imposed on them are both identified through stress management.

Trait Empathy

Another emotionality trait measured is empathy. Here, the individual's perception of how far they can commiserate and objectively see the world from the eyes of another person is identified and accounted for.

Trait Happiness

The happiness trait, on the other hand, deals with how a person perceives their ability to be happy, how happy they think they are, and how satisfied they are with their own lives. Hence, the well-being of an individual is judged in part by the happiness trait.

Trait Optimism

The last trait is measured by trait optimism, which, as a rule, checks how likely an individual is to confidently look at the positives - or on the "bright side," as people put it.

With EQ tests measuring different parts and many other factors, it is clear that emotional intelligence plays a critical role in terms of predicting job performance. As such, it has a very specific impact on contextual happenstances. It practically means that there is a positive correlation between the two. Emotional intelligence can be used to approach organizational behavior as a tool, which will not only help explain problems in the workforce but actively and effectively navigate through its waters as well.

50

Chapter 4 – Emotional Intelligence At Work

Leaders who have high emotional intelligence are able to understand and respond to emotions, overcome stressful incidents, and are mindful of how they affect others. They are able to accurately gauge the needs and wants of the members of their teams. They also know what their people expect of them and of their organizations. They use their understanding of their own emotions and those of their team members in designating posts and delegating tasks.

Low emotional intelligence in leaders can have detrimental effects even if their knowledge and technical abilities are unparalleled.vLeaders who immediately react to their emotions without thinking and filtering them out first can create mistrust, confusion, and frustration among other negative feelings. Working relationships are bound to be jeopardized as a result of not being able to manage emotions properly. At some point, this could damage the company's overall culture and erode the employees' positive feelings towards the organization.

What makes emotionally intelligent leaders stand out from the rest is the way they inspire what is referred to as discretionary effort. This means that the employees are motivated enough to go above and beyond what their job description states. Employees and team members exert extra effort not out of fear that they could lose their jobs and not even out of the ambition to climb the corporate ladder. They do it out of respect and admiration for their leader. This is the kind of leader that you want to be.

How To Create a Team Building

In team building, you define structure as the inner order that will make the process of team-building enjoyable and fun without playing games. You cannot do things just for creating structure and expect them to work. In order to benefit, you need to put together the right elements and see to it that the structure:

Fits the objectives of the team best

Is coherent, clear, and reasonable for the team members

Does not confuse the members believing that efforts and results are identical

In general, you will find three kinds of team structure, all of which will produce results if you choose the best fit and you use it correctly. These are the following:

Tactical or Strategic Team Structure – is best for clarity. There is a clear definition of roles and norms in achieving the strategic goals of the team.

Problem Solving Team Structure – develops and nurtures trust among team members. Together, team members focus on finding the best resolution where the team values the contributions of each member.

Creative Team Structure – focuses on independence where team members can engage in casual communication in arriving at the results.

The Importance of Team

With high levels of emotional and situational awareness, a leader has a detailed image of every individual in his/her team.

Great believers in a team effort, they are able to effectively dissect every task and challenge and fully utilize each person's abilities in meeting that challenge. Leaders are rarely selfish when it comes to the desire to steal the spotlight and get all the credit and fame. Research has demonstrated a clear orientation towards group activities like brainstorming, sharing knowledge and focusing the collective mind power towards the achievement of a goal. This entails employee empowerment and delegation. Achieving great things is never a one man show, so both teams and individuals are allowed degrees of freedom to independently assess and decide on the outcome of particular tasks in their field of expertise. That way a leader ensures that every subtask is met with the highest degree of experience and knowledge available in the team. In addition, implementing a practice of shared work and delegation sends a message that the leader believes in his subordinates. As a result effective delegation can increase the enthusiasm, morale and confidence of team members in their own abilities.

How To Create a Positive Atmosphere

Make yourself readily available for your team. A good leader is the first among equals. This means that you just don't delegate tasks or order them what to do; instead you show them you are the example. What they do, you do and you are there all the time to help your team achieve its goals.

Help your team members recognize and appreciate the value of their work and working as part of the team. If you are quick to call their attention when they commit mistakes, you must also be quick to commend them for a job well done.

In other words, they point out their good deeds and mistakes and the intention should always be to help them reach their full potentials as a team member. Make them feel their importance as team members. There is so much wisdom to this since human beings are basically social beings that value their emotions. Pay attention to the best advertisements, they have one thing in common and that is they all appeal to the emotions of consumers. If you ask that your team members trust and respect you, it is both necessary and important that you trust and respect your team members first. You have to give it first in order to take. These are cardinal and unwritten rules that will make anyone one of the best leaders-managers. Increasing employee engagement and building and sustaining the motivation of the team is critical to success. You can never compromise these two critical factors without compromising the success of your company, business, or organization.

Understanding Stress

Lack of Awareness and Understanding – often, the source of conflict among members is they do not understand clearly their roles, the goals of the team, as well as the code of conduct and cooperation.

As a result, team members usually resort to finger-pointing, blaming one another, using scapegoats, and being hypercritical of one another's actions and ways. Increasing their level of awareness and understanding of their roles, goals, and implementing a code of conduct and cooperation will enable team members to de-focus on others and focus on themselves.

Lack of Conversational Capacity – Team issues usually escalate during critical times or when under pressure. The major cause is the lack of conversational capacity.

Weber Consulting defines this as the team's ability to engage in an open discussion without prejudices or biases.

Teams with high conversational capacity may still disagree but their disagreements are part of resolving the issue. Teams with low conversational capacity are more likely to disagree often and over trivial matters that affect productivity and performance.

Misplaced Goals – while the spirit of competition may spark or stimulate enthusiasm among your employees, your team building goals should refrain from centering on the competition. Instead of competition, encourage and inspire your employees to cooperate.

While it is important to improve individual competencies, the team members should not attempt to outshine one another. They should be able to respect the identity of their team, and pull each other up to meet team goals. The interests of the team should be more valuable than self-interests.

Management Attitude – admit it or not, but most times, the management looks at team building as the process to enable staff to change, improve, and work with one another cohesively. Management rarely, if they do, include themselves in the picture.

The thing is that the participation of the manager or the leader is the most critical. Any organization cannot build a solid team unless the management is willing to look into its own contributions and improve as necessary.

Chapter 5 – Motivating People

Another vital way that can help you control the emotional environment of the workplace is to inspire motivation. One of the main causes of stress and anxiety within the workplace is a lack of motivation. Whenever people feel overworked, underappreciated and generally disillusioned with their job they will begin to lose the motivation that encourages them to put in their best effort. The end result is not only a lack-luster performance but also a loss of interest in the task at hand. Even worse, the longer a person lacks motivation, the more stressed they become by having a job that doesn't make them happy. Therefore, inspiring motivation is the key to creating a positive emotional environment. Additionally, you can actually spread emotional intelligence to those around you through motivation. When you show people how to handle the pressures and stresses of the workplace environment through your own actions, you can help them to develop better habits and behaviors of their own. This will cause them to develop emotional intelligence without even realizing it. The important thing is that you always demonstrate emotional intelligence in the things you say and do, thereby setting the standard for others to follow.

Lead by example

There are countless books available on the different styles of leadership and the benefits each style possesses. One thing most books will tell you is the importance of leading by example.

While this may sound like a revolutionary concept, the truth of the matter is that every person in charge leads by example whether they realize it or not. If a manager overreacts to every little setback that they face they will encourage each and every employee to do the same. This is because they create the idea that setbacks are devastating by reacting the way they do. Therefore, even though they don't mean to, these managers increase the stress and anxiety in their environment by reacting in an emotionally charged way. This makes a lot of sense when you realize that people are no different from animals in nature when it comes to learning. Every animal learns by watching and mimicking the actions of their parents or other animals. This is how ducks learn to swim, sparrows learn to fly and lions learn to hunt. While people are taught new skills at school or with the aid of instruction manuals, the same observational process is still present. Thus, people will develop skills and behaviors based on what they see and experience more than in any other way. This is why leading by example is so vital for controlling the emotional environment of any place, not just work. Once you realize how leading by example works you can begin to use it to your advantage, as well as the advantage of those around you. The first thing to do is to actively avoid negative behavior. It's not enough to never appear to engage in negativity, however. Instead, you actually have to actively avoid and condemn it. One example of this is how you react to setbacks. Every time something doesn't go according to plan, you need to demonstrate your emotional intelligence in how you respond to the situation. Rather than getting stressed out and lashing out, simply show your confidence in being able to solve the problem at hand. Furthermore, demonstrate the fact that you don't see setbacks as problems in the first place. This will prove that your confidence is more than just a façade hiding your true feelings.

Another way to lead by example is to set the standard regarding principles and ethics. You can't expect others to take punctuality seriously if you are always late or behind schedule. However, when you show up at work on time each and every day and have tasks completed by their deadline, you will encourage others to focus their efforts on always being on time. Additionally, showing integrity is absolutely vital for creating a positive emotional environment. aBy always being honest with others you will encourage others to be honest with you. This will significantly reduce the stress and anxiety that comes from dishonesty, underhanded actions and other similar elements that only undermine a person's emotional stability.

Reward hard work and success

Numerous studies have shown that another effective way to inspire motivation in a person is to reward hard work and success. All too often the focus in any workplace environment is the consequence of failure. Many companies believe that the best way to get a person to perform at their best is to keep the threat of being fired for failure always present in their minds. Such methods have been shown to not only cause untold stress and anxiety, but also undermine a person's performance rather than improving it. In the end it seems that negative motivation only ever leads to negative results. Alternatively, it has been discovered that when people are rewarded for hard work and success they tend to perform better on a more regular basis. This is a critical point to understand when it comes to influencing the emotional wellbeing of those around you, especially in the workplace.

Every time you reward a person for good behavior you will encourage them to continue behaving in the same way. This holds true for any aspect of performance. By showing appreciation for a job well-done you will encourage a person to continue to perform at their best level. The simple reason for this is that pleasure always beats fear as a motivator. Therefore, always be generous in rewarding those who put in good performances and produce positive results. Perhaps the most important aspect of rewarding hard work and success is that it fosters a sense of teamwork within any workplace environment. The main reason for this is that most employees are aware of the fact that managers tend to get bonuses when they achieve their quotas. Unfortunately, the average employee is usually left empty handed, even though it was their hard work and effort that accomplished the goal. Subsequently, when you share the spoils of success with those who created the success in the first place it serves to make them feel more a part of the process. The more valuable employees feel they are, the more valuable their contribution will become, leading to even greater success as a result.

Motivation Theory

Motivational leadership isn't a generic concept that projects one specific profile. The caveats are strongly influenced by the unique strategy, model, culture, and context in which it's applied. However, in looking at the very basic components of motivational leadership, you can define it as a product of your own mindset, skills, philosophy and work ethic, and how you apply it to yourself and those around you.

The end result is a type of leadership that motivates you and those around you to actively engage in physical and mental abilities to strive toward achieving goals and objectives versus simply mindlessly following directives to get to a prescribed destination.

Instead of micro commands and archaic control measures, motivational leadership uses empowerment as the motor behind the engine of productivity.

Successful workplaces almost exclusively have one thing in common - motivational leadership. Few businesses can go from intellectual property/goods to consistent cash flow without the productivity of multiple workers from design, sales, and marketing to logistics, customer service, and HR.

That's a long chain that can easily kink or break if just a single employee isn't performing, and that clearly affects the success of the company both directly, and from the indirect influence such a worker has in infecting other workers with negativity.

This is where having a motivational leader becomes key to creating motivated, engaged, invested, and positive workers. There's an extensive, multi-layered explanation on the how and why. But it all boils down to a motivational leader's ability to meet a worker's human needs, also called Maslow's hierarchy of needs, which are psychological, safety and security, belonging, self-esteem, and self-actualization. Every human on earth needs these components to effectively function in life and work. Your responsibility as a motivational leader is to find and interconnect those needs with your company's vision and strategies.

The Process of Motivation

Type of Motivation

There are two types of motivation: intrinsic motivation and extrinsic motivation. Before learning how to harness their potential, let's look at what they are and what sets them apart.

What is Intrinsic Motivation?

Intrinsic motivation involves types of behavior propagated through internal rewards. Those that are driven by intrinsic motivation pursue their goals because they get internal satisfaction from these pursuits. Intrinsically motivated people to obtain fulfillment from the journey towards the goal rather than from the reward waiting at the finish line. People that devote their lives to helping others provide some of the most easily identifiable cases of intrinsic motivation.

What is Extrinsic Motivation?

Conversely, extrinsic motivation relates to the type of motivation where the reason for pursuing a goal comes from the potential of receiving an external reward. Being paid a bonus or getting a promotion are both things that others offer to give you the incentive to achieve a task or adopt a new behavior. Parents are often seen utilizing extrinsic motivation with their children to get them to do anything from studying harder at school to behaving in a public space. Childhood offers most of us our first brush with extrinsic motivation.

How Do They Differ?

Besides the source of motivation, intrinsic motivation differs from extrinsic motivation in the degree of effectiveness at driving different behaviors. Different people respond to different types of motivation at varying levels, and we'll discuss what motivates each personality type in the next chapter. There also seems to be a cutoff point past which each type of motivation loses effectiveness; a motivational law of diminishing returns, if you will. A study by the Institute for Evolutionary Anthropology has proved that giving too much of an external reward for a behavior that is inherently internally rewarding results in a reduction in intrinsic motivation. This is called the over-justification effect and can be counterproductive to a business that aims to increase productivity. To give employees the incentive to do better, a company can shift focus to elements that are not necessarily internally fulfilling. Not that extrinsic motivation has any use in a business environment. On the contrary, external rewards are a powerful tool in driving productivity when thought out and applied correctly. To better understand the implementation of the two motivations and the reward systems that support them, let's look at practical examples of both.

Intrinsic Motivation Implementation, Factors and Examples

Implementing a company volunteer program, whether related to the business's offered services or as something entirely outside the company's normal activities, provides employees with intrinsic motivation to excel in their work. Helping others is already intrinsically motivating for most people, so tying volunteerism into the company culture provides an internal reward that cannot be quantified in monetary value.

For example, if a company is in the food service industry, an activity that promotes intrinsic motivation and is related to the business's operations would be for employees to take time and distribute food to local homeless shelters. Intrinsic motivation can be facilitated by having the partners of a law firm engage in food drives and dedicating time to the same homeless shelters. The only difference is that with the food service company, the act reinforces a greater sense of purpose regarding the employees' specific field of work. With the law firm, it is not directly related to them, and providing pro bono legal services for the people in need might be a stronger motivator for them. As an intrinsic motivation, it can work in both cases. It just needs to be conceived and organized so it motivates people to contribute to their workplace and community and not be viewed as grunt work. Another example of intrinsic motivation in the workplace is offering employees more independence as a reward for their quality work. People respond positively when their contribution is appreciated. Independence and achieving a higher status within a company are internal rewards that improve an employees' quality of life and can be a powerful driving factor in productivity.

Approaches to Motivation

When you first undertake a project it is very easy to be motivated and push hard to achieve success and get the project off the ground. Unfortunately, once the project is underway it can often be difficult to keep the momentum going; they will be many more demands on your time and a variety of issues that need resolving; possibly even personnel issues.

Every drain on your time will make it harder for you to focus on the end goal and may leave you procrastinating at every opportunity you get. There are several essential tips which you need to follow to ensure you remain motivated and are able to motivate your team:

- Mini Targets

It can be very difficult to aim for a huge goal which may or may not work and is only a possibility at some point in the future. In order to stay motivated and avoid stagnating; it is best to break your project into small pieces and set yourself a host of achievable mini-targets. These targets should be kept small; ideally they should be achievable within a week and you should provide yourself with a reward every time you reach the target. This will ensure that you take a small step every week and keep your project on track. The small targets should gradually get bigger so as to ensure everyone is aware of where the project is going and where it may end up.

- The Game

Another good approach is to make the project a game; this is usually an effective way of making sure you not only hit your targets but do more than you need to. The easiest game is to set yourself a simple goal; such as working later every day than you normally do, or even coming in earlier. You can even up the ante slightly by trying to complete specific tasks in less time than you have done previously; but still to the right standard. Another version of the game is to complete a specific task in a different way to normal, without affecting the outcome and ensuring that it takes no longer than the usual path would have taken.

This can certainly get the brain thinking as you need to understand exactly how something is completed in order to arrive at an alternative solution.

- Deadline

One of the most effective ways to improve the amount of work being produced and ensure that you do not delay is to visualize your working day as the last possible chance to finish a specific project. Working as though you have a deadline will create a pressured environment that many people feel comfortable in; even if it is a more stressful working environment than the normal scenario you are used to. This is not something that is recommenced every day; not only will it increase the amount of stress you are under, it is also possible it will decrease the quality of the goods you are producing. It can be a very effective tool when being used to motivate you to achieve your goal.

- Positive Attitude

This trait is as essential as a 'can-do' attitude. No matter how bad it gets you must always look for the silver lining and find something to focus on. This can help to motivate you as you will feel positive about the future. This small amount of positivity will be enough to keep you pushing towards the ultimate goal and will help you to keep the project on track. A positive attitude will also rub off with the other people involved in the project and the culmination of this will help to drive the project forward as people feel good about the project and their involvement in it. The power of a positive attitude should never be underestimated. If people feel good then they will always feel more capable and achieve more, no matter what the situation.

- Distractions

One of the biggest reasons why a project does not continue as per the designed schedule is the level of distractions that exist at all times around you and the things you are doing. Absolutely anything can be a distraction; whether someone is riding a unicycle or simply showing a video regarding fishing!

The biggest distractions are the mundane items in your office, your coffee mug, or a blank internet page. The internet can be searched and your coffee mug cleaned, the list of things that suddenly seem important to look at can grow rapidly and take your attention away from the task in hand. No matter how good your intentions, there will be something that can distract you. The safest route is to remove all the items which can potentially distract you and attempt to focus on the project. Whilst this is a good place to start, it may still be difficult to actually achieve. It may be a better tactic to study the task you need to complete and break it in smaller goals, this may improve your motivation for each task as each one will be easier to achieve and quicker.

- Working Hard

One of the biggest problems with many projects is the sheer size of the project. The simplest way to adjust this is to break each part of the job into different tasks and tackle each task. However, even this more stimulating approach can succumb to a lack of motivation. Instead of focusing on a small section of the plan, you may find it more beneficial to break the plan into small, bite sized chunks and motivate yourself by undertaking one section of the project at a time. It is far easier to be motivated to do something which can be completed in one day than it is to commit to a much longer term goal.

67

You will gain a sense of satisfaction every day that you have reached your target and that will assist you with completing the entire project.

- Have a Purpose

In order to truly complete the project and stay motivated you will need to define the purpose of the project and remind yourself of it regularly. You may wish to add a relevant picture or postcard which will help you to remember why you are undertaking such a project and how close you are getting to the end result. Most people take on projects which are close to their hearts and this makes it easier to be passionate about your project. But even if your project relates to something you are truly passionate about, you will need to remind yourself regularly of your purpose; this will ensure you stay on track and deliver the finished project in time.

- Take it outside your comfort zone

Everyone has a comfort zone, the things they do on a daily basis which they are happy to do; they are known and can even be part of a daily ritual. The longer you spend on a project the more your comfort zone will expand and the less motivated you will become. This will generally mean a more relaxed approach to the project and the slowing down of the expected completion date. In order to stay motivated and focused it is essential to challenge yourself daily. The best way of doing this is to challenge you to do something outside of your normal comfort zone. This task should be tied in to the completion of a daily task, or mini-goal; making the challenge a useful way of staying focused as well a broadening your horizons.

This willingness to try new things will not only help to keep you motivated it should also inspire your team to try the same challenge and they will remain motivated because of your actions.

- Passion

You almost certainly started a specific project because you had an interest in the subject, or a desire to promote it to other people. It is essential to keep this passion alive whilst working on the project. This should not be difficult if you are passionate about the subject. Should you feel your passion starting to wane then you will need to remind yourself about why you love the subject?

It is essential to let your passion show, you should let people know that you are excited by the subject and enjoy what you are doing. Other people will respond to this and be more enthusiastic about the topic; they will also become eager to see what can be achieved and for the project to be a success. This is another way of leading by example; simply allow others to see your passion and they will respond positively.

- Learn Every Day

One of the most important lessons that you should acknowledge is that you do not know it all. There is always scope to learn more and every day brings a new set of challenges that can be dealt with in a new and different way. Your team will recognize that you are open to new ideas and opinions and will not be afraid to voice theirs. This should lead to frank and open discussions regarding the way forward and all participants will be able to learn from this.

Learning something new every day will ensure you remain passionate about your project and will motivate you to keep looking for new techniques and methods. This approach will show to your team and imbue them with the desire to follow you. Humility is actually an important leadership principle.

- Never Give Up

There will always be times when things go wrong and it may seem impossible to continue. But the sign of a good leader and someone who is personally motivated is when you are not prepared to give up. This does not mean stubbornly remaining on the same track when it is clearly not working! It means making you aware of all the options and all the avenues for assistance and using them all to find a way forward. Having a dedication to your project and picturing the end result will help to inspire you to continue. You may even find it useful to have a personal mantra which sums up why you want a specific project to work. This mantra could be carried with you or displayed in several key places; it will serve to remind and motivate you. If you show a determination to find a way forward then others will naturally follow you and partake in your desire. They will believe it is possible simply because you do; and that will open up many doors!

- Treat Yourself

In order to stay motivated and continue to motivate your followers it is essential to treat yourself occasionally. If you become obsessed with the project you will quickly stagnate and find yourself stuck in a rut; without being able to see a clear way forward.

Every small achievement should be rewarded, as well as the larger ones, but, more importantly, you should seek to have a small treat every week, ideally this should be time away from your project doing something else that you love. You may want to put all your effort into the project but you will be surprised how much easier it is when you have a little fresh perspective every week. It will help to focus your mind and allow you to see all the options; it will also refresh you and help you to stay enthusiastic and motivated.

Chapter 6 – Organize People

Not only do you need to have the right habits in place in order to be successful, but you also need to turn around your mindset. No one is born being organized with everything.

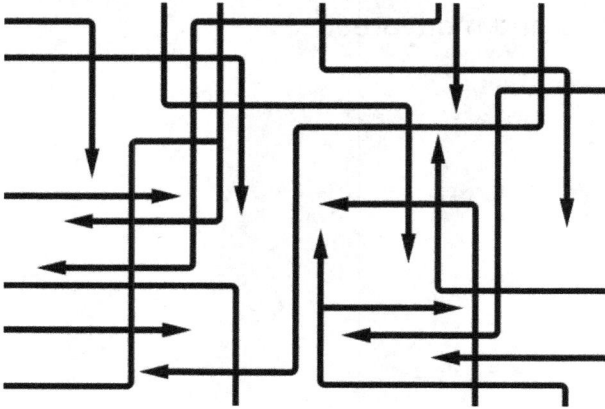

All of those you know who are really successful were not able to be this way overnight. They worked hard to develop the right mindset and habits that make them organized, and they continue to work on this throughout their lives. If these people can make it work, so can you. The right mindset is the first thing that you need to have. Here are some of the mindsets that you should have in order to become more organized.

Find the right tools

Life is difficult and getting ahead can be a difficult thing to accomplish. Things are not always handed to you, at least not in the manner you would like.

That promotion is not just going to be given to you without some work. You might find that with a bit of creativity, you can find the right tools and still get ahead in life. The most organized people are able to get out of any rut they fall into life. They realize that life is not always going to be good to them, but they make the best out of the situation they are given. They see the tools that are around them, and put these tools to work. For example, there are a ton of tools that you probably already own, but you are not using them to their full advantage. You might have a smart watch, smartphone, and tablet, but outside of using them to check Facebook and other social media sites, you do not put them to use. But an organized person would see some of the alternate uses with these items. They might see that they work to help organize and plan while also staying in contact with others who can make their work easier. These tools are used as a method to further their organization and to get ahead in life.

Learn their priorities

How many times have you worked hard on something that was not that important? Did someone ask you to work on this project but you really did not have the time to get it all done or you had some other important things that you should be working on?

The most organized people are able to figure out what is important to them and then they spend their time taking care of these priorities. No matter what is in store with your day, you need to know the proper methods to handle all of your priorities effectively. Even when the day starts to get a bit hectic, you still need to get all of your priorities handled. One method that you can use is to start the day with a to-do list.

Sit down when you first get to work and look at your schedule. Figure out what you need to get done throughout the day. Use different colors or highlight the things that have the highest priorities and need to get done first. These are the things you should work on first and prioritize, regardless of what else comes up during the day. If you are successful, you can get these urgent tasks done in plenty of time and then start to work on some of the other tasks that need to get done at some point.

Worry about the things that are relevant

Your mind will become occupied with a million different thoughts throughout the day. You have to worry about school, work, your family, and so many other things throughout your day. Keeping your mind on what is important can be difficult, but as you let more organization into the day, you will learn what is relevant and worth your time. Most of the topics that are floating around in your brain are not that relevant. You do not need to spend all day worrying about what to make for supper or if someone snubbed you in the hallway. And yet these simple and irrelevant things are what get your attention the most. This can take up a lot of valuable space in your head that should be spent on more important things. Those who are organized have learned how to get rid of these irrelevant thoughts and to just concentrate on what is important. They might try out some form of mindfulness or meditation to learn how to get rid of the negative thoughts. These kinds of people have learned that gossip, TV shows, and other nonsense is not worth their time, at least not while they are doing a big project at work, and so they avoid them. Basically, in this step, you need to learn how to clean out and organize your mind as well as the rest of your life.

You can spend your time thinking about things that are important and getting more done during the day.

Find the simple way to get things done

Often, people who are scrambling around all day long are doing things the difficult way. They don't spend time trying to figure out if there is an easier way to get something done. Instead, they spend their time doing things the same way and wasting a lot of their time. People who are organized are not considered perfectionists. They do not spend hours trying to get something done just right. But this does not mean they spend their time making things more complicated. They strive to find the easiest method to get things done. If they can use a program to finish a report in a few minutes rather than an hour, they will use it. If there is a shortcut to get to work, they will use it. You should not assume that you need to become a perfectionist in order to become organized. You just need to make sure that you will learn the right and simple way to get things done. This might take some time, but you will learn how to do it and soon things will get done so much easier with time to spare.

Keep things maintained

You cannot just sit down one day, organize it, and hope that it is going to stay that way. You need to actually keep up with things and maintain them all of the time. You have to pick up things that you take out. You need to make sure that the right papers are put in the right spots. You have to keep up with this work or your life is going to become disorganized again in no time.

Of course, things are never going to be perfect in your life. You will have times when things are going well and times when things are going poorly for you, even with an organized life. But even through all of these ups and downs, it is possible to take the right steps to keep your life on track and organized. And when you keep things organized, you can handle the downs much easier than when your life is already a mess. his is how people who are organized are able to stay on top of things, even when something happens to slow them down or derail their plans. They have things in place and a good system so that when something bad comes up, they can get back on track quickly. Those who choose to forego organization will come back and find things are worse than before and may never catch up.

Look to the future

The people who are the most organized are the ones who are able to think about the future. They know which path to take that will get them the most reward. They can look at each project that needs to be finished and determine the best reward. This gets back to the idea of working on the things that are the most important. Spending your morning just reading emails might make you feel important and like things got done, but you still have a long list of things that you need to finish in just a few hours. If you were more organized and have a list of things to accomplish, you can look it over and pick out the task that will give the most reward when you are finished. This can work for any part of your life. For example, an organized person would clean up the dishes right away because they can see that the reward of a clean kitchen and having less hassle later on is worth it now.

You might finish up the big project first so that you can take a break later on and relax while working on the smaller ones. Organized people look to the most benefit and work to meet that goal.

Throw out that clutter

The clutter in your life is going to hinder even your best efforts, whether your mind is all cluttered or if it's just your home. While those who are not that organized will live with this clutter and wonder why things aren't getting done, those who are organized are able to clean up the mess and clear out their lives. There is no issue of working around the clutter because the clutter is gone. Think of this process as making a straight path rather than an obstacle course to getting things done. Clutter is just hindering your progress in life so get rid of it. Take a few days of your life and just get rid of as much clutter as you can. Clean out your office, clean out the closets, and get rid of anything you no longer need. This is going to save you a lot of time and hassle, plus it clears out your head so you are able to work on some other important things in life.

Letting go instead of winning

You can't win everything. There are going to be times when your boss does not like the work that you did, that you need to take off a day when there is a ton of work, or when you just can't get the work done on time. Life gets busy and you are not able to keep up with it all. But some people are just so obsessed with winning in every part of their lives; they will keep going, even when it can cause them harm.

You will never see someone who is organized being that upset about the things they aren't able to control. They realize that things are going to change and that it is much easier to go along with it. When you get caught up in the particulars of something and you do not just let things go on, you are going to freak out a lot and have trouble keeping up. When you get used to seeing things changed and are able to move things around to make the changes, you can get so much more done in the day.

Change the routine

Wouldn't it be nice if you could just have the same routine each day? You show up to work and do the exact same things each day without having any change ever.

While this might be nice, it is not something that you get to deal with in the real world. There are times when things will not go your way or you have to change up your schedule. A routine is not a bad thing. It allows you to get more things done because you know what to expect from day to day. But if you begin to get upset and everything becomes a mess just because your schedule gets messed up a bit, you are not going to be very organized. The most organized people have a schedule, but they are able to change things around whenever necessary and still keep on track. No matter what your routine is, there are going to be things that cause it to change up. When you are organized, you can go with the flow a bit more and get back on track when you need to. It is not such a horrible thing when your routine isn't in order. You can still get everything done and have less stress.

Plan things out

You can't get very far in your life if you are just working on what is going to happen in the next few hours. What happens when those hours are all done and over with?

Planning things out for the long term helps you to know where you are heading. It also helps you to have an objective look at the steps you are taking to determine if they will further your goals in the future. Being able to plan out for the future can also help you to do your schedule. You can figure out which items need to be done first and get those done. You can see what is going to occur in the future to determine if you can take on more work or even to work ahead on projects. So many opportunities present themselves when you are organized and know what is going to happen more than one day out. Having the right mindset is the first step to being as organized as possible. You can use this mindset to get things in order and to get things done on time. Instead of rushing around and hoping that things will get done on time, you can bring the right mindset into the game from the beginning and see results right away.

Organizational Guidelines

Now that you know some of the importance of having an organized life, it is time to begin the steps to making all of this yours. While it would be nice to have a magic wand that you could wave and put everything in its place, it is going to take a bit more work on your part. This does not mean the whole process should be really difficult. Just follow some of the steps in the following chapters and you will see just how easy it can be to get the organization to become a part of your life.

With this first step, we will look at how to get in the right mindset of someone who is organized. It is impossible to bring an organization into your life if you still think that big pile of papers on your desk is just fine. This chapter will look at some of the habits as well as mindsets of those who are the most organized. This will give you a good look at some of the things you need to consider in order to bring an organization into your life.

The Habits of Organized People

First, let's look at some of the habits you can see in people who are organized. These habits might seem out of place or like they have no rhyme or reason, but these habits are meant to keep life organized. Being organized in life does not just come to people. It is something they have to work towards and often people will develop their own habits that help to keep things in line. You do not have to use the same habits that someone else has enjoyed. You might find that some confuse you or some just make you think too hard on the future. But over time, you will begin to develop some of your own habits that can make the organization easier in your life. There are a lot of different habits that you can start to accumulate over the years. It is often going to depend on the way that you do things, but there are a few topics you should keep in mind. These can help you to be on the right track to developing the habits that work the best for you to be organized. Some of these habits include:

Find out what you like—once you find something that works for you or that you enjoy, stick with it. When you change things up all of the time, it becomes hard to stick with one thing and your life will become a mess again. For example, find a filing system that you like.

80

You may find that one system is hard to use, even though others have promised you it is the only one you will ever need. Find the system that works for you and stick with it so that you can find your paperwork and never have to waste time searching for things again. Another way to look at this option is with your bathroom supplies. Just keeping up with shampoo, conditioner, face soap, lotions and whatever else you keep in the bathroom can be a hassle. Instead of letting this get in your way, pick one brand and type of each to keep in the bathroom. Never purchase anything else and only pick up the brands you like. Not only can this save you time in the store, but it also gives you the opportunity to only have to rustle through a few bottles of products rather than 20.

Learn how you can say no—saying no is really hard. You want to be there for everyone. You do not want to disappoint those around you and you want to come out as the person who is able to get everything done despite being overly busy them. This is going to break you very quickly.

The most organized people have learned how much they can handle and can say no when things get too tough on them. You do not need to do everything in life. Sometimes, people need to learn how to handle the work on their own. You have a life of your own and plenty of work that needs to gets done on the side. Do not say yes to projects that you are not interested in completing, that are someone else's responsibility, or that you just do not have time for. People will appreciate your honesty much more than your eagerness to please and then ultimate failure. A good example of how this works is during the holidays. There are always a lot of things going on during this time of year, plus you have to keep up with your regular work.

There is no way that you can make it to every party and event while still going on that family vacation, having some time to yourself, and keeping up with work. Learn how to be more selective on what you would like to do and just cultivate the tasks and relationships that are the most important.

Spend a few minutes each day organizing—keeping things organized all of the time can be a hassle. But the job becomes so much easier when you spend a bit of time on it each day rather than working on it for hours at a time a few times each month. You can pick out your own routine, but try to keep the clutter at bay as much as possible. For example, make sure to take out your trash as soon as the trash can is full. Look through the mail and throw it away each day so nothing accumulates.

When you have finished using something, put it back where it belongs right away rather than leaving it out and letting it get in the way. Yes, all of this can be a hassle, but a few minutes during the week can help to avoid the big mess and cleanup on the weekends while still keeping your life organized.

Do not worry about other people's messes—this one can be a bit difficult for those who are obsessed with organization. These people want everything in life to be as organized as possible and they can't stand it when someone else is being a mess.

You know what?

This is so not worth it. Other people are going to make messes and there's nothing you can do about it. Worrying about the mess is more hassle than it's worth. Spend your time on cleaning up your own area and getting things done and less on those around you.

Learn how to let it go—there are going to be a lot of things that bother you as an organized person. You want things to be perfect and others to work the same way that you do. There are people who will talk and procrastinate until the last minute and then whine because they do not have enough time to get the project done. This is a part of life and while it might be pretty annoying, it is a part you must deal with. Learn to let this go and just concentrate on what you need to accomplish. In addition, there are other things in your life that you need to let go of in order to be organized. Get rid of those clothes that might be nice, but you haven't worn them in a few years. Get rid of anything and everything that is getting in your way and which you never use. Unless it has some sentimental value, like a family heirloom and not something you picked up from an old boyfriend, throw it out and get your whole life organized.

Learn to make your bed each morning—this is going to help you to get in the right mindset for being organized all day long. This process will usually just take you a few minutes overall and you can be ready for the rest of the day. This can also help you to get rid of the rest of the clutter that is in your room, such as the clothes on the floor and the trash all over the place. Plus this is a nice treat when you get home from a long day at work.

Create folders for your emails—email is a big pain to keep in order. You can get hundreds of emails throughout the day depending on your business and who is trying to get ahold of you. This is difficult to go through and can make a lot of time go to waste. Instead of letting all of this happens, take a step back and find out if you can sort through the emails.

Are there some clients you can send to different folders? Are there topics that would work well in specific places?

When you sort through all of your contacts and send things to the right area, it can make things easier to find. You do not have to sort through a long list of emails, most of which are not worth your time. When you need to find some correspondence for a particular client, you can go to their folder and find what you need. This saves you a ton of time and keeps things on track all day long.

Do not fix what is broken—unless an item has a lot of value attached to it, you might want to consider just throwing it out. Too much time can be spent trying to fix an item. Does a small folder get ripped?

Just throw it out and get a new one. Your dress gets ripped and you need to sew it up? Consider throwing it out, especially if you do not plan to wear it again and getting a new one. You have to decide what your time is worth and if fixing the item is worth all of the hassle. Consider the effort, time, and annoyance that will go into your fixing project and decide if it is better to throw it out and get a new one.

Decide what is the most important—do not waste your time trying to keep up with a lot of things that are not that important. A lot of people will spend time working on small little projects and missing out on the important and big projects they need to get done instead. This makes them fall behind and often they will not finish on time, even though they are working as hard as possible. Rather than wasting this amount of time, it is important to work on the biggest tasks. You may have to take a step back and decide what is the most important and then work on that first. Keeping some of these habits in your daily schedule can help to make yourself more organized. They are simple and you can make them work in your own lifestyle and schedule.

But take time to use them correctly and you can see so much more success in your daily life and begin to get into the right mindset for this life as well.

The Organizing Process

Once you learn how to get rid of all the distractions and how to think like an organized person, it is time to actually put in the work and start being organized. This can include anything that works out well for you. Something that another person enjoys doing might not be the right decision for your day. You need to find the thing that makes you stand out and can help you see success. The following are some steps that you can take in order to become organized and to see some results for improvement in your daily life.

Create a Personal Success Morning Ritual

The first thing you should consider doing is creating a morning ritual that will set you up for success. This does not have to be a complicated ritual, but it should be enough to get you up and moving and ready for all that the day has to offer. If you are like most people, you will stumble out of bed just a few minutes before it is time to go. You run out the door while brushing your hair, maybe grabbing something to eat, and trying to put on your shoes. You may miss your commute or get stuck behind everyone else who is already running late. You stumble into the office, probably with your paperwork all over the place. You have barely been at work for five minutes and already your day is looking bad. Rather than start each morning in this manner, learn how to get some motivation and bring success to you early in the morning. There are many different ways that you can get this done.

Some of these include:

> * **Get up earlier**. This helps to prevent the rush of getting out the door on time when you are already late. Pick a time that gives you at least an hour to get a move on and put the alarm clock across the room so you never hit the snooze button. This gives you some time to wake up and get organized before it is time to head out the door.

> * **Eat something for breakfast**. Sometimes sitting down to a nice breakfast can help you to get energy for the morning. Consider eating something with some fruit, complex carbs, and protein so that you stay full and focused.

> * **Exercise**. If you have enough time in the morning, consider getting up and doing a quick workout. You only need to spend about 20 minutes or so on this, but it is often enough to give you the energy to complete your day.

> * **Organize your work**. This does not mean you need to get started on work early, although the quiet time at home before others wake up can be a great way to get more done. Just make sure you get everything put into your bag and have it all in place and ready to go before heading out the door.

> * **Have energizing music**. Many people find that putting on some music as they get ready for the day helps them to feel energized. You can listen to your favorite song while waking up and have a big smile on as you head out the door.

> * **Tidy up the house**. If you have been maintaining your organization for some time, this shouldn't take more than ten minutes.

Make the bed, rinse out your breakfast bowls and silverware, and clean up the bathroom when you are done getting ready. This can keep the home clean for when you get back. You can pick out the routine that will work the best for your needs. You can do a combination of these tasks or try something that is completely new and that works out the best for you. Make sure to pick something that is going to organize you and get you ready for an exciting and productive day at work.

Capture your ideas

The organization is going to allow a lot of thoughts into your head. You will have all of these ideas of the great things that you can do for your space and they can get jumbled around in your head.

This makes it hard to get things straight and to figure out what should be done first. It is great that you have all these ideas, but you must get them in order and figure out which ones to do first if you are going to see any success.

When you first decide that organization is something you want to pursue, sit down with a piece of paper and a pen. Write down all of the ideas that come to you on ways that you can do this project. In fact, write down everything that comes into your mind at all about this project. How does it make you feel? Where should you start? How can you go about doing the steps you have in mind?

Write it all down so it gets out of your head and onto something you can see and study. Keep this piece of paper near you for the next week or so. There are sure to be more ideas that come out of the woodwork that you can mess with. Do not judge the idea; if you have it in your brain it must have some merit. Write it all done for now. Later you will go through and pick the ideas that will work for your needs or that you think are completely ridiculous. When these ideas are out on paper, you can sort through them and see which ones might work well for your needs. You do not have to keep them inside your head. You can look through all of the information that you have written down and decide what you would like to get done to become more organized.

You're Inbox

Your inbox is one of the places that can get really messy in your whole life. You can get hundreds of emails each day depending on your line of work and this can make things really confusing for you. When more than one client is getting ahold of you, you might become confused about the right person you need to talk to or emails can get lost in the shuffle. When you are able to organize your email inbox, things can become so much easier. You get the chance to find things whenever you need them rather than hoping they turn up.

Often you will spend a lot of time searching around for that lost email each time you need it. To start this, make some folders in your inbox. When a new email comes in, set it up to go to the proper folder or move it there yourself. This way, all of the emails for each client are in the right place and you can save time with all of the searchings around. When you need to look for the client, you just click on the right file and there is everything you need. This makes things so much easier and with this kind of organization, which really only takes a few minutes, you can save hours searching for lost emails.

You're Task List

The task list is one of the best tools that you can have in your arsenal when it comes to being productive. You will be able to write down the tasks to complete during the day and then you can check them off as you get things done. This is one of the best ways to get your work done during the day without having the work rattling around in your head. So how do you get started with your task list? First, write down all of the work that you need to accomplish for the day. Doing this each day is best because then you can concentrate on a small list of things rather than having to keep up with everything that happens throughout the whole week. Write down all of the work that you must complete during that day along with when the work needs to be done. Once you have a small list of things that you need to get done, rank their importance. Maybe highlight the things that you need to get done today; these are the things that you have to get done right away. For the next group, you can pick out a new color; these are the things that you would like to get done, but can wait until the end of the day or until the next day if needed.

And finally, the third group is things that you need to work on, but they have a few days or even more than a week before they are due so you have a bit of room to work with. Now that you have this list, you can get to work. Go down the list and work on things based on their importance. Once you are done with the most important things, you can work on something else. Cross things off when you are done and you can watch as you're to do list starts to dwindle quickly.

Your calendar

Your calendar is going to become your new best friend when you are ready to organize. This is the place where you need to write down everything that needs to get done. You need to place appointments, projects, meetings, and anything else that comes up in your life. This gives you a nice overview of what needs to be done so you can plan out your life. The first thing that you need to do is pick out one calendar. Those who are not organized might have a calendar, but they will either not use them very much or they will have more than one. You can place your calendar on your phone, on the computer, on a wall calendar and even in a little planner. If you use all of these places, it is hard to keep track of everything. So to become a bit more organized, you need to pick out one calendar. Any of the options above will work, but do not put things down in different calendars. The more places you separate out your work the harder it is to remember what you need to complete. You might spend the day looking at one calendar just to realize at the end of the day that you forgot a really important project because it is on your other calendar. To start, pick out one calendar. Keep this with you all of the time.

Any time that you are assigned a new project, need to do some more research, have an appointment, or have something else come up, you need to write it down in this calendar. This can help you to keep everything in one place, plus you can open this up when it is time to make a to do list and rest assured that everything is in order. Soon you will see that everything on your list is getting done. You do not have to worry about missing out on projects or having more to do at the end of the day. You can look at your calendar, decide what all needs to be done, and then get straight to work knowing that it will all be done on time.

Chapter 7 – The Importance of Delegating

Coaching others is an essential part of developing and communicating; both as an individual and as a member of a group. A super leader will look to impart the wisdom and knowledge they have gained to ensure others are able to follow in their footsteps and, if necessary, continue what they started. The best leaders will inspire others to undertake a task that they may have though impossible on their own; yet with a little coaching is easily within their skill set. The sign of a great leader is being able to entrust these tasks to your staff and being able to guide your team even when they are going in the wrong direction. You must be able to assess how far they can go before they need correcting and give them as much support as possible along the way. The best leaders do not dictate what to do, but guide others in the right way and allow them to make mistakes and learn from them. A super leader will not judge a mistake made with the right intentions in mind; you should simply see it as an opportunity to grow and try other challenges.

- **Mindfulness**

  A great leader must always be mindful of the pressure that is being upon their team. But mindfulness is more than just being aware of your team. It is about leading by example, about learning to be compassionate and creating an atmosphere of self-awareness. In many ways you are creating an atmosphere that allows every member of your team to develop their own mindfulness for others.

If every member of your team is looking after each other you will have successfully gained a tight knit, committed team who will be ready and willing to undertake any challenge. Being mindful is having an awareness of the here and now, despite the need for plans, goals and dreams; it is important to spend some time simply existing in the current moment. Creating this atmosphere in your team allows every one of them to lower their stress levels and become more self-aware; this will allow you and your team to become more aware of your own flaws and the best way to work with them. Understanding these factors will allow you to have greater clarity and focus on all that you do.

- **Focusing the Brain**

Coaching others to be the best they can be is often a thankless task; this is because many people either believe they are already perfect, or, they are simply not interested in improving themselves or their life. One of the main aims of any coaching session is to allow your team an opportunity to step back from the pressures of the job and focus their brains on the day to day things. It is essential to focus on each part of the day and look at what you could have learnt. This attention to detail will force the brain to focus on one thing at a time and you may find there are suggestions and ideas which simply pop into your head. This is a good sign that the coaching is working as you are allowing your own creativity and inspiration to work their magic.

- **Awareness of Opportunities**

To ensure you get the most out of any team; both for yourself and the sake of the team; you need to be aware of any opportunity which could present itself to you. In fact, the idea that anything can be seen as an opportunity should be a basic principle of your team's development. The people who deal with the day to day processes will usually be the ones who see the most opportunities; whether this is to save money or focus on a new direction. Your team needs to develop an awareness of the world around them and how the general public reacts to the ideas and aspirations that the business believes in. This will help to focus your mind on what works and what does not; which means future projects can be more effectively prioritized and started, according to current trends.

- **Moving the Goal Posts**

Part of coaching a team and being a great leader is to inspire your supporters, but also to remind them that nothing is static, every goal moves depending upon outside influences and the changing perspectives of you and your team. It is important that all members of your team develop an understanding of not just the goals you are all aiming for, but also, of the underlying principles to these goals. This will ensure they are able to react to any changes and suggest ways of improving or modifying the goals to achieve better results. By coaching your team into the practice of watching and evaluating the goals you will take a huge amount of pressure off yourself and can enjoy focusing on the project development and the overall aim.

You can also ensure that all your team understands that there is no such thing as static in business or life, something is always changing and you must learn to move with it and make the most of every opportunity. A secondary part of this skill is to teach your team the value of setting their own goals and regularly evaluating them. The best leaders and coaches will encourage their team members to reach and exceed any goal.

- **Understanding the Basic Principles of Leadership**

Perhaps one of the most important skills that any leader should pass on to their team and those around them is an understanding of the principles behind leadership. A great leader is required to be fair, understanding and help to guide their followers along life's journey. Despite the number of challenges that will be faced by any great leader you will also need to be prepared to focus on your team and help them to reach their own goals; even if the only reward you receive is their gratitude. Leading others means setting an example for others to follow and accepting that this will not always be easy and others will not always be able to follow as they would like to. However, the mark of a great leader is in the optimism and belief they convey; that everyone has the ability to do great things and, with a little help and guidance wants to do so. Of course, if someone simply requires instructions they can also be a valued member of the team; a good leader understands the strengths and weaknesses of every member of their team and plans the way forward accordingly.

Coaching your team in the roles and principles of leadership will help them to understand your role and how they can become better leaders themselves.

- **Learning to Communicate**

As already discussed, communication is one of the most important traits of any super leader. It is also essential to coach others into this way of thinking and ensures that your entire team understands the power of communication. There are many different methods of communicating with others; they range from simple conversations, boardroom meetings, emails or customer facing service. The most important principle to be relayed is that every piece of communication should be conducted in a positive manner. Being positive is essential to building a relationship with the other party and obtaining a mutually satisfactory result. The same principle applies to all levels of communication and it is Important to build an understanding of the visual signals that the body gives off when people are discussing things that are important to them. Spotting these signals will enable you to connect with the other party and get the result you need or want. Listening to everything which is said is an important part of communicating and an essential lesson to teach your own team. The more the team emulates your own standards and behavior the more aware you will become that they have adopted the right approach to communication and others.

• Coaching as a Source of Information

Teaching your knowledge and techniques to others is an excellent way of passing on this information to ensure it is available for future generations and to ensure you are building leaders of the future. These leaders may exceed their own skills and capabilities and go much further than even you can dream off! However, coaching them with the necessary skills to become great leaders in their own right also provides an opportunity for you to connect with your team on a personal level and understand them, how they work, how they live and a whole host of other, useful information. The more you understand about your team the easier it will be to both coaches them and help them to grow, as people. It is important to teach your team how to handle and interpret information; they may struggle to see more than one point of view and you can help them to see other viewpoints by asking the right questions. Pushing decisions onto these team members will also ensure that become aware of the responsibility that they hold and that they are allowed to make certain decisions. This will create a feeling of self-worth in your team and encourage them to take on more responsibility and become more dedicated to the team.

• The Art of Delegation

Many managers' micro-manages and is extremely reluctant to hand over any control to other members of the team. This can stem from a belief that no one else can do a job as well as you or it can be out of fear that the more which is delegated the less you will be needed.

In fact, the best leaders learn to delegate all the time. If there is physically no work left to do then you have done a good job of training all your staff to take care of the everyday items and this will leave you free to focus on keeping your staff happy and ensuring the project or business is moving in the right direction. The bigger the project or business becomes the more important it becomes to delegate as many roles and tasks as possible; it will simply not be possible to undertake everything yourself and stay focused on your goals, progress and team satisfaction. The best leaders will pick the tasks they are most suited to and pass the others onto appropriate individuals whilst providing any training which is necessary to ensure they have the skills available to complete the tasks required of them. This is more than just delegation; it is a combination of all the coaching skills, as your team becomes capable of running the project and moving things in the right direction; whether you are there or not.

In many ways the ultimate aim of any coaching session is to ensure that a team can survive without your presence. Despite the importance of being able to delegate it is often one of the most difficult attributes to both teach you and coach others in.

Delegate, what it means

Delegation is not just another task a leader has to carry out; it is a skill to be developed. The effective delegation would have your entire team consistently motivated as each person would be carrying out tasks that draw on their natural abilities. As such they can remain motivated. The delegation also requires a balance of relevance among tasks; the leader must ensure that each person is aware of how important their assigned task is to the big picture; these tasks should not be rated merely on their complexity such that; those perceived as more complex are seen to be more relevant. The leader must emphasize the big picture and how every contribution is integral to success; such that; anyone without the other would be incomplete. Delegation is a great way to ensure more tasks get done; the option to this is undertaking all the responsibilities yourself. Overtime leaders that adopt this approach burn out easily and are unable to get the most of their people. When people feel redundant in a system they have a tendency not to apply themselves to any task assigned. To get the best from your team; refuse to do all the work yourself. Express trust in others and follow them up with confidence reinforcement that demonstrates your assurance in their capacity to produce results. Some people argue that delegation led them to failure in a previous leadership project. They hold firm to the saying; "if you want to get it done; do it yourself".

You may even have had a similar experience where by assigning tasks to others; they dropped the ball and that led to poor outcomes and unachieved goals. Yes; this could be the case; especially for new teams but then it is possible that the leader did not clearly understand delegation as such did not get the best results from it. Delegation is a skill; and here are four important stages in an effective delegation process:

Work Break Down Stage

Here the leader breaks down the process for achieving the overall goal into specific tasks. Each task would have its own mini goal and would form milestones within the entire process. This helps the leader break down the goal into stages, set expectations and most importantly choose which team member would be responsible for what tasks. Sometimes the delegation of task could happen democratically; where each team member chooses the one that best appeals to their perception of competence. This could be useful for new teams where each individual's competence is not known as such the leader can gain useful insight into each person by the kind of tasks they agree to undertake at this stage. On the other hand; mostly for established teams; democratizing responsibility may not be necessary as the leader already understands the competencies of each person and can easily assign them to roles that match these competencies. It is important that a leader does not skip this stage as this would help her think through all the activities to be carried out and how they tie in to the big picture. It may also help identify potential problem areas that would require more people or more time so as to set expectations clearly and identify key milestones.

Putting Round Pegs in Round Holes

A leader works to achieve a fit between the task and the one assigned to carry out the task. At its core, leadership is about people; understanding people in a way that you help them get the best out of themselves. So this stage requires getting to know your team mates more closely. You can do this by improving your interaction with them beyond the work environment; getting to understand more about their history and background. Now it is important to note that this does not suggest getting enthralled in their personal lives; seeking to know more than necessary or being uneasily clingy to your team members. This would dissipate respect fast and may put you in awkward situations where you are expected to give a view point of petty squabbles, even within your team, that you should not even know about; let alone react to. However getting to know your people is necessary; in a professional way that shows a measure of genuine interest. You can also fit people into positions by experimenting. Try to give them tasks and see how they do on each one. Some leaders constantly move responsibilities around within their teams; this is to get everyone to develop relevant skills but also for the leader to locate those who are best at certain tasks. This experimentation strategy should however be used with caution as when the stakes are high; you may not be able to afford a 50/50 chance of success. So you should experiment with the smaller task as you make up your mind for how roles would be assigned when failure or success below a specific standard is unacceptable.

Communicate Relevance

It is not enough to give people tasks and say "you do this". It is important how the task is communicated.

In communicating a task, a leader should pay attention to expressing two key things; 1) Your trust for the person to carry out the responsibility excellently and 2) the relevance of that task to the overall project goal. People like to know that are part of something big; and that their contributions are integral to the success of the entire project. A leader does not assume that people automatically know these things as such she takes out time to effectively communicate the relevance of each task to team members. Now take note that this is carried out with clear integrity and you are not merely working people's emotions to somehow influence them to work better. The task assigned must mean something to you and this is what is communicated. If people perceive that you are merely trying to make them feel good with nice words about their „supposed" relevance; they begin to distrust you. And trust, you would find, is one of the leader's greatest assets. So communicate clearly; without deception; the actual relevance of a task to the entire team. This may require you as the leader to think more deeply about how to get your people to make an emotional connection with their tasks. It would require thinking through ways things can be said to maximum effect. It is not automatic; it is an art driven by skill which can be learnt.

Be Available For Follow Up

After the tasks have been broken down and duly assigned; the job of the leader is not yet done. Understand that in delivering their responsibilities, your people can make certain assumptions that may prove to be wrong and then get stuck in carrying out their tasks. You would be responsible for untangling such situations for them; usually by guiding them to think of new ways to approach the task. More on this in the next chapter.

Encourage your people to reach out to you for help when things are getting complicated. If they make a mistake; correct them without condemning them. Focus on the task and never attack the personality of a team member who makes a mistake. This would encourage people to speak up when they are unsure and own up when they have made a mistake. As a leader you are a helper; and you should ensure you are within reach. Some leaders create walls of processes that make it difficult for people to reach them; this is what is often called bureaucracy. While a single leader should not be made to respond to every problem within large systems; teams should be structured in a way that direct subordinates have access to the leader; and can get quick responses from her; especially in a crisis situation.

The delegation process

The following techniques may help you to become better at delegating:

Evaluate the tasks which take up your time during the average week. Consider how much time they take and what skill level is required to so the job properly. Then think about what else you could be doing with that time. You will realize that the time can be far more productively spent and this should convince you to delegate this task to a member of your team. The most difficult part may be deciding which team member should be entrusted with this task. Instruct your chosen team members carefully, you must be certain that they fully understand what is expected of them and that they will continue to do the job as you have done it.

You should be open to the idea of them changing the method, providing the results are still accurate and within the parameters given. However, no employee should change a system without having first used it for an appropriate amount of time; this will ensure they understand all the ramifications of changing it. One task should be delegated at a time. This will help you to feel more comfortable about someone else doing one of your tasks and will allow you to keep a close eye on the results. As the first task is shown to be completed successfully then you can start to plan the next item to delegate; gradually the pace of delegation will increase as you hand over all the daily tasks, and you will find yourself as busy as ever. The key to delegating successfully is ensuring that the chosen team member understands fully what is expected from them and works towards the same goal as you and the rest if the team. Delegating anything is probably not a skill that many business owners have in abundance. However, it is an essential skill to master and will allow you to focus on the things that are relevant to your project.

The Difficulties of Delegation

If followed through, you are most likely to achieve success in delegating responsibilities within your teams. However it is important you avoid these two things after you give delegated tasks to your team members;

Reverse delegation: This happens when; even though you have assigned a task to a person; they still expect you do most of the work involved; as a way to supposedly "show how" things should be done. A good leader would avoid this; encourage your people to think through their responsibilities; take on tasks and own their outcomes.

Micro Management: A leader cannot be too far from her people; but she should keep a safe distance from constantly interfering with their work. At certain times you may not understand what they are doing and what stage they are; you can ask questions to seek understanding not that you take on command and begin trying to get people to do things just like you would. Give people the opportunity to succeed and sometimes the experience of failing before you interfere with their processes. Sometimes this cannot be afforded and you would have to step in and take on the wheel; ensure this is rare and only used when it is absolutely necessary.

The Benefits of Delegation

There are many different aspects of coaching and delegating effectively; used properly these skills can be developed and improved to establish a group of people which will assist you in leading your team and reaching your goals:

- Understanding the Current Skill set of your Team

In order to fully appreciate and drive your team forward it is essential to understand them and what motivates them. This is the best way of establishing a good knowledge of their skill set and of which approach is best to obtain results. Once you understand what your team is capable of you will be able to identify where improvements can be made and the best method for achieving these improvements. This is stage one of coaching, identifying their needs and building on their current abilities; this will ensure your team is constantly challenged and open to new experiences and goals.

In the majority of cases your team will welcome the additional responsibilities and opportunities. Pushing your team to be the best they can be will ensure that they are always providing maximum effort at work. This means that both you and your project will benefit from their personal growth.

Understanding your team and their skill set will also ensure that you allocate them jobs within or near their comfort zones whilst gradually coaching them into a new area, or improving their existing skill set.

- Providing Opportunities to Grow and New Challenges

The natural follows on from identifying the current skill set of your team is creating the opportunities and challenges for your team. There are many tasks completed daily which can be handled differently and it can be a great learning experience to allow someone, with the right experience and attitude, to tackle these tasks and find their own way of competing the challenge.

Chapter 8 – Introspection and Outrospection

Introspection is a vital element when it comes to the expansion and comprehension of every individual business's inherent building blocks. The easiest way to understand introspection specifically in terms of business leadership is by thinking about it as an opportunity to understand the inner workings of one's own mind. Intelligent business leadership, of course, views introspection not as a byproduct but as a fully functioning tool, which is used to weed out inconsistencies and hostility in the business environment. The reason is that introspection, when properly conducted, does not merely work on building a clear understanding of one's company or leadership. More importantly, it uses the opportunity to focus on a leader and a business's ability to regulate or control one's impulses and motivate them. All these three factors matter for the expansion of a business and the true establishment of a well-rounded business leader.

Self-Awareness and Introspection

This need to properly introspect business leaders and their motives brings us to the ageless concept of self-awareness. The idea is simple: use the truth, a clear unvarnished version of it, to recognize, accept, and embrace the changes required for you to become a business leader. It's like being a president who doesn't always go off saying that he has the best words. Rather, he makes a point to listen to the concerns that people raise, as well as works to address them instead of suppressing them.

Running a successful business is no different from running a country, after all. It's not always about gaining more traction or adding more land; it's also about how you rule and make sure that you know the best possible ways to do things. Remember that a strong foundation is nothing but that. When you are watering the soil it is standing on, the minute you stop, the very thing you are standing on goes from solid ground to shifting sand. Then, your traction, footing, and ability to remain upright - much less your ability to move forward - are all automatically compromised.

1. Self-Esteem vs. Values and Priorities

Two of the hardest things to do as a business leader are finding time for the things that the company values and prioritizing and balancing that with the self-esteem quotient of the people you seek to lead. This is particularly prominent in terms of schedule-based management systems in which the production of a specific outcome is practically the most important thing on the agenda.

Or is it?

Individuals with low self-esteem will say 'yes' and stick to the safe bet. They do as they are told, but if you are not questioning and implementing specific judgments, why are you even bothering with hiring people? Just stick to AI. The fact of the matter is that your strategic goals are what you need to look out for as a business leader. You need to ensure that your employees feel empowered enough to find better ways to keep on putting these values and priorities ahead of company culture and past trends.

Think about Goldman Sachs and E*TRADE for a second. Both of these companies work with financial services. Now, considering Goldman Sachs is so much bigger and more famous than E*Trade, the latter has sought to emulate the former's model to a T. How successful would they be? **Not very.** Do you know why?

If you tried to measure your success on the same scale, you'd still feel like a failure, and so would your employees. The reason is that they are not the same company. Goldman Sachs works with high-end customers and needs to focus on one individual sale, whereas E*TRADE is more grassroots and gets its push from the mass influx. While Goldman Sachs can rely on client relationships, E*TRADE has to set their eyes on being competitive, as well as more technically advanced options. You need to teach your employees and future leaders how to see things in context, especially when you are trying to introspect. After all, you can't judge the skill of a fish by how high it flies. Furthermore, the self-esteem of the employees you are working with is critical. The better they feel about themselves, the more invested they will be in their jobs. By teaching them how to replace their negative behaviors or perceptions with positive actions, you give an idea on how to identify the company's priorities and needs over their insecurities. That is essential for building a better tomorrow for your business.

2. Self-Confidence vs. Curiosity

Self-confidence is the next major wing of self-awareness. It also has a big part of what allows you to change and grow, as well as shepherd such growth as a business leader. In fact, curiosity is perhaps one of the most important elements of effective self-awareness.

It gives you cause to question what lies beyond the limits of your knowledge. As such, it constantly lets you accept and seek out more. The only potential roadblock here is self-confidence, which is considered as an important part of leadership. Now, here's the thing: does confidence still matter when it comes to the realm of business leadership? **Yes!** Every successful business leader needs to always seem like they know exactly what they are doing. You will not be able to move forward or lead if your words or decisions do not sound absolutely certain. A business leader is a rock in everyone's eyes. They know; they don't guess. They lead; they don't flounder. While all that is true, the only true way to foster growth is to keep reaching into the abyss and pulling you forward. Believe it or not, even business leaders don't know what to expect.

They aren't supposed to.

They are supposed to be curious and constantly seek information. A good CEO isn't necessarily the best financial graduate that has walked out of Harvard or MIT. It's the kid who knows he or she is not the best but is willing to ask the right questions and push the company and employees in the direction of prospective change while confidently maintaining the economic status quo. Curiosity is something that can be built into businesses. It was done by 3M whose concept of Post-It Note was developed by Dr. Spence Silver during the company's allocated curiosity window.

3. Assertiveness vs. Feedback and Circumstances

Another important part of self-awareness, particularly when you are a business leader, is the whole notion of being assertive or forthright in one's own opinions. Assertive matters, but it is also equally - if not more - essential for every leader to know how to temper this characteristic with the feedback that they receive and in light of the circumstances they are in. These two factors are the basis of accountability, which is perhaps one of the - if not **the** most - crucial parts of leadership. When a business leader is assertive when they are unaware, unwilling, and unable to admit their mistakes or the reality of the situation. The same thing occurred with the former CEO of Turing Pharmaceuticals, Martin Shkreli, who famously increased the prices of Daraprim (a drug used to treat toxoplasmosis, a disease that targets the immune system of cancer patients and HIV positive individuals) from $13.50 to $750 per pill. This markup of $736.5 was not the only thing that costed the company, however.

4. Identification of Personal Emotions

As a business leader, the most important reason that any individual needs to either cater to or learn to reign in is our emotions. There is a theory that our thoughts control our actions. In truth, actions are never controlled by thoughts unless they are specifically allowed to. That is exactly where mindfulness comes in. Mindfulness is like the express version of self-awareness. Whereas awareness centers around your ability to act on autopilot - that is, to do something without even thinking about it, without resistance or judgment - the whole purpose of mindfulness is to use these same tools to identify and label your thoughts. Instead of avoiding them, you challenge yourself to understand and accept how you are thinking and why you are thinking in that specific manner by objectifying your ideas. All of this is important because, to truly understand ourselves and our personal motives, we need to stop being overconfident. That is impossible to do without identifying the emotions surrounding us. Once we manage to do so, however, we are afforded key insight into our own values and thoughts, which allows us to bridge the disconnect that we've had between our functioning self and our theoretical self. This, in turn, allows us to become not just more productive but more successful as well.

Self-Regulation and the Control Paradigm

The thing that most people tend to forget about emotions is that they are, for the most part, biological impulses. While the impulses themselves may be hard or even impossible to control, the actual emotion itself is not. Having said that, we will concede that, in the heat of the moment, it is easy to forget that our conscious choice to manage or ignore emotional reactions will determine how you function as a business leader or even a regular person. Self-regulation is about more than just making room for emotional intelligence. It is liberation from the shackles of impulse-based behavior and the responsible undertaking of reflection and control in the face of current climates and uncertainties. They are all tempered by integrity, which gives individuals the choice to say 'no' to those impulsive tendencies.

The thing is, regardless of how it is perceived, self-regulation is a crucial part of business development.

In truth, it is one of the most underrated skills that the business leader needs to have. Why is this even more important now more than ever? Well, for one, businesses today require extremely higher productivity rates in order to stay competitive in the market. The only way that business leaders will be able to sustain high productivity while maintaining safe and fair environments for their workers is if they make a point of creating environments where high-profile, effective, and competent workers want to come and work for their companies. Frankly, this is something that they cannot do if they have a reputation in the industry for blowing their top all the time or creating drama. Furthermore, self-regulation builds its way into the concept of trickle-down economy. The more the leaders apply this technique, the more the employees will follow suit. Remember, as a leader, your actions will be emulated, so make sure that your workers can pick up characteristics that will take your company forward.

1. Basics of Self-Control

As a business leader, one of the major problems that we tend to face is the manner in which our emotions and logical brain seem to clash or face off. It is only natural for leaders to battle with their emotional reactions and be expected to provide rational decisions at some point. Despite that, this is where emotional self-control comes into play. Destructive emotions and impulses are a regular part of our day-to-day lives, even if we don't always recognize them as such. Something as simple as not wanting to wake up early in the morning - although you know that you have to be early at work - is a prime example of how destructive emotions can be to your behavior.

It can also control the actions that are taking place - and will continue to take place - as the leader of your workforce and company. So, how do we get a grip on our emotions and start to decide on what we're going to do, logically and not impulsively speaking?

Well, why don't we start with Dr. M. Seligmans' ABCDE model of worry management? The reason why you should use such a tool, in case you have not already guessed it yet, is that worry is the exact polar opposite of control. Meaning, if you can manage your worries, you will automatically be putting yourself in a position of control!

A - Adversity

The first thing that you need to do in order to establish self-control is to describe your adversity. Who is the problem? What is the problem? When did this problem arise? Moreover, where is this problem taking place?

By making sure that you are using specific terms to accurately describe the adversity in question, you automatically ensure that you are establishing objective statements. That will help you to form a rational decision in the near future.

Sample Scenario

Imagine that a product that you have launched has failed in the market. This failure is adversity. It's not about you feeling unwell or sad. It's not about the fact that your distributors were an hour late to the launch last week either. The problem is the product itself and its failure to attract consumers. Once you know and accept this, you can start working on the problem directly.

B - Belief

Considering you have identified the adversity, your next job is to recall what you say to yourself when facing such a dilemma. This is extremely important because much of what you speak of later translates into actual beliefs. For instance, if you are dealing with a tough problem, you may tell yourself, "I can't do this" or "I just can't cope with the pressure." You will honestly be unable to cope with the pressure because you have taught yourself to believe that you are incapable.

C - Consequences

This is where the concept of consequences starts to form. Once you have identified your adversity and then recorded the belief pattern that you have either verbally or mentally established, you may take note of the subsequent consequences of your ideas. For example, when you told yourself that you could not cope with the pressure of work or do a certain thing, how did you feel? Did it empower you, as if it was something you could do? Or, did you feel even more helpless, like your ability to overcome obstacles had been completely taken away? This idea is not that uncommon. Keep in mind that the feelings and emotions that you deal with stem from the beliefs that you instill in yourself.

D - Disputation

Now, let's move on to the action items. Go back to your beliefs and ask yourself objectively, "What is wrong or inaccurate with the belief that I put forward?" Identify it, then dispute it. For instance, when you said that you could not cope with the pressure, you could challenge this event by recognizing the multiple instances in which you managed to deal well with pressure.

115

E - Energization

That's how you bring yourself to energy and organization. Energization is where you identify how to apply your energy in an organized form so that you can build towards a better future. Instead of saying "I can't do this," try telling yourself that you need to work harder and make sure that you will.

2. Importance of Identifying and Quelling Impulsive Behavior

The biggest problem with impulsive behavior is that it can be downright destructive when it comes to the success of any business. As a business leader, it is essential to not only have the ability to organize and coherently plan but also be able to lead by example and ensure that your behavior is both rational and deliberate. Let's put this into context, shall we?

Imagine that you are the CEO of a multinational company. Among your current goals is to improve productivity during work hours, and you believe that the best way to do this is by avoiding unprofessional working environments. One morning, you walk past the office kitchen and notice a gathering of five or six employees who are chatting as they make their own coffee. You instinctively decide that workplace conversations such as these are responsible for the lower productivity of the company. Therefore, you issue an e-mail to all of the individuals you have seen, stating that employees are no longer allowed to visit the kitchen for a coffee break. If they want to have coffee, they merely have to push a button, and a server will bring them coffee. The only problem here is that you have not consulted the chief operating officer or head of human resources. Also, you don't exactly have a coffee server at the moment.

Almost immediately, your organization is in a state of absolute chaos. It can effectively extend to smoking breaks; if it does not, then smokers have an unfair advantage over non-smokers. So, you suddenly find yourself bombarded by thousands of questions from hundreds of employees. This problem may have been avoided by holding a small meeting with the COO and head of the HR department first. What's worse is that your impulsive behavior has led your employees to label you as an irrational and erratic leader - a name that is obviously not for PR.

3. Emotion Management: Leveraging and Controlling Positive and Negative Emotions

The thing is, emotional management is difficult to do, especially when it comes to stressful situations at work. Unfortunately, it is also much more common. But this doesn't mean that you need to allow yourself to be controlled by negative feelings. So, why don't you start by trying to identify the calm and negative emotions that can be found in the workplace first?

Remember that being aware of your emotional state is the first step to controlling your emotional state, just like we have laid out in the mixed model for emotional intelligence. Now, coming back to the negative emotions that we are faced with, one of emotional stress in the workplace arises from frustration or irritation. This is generally stemming from the form of helplessness. Say, you have a boss who is deliberately sexist or racist. If you want to get out of this situation, you first need to stop and evaluate if such labels are truly applicable for your superior.

Then, ask yourself if that is why you are feeling this way. Is there a better more tactful way to deal with this issue?

Take your time to think things through. After doing so, you will find that you feel calmer and more in control. Now, you can move on and look for a positive way to deal with the situation. One suggestion is to recall the similar incidents that you or your peers have been in and see and learn from how those situations have been tackled. Nevertheless, this is not merely about frustration and irritation. Every other negative emotion that you may experience in the workplace, such as worry or anger, nervousness or aggravation, dislike or disappointment, and unhappiness or dissatisfaction, can be resolved in the exact same manner. It's all about understanding what negative emotions you have and finding a rational and effective way to deal with them. It is important to keep in mind that introspection is a major part of running any business. As a leader, the ability to examine your own motives and feelings matters not only because it will give you a clear vision of what you see yourself doing in the future but also because it will allow you to lead the people who follow you with much more clarity.

Self-Motivation

In a world of over seven million people where no two people are the same, diversity is the lifeblood of businesses, as well as all the possibilities that lay before you. But what are these things? Furthermore, how do you teach someone that the #1 thing you need is the motivation? Frankly speaking, employees are a dime a dozen; great leaders, however, are not. The only question is: How does a leader become great?

For one, a great leader must be self-motivated.

They must know who they are, what their needs are, and how they intend to fulfill their needs. Most importantly, they should have a strong, unbreakable drive to achieve their goals while simultaneously ensuring that their personal objectives are in tune with the needs and goals of the organization that they lead. How do you ensure that you have maximized your self-motivation as a leader? Well, why don't we start with nine easy tricks to get you going?

1. Use Words to Boost Your Motivation

Talking to someone about the things that you want to do is an excellent way to motivate yourself. Not only does talking help communicate your ideas to your team; it also helps you! By simply hearing your own ideas spelled out aloud, after all, you can see what other people see, hear what they hear, as well as identify where you have gone wrong or where you need to refocus your attention.

2. Be Optimistic

Another great way to make sure that you are holding onto your personal motivation is by looking at everything through rose-colored glasses. In other words, be optimistic. Remember that obstacles come and go; the one thing that remains constant throughout is your approach to dealing with these obstacles. Are obstacles going to scare you, or will they be seen as another challenge that you can soon overcome? The choice is yours.

3. Find Out What Interests You

It's hard to stay self-motivated if you are neither interested nor absolutely in love with what you are doing. If you can't find something to love about the task that you have been given, try to look at the bigger picture and mentally envision how you do minor tasks as a building block for the ultimate big picture.

4. Acknowledge Your Achievements

Another important step is to make sure that you acknowledge the achievements that you have. It is challenging to stay motivated when you constantly feel like a failure or as if you are not achieving or amounting to anything. Instead, try making sure that you take time out to acknowledge things that you have achieved something, then point yourself towards the things that you hope to attain in the future.

5. Monitor and Record Your Success

Speaking of self-acknowledgment, try keeping a record of how successful you are. Having your failures and successes written down in black-and-white will not only allow you to physically see how far you've come. Instead, it will also act as a map and indicate how much farther you need to go in order to achieve the success that you wish to have.

6. Boost Your Energy Levels

Motivation, however, is hard to hold onto unless you have the right energy levels. Besides, maintaining the right energy levels means maintaining a healthy lifestyle. Eat right, sleep right, and make sure you exercise. Your body is your temple. While businesses may seem to want your brain more than they do your body, it's not really possible to have a brain that is fully functioning if the body it's attached to is failing.

7. Motivate Everyone You Can

Another technique to boost your own motivation is by sharing your own ideas and thoughts to boost motivation among the people you surround yourself with.

Healthy, motivated peers can automatically recharge you and keep you motivated and on track.

8. Be Open to Learning

Always, always, always be open to learning. There is no such thing as "enough knowledge." More importantly, as cliché as it may sound, knowledge is power. Always keep your mind open and take on each obstacle as a challenge that you not only need to overcome but learn from as well.

9. Break It Down

As a pro tip, when it comes to self-motivation, you should always use stepping stones to make your way to your bigger goals. Having such things can seem daunting, but what's even scarier is not even wanting to take it on because your motivation levels will be low. Instead, breaking your major project into smaller, more approachable pieces not only ensures that you are more confident. It also ascertains that your project gets done on time. A win-win situation, indeed!

Recognizing Emotion in Outrospection

Although emotional intelligence models have already taught us the importance of clear emotional perception, the specific use of emotions and the thorough understanding of emotions still seems to escape us. This is why trait EQ models focus heavily on the characteristics of various emotions, as well as the impact that they have on themselves and other people. At the moment, we have already figured out how to understand ourselves and manage our own emotions. As leaders, we cannot merely perceive what our customers and employees think about and how they feel.

We also need to find a way to share the experiences they endure since that is the only way to genuinely figure out what motivates them and what holds them back. We will go through this process in the same way we have approached the EQ models. It will start with understanding and recognizing emotions. Then, we will make our way down to the complex side of managing and controlling them. Imagine being able to read people's minds. How much easier would it be when you walked into a board meeting - or any business conference for that matter - and practically knew exactly what your opponent was thinking about, how they felt that way and why, as well as how there emotional state was without playing word games or throwing shade at each other. Imagine knowing how receptive someone will be to an idea after having an idea of what to say, when to say it, and basically be Jean Grey in a suit. Well, buckle up because we are about to teach you exactly how to do that!

Facial Expressions

Remember all those primary emotions we talked about back in Chapter 1? Well, it turns out that you can literally express almost all of them simply by using your face! As a beginner on the topic, why don't we start you off with the seven common micro expressions first?

1. Surprised Micro Expression

Usually, a surprise is identified by raised eyebrows that are generally curved in nature, horizontal forehead wrinkles, the whites of the eye showing both above and below the pupil, and on occasion with a dropped jaw teeth generally parted, and a tightly stretched brow.

2. Fearful Micro Expression

When depicting fear, human beings have a tendency to raise eyebrows once again. However, such brows are drawn together usually in a flat line instead of a curve. Their eyes are also enlarged, but the lower whites of the eyes are generally not visible and the mouth is typically drawn back in a taut expression instead of simply leaving it open.

3. Disgusted Micro Expression

Disgust is generally depicted with prominently raised eyelids and a curled lower lip. The nose wrinkles, as well as the corners of the eyes. You will also notice that individuals depicting disgust also tend to have raised cheeks, which combine together to show an overall sense of revulsion.

4. Angry Micro Expression

When it comes to anger, the facial expressions are very similar to those of disgust, the lower lip is tensed but usually not curled as it is with disgust, the eyes are hard and protruding, while there are lines between the brows again, although these are anger lines, which are vertical and not horizontal, like the worry lines we have noticed earlier. The lower jaw is also prone to be jutting out, and the nostrils have a tendency to be flaring, depending on the individual's level of rage and breathing capabilities.

5. Happy Micro Expression

The micro expressions that denote happiness are almost the exact opposite. The teeth are generally exposed, the lips are upturned, and a wrinkle is forming from the nose to the outer edge of the lip. The cheeks are also raised; depending on the age of the individual, you may notice wrinkles near the corner of the eyes as well. This last factor distinguishes genuine laughter from fake laughter.

As such, it can be extremely important when dealing with client satisfaction.

6. Sorrowful Micro Expression

Sorrow is also quite easy to spot. The eyebrows are a definite factor, the inner corners of the eyebrows are pulled toward the center and then upward, the lips are drawn downward, and the jaw comes up with the lower lip protruding outward. Because of the complexity of the factors involved, this also happens to be the hardest micro expression to fake.

7. Hateful Micro Expression

Then, we have hatefulness. Also projected as contempt, it is depicted with relaxed eyes and brow and a lower lip smirk to one side of the face. While it is relatively easy to express emotions when your entire face is projecting the same thing, micro expressions also allow you to pick up the tiny non-verbal cues that perhaps haven't even registered to the individuals themselves regarding how they feel.

Bodily Expressions

Facial micro expressions are not the only way to recognize what a person is thinking or feeling, though. One of the more prominent forms of non-verbal expression is the use of bodily cues, such as crossing arms, which indicates defensiveness, or crossing legs, which shows being closed off. Similarly, standing with one's hands positioned on their hips is an almost universal sign for aggressiveness or alternatives for strength and control.

Holding one's hands behind their back is indicative of boredom or anger, while fidgeting or repetitive motions can be used to identify impatience, frustration, and even boredom. All in all, being able to identify micro-reactions, both in facial expression and bodily cues, allows individuals to not only communicate more clearly but also allows interpret and understand the non-verbal signals being put out so that they can adapt their verbal communication to be more effective and impactful.

How Should You Respond to Other People's Reactions?

As a leader, you will soon find that a large portion of your time is spent trying to understand the needs, actions, and reactions that your employees or team depict. The problem a lot of leaders tend to face is that they don't know how to react or respond best to these external actions or reactions coming at them from all corners. The thing is, they are not based on actions or decisions that you have taken. On the contrary, external factors play an extremely large role in workplace reactions, and you will never be used to distinguish between how much of that reaction is genuine and how much of it is stemming from an outside factor until and unless you teach yourself to stop and listen. So, let's make this easy, shall we?

Instead of always assuming that there is a backstory, you can try using a leadership response technique. Dr. Rathe of the University of Florida developed a technique called Background-Affects-Trouble-Handling-Empathy (BATHE), which he began to use to communicate with patients and found it extremely helpful. According to BATHE, the first thing you need to do when you are dealing with employees is to initiate a conversation about the background of the issue.

Ask yourself, "What is going on?" "When did it start?" "How did it happen?" "Who was involved?"

Once you've assessed the incident, ask about how the situation impacts or affects the company or team. When the topic arises, you will soon find that the employees will start to discuss the troubles they face. As they make a point to ensure you are listening actively to their problems, you'll find this helps you understand their pulse a little better. In turn, it helps to tell you how to handle the crisis best. Usually, showing parallel examples and offering fresh solutions bring back positive emotions, which you can then reinforce with empathy and understanding. The BATHE technique not only provides a structure; it also gives leaders time to think and process. Instead of being forced to automatically react to situations, they now have the flexibility to rely on a specific structure to give them the same information that they will get through a complex conversation. The best thing is, this doesn't take away from the leader's ability to take knowledge or information; it just gives them a little more room to breathe.

How to Leverage Positive Emotions in Other People

Quick question: On a scale of one to 10, how happy do you feel when you go to work - a five, maybe a six, if we're lucky?

Now, ask yourself, "How long do you spend at work?" Most of your waking hours, right?

Do you feel that regret building in your chest? Imagine, if you could fix that, if you could do something that made going to work in the morning to look forward to.

126

How much more productive do you think you would be? According to corporate studies, a lot! Why don't we teach you a few tricks of the trade?

Express Gratitude

One easy way to increase the positive emotions in your employees and team is by creating a culture of positive recognition. Think about it; just saying something like "thank you" can make the recipient feel recognized and valued. By learning to count your blessings, particularly in a business atmosphere, you are fostering positivity in every individual team member. Because positivity is a reflective emotion like empathy, it tends to reflect back and add value to the team as a whole. Ideally, a great technique to inject gratitude into daily business dealings is by starting meetings with a positive feedback session. Meaning, talk about the good and reinforce it before you even touch upon the problems that need to be addressed.

Build Connections

Another important way in which leaders can build positivity into their teams and companies is by encouraging the employees to build connections among their own teams. Happiness research has shown that positive moods are practically contagious, which means that even if you are personally not in a good mood, simply being in contact with someone who is can help with your mood and those around you. You need to encourage staff to celebrate little successes or personal achievements; small companies and family-owned companies tend to do this by employing "employee of the month" or "manager of the week" strategies, which can entice employees to do better.

It also gives the staff a sense of community; that, in turn encourages, workplace friendships, which is very beneficial to productivity and company growth.

Embrace Strength and Values

Another pro tip is to use goals and opportunities to attract employees to work on their strengths. Goals give employees a sense of purpose, particularly since the big picture isn't always easy to imagine. By allowing employees to do what they are good at and giving them more opportunities to shine, we are effectively strengthening organizational goals and facing developmental challenges with the best possible candidates for the job. Doing something well in itself is a good feeling; as such, it makes it easier to make people feel good about themselves as well.

How to Deal With Negative Emotions in Other People

Unfortunately, leaders don't always get to deal with positive emotions. In truth, a big part of being a leader means dealing with the problems and crises that your company and team are going through. As you experience these negative incidents, it's easy to get sucked into a vortex of negativity, which is something that you can't afford as a leader.

The trick here is to center yourself and your employees. Before you let the problem swallow you whole, ask yourself, "What is its source?" "What is its result?" "How can you or your employee fix it?"

Action plans play a big role here; use your expertise to mentally guide your employees through possible solutions. As you do, teach them to process information productively instead of panicking. This allows you to use negative situations to your benefit, which later helps diminish the sense of panic your employees or team feel when faced with difficult situations. Always remember that, as the leader, you need to lead them forward no matter how difficult the situation is. Meaning, **you** don't get to panic or feel overwhelmed. There is nothing you can't handle.

Conclusion

An increased level of emotional intelligence is believed to be a predictor of success. You can learn to be emotionally intelligent no matter who you are or where you stand in the hierarchy of your workplace or of the organizations you work with. Mastering your emotions is one of the critical steps in becoming a brilliant leader. You can achieve this by practicing the tips in the chapters of this book. Thank you again for downloading this book. The next step for you is to start getting to know yourself and assessing how emotionally intelligent you are. Draw out your emotions. Be truthful to yourself and hold off any personal judgment. Understand how and why you feel these emotions. Connect with others and understand their emotions as well. Use your EI skills in your interactions and be on your way to success. Remember that you have to continuously enhance your emotional intelligence through constant practice. Do not fall into the trap of trailing off and getting too caught up in achieving your goals. While you never have to lose sight of where you want to go, you should not lose touch with your employees or team members. Keep your EI high and strong. You will soon realize that you are closer to your goals than you originally planned. Use your emotional intelligence properly and acquire the skills necessary to become a brilliant leader. Listen to your people. Find out how they are feeling and provide the emotional support that they need to carry out the tasks assigned to them.

The Power of Influence

Ultimately, having sufficient EQ affords you the ability to influence not only your decisions, actions, and reactions but also that of others, and not many people don't know this. The way you choose (train yourself) to respond to certain things can influence how other people react to those things as well.

For instance, let's assume you, as a leader, are informed that one of your subordinates has initiated a potentially unforgivable error. What will you do? Note that the monumental error puts your company, business, or brand in a tough spot.

Low-EQ leader: This leader will most likely lose it and go bananas. Abusive words will follow, and shouting, scolding, and an attempt to embarrass him or she publicly will be the aim of such a leader. Why? This is because this leader lacks a handle on his emotions and can neither process his or that of the victim of his or her verbal assault.

High-EQ leader: This leader will not act as the other leader above. He or she will take steps to first process their emotions in a bid to figure out if anger is the right way to go. This leader will also take into consideration if it does anybody good to publicly embarrass them and then to what end it will benefit the company. A leader with an EQ will command the situation. Instead of raining insults and abuses on the staff, they will try to find out how the error came about in the first place. After either proffering a solution or seeking out one, an emotionally intelligent leader will then proceed to use words of wisdom in rebuking the staff's behavior. The scenario painted above is a teachable moment to other members of staff that you do not need to scream your lungs off on impulse when such a thing occurs. The leader with the high EQ would also succeed in influencing how everybody in that organization views leadership. For the umpteenth time, leaders who can control their emotions in various situations in the presence of others will passively influence how they respond themselves. A lot of work is done to first influence what will otherwise be your natural response to such situations, but through intentionality, a leader will eventually attain mastery of his or her own emotions.

Emotional intelligence allows you to shatter all forms of limitations that stem from impulsive behaviors or unfavorable and spontaneous reactions. The average EQ score is between 90 and 100. However, a high EQ score is typically placed upward to 160. It has been pointed out that a high or at least an average EQ is paramount in leadership. If you have a low EQ, you need to take the steps needed to rectify it and boost your EQ serious. However, if your EQ is average, there is also a need to improve it. Mastering oneself and behavioral patterns take a bit of time and precision. To be better, you have to be deliberate, be emotionally mature, and practice daily. Until absolutely nothing can tick you off anymore, you must continue to manage your emotions and that of others.

Breaking Barriers

There can sometimes be barriers to communication between the leader and the followers. These barriers if not broken can negatively affect productivity in the workplace. Sometimes leaders with no EQ tend to feel these barriers more because they lack proper skills in communication. Leaders with a high level of emotional intelligence might sometimes experience it, but these barriers are not unbreakable. Some of the strategies that leaders can employ in breaking the barriers are :

1. Give clear instructions and to the appropriate quarters. Do not give to those below the appropriate recipients, but make it clear that you will like to be able to access information at any point.

2. Make sure your intentions and objectives are clear. There will be a better response when there are clear intentions and objectives.

3. Trust and listen to your instinct. If you have a feeling something is not adding up, dig deeper.

4. Encourage everyone to be as open as possible. Request for both negative and positive parts of a report and do not only acknowledge one part but acknowledge both parts when reported.

5. Foster deep connection with people. A deep connection with a leader breeds consistency on both sides.

6. Have a precise way of managing information, but make sure this is not your only way of getting facts.

7. Do not place title over people.

8. Contribute to discussions after your followers have shared their views because if you share your views first, they will simply agree most of the time.

9. Probe further if you feel you aren't getting enough information on reports.

10. Create time for one on one meetings sometimes rather than depending on phone calls and emails always.

11. Be clear about your vision and use it to inspire and unite your followers in a simple direction.

12. Know yourself so well that you understand all your weaknesses.

13. Have a well-grounded knowledge about your industry so you can ask the right questions.

Dark Psychology Secrets

Stop Being Manipulated, Learn the Efficient Manipulation Methods and the Art of Reading and Analyze People

By: Adam Goleman

Part 1: Dark Psychology Secrets

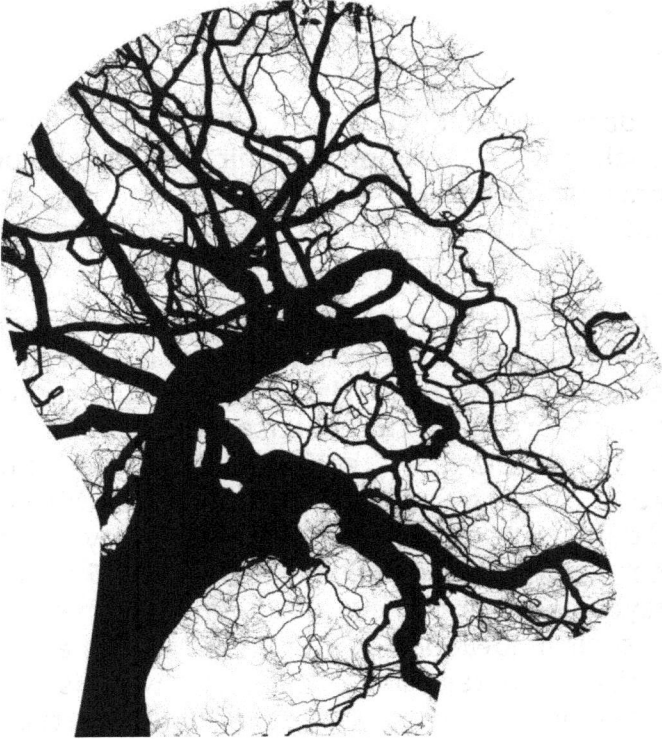

Introduction

What Is the Dark Psychology Secrets and What Does This Book Help You Achieve?

What is dark psychology, and how does it impact how we think, feel, and live? When we think of psychology, we may consider its broad definition: the scientific study of the mind, behavior, and how they are affected by many factors.

These factors include social interaction and behavior, mental health, cognitive processes, and overall human development. The term dark psychology refers to a specific area of study that focuses on aspects of mind control, manipulation, exploitation, and how to understand how they affect us. Essentially, this is known as the "dark" side of the mind or psychology. There are many secrets or lesser-known facts about the impact of dark psychology because it happens to many people without their knowledge. To understand the secretive nature of the darker side of psychology, this book will provide details on how to understand different techniques used and identify them.

This includes methods of manipulation, exploitation, and forms of persuasion: how to identify and analyze them in order to avoid their negative effects.

Chapter 1: Persuasion History

The History of Persuasion and How People Applied Techniques in Ancient Times

Persuasion has a long history, going back to when humans discovered how to use it to our advantage. Persuasion is defined as a type of behavior that is employed as a means to influence someone's way of thinking, beliefs, decisions, motivation, and behavior.

It can be subtle and undetectable, done in a covert fashion, or more obvious, such as a form of encouragement. The reasons for persuasion vary and are commonly used for personal and/or financial gain. It's a method applied throughout history for political and social gain. One notable example is how the Greeks viewed forms of persuasion, as a way to measure the suitability of a politician or position of authority. The ability to persuade was valued highly, and those who were successful were regarded as worthy of election. Aristotle, a Greek philosopher, regarded persuasion as an essential skill to acquire and develop for a variety of reasons. It can be argued that persuasion, if used in its most skillful form, can deflect a lot of negative attributes and help someone gain favor, regardless of the circumstance. An example of this is a court case, where a defendant or their lawyer can argue their innocence by way of persuasion.

Even where a defendant is believed to be guilty, persuasion can (and has) convince a judge or jury that evidence is circumstantial or that a witness's testimony is not credible. There is more to this method than simply convincing an individual or group of a certain belief or concept with a smooth presentation and convincing words; it includes a far more in-depth study and observation of the people who are to be persuaded. Many of these attributes are useful in winning an argument or a case, whether the person employing the persuasion techniques is correct or not. In some cases, it's not about right or wrong, but instead, a variance in opinions or beliefs where persuasion can go a long way to convince people to see the other side of the debate.

What are the Different Types of Persuasion?

Rhetoric is a powerful method of persuasion, which involves the careful study and observation of people, either in groups, as individuals or in society, to better understand how best to apply the "art" of persuasion. Observing people would entail a lot of studies, including employing skilled writers, artists, and speakers with the expertise and talent to persuade. A modern example of this method can be seen in advertisements aimed at specific demographics to promote the sale of a product, or a political campaign targeting undecided voters, with the intention of swaying their decision one way or another. The goal is not only to get your attention but to maintain it by "speaking" to you in a way that evokes an emotional response or action. This could result in an emotional plea to support one political party instead of others or to purchase a certain product or service because of a certain nostalgia or connection with family or co-workers. The reasons for using persuasive techniques is not always secretive or malicious: it can be a good way to convince someone to reconsider making the wrong decision that could result in a detrimental outcome, or serve as a form of positive encouragement or reinforcement as a form of empowerment, such as "you can do it" and "what have you got to lose, come on!" When persuasion takes on a more direct tone, it may seem like a strong form of encouragement. While this may work for some people, it doesn't have the same impact on others. Some people thrive on overt persuasion and may otherwise not achieve a milestone or "go for it" without that persuasive push. On the other hand, there are people who prefer more autonomy and do not respond well. This is where covert or more subtle forms of persuasion can be useful in influencing them.

Recognizing the different signs of persuasion is key to knowing if someone is using these methods on you. It may not be as obvious as coaxing someone to change their mind or try something new. Some forms of persuasion may be subtle and difficult to detect initially. Understanding the reasons behind persuasive techniques and the different purposes they serve can help determine if you may be on the receiving end and the reasons why.

Three Basic Forms of Persuasion

There are basically three types of persuasion: ethos, logos, and pathos, according to Aristotle. Each method appeals to a different source and has its reason for use:

Ethos

Ethos is known as the persuasion using ethics or morality as a basis. In this method of persuasion, the speaker or individual applying this method is trustworthy, credible, and knowledgeable. In their speech or debate, a credible person will make use of their related expertise and knowledge to support their argument. This is done by citing relevant sources and using their own credibility as an expert to persuade the listener of their legitimacy. This method is regarded as respectful in that it doesn't intend to sway the listener for unethical gain or advantage. The speaker's reputation and status carry a lot of weight in terms of credibility, though this can also be established by using carefully constructed arguments that show that they are ethical.

Logos

Logos is based primarily in logic, or the application of logic to reason with or persuade someone. This method involves using evidence and related studies to support an argument. It's a clear, concise form that doesn't convince someone based on pseudo-science or skewed facts, but rather, it appeals to people who are not easily persuaded unless facts and their related sources support the argument. The format of logos is usually presented in a clear, sometimes chronological and progressive manner to show how a subject or topic began as disputable, followed by studies and observation to gain factual information to support the argument.

Pathos

Pathos is a method of persuasion that uses the emotion of the recipient (the person being persuaded). This is one of the most powerful and frequently used methods of persuasion. Pathos appeals to an audience's emotions, including their passions, imagination, creativity, and sympathetic nature. While the aim of this method is similar to logos and ethos, pathos can become very deceptive is using a vulnerable person's or group's emotions to their advantage. This can be seen in high control groups, where the promise of making lots of money or reaping the rewards of following a set of rules or belief system. Emotional persuasion can also be powerful in helping the audience identify with the speaker and/or their supporters, by sharing personal experiences and anecdotes that have the ability to convince people they are sincere and genuine, or "just one of us." The danger with employing pathos is how it can be misused to take advantage of a vulnerable or gullible group of people who are looking for quick answers and solutions to their problems.

141

Elements of Persuasion

There are characteristics of persuasion that can determine how successful the effect is on other people. These attributes are key in focusing attention on the listener or recipient of the persuasion, often to observe their reaction and level of engagement. Some people are more easily convinced than others. There are people who require a high degree of credibility and factual information before they will consider agreeing with a specific side of an argument. Others, on the other hand, are more easily swayed with far less effort.

Likeability

In order to persuade someone, they must like you or at least share a common ground. A company representative, for example, may not be successful in persuading or "selling" their products or reputation unless they first develop a rapport with their audience. Initially, a person in a representative position may seem intimidating or unrelatable, so they will often find common ground or likable traits to connect with people before they apply their persuasion techniques. An example, they may share an anecdotal story about their immediate family or personal experience that resonates with others. This is essentially their "gateway" to establishing a connection and further their pitch. Most people want to be liked. If an individual or group of people feel marginalized or ostracized in any way, a display of acceptance or being liked can feel empowering. Unfortunately, it can also pave a dangerous path to being taken advantage of, as the person showing approval may have malicious intentions of trying to swindle them or use their plight to their own advantage.

Building Trust

Without trust, there is no success in persuasion. People tend to question who they don't trust or agree with. If you are tasked with persuading someone to comply with the opposite side of their views, it will likely never happen, unless they have a great deal of trust and confidence in you. Even in cases where trust is established, persuasion can be challenging, though combined with other elements, it becomes easier. Building trust takes time and doesn't always happen immediately. If there are similarities between you and the person looking to gain your trust, it becomes an easier process. Once trust is established, the recipient of the persuasion may let their guard down and become more susceptible to influence than before. When you feel that someone is worthy of your trust, it's important to continually question and evaluate how they communicate, as it is common to become more comfortable and less cautious once that barrier of mistrust is lowered.

Communication Skills

Using effective communication skills is important and tailoring the types of phrases and words used is vital to maintaining interest in persuasion. People will respond if you speak to them in familiar and understandable terms, instead of using elaborate descriptions and over-the-top speeches. If people feel that they can understand and relate, and reciprocate on the same level, then persuasion becomes useful and powerful. People tend to be drawn to others who share similar experiences, beliefs, and ideas. If someone is a smooth talker or conversationalist, they may also be a master of persuasion and should be approached with caution.

Maintaining Consistency

Keeping the conversation and expectations consistent from the beginning is important in maintaining engagement. When someone deviates from the initial goal, even with good persuasion skills, they lose followers and trust. A skilled speaker will keep things consistent, though it can be difficult to determine whether they are sincere in their goals (even with the ability to stay on track) or if their techniques are sharpened well enough to convince people of their legitimacy. There are many other techniques and common strategies applied in persuasion, which will be covered in this book. Persuasion, in its basic form, can be effective as a tool for many people to achieve a goal or status in life. On the receiving end, it may have its benefits, where the intentions are good and ethical. Unfortunately, persuasion can often be used as a way to influence our emotions and behavior to the degree of mind control, which can lead to exploitation.

The next chapters elaborate on the "dark side" of persuasion and how it can become dangerous where mind control is the ultimate goal.

Chapter 2: Emotional Influence Exploitation

How Influence and Persuasion Impact our Emotions and Make us Susceptible to Exploitation

There is a dark side to persuasion occurs when there are no ethical boundaries established. When using persuasion techniques, many people will draw the line at some point: when the person they are trying to convince may be harmed or suffer a loss of some sort, or when there is a chance that the persuasion itself may be done in bad faith. When ethos or ethics are involved, there is a limit to how far persuasion will go and the methods it is used for. A more malicious approach, or dark persuasion, does not take into account the detrimental outcome or how the effect of persuading someone will impact them; it merely serves the purpose of the influencer in getting what they want from the person they are using. In this form of persuasion, exploitation is the result. The initial stages of dark persuasion may seem harmless, as they are usually subtle. If the persuader is skillful, they may have observed your behavior and personality well enough to know or assume that you will respond to certain techniques. If you are hesitant, bashful, they may plot more carefully, taking these characteristics into consideration; whereas if you are outspoken and passionate about certain topics of items, they may draw you in, gaining your trust so that you may take them more seriously.

In any case, mastering dark persuasion takes effort on the part of the persuader to gain enough attention and for long enough to apply their techniques. How is this done?

Rhetorical Persuasion

Rhetorical persuasion refers to the method of persuasion that does not play by the rules, nor does it draw boundaries with regards to the consideration of others.

This form of influence doesn't use ethics as a foundation, and for this reason, the tactics applied are often deceitful and without regard to the person(s) being used. These methods appeal to our emotions and how we feel.

For example, when someone compliments us on our physical appearance or displays approval for something we say or do, however minor or significant, it has an immediate effect. Initially, we may experience shock or surprise, if it's an unexpected response from a stranger or specific individual that we don't know too well. When the flattery occurs more than once and becomes more routine, we grow to rely on it, and in a sense, become emotionally dependent on it. Flattery is a way of giving someone a compliment without sincerity. It can be patronizing and seem insincere, though if a skillful persuasion technique is used, flattery can be convincing, even to the most skeptical.

How Emotions are Used in Achieving Control

When you react emotionally to an event in a significant way, it immediately causes a reaction. In some cases, a regular event or occurrence can provoke specific responses or feelings that are observed by others. For example, a bully may use their physical stature or "towering" pose to cause intimidation. Their target may physically shrink their posture and display signs of fear and avoidance as a result. If the bully doesn't succeed in intimidating their victim by posture alone, they may use insults or make snide remarks, usually in the presence of others to display a form of dominance. This is a powerful combination of techniques aimed to keep a person in a submissive state for the benefit of the abuser or bully. A childhood bully, for example, may use a variation of these to steal lunch money or an employer or supervisor may use them to look superior to their co-workers and subordinates. It's usually done overtly, though confrontation with the bully is often avoided by most people, because of fear. For this reason, bullies often get away with their unsavory behavior unless they are eventually confronted and stopped.

Fear used for Intimidation

Fear is a powerful emotion that can freeze anyone in their tracks and cause them to react in a specific way. It is often used to coerce and intimidate people into doing something they wouldn't normally do. One of the most obvious tactics is bullying, though subtler methods may include a more systematic approach of instilling thoughts of doubt and fear through common-held beliefs and concerns that most people share.

147

Certain advertising methods may use this technique to sell their product, touting better safety for you and your family. While they may not overtly state that not using their product will put you a greater risk of theft or danger, they communicate this distinctly by using words like "safety", "responsibility" and "family" interchangeably, thus impacting our emotional attachment to our own safety and of those closest to us. This tactic has the effect of making us feel safer or more responsible if we buy the product, which increases our chance of becoming a consumer, which benefits the company's sales. Coercion through fear can be done individually in a close relationship, or by a group or an organization, to yield more power over their members by keeping them afraid and obedient. Some religious and political organizations use these tactics to retain followers and keep them "in line" with the teachings and activities of the organization for the purpose of influencing their actions for the group's benefit. This may include recruiting new members, increasing funding to the organization, and keeping the current members from leaving.

The idea of challenging an individual or group's actions may seem normal to most people, though to a person heavily persuaded and under their control, it may be considered unacceptable or even forbidden. Fear of non-conformance can mean no longer receiving approval from others to losing them altogether. Fear is especially powerful as a method of control for people already in a state of dependence on emotional vulnerability. This may include someone mourning a loss or in a state of shock due to a disaster. In these situations, people who would normally question an act of persuasion thoroughly may simply not be in an emotional state to adequately do so, making them more susceptible to insurance fraud, and other schemes.

Emotional Blackmail

Emotional blackmail is used to directly influence a person's actions to make them malleable or easily persuaded to conform by using their emotions to produce obedience. This is used in intimidate or close relationships, where one person uses positive reinforcement and compliments to "reward" the other, to show approval of their conforming behavior. In this situation, flattery and encouragement are used as forms of approval to fuel a positive emotional reaction from the recipient, and this may continue, as long as they remain obedient or conform to the individual or group. Once they deviate, however rational or reasonable their reasons may be, they will experience the other side of the control: the withdrawal of approval, which may be replaced with insults, verbal or other forms of abuse, or complete silence until they return to the desired level of behavior.

This has a powerful and detrimental effect on a person's sense of independence, essentially placing them in an emotionally dependent state of constantly meeting the needs of the controlling group or individual. The blackmail of this technique is applied when the victim feels coerced into acting or behaving a certain way in order to retain or "win back" approval from the oppressor. The looming threat of having that approval removed or experiencing anger or disapproval conjures enough fear to keep them obedient. This is often used in abusive relationships, to "guilt" a spouse or partner into a state of emotional dependence. In some groups or organizations, favoritism and a reward system may be established as a way to show others in the group what is expected of them, by placing those who are seen as exemplary or ideal as their goal to "win" the highest level of approval. This technique only works until others reach this "goal", and then the bar is raised to make them strive further and work increasingly harder. The end result of emotional manipulation and blackmail is always the same: people will never fully receive complete satisfaction from meeting goals set by their manipulator, as those goals will always be moved further away, thus giving the manipulator more power to control and coerce others. Signs of approval may dwindle over time, increasing the victim's need for more, thus making people try harder to achieve the same "status" of emotional acceptance as before. The oppressor will never be completely satisfied as there is no actual achievement; the process of emotional and mental control is their goal, and this will continue indefinitely until it is no longer tolerated.

How We Are Susceptible to Exploitation Through Our Emotions

When individuals or groups have the ability to persuade us into doing things or acting in ways we wouldn't normally consider; they are using methods targeting our emotions to do so. This is successful because most people are guided, at least in part, by their emotional response and how others emotionally react and respond to us. In general, people are eager to please and "fit in" to a group or feel accepted. While many people claim they want to be accepted for the individuals they already are, most people are willing to change or adjust their thinking, behavior and in some cases, their appearance, to gain a higher level of acceptance. This drive for approval is emotional, though it also indicates our willingness to seek acceptance and embrace some level of conformity in order to improve our chances of better employment and relationships in life. Sometimes our level of conformity is linked or connected to our success in life, which increases the reasons for more people sacrificing their authentic individuality to achieve a higher status. While working towards a goal, such as a career or personal milestone, it is important that our individuality need not be sacrificed in the process. Any attempt by someone or a group to change or own an authentic self is a form of manipulation and should be avoided at all costs. The next section explains how to spot the signs of emotional control and manipulation that can lead to exploitation.

The Effects of Emotional Control and Exploitation: How to Recognize the Signs

The effects of emotional control from persuasion resulting in exploitation are extensive. In its infancy, persuasion may seem benign and playful, though it can quickly change into a more harmful tool to manipulate and exploit if used by a skillful manipulator.

There are some key signs that can give you an idea of what to look for if you suspect that someone is using persuasion secretly or subtly to influence emotions for the purpose of exploitation:

1. Doubting or Second-Guessing Yourself

If you are usually confident in your decision-making, and gradually (or suddenly) become unsure of the choices you make, even daily, routine decisions, this can be a sign that someone or a certain influence is causing you to feel doubtful. A good reason for this to occur may be due to a change in a home or work environment, which may cause you to re-evaluate your decisions. A more malicious reason could be a co-worker, or someone you know is causing you to feel this way by challenging your decisions and making you feel that your choices are inadequate. In a relationship, your insecurities may be used against you, so that you are constantly second-guessing any decision or idea you have. When a manipulative or emotionally abusive partner has an ability to convince you to no longer trust your own decisions, this can be a powerful way for them to gain more power and control over you over time. They may insist on making more decisions on your behalf and dismiss anything you suggest to the contrary.

As easy as it may seem to recognize this sign, many well educated and capable people have fallen into this trap because their emotional attachment to someone overrides the logical response.

2. Fear and Guilt

Unfortunately, some people experience these feelings regularly, especially if they are subject to abuse or neglect. If you feel a sense of fear or made to feel guilty for someone else's actions, this is a sure sign that you are being manipulated into taking the blame. A manipulative person doesn't want to assume any responsibility for their actions or take any blame for negative results. They would rather shift all of these onto their victims. On the one hand, a manipulator will convince you that you do not have the ability to make adequate decisions for yourself, therefore justifying their taking away this power for themselves, while on the other hand, they place all the blame on those decisions on you. It's illogical, though guilt and fear are used to coerce.

A victim may simply accept all blame out of fear that their oppressor will react angrily, even violently, if they do not. This level of abuse is dangerous and can escalate when a manipulator feels that their current technique is no longer working. If you feel fear for speaking up or making a decision on your own, this can be a dangerous sign that someone else taking the reins of your life into their own hands. This tactic usually begins subtly, with suggestions instead of demands, to "test" your willingness to bend to them and their persuasion. In a normal situation, expressing disinterest in an idea or a difference of opinion is accepted respectfully. In a manipulative situation, any sign of disagreement, however minor or impersonal it may be, is not acceptable.

153

The initial reaction may be silence, or the manipulator may appear to ignore your reaction, though they will try again to gauge your compliance. Always take note of subtle signs of dismay or dismissal when expressing your opinions or ideas, especially when they differ from the manipulator.

3. There's a Catch

You are presented with an offer that is too good to be true. If someone promises you a prize or reward that doesn't fit the cause, this is a red flag. It's a good reason to question a person's motives and determine what they will get out of it. This is tactic used early in relationships where a person wants to paint themselves as the perfect partner or friend. They will agree with everything you say and appear to be your "soulmate," though there is always a catch. People who use these tactics are heavily disguising their "dark" side, by distracting you with all their positive traits, often completing your sentences or making you feel as though they are the person you've always been looking for. Beware of anyone who appears too perfect. They will often advance quickly, which is another sign they are not genuine. Real, authentic relationships take time to develop and flourish. In sales and in some organizations, they will promote their products, services, and membership as the perfect solution to all of life's problems. In some sales pitches, references will be made to saving lots of money over a series of months or years for signing a contract, to having more time for family and vacation. Some of these scripts are so grandiose that there may seem to be no downside at all, though there are almost always hidden fees or high cancellation charges for ending a contract, once you learn of their true motives.

Many pyramid schemes and high control groups use these tactics to "sell" their image of idealism to individuals who are usually unsatisfied with their life or work schedule, making it an easier "sell." If an offer seems too good to be true, that's because it usually is. An honest business or sales pitch will include mention of the details and make you aware of them, even if it means risking not closing a sale. Always focus on the bottom line for the business and your needs. If the scale tips overly in their favor, avoid these types of agreements or contracts as much as possible. If possible, get a second and third opinion before making a solid decision.

4. Using One Favor for Another Large One

This is a common technique used by a lot of scam artists. It involves asking for a small favor that is easy to fulfill, only to be used as bait to ask a larger favor shortly after. Salespeople may use this tactic by asking you if you can spare a couple of minutes so that they can pitch their product or service. While initially, this isn't a negative situation; it can become malicious when they try using your hospitality to aggressively promote or "push" for sale by way of intimidation. People looking for a handout also uses this technique. They may be known for the asking often, and continuously avoided as a result. If they can convince someone to simply listen to a story or hear their plea for help, it may covertly persuade someone to help them, even a little. Using a small favor to "springboard" to a larger opportunity is not always malicious. For someone looking for gainful employment, convincing an employer to give them a chance in a job interview is the "small favor" that can lead to successful placement in a company and career advancement. In this instance, however, there is no hidden agenda or loss suffered at the hand of the employer or the employee.

In a case where the receiving party unwilling suffers a loss or is coerced to comply with a request by using the small request as "bait," this is seen as manipulative and should be avoided.

5. They Use Your Weaknesses Against You

This can take time to develop, and gives the manipulator a lot of leverage, once they learn what you fear and avoid. They see fear as a sign of weakness. All people experience fear, and for some, there are certain circumstances or items they fear more than others. Other characteristics that a manipulator may deem as a weakness include a lack of confidence or self-esteem or feelings of inadequacy due to not being good at certain activities or skills. An example of this tactic would be learning that a person is uncomfortable with reading because they struggle with pronunciation and forcing them in scenarios where they feel inadequate or unworthy because of it. A manipulator may force someone to read a passage in a book aloud in a group setting, knowing very well they are fearful of doing so because of their struggles. When a manipulative person uses someone's struggles or perceived weaknesses against them, it is a form of bullying and can have a long-term impact of distrust and loss of confidence in the victim. While it may seem as though we are "weak" because of certain attributes that we do not possess or lack of certain skills, it's important to note that everyone struggles.

When a manipulator uses someone's insecurities against them, it's a way to deflect their own feelings of inadequacy and sense of insecurity within themselves.

They are often internally aware of their own struggles and will use any means possible to "shift" those feelings onto another person, as they do with guilt, fear, and responsibility.

6. They Lie, Exaggerate and Change Stories Often

Most people will lie or exaggerate on occasion, about showing up late for work, not being able to attend a party or about the size of a cruise ship they spent their vacation on. These are usually done without any hidden agenda or ill intentions. When lying and exaggerations are constant and become a regularity, it's a sure sign of manipulation. It usually begins with one lie, which triggers another, followed by exaggerations and further lies to cover the original untruth. Manipulative people will initially appear as desirable and well-liked, which is how they entice others to believe and follow them.

This requires setting up a false set of characteristics and attributes, such as being the "nice" person, who is patient and forgiving, when the complete opposite is the case. Over time, their true colors will show, which prompts further lies and excuses to apply their own line of reasoning for this behavior. For example, a manipulative person that appears to be kind and patient to impress someone may suddenly explode in anger without provocation. When they explain their behavior, they may blame an earlier traffic incident that made them upset or a long, stressful day at work. There may be further lies and hidden motives: they may not even work or experience stress in the way they use these items as excuses, and as time goes on, the layers of lies and stories change and build to "cover" for or excuse their actions. How can lies and exaggerations be detected? Some people are convincing, starting off with small, seemingly insignificant stories to paint themselves in a positive light when, in reality, they are the complete opposite. One way to detect a possible manipulator is to watch for excuses. If they begin to behave contrary to the way they describe themselves, they will begin to explain their lack of decency with an excuse. While some people can act unlike themselves in difficult situations, there usually is consistency with their actions and behavior. With a manipulator, they will act in any way they see fit to get their way, including making use of lies, excuses and exaggerating situations or minimizing them, to effectively argue their case. It is another way they deflect responsibility from their actions. If this is developing into a regular occurrence, it's a sign they are not taking responsibility for their behavior, and this will most likely escalate over time.

7. "Intellectual" Bullying

This is a term that describes when someone uses their intelligence (or perception of intelligence), and/or accredited education and related experience to appear more intelligent or qualified than you. This is a common tactic used in the workplace, where one individual will argue a point by using their self-touted "expertise" on a given topic to assert the validity of their opinion over others. They may not necessarily use their own credentials, but rather use statistics or data they have privy or access to in their position to assert their opinion as well. This is also done to discredit others' abilities and opinions. They may site previous employment positions of authority or privilege to strengthen their side of the debate. If they are malicious, they may point at others' lack of knowledge or experience to "raise" their own sense of importance and validity above others. These tactics don't always work well, and in fact, make such a bully less appealing to associate with, as they are always "right."

This technique of "intellectual" bullying may be effective in groups where people look up to a specific person who possesses a level of education and/or expertise that they acquire for themselves. They may see this person as a "guru" or an expert on a topic, and give them a disproportionate amount of credit, even where it is not due. In a healthy group setting, all opinions matter and count as valid, even where there is a lack of expertise or education. This can be especially effective when an honest evaluation or observation is made that can help a project or group as a whole, which may not have any bearing on one's level of education or experience. How does one deal with an "intellectual" bully? In a small group, it's always best to give all members a chance to participate or voice their ideas and/or opinions without the threat of interruption or being criticized.

If there is a constant threat of being undermined or discredited by someone who feels the need to appear superior, it can ruin the entire group's efforts. Avoiding these types of bullies is ideal, though not always realistic, especially in a work environment. The best way to handle them is a careful, well-planned confrontation by explaining that everyone's opinion is valued. In a personal relationship, it can be challenging when one person, the manipulator, feels entitled to exert more control and power over the other because of higher education or experience. This can be demeaning, especially where the other person wants to be respected and valued for their own knowledge, even if it is not perceived as such by the manipulator.

8. Avoidance Tactics Are Used

This may not seem manipulative at first glance, though it is a useful way to postpone or distract someone from the deception of a manipulator. They may keep you busy with additional paperwork or describe some form of bureaucracy or administrative process that will conveniently delay fulfilling a request or task. This is often done by manipulative employees not performing their duties fully, or an employer is avoiding legitimate concerns or requests made by a subordinate. In a relationship, this may occur when something always "comes up" just in time to distract from a problem or other occurrence. An example may be when large, and/or an unaccounted amount of money or credit is spent on an item or expense that is not justified as necessary or as an emergency. This often happens in relationships where the manipulator has access to all or most of the money and is not responsible for using or budgeting wisely. When their partner questions outstanding bills and calls from the credit or collections department, is places them in a position where distraction and deflection is the most effective way to divert attention.

160

It may work temporarily, though eventually, their deceiving techniques will become unavoidable. When this happens, it's usually after the damage has occurred. In most cases, the victim's credit is used and impacted negatively as a result. For this reason, always keep track of your account and expenses, even in a shared or joint account. Avoidance tactics may be used when there is suspicion of betrayal, where the manipulator is trying to "cover" his or her tracks. They may simply brush off or ignore any questions aimed at getting an explanation. Another tactic to avert confrontation or blame is to accuse the victim of wrongdoing, in an attempt to "turn the tables" and making them part of the problem instead of addressing any wrongdoing on their part. Obstacles, challenges, and other reasons may be used to distract the victim long before any suspicion occurs, paving a clearer path for the manipulator to get away with their devious behavior. When someone is suddenly accusatory towards you for no reason, always consider they may have something to hide or divert attention from.

9. Being Let Down and Constant Disappointment

We all experience disappointment from time to time and may let others down when we simply cannot fulfill a contract or engagement. In these cases, there is usually a good or sound reason, such as an unforeseeable event or accident that can derail a clear plan with good intentions of fulfillment. A manipulator, on the other hand, will disregard their commitment and responsibility, and will frequently make excuses for not achieving their promise or goal. In some cases, they won't even apologize or make an excuse, and simply forgo any explanation with blatant disregard. When the behavior reaches this stage, it's not only disappointment but also disrespect.

161

Letting someone down, even with a plausible explanation, will often conjure feelings of regret of disappointing someone, especially if it is a result they are looking forward to. Making a commitment to someone or a project should be taken seriously. When it is not treated with respect, and this practice becomes a recurring trend, it's a sure sign that the person isn't considerate enough to fulfill their end of the agreement. This form of disengagement is manipulative, in that it is passive-aggressive in nature; it produces a negative result with little or no action with the very intention of doing so. The manipulator may pretend to be ignorant about their actions, acting as if they didn't make any promises, though it's their way of absolving themselves of responsibility.

10.   Playing Victim

We may be familiar with this tactic when we observe children blaming one another for different actions, such as teasing or taking another's toy away, resulting in a conflict. In some cases, one child will provoke another with taunting and bullying, only to play the victim when the other child speaks up in protest, therefore "blaming" them for the bullying instead. This is practiced by manipulative people, who will often exaggerate their personal circumstances or situations to gain sympathy or favoritism from others. In doing so, they may get away with actions or behavior that would normally be considered and even benefit from gifts or special treatment as a result. This behavior is exploitative in taking advantage of another person's kindness and sense of nurturing. People who often display sensitivity towards others or practice acts of kindness are usually targeted. They are usually seen as "prey" for this form of manipulation because they possess a sense of duty and care for others, and are more likely to provide money, items and attention or favors for those who exploit them.

When manipulative people play the victim and are successful in their attempts at exploiting others, they will repeat this practice. It may vary in form and types of requests, though it will normally happen more than once, which should be taken seriously as another sign of their negative impact.

11. Willful or False Ignorance

This is a disturbing practice, in which a manipulator will pretend to have no prior knowledge or information about a person or situation, to use someone else's information as first-hand knowledge about the incident or situation. This tactic is used to stall or delay performing a task that they would normally be expected to do with this knowledge, and therefore by acting ignorant, they are essentially "let off the hook" and excused. A simple term for this tactic is "playing dumb." Some manipulators are more convincing than others. Once they are discovered, they are less likely to be trusted or taken seriously, so they may try to keep as much distance as possible from the person(s) or issues involved with the situation to gain trust and confidence that they are genuine. If a person's lack of information or feigned ignorance seems unlikely or difficult to believe, consider this a sign they may be attempting to fool you. There are plenty of other signs that point towards manipulation, though the above examples provide a thorough idea of the most common tactics used by people who want to control and exploit others for their own gain. In general, anyone who appears to be out for themselves with little or no regard for other people should be avoided as much as possible.

If they make an offer that appears too good to be true, it's usually short-sighted or not a benefit at all. Overall, if anything or anyone appears to be too good to be true, it's usually a sure sign they are!

163

Chapter 3: Mind Control Explained – Who Uses it and How

What is Mind Control and How Does it Work?

Mind control is a broad term that can be defined as any technique or method that effectively influences the mind, in one way (or multiple ways) for the purpose of manipulation. Manipulation can produce a variety of outcomes, and used for a variety of reasons, from compliance and obedience to influencing how a person looks at themselves or others to evoke certain responses and behaviors. Essentially, when your actions and behaviors are influenced heavily from an individual or group, you may often dismiss your own doubts or feelings in favor of theirs.

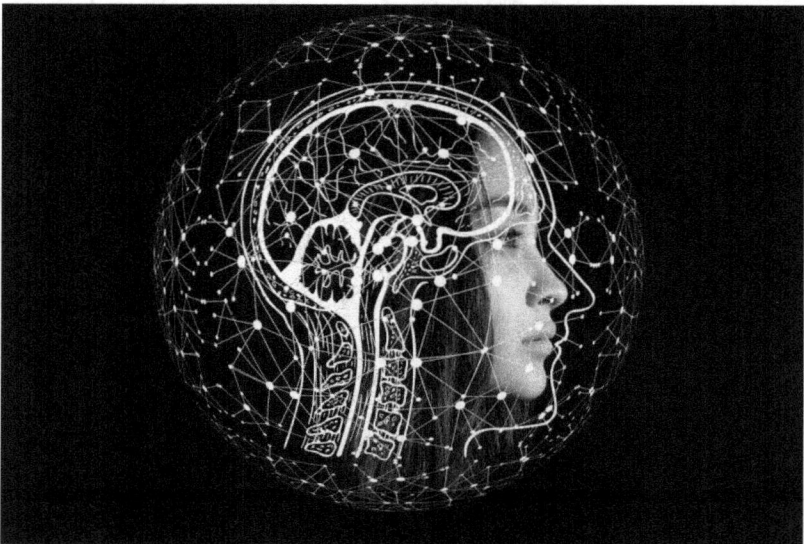

The effects of mind control don't work immediately in most cases, as this would be too obvious and easy to spot. How does mind control work? Mind control is the desired result of manipulation and related psychological techniques or methods that effectively influence your emotions and mind to bend your will and actions for another person's gain. It can be used to gain power, influence and money or benefits from another person, and maybe applied towards people who are in a position of privilege or in a state of vulnerability, making them a prime target. Once a person establishes a level of trust and confidence over another, they can be "primed" or targeted for mind control. The person seeking this form of dominance may be observant in the other person's habits and behaviors, learning how best to bait them with favorable comments and responses to gain their trust for further manipulation. Mind control and manipulation are almost always used for exploitation purposes. They often begin with seemingly more benign versions of persuasion or coaxing, which later develops into stronger forms of manipulative techniques.

The History of Mind Control and Its Effects Today

When reflecting on the history of mind control, you may think of brainwashing techniques used in prison camps and dangerous cults that have such a detrimental effect on people's minds to the point of permanent harm or death. Headlines of mass suicide or long-term psychological impairment, Stockholm syndrome, or post-traumatic stress disorder may also come to mind. In everyday life, mind control is just as prevalent as always, though we may not always be aware of it or recognize the signs.

The effects of mind control are not always obvious, and often, they influence our decisions, thoughts, and feelings in ways that we are not always aware of. Throughout history, mind control has been used as a means to instill fear and produce obedience among groups of people and can also be used within smaller groups or between individuals to yield powerful control over someone. When this happens, the power dynamic becomes severely imbalanced in favor of the manipulator(s). In countries or regions where people have very little freedom or liberty, certain regimes may have a stronghold over their citizens, by using the threat of imprisonment, punishment and other withholding fundamental rights as a result. Severe impoverishment and lack of proper food and water can often keep people in fear of disobedience or speaking out, for fear they may lose what little they have access to for their families and communities.

Today, mind control is widespread as it has always been. It occurs worldwide within governments, organizations, and between smaller groups and individuals.

In many ways, it's more obvious and present than ever, though we often ignore the signs. Commercial influence and the ability to convince people to buy products they don't need is powerful, especially when people are willing to go into debt or sacrifice their hard-earned income for something less important. Some forms of media and publications may often broadcast or publish certain headlines and events more often than others to provoke a sense of fear or urgency about home invasion or public safety. They may use emotive words and phrases to evoke responses of fear or shock, which causes people to live more cautiously and carefully, without deviating from the "norm."

What are the Signs of Mind Control?

Like manipulation, mind control aims to persuade and influence a person or people's ways of thinking, acting, and behaving to gain a benefit. When people are easily influenced and manipulated, they become more susceptible to practicing or doing things that would normally not consider as an option. The effect or success of mind control can vary depending on the techniques used, the target(s) and the environment. These factors, among others, play an important role in how successful and powerful mind control can be and also provide information on how to spot these signs before they develop further:

1. Isolation

This may seem like a severe case of solitary confinement, though isolation can refer to simply keeping you from friends and family. This tactic is often used by an abusive partner or spouse to keep their partner away from the comfort and support of friends and family. Isolation can be psychological, in that the manipulator will gradually convince you that one or two family members are trying to control you when they are the one doing the controlling. Over time, if they are successful in persuading you that your family is deceptive or manipulative, they may continue to target friends and co-workers or acquaintances as well, telling you there is something wrong with them, or making you feel as though your friends are insincere, jealous or not truly worthy of your friendship. After a while, friendships and family members fade into the background, and you find yourself more emotionally dependent on the person practicing these mind control techniques. Isolation can effectively keep you from seeking help when you finally realize the dangers of being left alone with someone who does not have your best interest at heart.

167

Recognizing the early signs of someone or an organization to isolate you from others, even subtly, is vital to avoiding a long-term disaster. Any type of discredit or negativity towards good friends and family should be regarded as a possible sign of control. This tactic will usually occur early in a relationship, where the manipulator realizes a strong bond between you and others. They see this as a threat to their ability to control you and will do anything in their power to break these relationships to keep you vulnerable to their will. If a group or organization appear inclusive and friendly yet questions the nature of your personal relationships and friendships, it's a sure sign they are seeking to gain more control of your life.

2. Mood Swings and Erratic Behavior

If your partner becomes easily agitated or angry when you disagree with them or makes you feel unworthy of their affection for expressing an honest opinion, they are grooming you to bend to their will. For the manipulator, there is little or no room for any variance in opinion or thought. They will only accept complete submission and agreement. Anything less will result in erratic mood swings and unpredictable behaviors. In extreme cases, some manipulative people become violent or aggressive. The very threat of this possibility will convince their victims to remain obedient simply out of fear. Recognizing severe changes in mood or emotion, especially when there is no reason or event to trigger the change, is a good reason to avoid someone. Over time, this behavior will escalate and become worse, especially once you discover their tactic and need to escape their manipulate grasp.

3. No Compromises

Mind control, when effective, requires complete and total obedience. There is no room for other thoughts or compromising. In a healthy relationship, all opinions expressed are regarded with respect, even if disagreements or debates are surrounding certain topics. Not allowing another person to express their thoughts without ridicule or judgment can convince them that they are not worthy or compromise. It is also a form of psychological and emotional abuse. This is an easier sign to recognize when even the smallest of decisions or ideas are bent to the will of the manipulator. This can mean anything from choosing a restaurant for dinner or film to watch, which later affects more significant decisions, such as a mortgage or starting a family. Knowing when to spot a lack of compromise can save you a lot of grief later in life, especially where a long-term relationship may form.

Who Uses Mind Control? Organizations, High Control Groups, and People We Know and Encounter in Everyday Life

Who uses mind control, and for what purpose? Many people who are susceptible to the influence of mind control don't often realize they are. There are different people (individuals) and groups that employ mind and thought-control techniques for a variety of reasons. Understanding their purpose also provides a good explanation for why certain techniques are used and how to recognize them.

When we encounter everyday situations, from commuting to work or school, shopping in a grocery store or running errands, we may experience a form of influence or covert manipulation through a sales pitch or billboard ad, without realizing its effect.

If we stopped every time, we noticed an ad, a promotion, a person or representative attempting to "pitch" a sale or ask for a donation, we would then realize how bombarded our mind is with persuasion. In reality, only certain ads or people will catch our attention, while others will slip away. The following chapter looks at a technique called NLP, or neuro-linguistic programming, which is a more non-verbal method of using manipulation and mind control techniques.

Chapter 4: Neuro-Linguistic Programming

Learning your Mind's Language: Neuro-Linguistic Programming or NLP

NLP or Neuro-Linguistic Programming is a method that changes a person's way of thinking and behaving, with the promise of helping people to achieve more in life. Richard Bandler and John Grinder developed this technique and quickly became popular in different marketing, political, and other movements beginning in the 1970s. Today, NLP continues to be used as a treatment aimed at changing people's thinking and behavioral patterns for a variety of reasons, including the treatment of certain types of anxiety and phobias. This program or series of techniques is often promoted with the promise of improving communication, performance at home, work, and overall better enjoyment of life.

What is NLP, and How Does It Work?

Neuro-Linguistic Programming was developed on the basis or belief that people's thoughts and behaviors could be detected by observing non-verbal cues and movements. It was further believed that these non-verbal signs of communication formed specific patterns to coincide with specific thoughts or feelings, making it easier to "read" people and their intentions, even when they are not expressed verbally.

171

Furthermore, NLP aims to understand these patterns of non-verbal communication as a means of learning how to form an individual's internal "map" or experience in life through these expressions, making it possible to respond in a similar way, then by changing those "patterns" of behavior as a way to gain trust and connection with them. Therapists and consultants use this method as a way to establish a sense of familiarity and build a rapport. When NLP is applied for the benefit of treating a specific disorder or condition, there are several techniques used:

- Physical behaviors, such as gestures and facial expressions used by the person being treated may also be used by a therapist to facilitate a sense of connection and display empathy to improve communication
- Changing behavioral actions to provoke a different response, or as a means to help someone change a pattern of behavior that is seen as destructive or harmful.
- Sensory techniques, such as visual and auditory cues, may be used to stimulate certain reactions and feelings about certain events or experiences.

This may be used to promote coping while removing certain negative characteristics associated with these experiences. While NLP has been regarded as useful and helpful for many people suffering from anxiety, depression and post-traumatic stress disorders, it has also been equally scrutinized by the scientific community, citing a lack of study and evidence of its effects. Although there are limited studies, some have shown promising results, while others were not conclusive.

Like other disputed practices, such as hypnotherapy, many people support NLP and the various methods used, which continue to be applied today in many practices. For people who support the results of NLP use in therapy, they reported improved psychological well-being and a better quality of life.

How is NLP used to Manipulate or Control the Way People Think and Behave?

While the NLP technique can be used as a method to change people's behavior and thought processes for positive results, the same or similar techniques could be used to manipulate and control other people by applying the same observation and use of non-verbal communication. While some forms of control through the use of therapeutic techniques may seem necessary, and beneficial to change harmful habits and behaviors into more positive patterns, it can signal a prime opportunity for control and manipulation in the process. In some cases, overt control over someone else's behaviors and actions may not be done with ill intentions, if the practitioner or therapist believes the NLP methods used are going to achieve improved results. The danger of this method arises due to the imbalance of control from one party to another, and the idea of placing a great deal of trust or confidence in someone else and trusting a process that may or may not work for the best interests of the recipient. When we communicate with various non-verbal cues, such as head movements, eye motions, and hand gestures, to name a few, we inadvertently influence others to communicate or reciprocate similar cues in response.

This is an example of how NLP is used in communication; one person responds in kind or with similar gestures or movements and establishing familiarity and building a comfort zone where the other person may feel more at ease in disclosing more personal information and letting their guard down. When NLP is used for the purpose of manipulation, it can be very effective in getting results, especially when people respond by changing or varying the pattern of non-verbal communication, which can alter or change how the other person behaves. This switching or patterns or behaviors can occur without the other person's knowledge, and although it is a conscious technique, it may appear to influence people on a subconscious level as well strongly. A strong development and experienced application of NLP programming can have an equally effective change or influence on many people, such as motivational speakers or successful salespeople who appear so convincing in their tactics that they can easily sway or persuade others to join their organization or invest in them. NLP techniques used in marketing and for other political or commercial influences include using subtle verbal cues in conjunction with strong non-verbal signs or gestures, having the effect of layering both to simultaneously affect a person's behavior through the conscious and subconscious at once. This strong impact on a person can impact their behavior almost immediately, though it may not always last for a long period of time. When these techniques are used, their aim is to produce results quickly and for the benefit of the manipulator, though their long-term effect may dwindle over time, once the techniques used are discovered and recognized.

Recognizing NLP as a Method of Control

NLP is a complex layer of behavioral and communicative techniques that can be detected in larger-than-life personalities and "gurus" or self-help celebrities making appearances at various conventions or promotional events. While on the surface, their advice and presence may be positive and seem helpful, many of these speakers use NLP techniques to provoke engagement with their audience on a deeper level. On a smaller scale, a manipulator not familiar with NLP may still use similar techniques to persuade or gain your trust. They may mimic or copy certain terms or words you use, to show agreement, or "reach out" to you with a congratulatory pat on the shoulder or similar approving non-verbal cue as a way to gain your approval and influence your actions.

Chapter 5 : Recognize a Manipulator – Common Character Traits of a Manipulator

What Are the Traits of a Manipulator?

When we think of a manipulator or a person with the ability to use mind control techniques, our own mind may imagine someone with a specific look or style and spiel or script. If this was as easy as noticing a certain appearance or obvious clues, it would be fairly easy to avoid manipulative people and their practices altogether. Unfortunately, people who apply methods of mind control, manipulation, and persuasion for their benefit come from all walks of life and on the surface, they look, behave, and seem like anyone else. While it's not always easy to detect a person's intentions to manipulate, there are certain types of people who are more likely to use mind control techniques than others:

- **The over-confident employer or boss**. This person may show signs of superiority and contempt for anyone who doesn't agree with him or her. They may balk at any opinions or ideas that conflict with their own, even if it's for the benefit of the department or company. Their over-confidence is a mask to hide feelings of inadequacy, and they may use their position of authority to exert control over staff every chance they get.

- **The possessive spouse or partner**. The relationship begins on a strong note with heavy signs of affection and attention, only to later develop into a possessive and manipulate relationship where the manipulative partner seeks to control all or most aspects of their spouse or partner's life, including who they associate with, where they go and how they spend their money. These traits will escalate into abuse and will worsen over time until the relationship ends. Following the breakup of an abusive or toxic relationship, the ex-partner may cause more damage by stalking (online or in-person), contacting friends or family to spread negative information or rumors and trying other techniques to discredit and effectively "destroy" as much about your life as possible.

This can be specifically dangerous when a manipulative person has a history of violent or unpredictable behavior, and where there is a family (or kids) involved in a custody battle.

- **Passive-Aggressive Behavior.** This method is used as a punitive technique that involves getting back at someone in a covert way. For example, when a person is angry that their best friend showed up late, they may simply state, "What took you so long! Everybody is waiting!" This is considered a reasonable reaction in this instance, whereas the passive-aggressive tactic may involve the following:
  - Instead of confronting the friend for showing up late, a passive-aggressive person will continue as if nothing is wrong, and may even dismiss the tardiness
  - Later in the evening, a cup of wine or food might be "accidentally" spilled on the friend, or, they may be purposely ignored for the remainder of the evening.
  - These examples indicate how confusing and ruthless passive aggression can be. It aims to punish someone in such a way, that they don't expect it to happen at all, or in such an indirect manner. When a person is confronted using passive-aggressive tactics, they may simply ignore the accusation or deny it. This can become very frustrating and lead to another technique known as gaslighting.

This occurs when a person is made to feel as though their suspicions, thoughts, or feelings are manifestations of their own mind and not based on anything legitimate. For the person impacted by gaslighting, they may feel that there is something wrong with them and their own perception, while the person convincing them of this is usually the one responsible for their suspicions in the first place.

Chapter 6: Stop Being Manipulated – Detect When Manipulation Techniques Are Used against You

How to Avoid Manipulation and Spot the Signs Early

Avoiding the trap of manipulation is easier when the signs are noticed early in a relationship, a friendship or upon being introduced into a group or organization. There are often small, seemingly insignificant signs that can provide a good hint at what to expect later. There are also good practices to develop in order to prevent someone from manipulating you or choosing you as their next target. Always remember that manipulation is often aimed towards people seen as vulnerable, isolated, or "weak," even if this is not the case. Perception is everything, and maintaining a strong level of communication and circle of support can prevent manipulation and mind control from wreaking havoc on your life and other people in your life:

1. Keep close contact with family and friends If you suspect your new partner or friend is attempting to isolate you, watch for their reaction or signs of dismay when you make plans with family. Their possessiveness may be disguised as an excuse to spend more time with you and get more acquainted with you, though even in a new relationship, there are other commitments and people that play an important role in our lives.

If you suspect there is a more aggressive attempt to keep you away from family and friends, make sure to discuss this concern with someone close, so they are aware of the situation and can be there for you in case, the relationship takes a turn for the worse.

2. Don't tolerate a lack of respect or manipulative mood swings. If you find yourself on the receiving end of an emotional or angry outburst, don't allow it to continue. Calmly explain that you will leave momentarily and return when the other person is in a better state to communicate more civilly. If you suspect this type of behavior will occur beforehand, make sure you are situated close to an exit, in case, the situation escalates very quickly and unpredictably. You have a right to feel safe and to find a quiet, peaceful place if things get out of hand.

3. Make your opinions and expressions heard. This might be easier early on in the relationship or experience with a manipulative person, as they may realize the need to approach with caution. In fact, if you make it clear that your opinions and thoughts matter, without any dispute about who is right or wrong, a manipulator may decide that your strong resolve is not worth their efforts, and they will move on. When this happens, it may seem disappointing at first, though it can be a lifesaver in the long-term.

4. You have your own personal goals and priorities. Don't let anyone convince you that their personal goals or needs come first. In a relationship, both parties deserve equal consideration and respect. Anything less is not acceptable, as it tips the balance of power unevenly.

For example, if you have a career goal or a long-term plan for your health, make it a priority and explain that it will remain as such. Anyone who attempts to discourage you from your goals by using demeaning comments and belittling as a way to make you feel less value is not worth the effort.

5. Don't let anyone convince you that it's "all in our head" This is how gaslighting begins, by gradually convincing someone that their concerns are a product of their imagination and nothing more. Any form of dismissal about a thought, feeling, or emotion should never be discarded by someone as unimportant or unworthy of attention. When we have a serious concern, it should always be considered as such.

6. Always assert yourself, when in doubt. If anyone tried to make you feel unimportant or that what you have to say doesn't count, it's a sign that they are trying to devalue your sense of self-worth and confidence. When you feel that someone is mistreating you or maybe trying to manipulate you, check-in with a friend or family member, and let them know what's going on. Sometimes, we internalize much more than we should and forget that there are people ready to support and help us when we need it.

How Organizations and High Control Groups Use Mind Control

Mind control is used by individuals and groups alike. Essentially, the same basic techniques are used for both, though in a group or organizational setting, certain tactics can yield powerful leverage and results in keeping people "inline" with organizational or group goals.

181

While it may seem like an individual sacrifice, in some ways, is beneficial for the group, such as time and community commitment, there are also negative results that can occur when motives are questioned, or a difference in opinion is expressed. The following techniques are commonly used by organizations and groups that practice forms of persuasion and mind control to keep their adherents "inline" with their practices:

Love bombing

This is a technique used in organizations that are also known as high control groups. They can be political, religious, philosophical, corporate, or promote some form of lifestyle. In all high control groups, the key component is more about the tactics used to recruit, control, and manipulate than what they are claiming to promote or teach. Love bombing refers to showing or displaying approval, social engagement, and even some forms of affection early in a relationship or at the first meeting. This has the effect of making you feel like "one of them" or "one of the groups," so that you feel more inclined to follow, join and susceptible to their influence and behaviors of the leaders and of the other group members. Often, people will form friendships and bonds before they actively try recruiting. This method is common in certain pyramid schemes or high-pressure sales groups. It essentially places you in a position where you continue to please and follow the group as much as possible so that you can continue to experience the sensation of acceptance and care that love bombing provides. If you withdraw from the group or don't perform up to their standards, those same people showing the love may withdraw and become cold and demanding, possibly raising the bar of expectation until you jump higher and higher for the same effect.

This technique is very common in many self-help groups with charismatic leaders or "gurus" that profess to know the secret to solving all of life's problems.

The Group's Philosophy and Promises Are "Too Good to be True"

This is almost always a sure sign that something isn't right. Every friendship, acquaintance, or team has many elements, and not all of them are aligned perfectly without error or fault. Anyone or any group claiming to be the true way, or the best should raise a red flag immediately. Some high control groups state that their organization, philosophy or belief system is superior to all others, and may even cite their own written documents or literature to promote this level of confidence and obedience within its ranks. They may promise rewards and wealth, and act as if they hold to key to making your life better. Even people with good intentions can be caught up in a certain philosophy or belief that later becomes a disappointment when it is not fulfilled.

Controlling of Information

If you have doubts about the legitimacy of an organization or group, you may take the initiative and research. If your research produces highly concerning results about the group and/or their practices, this can cause a lot of friction. For this reason, high control groups often discourage or outright forbid referencing literature or documents about their practices outside of the organization. This may seem like a red flag that should not go unnoticed; however, many people will "buy into" a group's philosophy and eventually become convinced, without question, that their teachings and/or practices are superior regardless of outside research and findings.

The control of information and access to alternate resources is a powerful way to keep people compliant. In situations where people have committed a great deal of their life and time to a group, relationship or organization, they may suspect something is amiss, though avoid research or questioning because of the fear of what they may discover.

Propaganda

This is a useful tool by many groups and some forms of media. In smaller groups or relationships, one person may belong to a group that promotes propagandistic information that they use to their own benefit to recruit or convince others of their legitimacy. While this method works on some people, many others will use due diligence to research and find information from more credible sources, effectively discovering the hidden agenda. Propaganda is often used by highly controlling governments and organizations that already have a strong level of authority. In these situations, there is already limited freedom available to the followers or recipients of the propaganda and other techniques of mind control. For people who are skeptical and rely on substantiating everything they read, propaganda can be largely ineffective.

Brainwashing

The techniques vary considerably and inconsistently, though brainwashing is a broad term that covers many types of mind control tactics. Often, brainwashing is associated with cults and highly controlled regimes and governments that forcibly imprison and/or convince people to behave or think a certain way.

In its most frightening and severe state, brainwashing involves forceful confinement, interrogation, and repetition of phrases or passages that are meant to "program" a person or group. Many of the extreme cases of brainwashing are considered forms of torture, due to the psychological harm and distress caused to many people, some of which never fully recover, even after years after their escape. Today, there are many groups and authoritarian regimes or governments that practice various forms of brainwashing, including the following methods:

- Lectures and "talks" that last for hours, with little or no breaks for food or relaxation. These are usually repetitive in nature, to "implant" a series of thoughts, ideas, and beliefs into the listeners or adherents.
- Limiting association with people outside of the organization or group, to strengthen the individual's reliance and dependability on the group, therefore making it easier to follow commands and become more malleable.
- Isolation through the use of "retreats" where groups are often separated from the rest of society. This is a more extreme measure used by small cults, to give people a false sense of importance or belonging. It's also an opportunity to cut off their connection to resources such as family, friends, and financial assistance if they feel the need to escape.
- Repetitive words, re-defining common words to fit a certain belief structure of philosophy, and using loaded language. These are effective on a subconscious level, where people become gradually used to changing the way they talk or converse with a new "language" that only they fully understand, giving them a sense of importance or inclusivity.

Generally, any organization or group that attempts to limit your ability to question or seek information from the outside should raise concern. A reputable person, representative or group should welcome criticism and questions, as a means to validate their legitimacy, though when they tighten the reigns of control and use methods of deception and distraction, it's a sign that they are not looking for your best interest. If there is any doubt, even a slight question or a group's intentions or purpose, always take this seriously. As often as we may be swayed or persuaded subconsciously by high control groups and companies, we may also "pick-up" or make subconscious observations that cause us to feel uncomfortable, even slightly uneasy. When this happens, it best to not ignore these feelings, as they are genuine and may signal a more significant problem.

Recognizing When You Are Being Controlled and How to Cope and Strategize Your Way to Freedom from Manipulation

If you are in a position of being manipulated or under undue influence from an individual or a group, know that you are not alone. Many people, upon learning that they have been "duped" or fooled by a manipulator or set of mind control techniques, may immediately feel that they were not intelligent enough to recognize the signs. Some people may feel angry or frustrated, especially if they are generally confident about their experiences in life and knowledge of people and their behaviors. It may often come as a surprise that many intelligent, educated, and well-grounded people can be susceptible to mind control and persuasive techniques, under the right (or unfortunate) circumstances in life.

186

Most, if not all, people have been subjected to some form of manipulation or mind control at least once in their lifetime. It may last for a few minutes when a salesperson momentarily convinces you to consider signing a contract for a new energy company, or it can be a long-term relationship with an abusive, manipulative individual that can take years to overcome. Some people join pyramid groups, religious, or political groups that are defined as high control groups, due to the strong influence and control they have over their followers. For some people, it may take months or years to truly realize that they have been subjected to a form of mind control. When this realization occurs, what can be done to reverse the damage? How can someone in an abusive or manipulative situation find a way out and cope following the aftermath?

To understand how to leave a high control group or individual, it's important to recognize the reason(s) for getting initially involved. For some people, joining a new community and finding a new purpose in life becomes meaningful, especially if they have experienced trauma or feel vulnerable. For others, getting involved in a relationship where the other person is manipulative may not have been apparent, and the signs may have been subtle in the beginning. At some point, many people, even those who are more susceptible to mind control and persuasion, will realize that they are effectively being controlled. It's a difficult situation to acknowledge and to realize that someone has "duped" you into following a set of rules or allowing someone to control your life.

It's a hard reality to confront, though there are ways of coping when you realize that you are a victim of mind control:

1. Find a support system. Today, the internet provides many support groups for victims of abuse, including resources and communities that provide invaluable information and comfort, especially in the initial stages of "escape."
2. At first, you may feel alone and unworthy. Connecting with other people who share the same or similar experiences is key to understanding that while your situation is not unique, it is valued and important that others know as well. Many people use online support groups anonymously, which provides a sense of comfort and safety.
3. Seeking help from a therapist. After leaving a manipulative situation, therapy is a valuable way to learn coping mechanisms and establishing new boundaries and goals for your future. When leaving a difficult situation, finding a therapist that you can connect with may not happen immediately. Some professionals may specialize in certain situations, such as relationships or familiar abuse, where others may be more familiar with high control groups and their impact on individuals.
4. Time is your friend It's important to get the help you need to cope and move on after leaving a mentally and emotionally toxic environment, though it's equally vital to understand that the hurt, betrayal and emotional upheaval experienced in the initial stages will lessen over time. It's natural to feel all sorts of emotions and feelings. You may feel a sense of loss or grief, reminiscing about the "good times" and relationship(s) that are no longer.

In time, you'll also realize that all the positive experiences in the past were heavily clouded by the negative elements of mind control.

5. Enjoy your freedom Everyone experiences or celebrates their sense of freedom differently. For some people, the idea of breaking free from mind control is immediately satisfying.

6. For others, there is a grieving process that takes time, and the sensation of being free isn't necessarily experienced as such. This usually occurs when a person leaves an emotionally and psychologically abusive relationship. They may miss the other person and crave their attention, and yet they are aware of the dangers of returning to them. In time, however, becoming less dependent on pleasing others and finding a new sense of self.

7. Don't blame yourself. One of the first reactions we may have, once we realize that we've been manipulated, is to blame ourselves for not being more aware. We may imagine that the signs should have been obvious to us, and not recognizing them puts the blame on our own lack of knowledge or awareness.

8. While there may be some signs early in the manipulation process, there are many variations of the techniques that hide their intentions. For example, when a person attempts to recruit others into a group or organization, they may not overtly explain the true intentions of the group, and instead, extend an invitation to an "open house" or "dinner event" aimed at building community and fostering discussion. They may appeal to the idea of community and being social, which many people are drawn to.

Even during some meetings or group events, the intentions to recruit people to a pyramid scheme or high-pressure sales group may not be initially apparent. They may draw you out, learn more about what you want first so that they know how to "target" you later. Many educated and experienced people may succumb to this technique because it feels very social, legitimate, and it may appeal to their interest in networking and meeting other people. They may begin to socially invest in the idea of building a rapport with new people, only to later be persuaded to join a sales team and become part of a group they wouldn't initially consider.

Part 2: Reading and Analyze People

Chapter 7: Analyze Yourself – The First Step

Steps to Self-Analysis

Self-Analysis is a powerful tool that can help us evaluate a lot about ourselves. When we analyze who we are, it can reveal a lot about how we reflect on ourselves, and the various factors that impact us, such as our childhood and upbringing, to other environmental and emotional elements that we may not always be aware of.

Self-analysis is most effective when it is done through a series of steps that focus on one aspect of our life at a time:

1. Childhood and Upbringing

Whether we realize it or not, most of our adult experience, including behaviors, actions, and decisions stem directly from how we were raised as children. Our childhood experiences also shape who we are and how we see ourselves. Self-reflection, our attitudes, and beliefs are also deeply rooted in our upbringing. If we were heavily criticized or ignored, mistreated on a regular basis, we might have formed a low opinion of our own thoughts and beliefs, and not viewing them as valid. On the other hand, if we received a great deal of encouragement and support in childhood, we may find more value in our opinions and a greater sense of self-confidence. Childhood abusive, neglect, continuous berating, or mistreatment are all factors that contribute to negative self-reflections in adulthood. We may strive to seek approval from our family, even the same people that mistreated us in childhood, as a way to build our confidence. Even where the fault is found and accepted by those responsible, the damage done lasts into adulthood, and until we recognize the impact it has on our own self-esteem, it is impossible to make progress. Many victims of abuse blame themselves, and when they come forward to confront the abuse, they are shamed for doing so, and often held responsible for their own feelings of inadequacy.

While childhood trauma is serious and is best addressed with a professional therapist, there are helpful support groups that can provide a non-judgmental forum for discussion and connecting with others who have similar experiences. It is also important to acknowledge that mistreatment and abuse in childhood do not define who you are, and it is never acceptable to excuse such behavior.

2. Check Your Inner Voice and Mood

Tracking your mood changes and what our "inner voice" says is an important way to look inward and discover how we are affected by our environment. When considering what our inner voice says, it's important to acknowledge that it not truly our voice speaking to us, but a collection of different statements, opinions, and comments made to us over time. Often, the most negative statements are the ones that "stick" with us, which has a direct impact on our moods and sense of worth. If we often hear phrases like "that's good, but you need to do better" or "you can be better if...", they may seem like forms of encouragement, though they may feel a sense of inadequacy and convince us that we are not good enough. For some people, the inner voice is positive and affirming, which is mood-lifting and gives a sense of satisfaction. In order to achieve and continue that positive mantra internally, we feel encouraged in a more productive way. When someone provides us with a comment of approval or acceptance, we internalize this as well. Realistically, we will receive criticism, along with acceptance. Not all criticism is negative, if it is constructive and helpful, though we often internalize what others think and work harder to improve based on the inner, or collective voice. To gain a better understanding of how others' expressed opinions and comments impact our own thoughts and internal dialogue, it's a good idea to keep a journal or diary to record any negative or affirming comments we hear. It can be a compliment from our spouse or constructive criticism from a co-worker, to a more critical comment from a bystander or neighbor. As insignificant as some comments may appear, especially if they are from someone we do not know well or a complete stranger, they still have an effect on how we view ourselves.

3. Keep a Log of Your Thoughts

This can be done in conjunction with the second step, by recording what others say as well as how we think or feel following those responses. Sometimes we may have thoughts that appear to be random, and completely unrelated to our current situation.

These ideas or thoughts are often subconscious and may stem from previous experiences or influence experienced on a more subliminal or covert level. When we experience a specific thought or idea, it's essential to take note of it, but also to notice how we feel at that very moment. Is it a stressor that originates from a previous incident or experience that triggers this feeling? A more straightforward way to analyze the thought or series of ideas, is to ask the following questions: "Why does this make me feel this way?" "Is there more to this? What else does this thought or idea relate to?" in probing deeper, we may eventually find the reasons why a specific thought or feeling may occur out of the blue.

When we feel a certain way because of a current issue or situation, it's much more relatable and understandable. It's also important to record these experiences as they may recur at some point in the future and have an impact at a later time. If a simple gesture or comment caused us to feel angry or anxious, we might dismiss it at the time, only to revisit it later and have it impact us more than expected. We can record the experience to read the statement made, followed by our immediate reaction and/or feeling. At the moment, we may not have a clear picture of how or why we may feel a certain way until we are able to sift through our thoughts and feelings for further analysis later.

4. Thinking Patterns and How They Develop

As we become more aware of how others' comments and behaviors impact our own, including our innermost feelings and thoughts, we may notice certain patterns in our own thinking and behavior emerge, as a result. For example, if we work in a high-stress environment where there is constant pressure to achieve and exceed a sales quota, we may apply a harsh set of thinking or self-depreciation when we fall short of our goal. This may apply to work, or other commitments and/or goals we set for ourselves. Instead of seeing progress as a long-term process, we may only fixate on one small failed attempt and not acknowledge enough of the positive achievements we make. One pattern that may develop is an all-or-nothing approach to every project you embark on. If you take a test or accomplish a goal, you may be focused too much on one or two minor errors instead of viewing the entire project as a success. This type of thinking can result in perfectionism, when we become so fixated on reaching for the unattainable goal of perfection, only to realize that we never will and that it is not necessary, as long as there is progress. Another pattern that can develop is seeing people and situations in generalizations or applying labels to them. This can be harmful in how we associate with people, as we may jump to conclusions and underestimate them with little or no information. We may also fit ourselves into a category and feel "trapped" or limited in some way, though the only limits we are subjected to, in most cases, are the ones we place on ourselves.

Recording our thoughts and feelings will help determine if a specific pattern of behavior or thinking emerges, which will give us a better sense of how we can improve how we view our own value and self-worth, which is covered in the next step.

5. Assessing our Self-Esteem and Sense of Self-Worth

A positive sense of self and self-esteem is essential in making sure that we gain the most positive experience out of life. When we feel unworthy or experience self-doubt often, it is often reflected in how we view our own sense of self-worth. It may stem from childhood trauma and neglect or abuse, or due to feeling of inadequacy. We may seek approval or acceptance from others as a way to increase our sense of value or feel that we must constantly compete with other people to make ourselves feel better and more worthy of praise. It is common for many people to have negative or low self-esteem. This way of thinking or self-reflection manifests itself in different forms, and we may identify with one or more of these types, depending on our personal situation or experience:

· Some people will consider themselves the victim. This may be accurate when they are the target of bullying or abusive behavior. This may also be a tactic used to gain acceptance from others by encouraging people to feel pity for them. They may relay negative experiences about their past or current events to gain attention, as a distraction from their own lack of self-esteem. People who feel like the victim are often unassertive and lack the ability to speak up for themselves when they feel targeted, often relying on others for reassurance and acceptance.

- In an attempt to mask low self-esteem, some people will act happy and satisfied outwardly, while continuing to feel inadequate and unworthy inside. They are usually afraid of failure and strive for perfection, and often compete with others to assert themselves and feel a sense of accomplishment, though it is often short-lived and temporary.

197

When people strive for perfection, it can be exhausting, as it is an impossible goal to achieve, and often results in burnout.

- For some people, anger is the result of not feeling worthy. Instead of trying to gain acceptance, they may "rebel" or resist any direction but their own. They may not be happy with themselves internally, though, in an attempt to divert their attention from ridicule and criticism, they carve out their own path instead. If they "fail," they tend to blame other people for their mistakes and are generally seen as anti-authoritative.
- Self-analysis is most effective when it is consistent and done over a period of several months, or longer. It is a "window" into our why and how we certain internal feelings, thoughts, and reactions. It can also help us determine the reasons why we behave and react in different ways and how our moods are affected.

Why is it Important to Analyze Yourself?

We often think we know more about ourselves than we do. This isn't because we don't know who we are, but rather, we may not be aware of how influenced we are by certain situations, other people's behavior and comments. This exercise gives us more clarity on what lurks beneath the surface and gives us a better understanding of the "how" and "why" behind our behavior and thinking.

When we feel inadequate or suffer from low self-esteem, it isn't simply by chance, but rather, it's a deep-rooted belief held that we are not worthy in one or more ways.

Exploring our own patterns of thinking can reveal a self-destructive trend of self-beratement and criticism that manifests based on what other people may say.

Once we become aware of the impact negativity has on our own well-being, it becomes easier to recognize patterns of behavior that we can avoid or notice. It empowers us to take action to reduce harmful relationships with people or situations that impact how we feel about ourselves. As we become more aware, we build a stronger sense of self and become more careful about the people and groups we choose to associate with, so that we can maintain a healthier level of self-worth and awareness.

Chapter 8: Body Language

Body language is universal. It transcends the verbal language barrier and is an effective way to "read" someone's feelings, thoughts, and in some cases, what action they will take. We use our body language to convey interest or disgust, to indicate approval, among others.

Reading Body Language of Other People: Key Signals to Look For

Body language and non-verbal cues are an important means of communication that we may not always recognize. When we converse with someone verbally, we may notice that their gestures, posture, and/or facial expression match what they say, and at other times, it may be contrary to what they express.

When the gestures or non-verbal cues are obviously different from verbal communication, this may be an indication of dishonesty or an attempt to hide or mask a certain thought or feeling. Non-verbal communication, in many ways, can speak louder and more accurately than words. There are different types of gestures and bodily movements that are commonly observed during conversations, such as eye movements, hand gestures, and changes in postures. Folding your arms across your chest may signal being "closed off" or guarding yourself against another person or situation, while different types of handshakes or facial movements may send other signals or say something about a person that they may not verbally reveal. The next two sections will explain further how body language is useful for reading other people and how it can be used to manipulate others.

How to People use Body Language to Communicate and Manipulate?

Just like verbal techniques in persuasion, body language, and non-verbal communication can be used to manipulate other people. Many signs we make with our hands, or gestures we make with our face or body, will send a message and convey a certain characteristic or trait. For example, when someone appears timid, by concealing their face or hunching their back and shoulders forward, they may be perceived as weak or having low self-confidence. When a manipulate person exerts a dominant pose or leaning forward with their head held high, it can cause someone to feel intimidated and eager to comply with their requests and without question. Many people are affected by bold, forward gestures and movements that invade personal spaces.

These movements have the intention of placing others in a position of submission or compromise, so that manipulation becomes successful. Maintaining an upright posture, clear voice, and confident pose can go a long way to keeping people from using their need for dominance against your best interests.

Chapter 9: Analyzing Cognitive Functions

Cognitive functions are defined as mental activities that involve knowledge, reasoning, memory, language, and other information that are used to make decisions in our lives and for the purpose of communication. We use what we learn to achieve tasks in life, such as making decisions, budgeting our finances, translating from one language to another and/or finding the reason(s) and/or purpose(s) behind something. How we acquire information, process it, and use it later is vital to our development and communication with others. It can also be heavily influenced by our relationships with other people, places, and situations. There are several ways in which our mind acquires and absorbs new information:

Extraverted Sensing

This refers to how we acquire information through our five senses (taste, smell, sight, hearing, and touch) and how these experiences are translated into our mind to retain and develop this information. When we taste a new food or observe a new species of animal, it becomes a learning experience that we acquire and "file" in our mind for future reference and knowledge.

Introverted Sensing

This refers to recalling a previous experience as it was remembered. This new scent of a flower discovered a week before, or the sound of someone's voice you recently met at a conference. The more impactful or unique the experience, the more likely you are to remember and recall the event, person, or item more vividly.

Extraverted Thinking

This is a process where we make a judgment or decision based on external facts or items that we take into consideration. An example would be making a quick judgment immediately following a vehicular accident, that involves contacting an emergency without hesitation. This is a quick or "snap" decision based on external information available at the time. In cases where there is an imminent danger or appears to be a threat (an upcoming natural disaster or fire), the decision to vacate, then make other plans is part of the extraverted thinking process. These choices are made based on objective, external facts that may impact our emotions, though they require only observation in order to determine the next step(s) and decision(s) to make.

Introverted Thinking

This decision-making process is based on internal, personal needs and values, as opposed to external, objective items. Often, judgments or choices made through introverted thinking tend to be more emotionally based and personal in nature and may or may not consider external factors.

An example would be to abruptly leave a room or conversation when someone makes an offensive joke or comment or to respond with an objection if the comment has a personal impact. How we process, retain, and use information that we acquire varies depending on how we perceive and remember it. This process also impacts how we communicate with other people and how they read our verbal and non-verbal cues. It's important to become familiar with different types of communication, as these can serve as a "window" into understanding more about how we are perceived and how we communicate with others.

Verbal Communication

The way we express ourselves verbally to another person or within a group is the most common form of communication. How we speak to other people and how they communicate with us has an impact on our response and perception. While non-verbal cues and communication are important to understand, there are elements to a verbal expression that is equally vital to become familiar with:

- A person's tone, emphasis, or lack of emphasis on certain words, phrases, and speech can vary widely depending on their intentions. For example, a simple phrase may seem uneventful or unimportant if spoken in a monotone or unenthusiastic tone of voice. If the person is known for making sarcastic remarks or statements, a dull expression may indicate sarcasm or simply a lack of interest. If the same phrase or statement is spoken with more enthusiasm or excitement, it may generate more attention and an equally excited response.

Sometimes it's not what we say, but rather how we say it.

- The volume and speed at which we talk and be an indicator of our mood or attitude surrounding a specific topic or event. For example, if we state "I have to go to school" in a slow, quiet and monotone voice, it may signify boredom or displeasure in attending school.
- On the other hand, if we make the statement with more cheer and express it loudly, it may indicate something more positive. Speaking quickly and stumbling over words may indicate nervousness or fear, whereas speaking loudly with a deliberate tone may denote anger or frustration.
- Verbal sounds, such as sighing, laughter, pausing or using "filler" words such as "umm" or "uh" can indicate a variety of different moods or impressions.

Pausing during a sentence or conversation may be a sign thinking before you speak, or simply "searching" for the right words or description to use as a response. Sighing can be a sign of frustration, despair, or grief. It can also indicate being tired and not wanting to talk any further. Laughter usually indicates a light-hearted or humorous comment, or it can indicate nervousness. Some people will use laughter to convince others that they are happier or more content, whether that is the case or not. The style of verbal communication can indicate a lot about how a person feels. Interpreting verbal cues or changes in speech patterns or mood can signal when it is appropriate to respond, how to respond, and when merely leaving the conversation is the best option. For example, if a person sounds nervous or anxious, providing comforting words and encouragement may be appropriate.

If someone sighs or shows signs of frustration, asking them if they need assistance or simply giving them space for reflection can be a useful way to communicate.

Facial Expressions

Facial expressions and gestures are an essential means of understanding what people mean to say and how even when they may not verbalize their innermost thoughts and ideas. Most facial gestures or movements are easy to understand and require little or no explanation. If a good friend or family member smile upon meeting with you, they are displaying joy and contentment. During a tragic event or mourning a loss, people may display a somber expression of sadness. Other emotions and experiences can trigger many different facial expressions, and some are more obvious than others. In cases where a person is confronted with making a decision or asked if they accept or agree with a certain rule or decision, they may state "yes, sure," yet frown at the same time. These two concurrent, yet conflicting lines of communication can mean that the person wants you to believe that he or she is in agreement, but their facial expression indicates they do not agree. Sometimes, facial expressions are obvious and other types they can be contrary or opposite to what a person may say. Examples of communication through facial gestures or expressions often convey true emotions, including fear, anger, sadness, confusion, excitement, shock, and happiness. If a person's facial expression matches how we perceive them or how they speak, we tend to trust them because they are showing consistent or "true" feelings.

In several studies conducted on the impact of facial expressions and their impact on other people, it was noted that more people recognized happier, joyful expressions as being more confident and intelligent, whereas angry, frustrated expressions were not valued as highly. Some people may use a smile or friendly face to mask true feelings of sadness or anger so that they are not perceived as they truly feel.

Eye Reading

Eye movements, gazing, or avoiding contact are examples of communication. Eye expressions are often used with other facial gestures to show a variety of emotions or reactions.

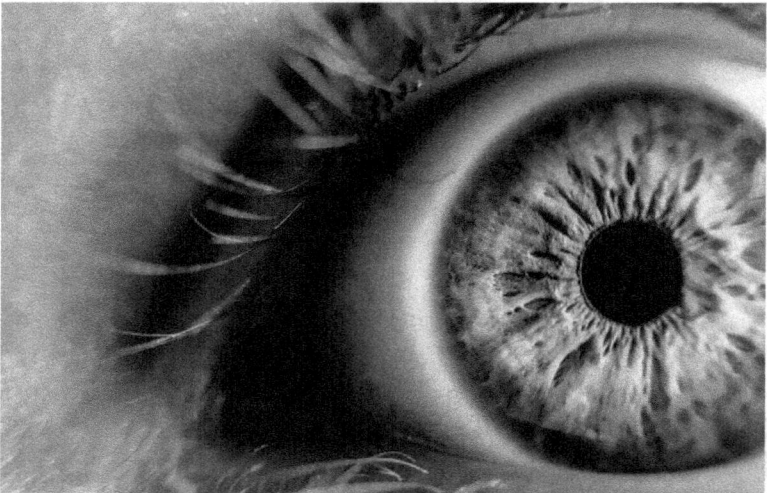

They can also indicate whether a person is paying close attention if they are interested in what you have to say, or whether they prefer to avoid the conversation altogether. In studying the various types of eye expressions or movements, we can gain a better understanding of how they communicate with us:

- If a person maintains consistent eye contact with a continuous gaze, they are likely interested in you and what you have to say or offer.
- If you maintain eye contact with someone, they will likely "read" this gesture as a show of interest and attention. People respond well to attention and will often go to great lengths to maintain it once they have your undivided attention.
- Avoiding eye contact and/or frequently looking away is a sign of disinterest or boredom in a topic or person. If you have to continuously remind someone to notice you or speak louder or more enthusiastically to hold another person's attention, it's likely because you've noticed a lack of interest. They may dart their eyes away from you and look elsewhere. If they are tired or overworked, it may simply mean that they don't possess the energy to pay attention at the moment, though they may show more interest at another time. Another reason for avoiding eye contact may occur when someone feels embarrassed, uncomfortable, or attempting to hide their true feelings or thoughts on a topic or situation. While some people are eager to debate or challenge a subject, many people prefer to avoid the discussion altogether. They may not express this verbally, though their lack of eye contact is a sure sign of avoidance.
- Blinking may be a sign of excitement or nervousness. Some people may often blink or on occasion. They may not even be aware of it, as it is a normal function that occurs whether we realize it or not. In situations where a person may be overtired or bored, they may purposely blink to keep their focus. Blinking may also be a habit or circumstantial and have not related to expression or communication at all sometimes.

- Eye rolling or making deliberate movements in direct response to a joke or comment are other examples of eye expressions. They are usually specific in nature, such as responding to a silly joke with eye-rolling or closing your eyes momentarily to show displeasure or disagreement with a statement or opinion.

In addition to eye expressions, facial movements, and verbal cues, there are many other verbal and non-verbal signs that can give us an indication of someone's true feelings or intentions. Examples of hand gestures, postures, and other non-verbal motions are described in more detail below:

Hand Gestures

The way we gesture with our hands, arms, and fingers can show enthusiasm or excitement about a specific topic in general. There are specific movements and symbols or signs we make that can be more indicative of something we want, request, or to show approval. One simple gesture of the fingers or sway of the hand can mean the difference between dismissal and approval. Other movements are habitual and maybe a specific characteristic of a person's mannerisms as well:

Fingers are often used to communicate in a quick and simple way, especially when verbalizing isn't an option (due to a long-distance or busy crowd), and a clear sign is needed.

For example, giving a "thumbs up" is a sign of approval or agreement. It may also confirm that everything is in order and "good." "Thumbs down" can indicate failure or disappointment. Pointing fingers can be an accusatory action and used to aim or point at someone to blame them for action. This gesture can also be used, in some cases, for emphasis or as a way to describe a situation or scenario while keeping your attention. In most cases, finger-pointing is considered rude and even obscene. It can make someone feel targeted or humiliated and should be avoided. An upward "V" was used as a sign of peace in the 1960s or as a symbol of victory. Forming a circle with the index and thumb, with the remaining fingers spread indicates everything is "ok." It's also a signal that a plan or event is in good order. It can also symbolize perfection. To curl your index finger towards someone can summon them. One of the most positive finger symbols worldwide is the crossing of the index and middle finger. This indicates good fortune and luck. In some countries or regions, these and other hand signs could be interpreted as something negative, such as an insult or lewd comment. It's always a good idea to research hand gestures and other customs before traveling, to ensure appropriate and respectful communication is used.

A flat hand will often mean "stop" or stay back, to limit contact with someone or signal for them to cease acting or behaving in a certain way. This sign can similarly mean "stay" or to hold a specific thought or position.

It can also translate into "talk to the hand," which basically indicates a lack of interest in communicating with someone, therefore, using your hand as a barrier. In some cultures, this hand sign can indicate reassurance, or as a way to summon or ask someone for their assistance.

Body Posture

Our posture and how we pose can give away our innermost thoughts and insecurities. When a person is often slouching forward and looking downward, it's a symptom of shame or a lack of self-confidence. It may be a pose or position that we don't intend to portray, as it may reveal certain feelings of insecurity or weaknesses that we would rather hide. When a person sits or stands with their arms open and with a straight, upright posture, it shows engagement and confidence when they speak or listen. They are interested in what the other person or people have to say and want to contribute. Some people may go further to lean forward to acknowledge when someone makes a comment. Signs of avoidance, tension or feeling defensive are often conveyed through body language and a variety of poses and positions, including sitting with arms folded across the chest with a stern facial expression or none at all. In this position, the upper body may be turned away from the person communicating to indicate their disapproval or a clear message of having no interest in reciprocating. In a standing position, a person showing avoidance may simply walk away, usually with their arms folded and all forms of contact, with their eyes or face are minimized as much as possible. Other signs of avoidance or limiting contact may include fidgeting, looking away, or gazing in another direction to display a clear message of disinterest. Displaying confidence and a willingness to communicate is often shown with open gestures that symbolize and an invitation to talk or share discussion. In this situation, the posture is confident, and hands are usually used minimally unless gesturing to supplement the description of a situation or item. When people display a confident, upright posture with direct eye contact and a firm but a friendly disposition, they are more likely to grab your attention and keep you listening.

Some people are natural with social engagement, while others practice these techniques to improve their performance in business, networking, and sales.

Head Movements

Nodding, shaking from side to side or tilting to one side are all examples of head movements that convey a certain feeling or emotion. Tilting the head to one side is a way of saying, "I'm interested and want to know more." When someone displays this action, it usually means they want to listen to you and are interested in what you have to say. In some cases, it can be a sign that feels attraction towards you, and for this reason, they want to know more about you. In some situations, where a person is observing an event or piece of artwork, they may tilt their head when they are trying to understand or interpret its meaning or message. This may occur when the image or item is complex or enigmatic, and tilting your head to adjust the gaze or perspective can provide more options for viewing and understanding. Tilting the head upwards to extend the chin is a show of dominance or feel above other people. It can also indicate a strong sense of confidence in leadership. It's often used by executives and politicians when they speak to a crowd or group. This gesture can also be read as a form of arrogance or superiority, which may effectively hide any insecurity and convey a sense of fearlessness. On the contrary, by tilting the head and chin downward, this could mean rejection, bashfulness, or a sense of shame. It also indicates a lack of confidence and can make others see you as more sensitive to criticism. Facing forward with your chin pushed inward indicates a defensive gesture or a sign that someone feels threatened by a new event, situation, or change.

This gesture may spontaneously occur when another person "steals" the spotlight from someone else. Nodding of the head is a common non-verbal way of saying "yes" or "I agree" with someone. If done quickly and anxiously, a quick nod may indicate a strong eagerness to agree and coincide with another person's comments and ideas. Shaking the head from side to side is usually the opposite of nodding, indicating a "no" or non-approval. Playfully tossing the head from one side to another during a casual conversation may indicate signs of attraction towards someone in the group. It also displays a measure of comfort and willingness to submit and engage on a more personal level.

Handwriting

The way people write says a lot about their personality and how they express themselves. Often, people tend to use texting and online communication as their main source of written expression, though handwriting still remains important for taking notes, signing paperwork and adding a personal touch or expression to a card or letter. The most common use of handwriting, especially in business, is a signature. The formation of letters, their spacing, and size are factors taken into consideration when analyzing a person through their handwriting:

- Letters spaced apart and written in a medium to large size can indicate a sense of freedom and sincerity. This may also indicate a tendency towards being more generous and sharing, and a sense of independence and a free-spirited attitude.

- Letters or words that were written closely together may indicate that a person is not aware of personal space or boundaries and may be intrusive or step over the line sometimes.
- Printing lightly with a pen or pencil indicates a degree of sensitivity and care, whereas a heavier hand can mean a more tense and angry attitude. An evenly, moderately printing pressure is ideal, as it can indicate a level of consistency and commitment in the writer
- Some signatures are clear and easy to read, whereas others may appear like a scribble or illegible. People who sign with a deliberately clear print or handwriting are easier to understand and desire to be understood. They tend to be straight-forward and an "open book." People who use messy or less legible styles of signatures tend to be more private and concealed.
- The way t's are crossed, I's are dotted, and other letters are formed also provide ways in which we read other people by their writing habits.
- Some analysis of even seemingly insignificant styles in writing, such as how closely an "I" is dotted to the openness or closed loop of a lowercase "l" can seem trivial, though they are all signs of specific personality types and practices. For example, when an "I" is closely dotted, this may indicate an organized mind and lifestyle. Dots over an "I" or "j" that are more playful, such as a circle or heart, may be interpreted as creative and inventive. If a person crosses their "t" high, they may have a goal-oriented way of living, where they aim high and strive for greatness, whereas crossing a "t" low or barely at all may be a lack of ambition or drive.

In handwriting a lowercase "l," a large loop may show a sign of an open-mind and ready-to-learn mentality, whereas a smaller space within the loop is likely a sign of close-mindedness and stubbornness.

- Round, circular letters indicate a potential for creativity and artistic talent. If letters are both round, curvy and large, this may indicate a combination of showing generosity along with a talent for the arts, with a willingness to share their talent and abilities with others for greater appreciation. Pointed, sharply written letters and words indicate a sign of intelligence and logic.
- The way letters are slanted in handwriting can indicate.

Chapter 10: Analyzing Personality Types

There are many personality types and even more variations within each general type of personality. Learning about the different types of people, in general, and their most common characteristics or attributes can help understand the way they think, feel, and communicate. When considering the types of personalities and people we know in our own personal life, we may be quick to generalize or categorize each person to "fit" a specific type. Realistically, many people can fit into more than one category, or barely resemble any at all, though generally, each type of personality indicates an overall trend or group of characteristics that collectively resemble certain people better than others. Understanding and analyzing different personality types can help us communicate and "read" other people's thoughts, feelings, and intentions.

What are the Different Personality Types?

Becoming familiar with different personality types and people is a beneficial way to understanding what "makes them tick" and how we can communicate with them. Some personality types may be challenging or difficult to deal with, whereas others may be more approachable and easier to address. Overall, most people will identify themselves with at least one personality type, then decide how other people they know fit into the others.

The following personalities are generally easy to spot and can provide a good foundation for understanding a person's motives and aspirations, as well as how to communicate and become more familiar with them:

The Analyst

This type of personality focuses on understanding and studying everything for greater knowledge and curiosity. The analyst is usually very logical and intelligent, though they are not the majority. This personality tends to make up five percent of the population. They are goal-oriented with a focus on achieving results, and often feel most comfortable on their own or with similar, like-minded people. They can have a sense of imagination, with the capability of inventing and discovery. Analyst personalities are a quick study and are continually reading, studying, and learning. They are ambitious to a degree, though not excessively, and maintain a more acute focus on specific goals or areas of study.

The Authority

People with a leader or authoritative personality type are often considered confident, charismatic, and with unlimited ambition. They are brazen, blunt, and direct in their communication, to the point of ruthlessness. Like analysts, authoritative-type personalities tend to dominate and control the environment, or at least strive to do so. They will go to great lengths to climb the corporate ladder, without regard for stepping on anyone else on the way up. While they are challenging to communicate with on a personal or one-to-one level, they are charismatic and magnetic in a group setting. They tend to fit into leadership positions where they can persuade and motivate people, often to their own advantage. Like analysts, they make up a small percentage of the population.

The Idealist

This personality type may seem very different from the first two types, though the idealist shares a common trait with both the analyst and authoritarian: achieving a goal. They have a deep desire to achieve greatness, though it may not necessarily be for money, fame, or a career. The idealist is creative and poetic, often looking for the inner good or positive in people. They dream of a better world for everyone and may advocate or protest for specific causes and/or goals. The idealist may be a dreamer with more passive goals or interests or engage in hands-on rescue work or volunteer missions. They may be easy to converse with and engage, and still hold strong beliefs and/or opinions. Overall, the idealist wants to make the world a better, more "ideal" place for everyone.

Natural-born Leaders

Like the authoritarian personality type, natural-born leaders are good at taking charge and engaging people. They may possess some of the same attributes of the authoritarian personality type, without the same level of ambition and ruthlessness. Natural-born leaders tend to take on the role of the teacher or coach, with a genuine and sincere ability to help others through guidance instead of dominance. When they coach or counsel, it is done in an unintimidating and unauthoritative way. They are charismatic and display a lot of passion for their goals and work. Their confidence is not inflated, but natural and genuine—not egotistic. Their motives can vary, though they are usually more altruistic than the ambitious executive or aspiring politician, instead of taking a more modest and authentic approach to leadership. If they do aspire in politics, their platform or speeches may focus more on community issues and people than business.

219

In this way, they can be seen as a protagonist or the "good guy" personality that comes up with the right answers and works towards a solution within the leader role. These types of leaders make up around 5-7 percent of the population.

The Free-Spirit

The life of the party, the socialite is the free-spirit personality type. This type of person is less focused on logic or business, and more on the emotional connection they make between people.

Their view of the world may seem like an analyst, in that they see their environment as a series of puzzles and sections that fit together, though instead of using equations or logical reasoning, they see the world in shades of emotional and intuitive connections.

Their enthusiasm for people and connecting with them will often make free-spirited personalities an exciting experience to socialize with, though they usually don't want this level of attention. They are more interested in creative ideas and exploring them with other people than to become the center of attention. When they are in a party or at an event, the free-spirit personality can easily shift into dancing, laughing and enjoy socializing with everyone, and also find unique commonalities with individuals. They value other people's feelings and emotions, to the point of encouraging them to express their thoughts. They are reliant on their intuition and feelings and often use their interpretation of these to make decisions in life.

The No-nonsense Personality

If you've ever known a person that follows the rules, only relies on facts and focuses on straight-forward goals with little wiggle room, this is typically referred to as a logical, no-nonsense type of personality. They tend to keep within their own lines or boundaries and achieve their tasks, regardless of how difficult or challenging they may be. The no-nonsense type will take responsibility for what they've done, and strive to improve on their performance, even to the point of perfectionism. They generally have no tolerance for laziness or procrastination. If they are in a position where they must work within a group of people, they do not heavily rely upon others to complete a project but would rather take it on themselves to ensure that it gets done correctly. This personality type is reliable and dependable, though not always flexible when new ideas or suggestions are introduced. They value honesty and integrity over satisfying another person's emotional needs. In this way, they may appear blunt or insensitive, though consider it justified when they are speaking honestly.

Generally, they tend to prefer solitude than in the company of others and make up about 10-15 percent of the population.

The Socialite

Socializing is a key component and foundation of this personality type. Almost every decision, career move or decision they make is based on their ability to socialize widely and gain popularity and the spotlight. They may get involved with sports, dancing or performance arts and enjoy both the attention on stage and the social network opportunities attached to their image. While they crave attention and social interaction, they can be very supportive of their peers, friends, and family, and continue to coach and support them in the same paths they have previously taken. They aim to please and make people as happy as possible. In the spotlight, they enjoy high approval ratings and rave reviews, though they do not need to be an authority or seek a position of superiority over others. When it comes to social events, they are experts and coordinating and organizing everything, focusing on appearance and making an impression. They are not conversationalists about politics or science but would rather discuss fashion trends and issues associated with social status.

They will show a genuine interest in someone when they ask, which makes them sincere and pleasurable to converse with. When they are in the spotlight, they do not become arrogant or egotistic, but rather, use their fame to promote and help others. For this reason, they tend to be more altruistic and well-intentioned. They are loyal and respected people, often valuing traditional or widely accepted rules as a basis in how they live.

The Explorer

These are the adventure-seekers of society; the people who are always looking for a new destination to explore and report about, often pushing boundaries and limits to establish a new path or seek out a new idea. Explore personality types tend to follow their inspirations and connections with people, ideas, and places. If they are not physical travelers or explorers in the literal sense, they may be experimental in other aspects of life, such as extreme sports, controversial arts, and literature. They may challenge another person's point of view for the sheer purpose of exploring a new idea or to belief. Although an explorer may seem to embody sufficient interesting ideas and traits to make them social, they often remain introverted and often misunderstood because they often step over boundaries and limits that other people are not comfortable with. Explorers are risk-takers and more susceptible to gambling, experimenting with drugs, sex, and other compulsive behaviors. Approximately 10 percent of the population is considered the explorer personality type. When they are carefully and diplomatically criticized for their behavior, they may either handle it well. If criticism is blunt or direct, they may react suddenly and lose their temper. Often, they are unpredictable and can display an array of intense emotions when confronted, though, in the long-term, they tend to be forgiving and embody a "live and let live" mentality.

The Entrepreneur

Like the explorer personality type, the entrepreneur is willing to take risks and "jump" into situations that may present a sense of danger. They are good conversationalists and tend to favor intelligent, relevant, and meaningful conversations over dull small talk.

When they take a risk, it's usually a more calculated one, than the explorer. When they jump into an opportunity head-first and encounter many errors and difficulties, they make an effort to "fix" these as they go, choosing to "swim" in a "sink or swim" scenario. While they may be good at responding quickly and effectively to minimize trouble, they are natural risk-takers and don't mind being in a sea of chaos. They take delight in the excitement of passion, drama, and the thrill of chasing the next risk. While they are good at solving problems quickly and on the go, they tend to not perform well in structured, organized environments where they are expected to adhere to a routine. They are quick studies and tend to prefer learning as they go, rather than learn first; practice later. When it comes to societal rules and standards, the entrepreneur's personality doesn't feel the need to follow them. They may often bend, and even break the rules where it satisfies their own needs and goals. This personality type tends to rely on their own sense of values and morals for guidance, which may conflict with society. They are good in emergencies when a quick fix is needed, using a mix of reason and creative "out of the box" thinking. In a hurry, they can assemble a team of people and tasks to get the project done, though they may not be sensitive or always personable with others when there is a high demand or pressure to perform.

The Maker

Makers enjoy using their senses to explore the world and learn best with a "hands-on" approach. They are not afraid to get dirty to get creative or make a few mistakes along the way before accomplishing their goal. Instead of or learning by reading or study, makers progress better when they practice through trial and error.

When they finish a project, they take note of their experiences along the way and enjoy sharing those with others to help them progress as well. In this way, they can become excellent coaches and teachers in trades, mechanics, and other skilled professions. Their curiosity makes them naturally exciting and creative, though they are not always consistent or straight-forward in their approach. They tend to value realism and directness, though not always mindful of how others feel about their approach, often interfering or interrupting standard processes already in place. For example, they may interrupt a well-organized plan or structure when they suddenly brainstorm an idea that they want to share. While they may have good intentions, their ideas may fall on silent ears and result in frustration and a sense of misunderstanding. They can be kind and considerate, though often directed by their passions. In expecting that others will understand their methods, they may become frustrated with their enthusiasm and passion is not reciprocated.

The Independent Thinker

This personality type loves to debate and stir up controversy. They seek a thrill out of arguing on the opposing side to determine what will come of it. While some people will use this exercise to better understand the other side(s) of a case and to evaluate a viewpoint from different perspectives, the independent thinker debates simply for the sport. They see this as an exercise or battle of wit, and nothing more. They may even argue for a side that they are typically opposed to, just to see other people squirm and tense up in the debate. This is the independent thinker's rollercoaster ride. Although they may not choose to debate for a meaningful purpose outside of the argument itself, they can become more sensitive and understanding of all sides, which may effectively increase their awareness and compassion.

What they originally see as a mental exercise or challenge, they don't seek attention or praise in taking the opposing side in a debate. They enjoy the challenge of being challenged and being in a disadvantaged position for the purpose of the exercise. Independent thinkers are good at visualizing the big picture and coming up with ideas, though they are not well suited to developing strategies and plans to follow through on those ideas. In a work environment, they want to be appreciated and acknowledged for their ideas and suggestions, though they do not always pick up the responsibility associated with making it happen and relying on others to do this instead. This personality type makes up less than five percent of the population. There are many other personality types, including combinations of the above examples. The next section delves into the advantages and disadvantages of each personality type and how they can be dealt with successfully.

Advantages and Disadvantages of Different Personalities and How They Affect us

As we learn about different types of personalities, we also encounter that certain personality types are more challenging than others. For example, a person who is more authoritative and dominant in nature may be more difficult to communicate with because they view their own ideals and beliefs as superior to others. An analyst, on the other hand, maybe more open and patient to listening, though it will only take you seriously if you can present sufficient evidence and facts to support your views. Overall, all personality types can present both advantages and disadvantages.

It's important to become familiar with these challenges, especially for distinctive personality types that you may encounter in everyday life. The following chart indicates the different hurdles and advantages for each personality type described in the previous section:

Personality type	Advantages	Disadvantages	Suggestions on Communication and Dealing with Challenges
The Analyst	Focused, rational and deals with facts only. They value hard evidence and facts to base their decisions on, making them consistent.	There is little room for debate once they make a decision, as they do not take into consideration any emotional or personal consequences or impact	Cite factual information and sources to communicate with an analyst. They will place more value on facts than feelings.
The Authoritarian	Charismatic, magnetic and motivational in a group setting or on stage. They are driven and ambitious.	Ruthless, blunt in their approach and not always sensitive or approachable. They look out for themselves first, and	Always take into consideration their advantage when approaching an authoritative personality on a specific

		strive for the top only, and are not afraid to step on other people's toes.	issue or topic. They are more likely to listen in favor of what you have to say, if it benefits them in one way or another.
The Idealist	They are altruistic and looking for the ideal solution to every problem. Their goals are selfless, and they can be strong advocates for vulnerable people and situations in need of support. When they are ambitious, it usually entails volunteering on a rescue mission or taking part in rebuilding a community	Sometimes, the idealist can be too passive or vague in their direction. They may be unrealistic and dream more than they achieve. When some idealists are actively trying to make the world a better place, they may become disillusioned with one cause and	Speak clearly and passionately. If you are perceived as genuine in supporting a cause, the idealist will relate to you more.

	damaged by a natural disaster.	not see the big picture or acknowledge if the effort is worth the end result.	
Natural-born leaders	They are excellent coaches, teachers and aim to improve the lives of others through their natural ability to lead and achieve. They are not authoritative but are revered and respected as authorities on their subject of expertise.	Generally, there are no drawbacks or negative aspects of this personality type. If they occupy a position of power, they may be misunderstood as a more authoritative personality in some situations, where they may express a passionate comment or opinion (politics can be an example). They are often very successful in their	Natural-born leaders can be in high demand, as they are approachable, genuine and supportive. If you have an opportunity to speak with one, always prepare what to ask or state in advance, to save time and get the most out of the experience. Speak clearly the problem or situation you want help with and how you wish to resolve (or

		profession and may not have much time to spare for individual communication, which can be a drawback in some situations.	which end result you wish to achieve). This will give this personality type the best possible basis to give advice and guidance.
The Free spirit	They are fun, enthusiastic, and passionate about connecting with other people intuitively and emotionally. They can be enjoyable conversationalists and "liven" up a social event with their ability to adapt and blend into a variety of different social landscapes.	Free-spirited personalities do not respond well to conversations or topics involving logical or statistical information. They tend to base their experience and knowledge solely on emotion and intuition, which can be difficult to relate to or quantify.	Appealing to a free spirit means speaking to them in a way that they feel connected to you. This can be as simple as mentioning a favorite type of music or an ideal place to go on a retreat or vacation to get the conversation started. If they relate to you on this basis, it can be a

			good start for further communication.
The No-nonsense	The no-nonsense type of personality will always take the practical, always-tried-and-true method of getting things done. They prefer to follow a straight-forward, honest approach instead of wavering from the norm. They value rules and stick to them. This personality type will always tell it like it is.	They can be blunt and insensitive without warning, though it is not often their intention. Their approach leaves little or no room for change, and they are not open-minded when new ideas or suggestions are expressed. They are generally resistant to anything new or untraditional.	Approach this type of person from their perspective: if a new idea is beneficial in making an established process more efficient, or if it can be described in such a way, this may sway the opinion of the new idea or thought in a positive direction. In this way, the idea isn't viewed as a "challenge" to the original, traditional process, but rather as an enhancement to it.

The Socialite	Socializing is one of their strongest traits. They are naturally likable and aim to please everyone. The socialite personality is loyal, committed and supportive to friends, and family. They are good event organizers and often seen as the "star" of the show.	When it comes to conversation, they tend to focus on social status and related topics that focus on status and appearance. Delving into the deeper subject matter is a challenge. Socialites may take criticism very personally, even if it is constructive, as they are focused on making everyone happy, which is never achievable.	Keep the conversation light and positive. Getting to know social people and gaining their support is valuable in networking within their circles. When giving a socialite a compliment or positive encouragement, always be sincere, and it will be appreciated.
The Explorer	They are exciting, interesting and never boring. Their unconventiona	They are natural risk-takers and almost never err on the side of	Showing interest in an explorer's quests or stories is sure-fire way

	l nature allows them to challenge the status quo and make people take notice. At a party, they are the guest that everyone will remember for their liveliness and adventure-seeking attitude. They tend to be likeable people.	caution, which makes them unpredictabl e. They are prone to danger because they don't weight the consequence s of their actions beforehand. Getting into a long-term friendship or relationship with this personality type may present a lot of challenges because of the risky behavior. They also may have difficulty maintaining steady employment because of their erratic lifestyle.	to gain their attention and understand them better. They are often easy and fun to talk to in a casual setting. If you share their enthusiasm on a specific area of interest, this can help them focus better and communicate more effectively.
The Entrepren	They are adventurous	Their ability to take risks	Appealing to an

eur	and take calculated risks that they are willing to "fix" and make work in the long-term. If there is a problem, they will find a solution. They are fast learners in the process and always seem to land on their feet. Entrepreneurs achieve success on their own terms.	and thrive on them makes their lifestyle unpredictabl e, similar to the explorer personality type. For this reason, they do not perform well in structured environment s, making it difficult for them to maintain a stable livelihood.	entrepreneur from a standard, traditional approach will not interest them. They respond better to something thought-provoking and fun, in a challenging way. A unique business venture or unusual style of handling a situation may interest them more.
The Maker	They are creative on their own terms and enjoy experiencing the world around them with a "hands-on" approach. Makers have the ability to invent solutions and	Some makers may lack certain academic skills or have an inability to translate their creations into a more standard format for teaching and learning.	Makers take pride in their work. When others don't share in their joy, they tend to keep to themselves. Showing an interest in their creation and skills is a good way to

	create new possibilities from scratch. They have the advantage of seeing their ideas materialize through their own creations. Their skills are valuable and can make them ideal teachers and coaches.	They are quick to enthusiastically display their talent and creations, sometimes without considering any practical use for them. This can frustrate others who are accustomed to following specific procedures and plans.	connect with this personality type. Aside from this, they are easy to talk to and straight-forward about their life.
The Independe nt Thinker	Independent thinkers enjoy a good debate, and for this reason alone, they can be entertaining. They are often witty and skillful and debating any topic and from any perspective.	They can be very direct and sometimes misundersto od because of their methods. Their constant need to argue to display their knowledge and wit may seem short-	Ask the independent thinker questions about why they choose their side. In many cases, they choose the side they oppose, and simply view the whole debate as merely an exercise. It

		sighted and not very useful. In some cases, where they choose to defend a controversial "side" of a debate, communication can become very frustrating and charged.	can be a good opportunity for them, and others, to learn from the experience.

All personality types present challenges, and not everyone we know, or encounter will fit into one category completely. Some people may be mildly free-spirited and more of an explorer, while others may be a mix of other traits, such as an independent thinker and authoritarian, to a lesser or greater degree. There are people who are difficult to read or understand until you get to know them, and once certain attributes emerge, it can be easier to pinpoint with style(s) or method(s) of conversation work best. The best option, in almost all cases, is to exercise diplomacy.

It may seem trivial at times when we want to speak up and vocalize a passionate opinion, though it goes a long way to making communication work and maximizing its effect. The next chapter deals with examples of when to recognize manipulation tactics in everyday situations.

Chapter 11: Danger Signals

In our daily life, we may encounter situations that indicate a potential for manipulation, and in some cases, we may experience a technique that is not readily recognizable. Even when we are educated and aware of the signs to watch for, there are other factors that impede our ability to make a decision about a specific person or event. Sometimes, a manipulator is aware that during a certain time of day or in a specific place, we let our guard down and become more like "prey" to their predatorial tactics. Staying aware of our surroundings, especially when we are in an unfamiliar place or around new people, is especially important to avoid unexpected surprises.

Taking Control of your Life and Mind: How to Spot the Dangers of Manipulation and Avoid Pitfalls

The first section of this book provided a number of signs and situations to be mindful of in order to avoid the pitfalls of manipulation. Persuasion is initially and usually the milder, gentler version of manipulation, which usually follows once a persuasive technique becomes successful. Once a person is influenced by one form of persuasion, they've effectively taken the bait and are ready for the next step, which is manipulation. At this stage, there remains an opportunity to become aware of this process, and to get out of a toxic relationship, situation, or group, before it blossoms into a form of mind control.

This section will provide specific examples of techniques that can be used in everyday scenarios that can be encountered on the way to work, inside a store or shopping mall, at your place of business, at school or even at home. Realistically, manipulation and mind control can happen anywhere and from anyone. When we marginalize some people, who are victims of mind control, we often fail to realize that there are many different forms, some more subtle than others and that we are all susceptible to it. When we read a news article of an elderly couple who were scammed out of their life savings, or hear about a young man who was brutally attacked for showing a car he advertised for sale, we may feel bad for them, and yet dismiss these incidents with "I would never let that happen" or "I wouldn't fall for that scam", we don't realize that some people are more vulnerable, trusting and naïve than others. Even when a person is aware of schemes occurring, they may not recognize one when a different tactic or "bait" is used.

Examples and Scenarios of Mind Control in Action

Scenario 1: A New Business Proposal

Susan, a receptionist with a law firm, is on her way to work. She commutes on the train from the suburbs, where she lives with her husband, Ron. Ron is a computer technician and often works from home. When Susan isn't commuting to work, she's looking for another job, since she despises the two-hour travel time every day. On her way to work, she often passes by salespeople in the train station, who usually target tourists for cheap merchandise at high prices or city tours that only provide limited access. Susan often smirks to herself, noticing how easily duped people are.

She remembered back to when she and Ron took a vacation and were bombarded with the same offers. They were careful not to buy anything overpriced, and instead, researched local markets and tour guides before they went on their trip. We were smart, she thought. We weren't gullible enough to be swindled for all of our cash. Sometimes the train going home is delayed, and this means Susan must wait in the concourse of the station. One afternoon, the train announced a one-hour delay, with no other option but to wait. Feeling restless and agitated, after a stressful day at work, Susan decides to relax in one of the cafes in the terminal and enjoy a drink. She has one beer and realizes only fifteen minutes passed, so she orders another, and texted Ron to let him know she'll be late. A few minutes later, a young woman, similar in age to Susan (late twenties) takes a seat near Susan. There are several empty seats, and she leaves one in between them. Within a few minutes, they begin a conversation.

"Those trains are always so late, and today especially."

"Yes, it's going to be another forty-five minutes," Susan responds, checking the time on her phone. "I wish I didn't have to commute every day to work. It would make my life a lot easier if I could work from home as my husband."

"I know what you mean. I'm sick of commuting, too. It's time to try something different."

"It sounds as if we are in the same situation. My name is Susan, by the way."

"I'm Linda. Nice meeting you." The two women talk for about ten or fifteen minutes, and during this time, Linda casually mentions a seminar about starting your own business. It's a new business model that helps people looking to exit the nine-to-five grind and make it on their own terms. Susan is aware of direct sales companies, as her sister-in-law attempted to "recruit" her before, without much success. What Linda proposed, however, seemed different. It wasn't about selling anything, but more about starting a successful business. The seminar is free and may provide some ideas and options for Susan.

Was there a catch?

There was an announcement that the train would arrive in ten minutes, and Susan was about to leave when Linda hands her a card. "Here's my number, just in case you think of going to the seminar.

I might attend. Maybe I'll see you there?" They shake hands and leave to go home. Over the next couple of days, Susan contemplates attending the event. She reviews the card, which indicates that Linda is a business consultant for a firm downtown. Susan is skeptical, but she is also tired of being a receptionist.

She decides to discuss it with Ron.

"If you want to go check it out, why not? It's free, right?" Ron seems indifferent, as he has a lot of work to catch up on. He recently started a new contract that takes up more of his free time and makes it difficult to spend with Susan. He also knows that she's looking for a new career opportunity and learning about starting a business may be something she can try. Susan did consider becoming a virtual administrator online, and this could be a way to discover more opportunities associated with this field of work.

The seminar is scheduled for a Wednesday evening, which means Susan will have to take a later train home if she wants to attend. She decides to give it a try and calls Linda to let her know she'll attend. Linda explains that she wasn't sure about the event but is eager to go now that someone else will go with her. They agree to meet at the train station and walk to the event together, which is conveniently located downtown where they both work every day. Upon entering the facilities, Susan notices how extravagant the decorations areas if they are really trying to impress. Linda seems to be taken by all the fancy décor and mentions it to Susan.

They are invited to join a group of people in a spacious room with light appetizers, pastries with tea or coffee. Within the group, they notice a lot of well-dressed people who appear to be very professional and friendly. A few people already know one another and seem very happy, embracing each other and shaking hands as they exchange greetings. Susan notices that Linda is familiar with another woman, Diane, who happened to learn about this event on a social media group or women interested in starting their own business. Diane met Linda through another group and suggested coming to this event once they exchanged a few conversations online.

A few professional people who seem to be hosting this event make their rounds to introduce themselves to everyone, including Linda and Susan. Susan finds their appearance, warmth, and friendliness very appealing. Soon after greeting everyone, the professional hosts bring everyone's attention to a platform, where they begin a presentation about financial freedom and doing a successful business out of your dreams. Soon after their short presentation, they dim the lights and play a video, which further elaborates on the benefits of financial freedom, and how many people who learn their techniques for self-employment become highly successful.

They are able to buy their dream home, pay off their debts, and travel more.

When the presentation is over, several members of the audience are asked to give testimonials of their own success, further driving Susan's curiosity for more information. How did they achieve this? How can I take advantage of this opportunity? Linda seems attentive as well and mentions that she is very interested in this idea. Towards the end of the evening, the hosts announce that for a small "investment" of two hundred dollars, they will coach people on starting their own successful business. This takes Susan by surprise. Linda seemed to be contemplating the idea as well. While two hundred dollars isn't a huge amount, Susan takes pride in sticking with a budget, even though Ron is more liberal with his spending.

"I'll have to think about it,"

Susan explained to Linda, and both Linda and her new friend Diane are about to leave, then ask Susan for a drink.

"I should really go home; the last train will leave soon."

"It will leave in one hour. How about just one drink?"

Susan contemplates for a minute, then decides it would be fun to relax with her two new friends before heading home. They visit a fancy pub, where the drinks are overpriced.

Susan decides one drink is enough, though Linda offers to cover the tab and orders two drinks. Once the three ladies sit down, Susan notices two of the hosts from the event are at the pub. Within a few minutes, the two hosts join the ladies for drinks.

They talk extensively about business and how nice it is to sleep in and not have to get up early for work when you can set your own hours. Susan feels more convinced than ever that this may be a good opportunity for her. Before they all leave, she decides to sign up for the coaching session with one of the hosts on the spot, just before she catches the train home.

Analysis of Scenario 1

This scenario is an example of a persuasive technique that resulted in the successful recruitment of Susan to join a pyramid scheme. Susan isn't naïve to sales tactics, as she knows very well how people will try to coax others into buying things for more money than they're worth. Feeling confident that she would never be duped, Susan let her guard down when she met Linda. A common complaint about many people who commute is the time they spend in transit and the delays in traffic. Linda knew very well that Susan was likely a commuter and mentioned that train to fish for more information. Susan responded in kind, which led to a conversation about starting a business and working from home. Linda offered bait to Susan: an offer to attend a free seminar to learn about starting your own business, and she accepted it. Susan let her guard down for two reasons: she was preoccupied with the frustration of having them wait for a later train and finding common ground with someone. When someone, even a complete stranger, makes a connection with us, it can make us feel as though we know them or at least identify with them. Two people frustrated with the same commuter delay = a common frustration. The reality is this: Linda doesn't take the train, nor does she need to commute to work every day.

She lives with her mother in a condominium downtown and can easily walk to work in fifteen minutes, where she works as a cleaner for an office building. She recently finished university, though she couldn't find gainful employment, so when her mother asked if she wanted to move in and look for work, cleaning was the easiest job to find. Linda wasn't satisfied with the paycheck and decided to join a group online that offered seminars on starting a business. This led to meeting the hosts, which Linda previously knew, though she pretended to be "new" to the event when she met Susan. When they attended the seminar, the room was full of other people, just like Susan, who were recruited with the same offer.

A few "experienced" people, who claimed to have reached success, were invited to share their testimonials, though the vast majority of attendees were as clueless as Susan. Diane, who previously met Linda, encouraged Linda to bring someone new, which resulted in the invitation to Susan.

Overall, the scheme works by continuously recruiting people and offering "coaching" to them for a fee. When the fee is paid, a meeting is set up with a consultant. The consultant or "coach" explains that the two hundred dollar investment will buy the products that they can promote online, though by recruiting more people, and getting them to do the work for them, they can "move up" the ladder and earn a portion of all the sales that the people working for them earn. Ultimately, the "coaching" session is nothing more than a pitch to convince a new recruit to sell products online. While the products themselves may be legitimate or made well, the tactics used to recruit people are highly suspicious and manipulative.

The manipulative strategy begins with persuasion from Linda. The manipulation begins covertly, once Susan attends the seminar. She observes people embracing each other and showing signs of affection, even though they may or may not know each other well. She finds the warmth of the hosts welcoming, though they feel "too good to be true." The type of affection feigned at the event is a form of "love bombing." Once new recruits become emotionally and financially attached to this concept, they are effectively under the influence of the company, and this is how mind control works. After a while, they may begin to question the practices of the company and their methods, though the bonds formed within the new community will be broken if they leave.

There is a certain magnetic pull or attraction to the extravagance of the organization, even if it doesn't feel completely right. Over time, most people will leave or lose interest altogether, simply remembering the whole experience as a bad decision.

Results of Scenario 1:

Susan signed up for the coaching session on Wednesday night and agreed to bring payment and meet one of the new hosts, Dana, at her office on Saturday morning.

She is excited about the prospect of beginning a new career, though it feels like there is something off or strange about the experience. Susan decides to call Linda, who is very positive and encouraging. Instead of showing indifference initially, "I might attend the event," Linda proactively and almost aggressively promotes the coaching. "It's life-changing" and "You'll be so much happier."

Susan feels pressured, though she also likes Linda. She doesn't know her, but she seems almost like a friend.

Susan decides to do some research on the company, but she doesn't know where to begin. The information on Linda's card shows "business consultant," though there are no further details aside from a generic-sounding company with initials and "Inc." Susan decides to perform a search on the name, which brings up a lot of unrelated items, so she narrows down the search by adding "coaching" and "seminar." The results are astonishing: the company is listed as a distributor of products through several online distribution sources. While there doesn't appear to be anything shady about the company itself, some reviewer sites state that it's a waste of time and money. The comments vary from "it's a good side job" to "it's not worth the 'investment'."

After a lot of thought and consideration, Susan decides to cancel the appointment. She is met with an unexpectedly strong response from Dana, the host, who alleges the company is one of the best and can make her rich. Susan eventually ends the call but decides she would like to stay in touch with Linda. When she calls to meet for coffee, Linda only wants to talk about the coaching and ask when Susan will begin. When she learns that Susan decided to cancel, the contact abruptly ends, and Susan continues working as a receptionist for the law firm.

Conclusion for Scenario 1

Susan realized that not all schemes or manipulative techniques are the same. Some may be immediate or obvious, such as a quick sale, while other methods draw you in and convince you that you can have everything you have ever wanted if you sign an agreement and hand over money. Not all recruitment tactics are upfront either, at least not at the beginning. A person may befriend you and make you feel special, only to bait you with an offer that doesn't live up to its expectations.

Scenario 2: Getting to Know You Better

Ronia was not interested in dating anyone after her last boyfriend until she met Alan. Alan was new to the neighborhood. He would often notice Ronia walking to the local coffee shop or walking one of the neighbor's dogs. She had met him briefly at a local community gathering and found him to be very friendly and polite. He seemed to have a lot in common with Ronia. They both loved dogs, enjoying live music and cycling. Since Ronia's last boyfriend was abusive, she avoided dating for almost six months. Her ex would use up all of her money, then leave for days at a time until he was breaking again. When she left him, she was nearly destitute and had to move in with a friend until she could find a new place to live.

With a full-time job as a dog walker and a small, decently priced apartment, Ronia was back on her feet and happy in life. Her parents lived out of town, though she would visit them once every two months. They too, were relieved when she started a new life on her own. Alan was a musician that worked nights as a bartender. He decided to ask Ronia on a date after they shared a few light-hearted and humorous conversations. As interested as Ronia was, she was also hesitant about dating again. She explained that she was interested but wanted to take it slowly and see if things would work between them. Alan agreed, and they began to see each other. Within a month, their relationship progressed quickly. Alan spent a lot of time at Ronia's apartment, helping her organize her pantry, and paint her living room. She was so thrilled to have someone who treated her with respect and didn't expect her to give him money. Alan was a very affectionate person, always holding hands with Ronia and offering to give her a massage after a long day.

By the second month, Alan jokingly asked for a key to the apartment, just in case Ronia needed him to help out with anything. She found it a bit odd but laughed it off as it seemed funny.

Ronia's best friend Maddy invited her to a girls' night out. She was excited to have a night off and texted Alan to let him know that she would be out for the night and that he could reach her the next day. After a few drinks, Ronia went dancing with Maddy and a few other friends, who made sure she arrived home safely in a taxi. The next morning, Ronia woke up to at least five texts from Alan:

"Roni? Are you there?"

"Are you still out with your friends? Call me."

"I miss you. Can you call me?"

There were several more texts, and at least one phone call. Ronia worried that maybe Alan was upset for some reason, so she called him right away. He seemed distant, and not his usual, friendly self. When she asked him if there was something wrong, Alan mentioned that he was hoping to spend time with her last night, and instead she chose her friends.

He wanted to spend the rest of the weekend with her, so she obliged, and they did. The following weekend, Ronia's parents invited her to visit them out of town. She asked Alan if he wanted to meet them, but he was hesitant, and instead, asked her how long she would be away.

Over time, Ronia noticed that any time she spent away from Alan, the more possessive he became. Alan also began to burst into fits of anger, even just for a moment, over trivial matters. He would also start to criticize Ronia's chose in clothing, even though he never seemed to care before, and always complimented her appearance. Sometimes, when Ronia would spend time with friends or family, Alan would not speak with her for a day or two. When he finally did respond, Ronia would ask what is wrong, only to receive the response "I was busy." One afternoon, when Alan was visiting Ronia's place, she decided that giving him a key would help him feel more secure in their relationship. He had joked about it before, and since then, he would bring it up on occasion, suggesting that he could look after her place if she visited family. That same afternoon, one of Ronia's friend's Erica dropped by to visit while Alan was home. They were startled to see Alan, as they had only heard about him, though they never met him. It seemed strange that he was in Ronia's apartment without her. Erica also felt that Alan was familiar for some reason, though she couldn't recall where she had met him or seen him before. Within a week of receiving a key to Ronia's place, Alan began settling in, as if he lived there, bringing some personal items and leaving them behind when he would go out. Ronia was concerned about him "moving in" so soon, and she confronted him about it. Alan became agitated, accusing her of being untrustworthy and unfair. She took great offense and asked him to leave. Ronia wasn't going to tolerate any mistreatment in her home. When he protested, then apologized for his behavior, Ronia reluctantly gave in, and let him spend the night again.

Erica and Maddy met Ronia for lunch and happened to see Alan crossing the street.

"That's him!" Erica stated, pointing to Alan.

"Who?" Maddy looked to see where Erica pointed, then noticed Ronia was watching as well.

"It's Alan. We've seen each other for a little while." Erica only met him when she dropped by Ronia's apartment, though Maddy didn't know much about their dating. At that moment, Ronia realized that Alan didn't really want to publicize their relationship, only keeping it private in the comfort of Ronia's home.

"How do you know him?" Erica asked. "He looks familiar. I thought this when I saw him at your apartment when I dropped by. How well do you know him?"

Ronia explained how they met, casually, and that dating him happened fairly easily and quickly. As she spoke, Maddy realized that Alan was more than a familiar face. He was basically homeless or at least living without a fixed address, and while he did work, it wasn't as much or as often as he led Ronia to believe. In some places of business, he was known to be temperamental and was caught stealing from a few local stores. As Maddy recalled this, she spilled it all to both Erica and Ronia. It was an emotional moment, as Ronia realized that her new boyfriend was only using her for a place to stay. If she had known that he was struggling, she would have helped him, though she felt betrayed because of his dishonesty.

Analysis of Scenario 2:

Alan had been living in and out of rooming houses and sharing apartments with people for years. It was a pattern he created: move in, stay for a few months, pay no rent, then get kicked out. He repeated this pattern regularly and successfully while maintaining some small, odd jobs cleaning and bartending. Alan did not want any responsibility. Every time he was kicked out for not paying rent, he would blame his roommate for mold in the bathroom or other fictitious conditions in the place. When Alan moved into Ronia's neighborhood, he was temporarily staying with an ex-girlfriend in a small bachelor. She clearly stated that he had just two months to stay, which was around the same time Alan asked Ronia on a date. Alan's ex-girlfriend set clear boundaries about leaving after two months and was familiar with this track record of irresponsibility. When Alan began working nearby in a bar, he made a point to observe people in the neighborhood, to get an idea of who the locals were. When he first saw Ronia, she was walking two dogs, and showing them a lot of attention. Alan decided that her kindness and sympathy translated into being gullible and easy to manipulate.

After dating for several months, and getting a key to Ronia's apartment, Alan was able to "move out" of his ex-girlfriend's home after two months.

She also suspected that he simply found another bed to sleep on. Alan showed as much affection to Ronia at the beginning of the relationship to "secure" a bond and convince her that he was sincere. When he secretly moved into her home, he wasn't expecting Erica to catch him settling in, and he knew that if other locals saw him staying coming and going from the apartment often, that eventually, they would figure out his plan.

Alan used several techniques to manipulate Ronia. He targeted her well in advance, observing her from a distance and assuming she was an easy person to persuade. Alan used deception to make it appear that he was gainfully employed as a bartender and a musician, though he barely worked two shifts a week and didn't appear to have any musical instruments. Ronia was immediately suspicious when Alan initially asked her for a key, though eventually gave in when she grew to care for him more. One obstacle that Alan hadn't considered was Ronia's close friendships and family. He became possessive and demanding to be with her more after she would spend several hours with friends or a weekend with family. When she offered to introduce him, he declined, stating that he wasn't ready yet. While this seemed to be a red flag for Ronia, she dismissed his decision and continued the relationship. Over time, as Alan settled into her apartment, she noticed that he would become less kind and more demanding, as well as critical of Ronia, her decisions, and even her choice in clothing. It wasn't until her friends revealed him for his true intentions that Ronia realized she had a choice to make.

Conclusion for Scenario 2

Ronia decided to confront Alan, and with both Erica and Maddie as support. She calmly and kindly explained that the relationship would not work and that if Alan needed help finding a place to stay, she would offer to help. It was a disappointing scenario for Ronia, who had already dealt with a previously difficult relationship. She realized that these types of situations follow a certain pattern, and once she becomes more familiar with it, Ronia can potentially avoid further disasters in the future.

She also acknowledged that there were a number of signs that she could have noticed earlier in the relationship:

- Moving into the relationship too quickly and smoothly
- Too good to be true
- Becoming possessive and controlling
- Isolation from family and friends

Both scenarios are common situations that can happen and in various ways. For example, one person may take advantage of another for a place to stay or money, while another person may use them for status in a company or other favors. Manipulation and mind control is used in many everyday situations that we may encounter, which makes awareness one of the most key components of prevention.

FAQs

Additional Tips and Suggestions for Stopping and Preventing Manipulative People from Taking Control of Your Life

Q: If a manipulative person becomes immediately obvious in their intentions to persuade you, how should you respond?

A: Be direct. Explain that you are aware of their intentions, understand their reasons, but would rather decline. Keeping communication open and honest is the best defense against a covert manipulation technique.

Q: What if someone doesn't take "no" for an answer?

A: This can mean several things; either your "no" wasn't clear to them (even if it was clearly stated), they prefer to ignore your decision, and choose to continue with their techniques anyway.

Q: What sort of things should I say or questions to ask to find out if someone is using me in a relationship?

A: Initially, asking too many questions can seem invasive and like an interrogation. If you are getting to know someone better over time, it's a good idea to ask well-thought-out and meaningful questions. Ask about family relationships, the type of work they do, and what their goals are in life.

If you encounter too many vague answers to questions, and they avoid talking about their life altogether, it's a bad sign. It's also a red flag when they talk about an ex-girlfriend, ex-boyfriend, or spouse who is essentially blamed for all of their woes. This is also a sign that something isn't right.

Q: When should I question whether someone is trying to scam me?

A: If you ask this question, then it's appropriate to question them. In fact, any doubt at all is a good reason to figure out whether someone has your best interests at heart, or if they are only thinking for themselves.

Q: I tend to lack self-esteem. Am I an easy target for manipulation?

A: Unfortunately, yes. There are changes you can make to improve your sense of self-worth and confidence, which can take time and will not happen overnight. In the meantime, standing tall, with your posture upright and head held high are all good ways to appear confident, even when we may have to work harder to feel this way inside.

Q: How do I know if someone or something is too good to be true?

A: They are perfect. The organization is perfect. They smile all the time and treat you better than anyone. It may sound unrealistic, and it is. Any group or individual that shows no sign of fault is hiding something because we all have it.

If in doubt, ask a person about their faults, and share some of your own, if you feel comfortable in doing so. It's important to be transparent, but also expect the same level of honesty and transparency in return.

Q: How can I learn more about high control groups and their impact on people?

A: There is a lot of controversy around what defines a high control group, as some groups disagree with this term and any reference to it. An organization that is considered a high control group aims to control is members as much as possible by limiting their access and bonds with people and community outside their group, including close family and friends. There are a lot of online sources and research on the subject that can provide a lot more detail and insight into how these groups operate, including their involvement with scandals and criminal cases.

After taking into consideration all that there is to know and learn about persuasion and manipulation techniques, always keep the following points in mind for quick reference. This is a useful list of tips, which can be modified or added so that it fits into your life. For example, you may want to personalize some of these suggestions for your own personal experience.

Tips

- If you feel uncomfortable or coerced into doing or saying something, don't!
- When someone makes you a promise, and they are insistent about it, always question their motives.
- Hesitation is your friend. If you act quickly and hastily in a situation where you feel coerced or persuaded against your will, always choose hesitation and make an excuse, then leave as soon as you can.

There are many forms and variations of manipulation and mind control. The more we understand these techniques and the types of personalities who use them, we have a better chance of avoiding potentially disastrous results in the future. One key point we can all benefit from is the strengthening of our own self-confidence and sense of self-worth. This means taking time for yourself, even if for brief moments, to acknowledge your worth in all that you say, do and feel.

The most important thing you can do for yourself and well-being is to acknowledge and understand your true value and guard against anyone who attempts to challenge it.

Empath Healing

A Comprehensive Healing Guide for Highly Sensitive People Enabling You to Stop Absorbing Other People's Pain and Overcome Negative Mindset

By: Adam Goleman

Introduction

The manuscript has been published to assist readers in understanding the different traits of an empath. In the chapters, you shall grasp basic lessons regarding what it takes to become an empath. You shall also learn more about the traits of different people who are known as empaths. Other than that, through these chapters, you'll grasp basic fundamentals regarding empathy and what it entails to take different roles of empathy in society. If you're one of those individuals struggling to understand what it entails to be empathetic to your loved ones, this manuscript is going to guide you. Also, you'll be in a position to comprehend some of the basics of handling empathetic people. That is if you're not one of them. Eventually, you'll also master the possibilities of becoming an empath in the long run. While in many cases, it's declared that empathy is in-born, some people, such as scientists, have always assured us that empathy can be learned. The same implies that there's a possibility of grasping lessons regarding how to become an empath. Still, while learning more about empathy and what it takes to change this world, you'll understand the value of caring for one another. The same applies to different cases where you're required to be considerate to some people. Empathy is all about feeling concerned about others. In the end, the chapters of this manuscript share basic knowledge regarding what it entails to care for others.

Chapter 1: Definition of Empathy

Empathy is a term that often gets thrown around without actually having a clear sense of what it means or what it represents in a practical sense. All too often, you hear this term being used in such a manner that is not consistent with a person's beliefs and values. That is why it is of the utmost importance for us to define what empathy is and how you can spot in everyday life.

The easiest way to look at empathy is to simply put yourself in the place of someone else. By this, we mean that you are able to truly understand what a person is feeling and what they are going through. However, this isn't always the easiest thing to do. It might seem that some people are more naturally empathic than others. Often, this is due to the fact that these folks have lived through a lot of life experiences. These experiences enable them to identify with the struggles, suffering and even pain other individuals are going through.

Think about it along these lines:

If someone has just lost a parent, you can immediately connect with them if you have been through the loss of a parent yourself. You can relate to what they are going through and offer your perspective. But if you haven't been through this experience yourself, then it would be a lot harder for you to truly gain a clear insight into the feelings of the grieving individual. It should also be noted that it is not a pre-requisite for you to go through the exact same experience in order to empathize with someone. That is a common misconception which generally permeates the mind of most people. Nevertheless, it is certainly a lot easier to truly relate to another person's experiences when you have been through the exact same situation. Moreover, having been through the same type of experiences leads empathy to become a bonding experience. In the military, for example, soldiers quickly bond when they realize that they have been through similar experiences. Perhaps they haven't necessarily fought in the same war or were part of the same unit but have been through the same experience quickly allows them to bond and connect on the same level. That being said, becoming and an empathic person does not mean you have to go through every single type of experience in the world. The fact of the matter is that we all identify the same types of feelings, fear, happiness, loss, grief, disappointment, love and so on. In addition, becoming a truly empathic person is something that you can learn. This isn't a quality that we are all born with and that's that. It is the type of quality which takes time to learn and time to develop. Of course, some people are naturally more empathic than others. But on the whole, anyone can develop their empathetic skills. This is why the words of former US President Barack Obama eloquently illustrate this point: "Learning to stand in somebody else's shoes, to see through their eyes, that's how peace begins.

And, it's up to you to make that happen. Empathy is a quality of character that can change the world".

From this wonderful statement we can learn several things. Firstly, that empathy is learning to see the world through someone else's eyes. When you learn to see the world from another person's perspective, you are able to truly being to step into someone else's place. Now, it is very easy for you to step into someone who thinks the same way you do. But when you begin to see the world through the eyes of someone who doesn't think the same way you do, then you are truly beginning to become empathic. In fact, when you are able to see the world through the eyes of your enemies, you are really become that much more empathic. Sure, you can see the world through the eyes of your enemies, but that doesn't mean you have to agree with them. Nevertheless, being able to see where your enemies are coming from in an incredible skill that allows you to diffuse potentially violent situations.

Consider this example.

You have going head to head with a co-worker for a promotion. In this regard, this person is your enemy. You both want the position just as much and are willing to do whatever it takes to get there. You put in the hours and get your respective jobs done. Then, your boss decides to give a promotion to your colleague. If you are not an empathetic person, you might become bitter and resentful that this other person was chosen over you. You take this decision personally and decide to take it out on everyone else around you. This negative reaction leads to a decline in your performance which puts your job in jeopardy. Conversely, you decide to flip the script and look at this contest from the perspective of your co-worker. They see a formidable opponent in you, but they want the job so badly because they have a family to feed. So, the raise they earn from the promotion will go a long way toward putting food on their table and making ends meet at their home. When your boss announces that your co-worker got the promotion, you figure they deserve it and that their family will benefit from the bump in pay. Moreover, you might even feel happy for your colleague because they won fair and square. Yet, if you can prove that your colleague got the promotion by torpedoing you or doing underhanded deeds, then you have every right to manifest your discontent. In such cases, you don't have to accept dishonest behavior from anyone.

As you can see, a truly empathetic person sees the world from the other person's point of view, feels things with their heart, so to speak, and doesn't take everything personally. While an empathetic person is not a pushover by any means, they are able to feel and not react like an automaton. The great American poet Maya Angelou once said, "I think we all have empathy. We may not have enough courage to display it".

These words ring true insofar as the willingness we have to demonstrate how we feel in the face of the circumstances that others face around us. We can find pain, suffering and injustice everywhere we go. And while we may feel for those who suffer, we don't necessarily have the willingness to do something about it. Of course, there are situations in which we can't really do anything. In such situations, it is best to step aside and let those who can do something, do it. We might even be able to contribute by supporting those who can do something meaningful in that situation. For example, you are concerned about a natural disaster that has destroyed a foreign country. While it might be impossible for you to get on plane and help out, you can help those who help, that is, contributing in any way you can to the organizations which have the capability of helping those people in distress.

Another great example is seen in animal lovers. They feel empathy for lost and stray animals but do have the means to adopt every single animal that is lost and hurt. So, they contribute to their local animal shelter in any way they can. Often, you don't need to contribute large sums of money. Even volunteering your time every chance you get is enough to make a difference. On the opposite side of the spectrum, you can show your empathy by not doing something. For instance, you are keen on the environment and would like to help out in any way you can. So, you were to stop engaging in activities that damage the environment and take on a more proactive role in recycling, reducing energy consumption and teaching others about how they can help the environment. These examples are all ways in which you can help a greater cause from your corner of the world. You don't have to be a champion for a cause and lead a crusade. You can lead a transformative life by just engaging in the type of actions and behaviors that can add up over time. But, this attitude begins with your ability to see things from the perspective of others. If you are a pathologically selfish person, you will stop at nothing to get your way even if it means destroying others. You won't care about what others are going through so long as you are comfortable and satisfied. The fact is that overly selfish people lead miserable existences because they need to prey on others in order to advance their personal agenda. For empathetic people, lead much more meaningful and fulfilling lives because they are able to contribute to the world through their actions. Empathetic people generally stand for something and adhere to values that are congruent with their personal vision of the world. Yet, they are able to take those values and flip them around to see how they stack up in the minds of others.

Again, an empathetic person learns to see the world from someone else's perspective though they may not

265

necessarily agree with that viewpoint. One other important point to consider in this chapter is the difference between empathy and sympathy. While empathy is a deep feeling of sensitivity toward the emotions of others, sympathy is a shallow feeling that merely acknowledges what someone else is going through. As such, being sympathetic only scratches the surface of a situation. That is why it is common to hear people say; "oh, that's awful" but then they turn around and not do anything about it. While being empathetic does not obligate you to act, empathy takes you to the place where another person is actually standing. Furthermore, sympathy is often confused with condescendence. When folks act in this manner, they attempt to appear to be coming from the higher moral ground.

They may even act judgmental particularly when they believe that a person's ill fate is the result of their own actions. For example, these types of folks see people going through tough financial times as a result of the loss of their job. They may utter a phrase such as "that must be rough. Losing your job is always tough".

That type of statement hardly reflects the attitude of a truly empathetic person. This is just an acknowledgment of a generally tough situation. Condescendence may even creep in when a person says something like, "how awful! I couldn't imagine losing my job!"

In this statement, it seems that this individual is taking a moral high ground saying, "I have a great job and I don't know what I would do in that situation because I am so fortunate not to have lost my job".

The fact is that a truly empathetic person would either be quiet and not saying anything that could potentially be misconstrued (especially if they can't really relate to the situation), or come back with something like, "that's rough. I remember when I lost my job..."

This statement clearly identifies how an empathetic person would react. After all, they have either been through the exact situation, or they can somehow relate to the circumstances other people are going through.

Ultimately, being an empathetic person is all about really putting yourself out there and showing your own vulnerability. No one likes to admit they too have been through pain and suffering.

By the same token, it is also hard to really be happy for someone else without boasting about your won accomplishments. As such, empathetic folks have known then it someone else's turn to be in the spotlight. They can understand that because they have been in the spotlight themselves.

If you believe that believe that being empathetic means suppressing yourself for the sake of others, then you need to focus on this: we are all equally important. It's just that there are times when others' needs preclude ours. You will be able to perfectly get that when you are able to see exactly what others are seeing through their own eyes.

Chapter 2: Who Is an Empath - Are You One? Knowing How to Tell

After having defined empathy, you might be wondering if you really fit the mold of an empathetic person. First of all, we all have the capability of being empathic. While some folks have a more naturally tuned sense of empathy, others may need to work on it a bit more in order to better develop this trait. Nevertheless, you have everything you need to become truly empathetic.

Perhaps the best way for you to get started tuning your empathetic skills is to consistently think about how others feel in any given situation. This is a mental exercise in which you can take any situation, both good and bad, and really try to place yourself is that person's shoes.

In order to make the exercise work, you must transport yourself to the situation in which that person finds themselves in. Then, you need to think about what you would or how you would do things if you were in that situation. From there, you can begin to gain a deeper insight into what that person is going through.

Let's consider this example:

A person you know has lost their beloved pet.

Now, if you have lost a pet before, it wouldn't be too hard for you to relate to this experience. In fact, hearing about this person's loss may take you back to when you lost your own pet. This may end up triggering feelings of sadness and grief as you recollect on what that experience was like for you. You may offer solace to this person by listening to their feelings and sharing your own experience. Often times, people simply need to hear that they are not crazy for feeling the way they do. Moreover, people take great comfort in knowing that what they are feeling is perfectly normal. The last thing anyone wants to feel when going through the painful experience is to feel like an outlier.

On the flipside, suppose that you have never lost a pet in your life. What's more, you have never even owned a pet. So, you really don't have a frame of reference from which you can derive meaning to comprehend what this person is going through.

Nevertheless, you try to become truly empathetic. So, you take yourself to the place where you owned a pet and subsequently lost it. Perhaps you might be able to identify with the loss of a pet *per se*, but you are certainly capable of identifying with the feeling of loss.

269

Perhaps you have lost a family member or have experienced other types of loss such as destruction of property resulting from a natural disaster.

When you begin to place yourself in the same place where the other person is coming from, your own experiences begin to serve as a frame reference. So, you might think, "I don't know what it's like to lose my beloved dog, but I do know what it's like to lose your home in a flood". That is where empathy begins to take hold of you. This exercise may even trigger feelings that you "gotten over".

As you begin to further develop your feelings of empathy, you will notice how you will become more susceptible to the suffering of others. By the same token, you will also begin to relish in the success and happiness of others.

For instance, one of your best friends is getting married to their sweetheart. If you are single and never been married, it might be a bit hard to place yourself in the middle of a wedding, but seeing the happiness and joy of the newlyweds, you being to think, "what is a truly happy moment in my life?" When you think about when you felt over the moon, then you can empathize with your friends and think, "if they feel anywhere close to the way I felt then, they are truly lucky to have each other".

In contrast, a selfish person would resent the married couple because the spotlight is not on them. Do you see where the difference lies?

Consequently, we are going to delve further into specific signs that will alert you that you are an empathic person and not just paying lip service to others who are going through a rough time.

You make others' emotions your own

Before we get into this, a disclaimer: this first point is not about taking on someone else's burden as your own nor should you attempt to take credit for someone else's success (even if you played a pivotal role in their achievement). What this first point highlight is the fact that you are willing to internalize others' feelings in such a way that you place yourself directly in their situation. You are keen on understanding what they are going through, both good and bad, as opposed to superficially commenting on what it must be like. In addition, you are willing to offer emotional support if you are asked to do so. Unsolicited support or advice may rub some folks the wrong way especially if they are too proud to seek help or advice. So, if you are willing to take the feelings of others to heart, then you are well on your way to becoming a truly empathetic person.

You experience sudden and overwhelming emotions

As an empath, you might find yourself suddenly becoming overwhelmed by emotions. These instances can happen at any time especially in the middle of a highly emotional situation. For example, you are listening to a testimonial from someone who has gone through a challenging situation. Or, you are listening to someone's story about how they overcame adversity.

271

Regardless of the specific situation, you find that you are very much in tune with the feelings of others who are attempting to convey. While it is certainly a lot easier to experience these sudden flashes of emotion in a personal, one on one setting, it is highly probable that might become overwhelmed by emotion in a public setting. For example, you are attending a church service. During the service, you listen to the story of fellow churchgoers who have overcome difficulties in life. The stories you hear are filled with so much emotion that it is impossible for you to contain your own emotions. As a result, you might begin to shed tears or overcome with joy. In other situations, you might be talking with a friend. This friend might have important news to share with you. When you hear about how good things are going for them, you automatically become overwhelmed by sheer joy and happiness. You are really putting yourself in your friend's spot. So, you might not have anything to say to them other than simply basking in their success. As you get more and more attuned to your inner feelings, you will find that it is not hard to connect to other folks on a deeper, emotional level. All you have to do is listen to their own feelings and then pay attention to yours. So, don't fight back, just go with the flow.

You get where people are coming from

This is a knack people develop over time due to their own life experience. As you get older and go through various experiences, you begin to appreciate where people are coming from, that is, what causes them to feel and act the way they do.

As such, you are able to connect with people because you understand the underlying factors that are motivating them to do what they do and feel the way they feel. In a way, you do not simply feel what they feel, but you can actually relate to the reasoning behind their actions and emotions.

Consider this example:

A friend has lost their job. They are devastated by the situation and decide they need a change of scenery. So, they take a job overseas that don't necessarily pay well but offers a fresh start. As an empath, you understand how distraught your friend feels at the loss of their job. At the same time, you understand why they need a change of scenery. In fact, you totally get it to a point where you would have done the same if you had been in the same spot. So, rather than judging your friend for "bailing out" you praise them for making a tough choice and moving on with their life.

Thus, you have connected with your friend at a deeper level. Since you really get where they are coming from, you end up being supportive of their decision. You might even offer your help in any way you can. Now, you might personally feel apprehensive about the decision your friend has taken, but you trust that it's in their best interest.

Others seek you out

Empaths characterize themselves for their lack of judgment. While they may disagree with the actions and decisions that others may choose to make, they don't openly judge anyone. In fact, empaths may even take someone else's side even though they disagree with their decisions. As a result, others seek your advice and wisdom. Often, they seek you because they know you're a good listener and won't judge them unfairly. This is so important when folks are going through usual circumstances or take unconventional roads. Moreover, when others seek your advice, they know that you really mean what you say. The words you utter are not superficially commented on shallow observations. You are sincere in your words and would not purposely say something hurtful just for the sake of it. As a matter of fact, if you call someone out on something, it is because you really have the moral high ground to do so. Yet, an empath would do so unless they felt it was beneficial to the other person. When you are recognized as a true empath (though people may not consciously know it), you will find people opening up to you in ways you would have never imagined possible. But please bear in mind that many times all you need to do is listen without jumping to any conclusions. Often, all most people want is someone who will let them speak their minds.

You are too sensitive to violence in film and television

Gratuitous violence on television and in the film has desensitized people in unimaginable ways. Children and teenagers are exposed to violence from a very young age. And while it is beneficial to become aware of the tragedies in life to a certain extent, empaths struggle with graphic scenes on television and in film. Of course, scenes in movies and TV shows are not actually real, they do depict situations which trigger feelings of pain and suffering for the people going through those acts. This is especially true if an empath has been through a similar situation. For instance, if you, as an empath, have been in a car accident, scenes of car wracks may trigger feelings of fear and pain stemming from your own experience. Consequently, you may choose to avoid watching such scenes altogether. So, if you feel easily offended and overwhelmed by graphic scenes in television and in film, you need not feel ashamed or embarrassed; quite the opposite, you should feel proud of being sensitive to the suffering of others.

You have a soft spot for kids and animals

If you find that you have a soft spot for kids and animals, then chances are you are far more sensitive than you think. Empaths are usually drawn to babies and cute furry pets. But feelings of empathy don't just apply to cuteness. True empaths love all kids and animals. They are concerned with the feelings of children in all circumstances while also being very attentive to the needs of animals.

An empath would never stand for cruelty to animals. In fact, empaths are the first to offer their help and support in the protection of animals. Similarly, empaths are always kind to children. They understand that kids are vulnerable and have very sensitive feelings. So, the last thing they want is to hurt a child's feelings. In fact, they will be the first to offer comfort to a child who is upset or hurt. Some of the greatest empaths you will meet will stop at nothing to help an animal in distress or comfort a child. The fact is that empaths are also vulnerable. They know what it's like to have strong feelings which they cannot control. Additionally, they can relate to a defenseless animal that might be in pain or in need. So, they don't just say "oh, poor thing" and leave it at that. They will try their best to remedy the situation. If you find that you cannot stand anyone harming and animal or a child, then you are on the right track.

You don't just feel others' emotions, you also share their physical discomforts

There is a term called "sympathy pain" meaning that one person "feels" what another person is feeling when they are ill. This is common in married couples, parents and children, or siblings. Yet, truly empathetic people are able to sense what others are actually feeling when they are in pain or when they are ill. Now, this isn't just a superficial reaction such as, "oh, that's gotta hurt!" This is a deep understanding of what the other person is going through. As a result, an empath may begin to feel physical discomfort mirroring what someone else is going through.

This reaction is not some kind of magical superpower. In fact, it is a logical reaction on the part of the brain. When an empath sees that another person has an illness, for example they have a cold, the empath's brain processes emotions in such a way that it begins to process its own feelings of physical discomfort mimicking the illness itself. While there is nothing actually wrong with the empath, the empath's brain begins to believe they are sick, too. In most cases, empaths will simply begin to feel upset when they encounter people and animals in distress. Most empaths report feelings of dizziness, nausea and headaches when they encounter people and animals in distress. These feelings often go away when the person in question receives medical attention or when the empath is removed from the situation. But if the empath does not see that the person in pain has been tended to, the feelings may still linger for a while.

Intimate relationships can become overwhelming

Intimate relationships can take on various facets. For instance, we could be talking about a romantic relationship or a very close friendship. Regardless of the nature of the relationship itself, getting very close to someone can become overwhelming at times due to the emotion connection and bond that is developed. The bond between two people, or perhaps as part of a group setting, can get pretty intense especially depending on the circumstances surrounding that relationship. Examples of this can be seen all over. For instance, you might find yourself developing a very close bond with survivors of a disaster or perhaps working with abuse victims.

One classic example is the bond that teammates of sports teams develop. Teammates get to be so close that the bond they share lasts a lifetime. Similarly, firefighters and police officers also form tight-knit groups. As a result, the emotions felt by one member of the team can spread like wildfire. If one member happens to be going through a tough time, then that emotion can blast through the entire crew. Empaths in particular may become overwhelming to a degree where their focus and attention will almost entirely focus on their mates even to the point of self-detriment. Ideally, empaths are able to balance the load so that they are able to cope with the circumstances surrounding them. That way, they can still offer support to their friends and mates, but also stay grounded and not be hurt in the process.

You can't understand selfish people

Empaths are unable to wrap their minds around anyone who is selfish. This perception is due to the fact that empaths almost always put others ahead of themselves. As such, being selfish is something that an empath simply cannot comprehend.

In fact, a selfish individual is, in many ways, diametrically opposed to an empath. A selfish person neglects others' feelings and needs in order to put their own needs first. This attitude generally means that a selfish person will achieve their aims at the expense of others. In order to be that ruthless, a selfish person needs to completely disregard the emotions, needs and wants of others. As such, this lack of empathy allows selfish individuals to get their way regardless of the cost.

Furthermore, a lack of empathy is one of the core traits of psychopaths. An individual with a psychopathic personality usually finds themselves completely ignoring what someone else might be feeling. This leads them to commit heinous acts of violence simply because they cannot identify with their victims in any way.

While psychopaths may seem a bit extreme in this case, the underlying psychological theory stands on its own. That is why an empath is prone to self-sacrifice. This trait has been evidenced throughout our discussion thus far though we haven't quite articulated it in that manner until now. So, if you are prone to putting the needs of others ahead of your own, then you might very well be a true empath.

Throughout this chapter, we have highlighted the main attitudes of an empath. It is safe to say that you have checked off many boxes while leaving a few of them blank. If you find that you lack in some of these areas, then now is a good time to reflect on the ways in which you can improve your overall skills. After all, this book is intended to help you find the right path that will lead you to sharpen your empathetic skills. While some folks are more naturally empathetic than others, all of these skills require honing and development. So, now is the time to make a conscious choice to build up your skills and continue on the path to becoming a better person.

Chapter 3: The Highly Sensitive Disorder

Do you notice or realize an elegant scent or sounds that do not annoy people around you? Do people often accuse you of being emotional? If such traits reflect your personality, then you qualify to be a highly sensitive person (HSP). More often, people misunderstand highly sensitive people to be weak characters, yet there are strengths that they carry around.

By definition, in order for an individual to be called a highly sensitive person means you react more intensely to environments than an average person. Let me explain. It means that you process both positive and negative situations more deeply. An HSP is usually overwhelmed by stimuli such as loud noises, high-pressure situations, and crowds.

In the opinion of one Dr. Aron, the author, as well as the publisher of, the category of the people who are highly sensitive up to 20%, makes a section of the world population. Furthermore, high sensitivity is innate, which means that they were probably born that way. An HSP individual can be an introvert, extrovert, or somewhere in between.

Symptoms of a Highly Sensitive Person

- **Abhorring violence and cruelty of any kind**
  It is an undeniable fact that everyone hates violence. For an HSP, hearing or seeing violence can be unsettling if you can't watch a scary movie or gory without getting affected or sometimes resulting in physical illness. To some extent, a highly sensitive person cannot stomach news that deals with brutality or animal cruelty.

- **Getting exhausted from absorbing other people's feelings**
  A highly sensitive person tends to absorb other people's emotions, just as empathy would. It is usual for a highly sensitive person to walk in a room and immediately captures the moods of all the people in it. Highly sensitive people are always aware of decoding matters, especially the facial expression, tone of voice, and body language. In the long run, a highly sensitive person will suffer frequent emotional exhaustion than others.

- **Time pressure rattling you**
  There are moments when you have too many things on your to-do list, and there is no adequate time to finish it. That a lot brings pressure, sometimes in school, your speed tests usually carried anxiety and eventually causing the individual not to perform well as he would. A highly sensitive person is typically sensitive to stimulation and time pressure.

- **Separation**
  An HSP will find himself withdrawing to a quiet place alone like a darkened room to reduce the stimulation level, recharge and soothe your senses. Such a scenario can happen to an introvert or an extrovert who needs enough time to meditate and come back to his normal feelings while alone.

- **Being jumpy**
  It happens when someone sneaks on you. Your reaction will be reaming unsettled throughout the conversation. It is more alarming to note that an HSP has a high startle reflex. The primary reason is, even in non- threatening situations, their nervous systems are always on a high alert.

- **Overthinking**
  One factor that distinguishes an HSP from the rest of the people is their ability to process information deeply. To some extent, the person is vulnerable to negative overthinking. As he continues meditating over and over, it results in the anxious thoughts.

- **Getting rattled by a sudden loud noise**
  Such a situation happens when an HSP cannot withstand loud noise. For instance, a loud vehicle sound that roars behind your door can shake you and displace your peace.

- **Clothing**
  Here, we mean being sensitive to what you have been wearing. Some scratchy fabric or restrictive clothing like tight panties may irritate you. A purely HSP individual will be careful to select their wardrobes well to avoid clothing of specific categories. If an HSP happens to wear some clothes that are not of his choice, the entire experience may result in total discomfort.

- **Inquisitive**
  HSPs are ever seeking answers to some big questions in life. They will always ask to understand why things are happening in a particular sequence while trying to discover possible solutions. As an HSP, you may wonder why some mysteries of the universe and human nature don't bother other people as you are.

- **Less pain tolerance**
  When it comes to pains of all kinds such as headaches, injuries, and other body aches, HSPs are more sensitive than non-HSPs.

- **Resisting change**
  HSPs may always be comfortable with routines. The key reason is that a brand new thing is less stimulating than something familiar. For that matter, an HSP will find it difficult handling any positive or negative change.

A perfect example is when an HSP acquires a new job or dates a new person; they feel equally stressed. It is an indisputable fact that an HSP will require more time to align to change.

- **The alive and present inner world**
The fact that you are ever deep processing your thoughts, it creates a rich inner world. Starting from your childhood, you may have had some imaginary friends or daydreamed, no problem. When you graduate into adulthood, you will have more realistic dreams.

- **Always misunderstood**
The society has consistently mislabeled highly sensitive people. They usually conclude that there is something wrong with you while calling you with some unfamiliar terms like shy or anxious. Furthermore, people refer to many HSPs as introverts since they share some traits like needing more downtime. It is a fact that around 30% of HSPs are introverts.

- **Resisting new environment**
Sometimes your unique situation becomes your undoing. You may find no excitement when settling in a new home or even traveling to new places. It happens because your senses are full of new stimuli.

- **Losing temper easily**
You can easily upset an HSP and become angry even with a small matter. The HSPs are also sensitive to changes in blood sugar levels hence get hungry quickly, especially when their stomach is empty for a while.

- **Stimulants**
  We have a category of HSPs who are very sensitive to stimulants, such as caffeine. They may only require a little of it to feel its effect. Other groups of HSPs are also vulnerable to the effects of alcohol and therefore avoid it.

- **Avoids conflicts**
  An HSP feels it deeply whenever there is a disagreement in her close relationship. It can worsen until an HSP is physically ill. As a remedy, many highly sensitive people avoid conflicts and try to say almost anything to keep the other person happy. It is an act of reducing tensions and eliminate hurts.

- **Resists criticism**
  Every word you utter matters to an HSP. Harsh words can make them crash to the ground. Positive words give them an edge; they use them to soar. Criticism is a dagger. Highly sensitive people never like negativity because it paralyzes their operations.

- **Striving to remain conscientious**
  While at work or school, highly sensitive persons try not to make mistakes. You are always giving things to your best and remain near perfect.

- **Driven by beauty**
  An HSP will prefer rich scents, exquisite meals, beautiful artworks, and stirring melodies that may have a high impact on someone. Some musical sounds may translate you in a near trance-like state. You may not have an apparent reason why some individuals are as sensitive to beauty as you are.

- **Perceptive**
  The highly sensitive person can be keen and insightful because they notice quickly things that others miss. As a young kid, people usually rate you as being wise beyond your years.

Categories of Highly Sensitive People

There are three categories of highly sensitive people:
- Sensitive about oneself
- Sensitive about others
- Sensitive about one's environment

1. Sensitivity About Oneself

The persons in this category have the following traits:

1. They usually hold on to negative thoughts and emotions for a very long time.

2. When something unpleasant happens during the day, this HSP experiences frequent physical symptoms like headaches and stress.

3. A bad day can affect his eating or sleeping habits. He may eat little and sleepless.

4. This kind of person will always experience frequent anxiety and tension.

5. The person is under self-inflicted stress when he fails to meet his expectations.

6. Such an HSP is still under rejection. Always upset by minor situations.

7. This HSP does a self-comparison, especially in physical, work, financial, and relational. He will experience unhappy feelings from unfavorable social comparisons.

8. There is a feeling of resentment about occurrences in life that appear unjust or annoying.

2. Sensitivity About Others

The following points describe a perfect description of this category:

1. He frequently worries about what other people are thinking about him.

2. This category of an HSP is prone to taking matters personally.

3. This kind of HSP finds it hard to forgive, especially when hurt by other people.

4. Easily offended by the actions of others.

5. Keeps negative feelings to self, believing it is embarrassing to expose them to people. He would rather hide negative feelings than share.

6. He resists accepting critical feedback, even if it was constructively and reasonably issued.

7. He usually takes others as judgmental also if there lacks no substantial evidence.

8. This category of an HSP will overreact to real or minor provocations.

9. He will feel uncomfortable with group situations and finds it hard to be oneself.

10. He is self-conscious about a romantically intimate relationship. He worries about the partner's approval and will unreasonably fear of rejection by the partner.

3. Sensitivity About One's Environment

This category of people will have the following traits:

1. When too many issues are happening at the same time, this HSP feels uncomfortable. It is evident and especially in the crowd or in a room that is full of people.

2. Feels an irritation when exposed to loud sounds, certain strong scents, or bright lights.

3. Gets typically upset when watching a scary movie or reading some negative news in the media.

4. He will sometimes feel unhappy when following people's posts on social media.

What Does It Imply If You Test as a Highly Sensitive Person?

When you prove to be an HSP by taking a highly sensitive person test, it means you have a dominant trait. It also means that you are part of 15% to 20% of the population.

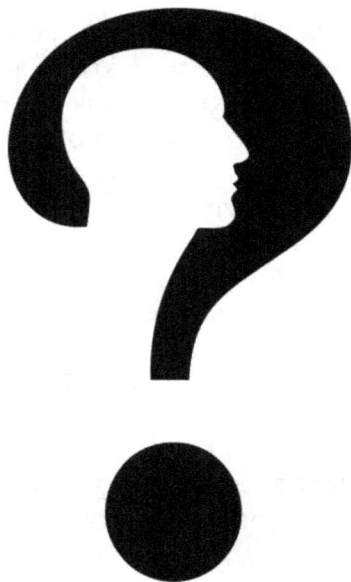

A highly sensitive person overreacts to situations than an average person would do. Their minds will process both positive and negative information more deeply. Consequently, some external stimuli, such as loud noises and high-pressure situations, will overwhelm them. Sometimes to be a highly sensitive person can be your biggest strength. It is a big gift but not always easy to handle. For instance, let's see the life of Mahatma Gandhi. Many folks believe he was an HSP who spent many years in prison. He realized how religious conflicts affected his dreams, but his leadership inspired others.

Mahatma left a great legacy of peace when he negotiated the independence of India without going to war.

Tips That Assists an HSP to Cope with over Stimulations

The first and most critical step is to identify the situations that overwhelm you. Once you know your triggers, you can employ ways to reduce your overstimulation. Use cognitive therapy skills to assist your reality check your emotional reactions. You can also do the following when dealing with hypersensitivity:

1. Honor your sensitivity. Choose situations that tolerate your temperament.

2. Step back. When reacting to a situation, calm down, rethink, and pause for reflection.

3. Reduce external stimulations by avoiding to do things that you may not handle well.

4. Use the noise-canceling headphones to control noise.

5. During parties, always retreat to a quiet place for every thirty minutes for a breather.

6. Adjust TV settings to equalize the volume, such as knocking down the treble.

7. When you feel stressed, always go for breathing exercises. Slow inhales and exhales, holding for a count of three to five.

8. Avoid stimulants like caffeine or nicotine.

9. Make sure you have enough sleep before facing a situation that will be highly stimulating.

10. Meditate and pray while using another relaxation method to strengthen your ability to deal with daily challenges.

Genes That Make You a Highly Sensitive Person

It's evident in various researches that an individual who is highly sensitive is a normal and healthy being. The same comes with a distinct evolutionary advantage. Sensitivity may be genetic but does not result from a single gene. The personality traits come from a collection of genes that are more than one. In this case, three separate genes play a role. Surprisingly, every single one of these genes affects your brain and nervous systems. Let's discuss these genes that make you a highly sensitive person.

The 'Sensitive' Gene (Serotonin Transporter)

Serotonin is an essential chemical in your body that performs many functions, such as stabilizing your moods. On the other hand, serotonin transporter is a chemical that helps to move serotonin out of the body. It is necessary for mood balancing in the experience of an individual.For highly sensitive people, they have a particular variation of the serotonin transporter gene that behaves a little different. Suppose you have this gene variant, which means you have lower serotonin levels; therefore, you will be a highly sensitive person.

The gene variant does not cause mood disorder on its own but makes you remain sensitive to your environment. Therefore, you will decode the nature around you and learn a lot from it. This type of gene is crucial to childhood development. Suppose you add this gene with an unhealthy childhood environment; you reduce the risk of depression and other disorders throughout your living. On the other side, when you combine the same gene with a safe environment, you will receive excellent outcomes as an adult. The gene boosts the effects of good and bad upbringing. To a highly sensitive person, your childhood experiences will have a more extensive impact on you as an adult. Alternatively, there is a space for you to get correct the effects of your rough childhood. The good news is that it does not affect you more than it does to others.

The Dopamine Genes

Dopamine is the brain reward chemical. There is a connection between sensitivity and a collection of ten different gene variants related to dopamine. For beginners, someone with a sensitive system would need to feel less rewarded by external stimuli. Furthermore, it makes good sense when for vulnerable people to get more rewarded by positive social and emotional cues.

As a highly sensitive person, you may find it strange for a set of people who go to a loud and crazy environment and find it tolerable. If it happens so, it is because you do not receive a similar dopamine hit from these noisy external stimuli. It is possible because of these gene variants at work.

The 'Emotional Vividness' Gene

Every individual will experience life more vividly, especially during emotionally charged moments. The degree of vividness differs among various groups of people. The high sensitivity has a direct link to the gene variant that controls it. The emotional vividness gene has a closer link to norepinephrine. The norepinephrine transmitter helps with the body stress response. Interestingly, there is one variant, which is usually common in HSPs that will turn up the dial on emotional vividness. If you prove to have it, your experience in the psychological aspects of the world will be more vivid. As a result, you will have many more activities in the parts of the brains that create intimate emotional experiences with your experience. The highly sensitive persons are always aware that they have stronger emotional reactions than an average person. They will more often notice emotional undercurrents where other people pick nothing. If you are an HSP, you have a brighter palette of emotional colors because of this gene variant. Besides, it directly drives the level of empathy and awareness you may experience for other's feelings.

The Best Things About Being Highly Sensitive

One Feels Positive Emotion Deeply

An HSP gets upset more at a higher degree than others. When a good thing happens, the HSPs will feel pleasure, happiness, and enjoyment more than others. A single compliment can make his day or extend to the whole week.

There are situations when something unusual happens that may lead that can radiate good vibes for the entire month.

Appreciating Art and Beauty

HSPs are perfect aesthetes. Well, aesthetes are people who are appreciative, too, and sensitive to art and beauty. An HSP can get moved by a movie or music and the nature of the universe, such as observing sunset and sunrise.

They are Empathic

It is the ability to feel the world in another's shoes. Research indicates that HSP is strong empaths than average people. HSPs will not just sympathize and feel compassion, but they can feel other people's feelings as if they were their own. Empathy is a positive energy that inspires HSP to assist people who may be in an awkward situation. Insight is the driving force for all HSPs.

Detail-Oriented

The brain of an HSP can process information more thoroughly than any person would do. He can pick up a minor indication that other people will not and use it for more insight. This ability helps the HSPs to excel in projects that require an eye for details, making them conscientious and competent throughout their working experience.

Insanely Creative

Do you know that sensitivity will inspire creativity? When an HSP feels exceedingly emotional, he will seek outlets to express himself. They can go to the extent of writing their experiences or even developing a piece of music. Such actions lead to creativity and progress in life.

Quick Learners and Deep Thinkers

Highly sensitive people process materials more deeply. The brain of a highly sensitive person will draw connections from experience and use them to bear a new solution. They have semantic memory. Semantic memory means that it is long-term, which deals with meaning, understanding, and other concept-based knowledge. An HSP can also pick up new information unconsciously. Such makes them have answers to most problems, which is an excellent asset to their work.

Chapter 4: Understanding the Different Energy Types

The concept of empathy is familiar with most people. If you are empathic, you can claim that you understand other people's feelings at an intellectual level. Most people believe they are empathetic, but it takes another level of extremes to be an empath. For instance, it is easy for a bereaved person to understand the pain that comes with grief. That is empathy. Being an empath, on the other hand, pushes someone to experience the pain and the happiness of others even when such feelings are unfamiliar to the individual.

In this chapter, we shall delve deeper into the unique attributes of empaths, and scrutinize how people can be able to determine if they are indeed empaths. It is important to note that we are all empathic. We need empathy to navigate through our social world. If you can read intentions and emotions, you qualify as an empathic person. However, an empath is a different trait where individuals operate from a position of awareness and intent. It has distinct features from being an empathic person. An empath experiences other people's feelings with their mind, body, and soul. Empaths are highly sensitive to other people's feelings and will often tend to have a heavy burden for other people. Over the years, there has been contention on whether this gift is a weakness or a strength, considering how tough it can be to be an empath in modern society. The ability to synchronize into other people's moods and feelings occur unconsciously in empaths. As a result, there are many instances of unpredictable shifts in the attitudes and emotions of such people. Yet, their primary goal is to make others feel better even at the expense of their happiness. Often, the term highly sensitive person (s) is used to refer to empaths. While the two words have close relations, they may not necessarily relate to the same thing. All empaths are highly sensitive persons, but not all highly sensitive people are empaths. Empaths have heightened sensitivity, due to their inherent abilities, which are uncommon to all highly sensitive people. An empath has a depth of processing that makes them uniquely different from highly sensitive people. An empath tends to analyze things critically and show extreme conscientious in their decision path. On the contrary, most highly sensitive persons tend to be highly reactive, which limits their ability to make well-reasoned judgments. But both empaths and highly sensitive people share certain similarities. Overstimulation is among the most noticeable trait.

297

The ability to pay attention to even the most subtle details is common among empaths and highly sensitive persons. The result in such cases is often a tendency to experience instances of emotional fatigue and apparent difficulty in adjusting or adapt to new environments.

Highly sensitive individuals, such as empaths, will also tend to be overly emotional. Empaths are likely to feel negative or positive situations in a more profound way than other individuals. Empaths have high levels of empathy. This aspect makes them detect what others might be feeling. Experiencing such instances of emotional extremes has often seemed as a disorder, because of the lack of adequate information on empaths. While empaths encompass different walks of life, a majority are artists because of their imagination and creativity. They have broad and varying interests making them multi-talented. There is no specific label that can describe empaths because they are of diverse genders, personalities, and careers. Researchers conclude that empaths are thinkers, problem solvers, and active listeners. They seek to look for answers in every problem and seek the peace of mind at all times. Empaths make great friends because of their emotional abilities. However, they can be susceptible to exploitation, and regular recharging is necessary. There is a popular notion that introverts are empaths. Is that so? Well, there is a correlation between empathic abilities and introversion. Yet, we can't conclude for the fact that all introverts are highly empathic. However, the inherent introspective nature of introverts makes them more observant as compared to extroverts. It becomes possible for introverts to pick up cues on issues affecting other people. On the contrary, extroverts can be oblivious about the emotional needs of others. They are ready to jump on the next activity without thinking critically about the extent of the emotional drain their counterparts are experiencing.

On the flip side, empaths experience the world differently, and they can be vulnerable to adverse situations. Empaths can be emotional detectives. Once they understand the energy in a room, they can try to tone down their sensitiveness to be acceptable. The situation can be draining because they engage in activities they don't like. Empaths can experience innate excitement upon getting a vibrant room. However, a dull mood can suck the life out of an empath. Unfortunately, empaths are likely to attract toxic partners or friends. Narcissists target empaths because they can get emotional support despite being abusive. Toxic people use empaths for their healing. Empaths show compassion indiscriminately, and narcissists can feast on this generosity for their selfish gains. Ultimately, an empath becomes drained, and failure to rejuvenate can lead to depression or anxiety. Empaths are open-hearted, which can make them absorb toxicity and negativity from other people. With these features, people trust empaths intuitively and are likely to share even the darkest secrets. The healing outcome satisfies empaths, but it also leaves them exhausted. They forget themselves in the healing process, which can be debilitating. Empowered empaths can have meaningful relationships while maintaining their emotional health.

These scientific explanations further expound more on empaths:

- **Emotional Contagion**

This finding shows that a considerable number of people embrace the emotional phenomena within their surroundings. For instance, an anxious mother can make other family members have heightened anxiety. Synchronizing the moods with others is the main factor characterizing empaths.

Studies on emotional contagion show that empaths are likely to hang around encouraging and vibrant people so that they can 'catch' these good feelings.

- **Mirror Neuron System**

Every individual has a group of brain cells promoting compassion. The cells allow individuals to share other people's emotions, such as joy, fear, and pain. For empaths, the mirror neurons are hyper-responsive.

- **High Dopamine Sensitivity**

Dopamine is a neurotransmitter, which increases the neurons' activity, especially when responding to pleasure. Introverted empaths are likely to react because of their high sensitivity to dopamine.

- **Synesthesia**

Empaths experience synesthesia, which is a neurological trait linking two unassociated senses. People with synesthesia can relate a color to a particular flavor or a musical sound to a number. In the case of empaths, the type of synesthesia is mirror-touch. It allows a person to relate to the emotional needs of others. The emotions might seem like they are from the empath, and in its excess form, it can cause neurological abnormalities.

- **Electromagnetic Fields**

Researchers conclude that the heart and the brain have electromagnetic fields that transmit information about the emotions and thoughts of people. For empaths, the input can be overwhelming because of their high sensitivity. The ability to regulate the heightened sensitivity remains a mystery. From the theoretical explanation, it is clear that the development of empathic abilities can be complicated.

While some are inborn, other empaths get their skills from early childhood experiences. Empaths have survival mechanisms that can make them navigate through life issues positively. However, they can be maladaptive in some instances. Following the comprehensive description of empaths, it is clear that several aspects characterize the trait. These aspects include empathic accuracy, emotional contagion, perspective engagement, concern for others, perspective-taking, and emotional regulation. These characteristics build one another to determine and empath. Most of these aspects are intentional, which leads to the query on whether empaths are born or made.

At times, it may be hard to conclude that a person is an empath considering that there is no standard of measure. Nonetheless, over the years, continuous research has made critical headway on what defines an empath and the traits that may describe this uniqueness. You may need to search deep to evaluate your inclination towards being an empath. Researchers are yet to establish a medical test to determine empathic tendencies. You can only verify if you are an empath through a detailed and honest self-review. After reading about empaths, you might ponder whether you fall under the category of empaths. The description of empaths is well laid down, and you can make an accurate guess if it fits your persona. Empaths are different, and understanding the types can enable you to know if you fall in any of the categories. The emotional empath is quite common. If you fall within this category, you are likely to pick other people's emotions and relate with them as your own. Emotional empaths can be overwhelmed with sadness when around a sad individual. You are a geomantic empath if you have a fine attunement to specific physical landscapes. Often known as environmental empathy, these kind of people are incredibly excited or agitated by certain situations or environments without reason.

You will realize that spending time in nature helps you to recharge. For religious geomantic empaths, sacred stones or shrines seem to have a healing power to your inner soul. You might also be a physical empath if you can pick or relate to the energy of people's bodies. Empaths in this category often follow the medical career as they gain satisfaction in 'healing.' They can understand a person's bodily needs and feel their need for treatment. The medical empaths can pick symptoms and feel them within their own body, which can be a downside in its extreme. The intuitive empath can obtain information from people by just being with them. With a one-time interaction, you can gain significant insights about a person. You can detect any cases of lying by listening to a person. Intuitive empaths can read other people's energy; they have correlations with the telepathic empaths.

Animal empaths have an unusually strong connection with different animals. These types of empaths dedicate their resources to taking care of animals. They spend significant time with animals and understand their diverse needs. Conversely, the plant empaths have a deep sense of the needs of plants. They know where to place different plants within a garden for them to blossom. Being an empath can be disorienting and confusing. However, it is essential to understand if you are an empath to know how to make good use of your abilities. An empath can be a great resource to friends and family. If people around say that your intuition is sharp, there is a likelihood you are an empath.

Most empaths can form strong opinions regarding a situation or individuals. As an empath, you can judge a person's character within a few seconds of interaction. Besides, you can detect if a person has ulterior motives despite using sweet and kind words.

Most empaths exhibit the character from childhood because the abilities are primarily inherent. If growing up, you had several instances of sensitivity to the emotional needs of others; you are an empath. As you grow up, the empathic pattern is definite. During the adolescent and teenage years, an empath is seemingly mature and hardly gain pleasure in peer activities.

Do your family and friends describe you as 'shy,' 'sensitive,' or say that you relate with the feelings of others? In other extremes, you might be labeled as sullen or aloof. Why is that so? Most empaths shun from stimulating situations leading to withdrawal, often viewed as unfriendliness. If you have been subject to such labels, you might be an empath.

Do artistic pieces move your emotions? Most empaths feel moved by evocative arts, including paintings, sculptures, or even music. Staring a portrait of a smiling baby can make an empath to smile. When listening to music, empath emotions are triggered by changes in pitches and tones. Such arts bring mental images, and a person can relate them to real or imagined situations.

You are unusually sensitive if the emotions in a movie or film affect you. While scriptwriters and producers create movies to evoke emotions, empaths get too overwhelmed. They can relate to a specific character and 'feel' his/her pain or joy. An empath can cry over the death of a character as if there existed a personal relationship. Besides, empaths have preferences on what to watch and are likely to avoid scenes that are graphic or violent. If you experience mental or physical sickness after encountering a situation that provokes your emotions, you are an empath. For some empaths, being around people can cause headaches. Conflicting situations leave you feeling physically and emotionally sick.

Empaths can also be more prone to intolerances and allergies. However, you should seek medical help if you experience physical symptoms to rule out other underlying conditions. Empaths can, at times, fail to enjoy physical and emotional intimacy with their partners. Sexual and romantic relationships can irk empaths leading to distress. The emotions exhibited by their partners can be stimulating and overwhelming. Some people might feel that empaths are unloving, emotionally detached, or withdrawn. Such features show a highly sensitive and empathic person. In such a situation, being an empath can cause you to have unfulfilling or strained relationships. You are an empath if you have a constant desire to lessen the suffering of other people. An empath feels obligated to step in for someone who seems in pain, whether a stranger or a friend. Another characteristic that can make you know if you are an empath is your circle of friends. Empaths value quality friendships and might not be keen on building an overly extensive social network. Many get-togethers with the larger family or group of friends might not be ideal for an empath because of the resulting overstimulation. If you are content with your own company and the few friends you have, there is a high chance you are an empath.

Empaths react differently to caffeine and medication. For empaths fighting anxiety and depression, a lower dose can lead to the desired effect. The high sensitivity in empaths is also notable in medication, and the conventional treatments can be intolerable. Trust your body and inform your doctor in case a drug produces the unintended response. However, be ready for counter-responses even from professional physicians who are not highly empathic.

Other than the described features, a wide range of matrices may be useful in answering this question, 'am I an empath?' The following items can be an essential starting point if you want to do a quick self-analysis.

1. Do other people often label you as overly sensitive or extremely emotional?

2. Do you find yourself carrying other people's burdens to extremes?

3. Are your feelings easily hurt?

4. Do you crave alone time?

5. Do you experience a constant feeling of being emotionally drained?

6. Do you often feel agitated by excessive talks or big crowds?

7. Are you highly sensitive to noises, smells, and emotional fluctuations?

8. Do you overeat when emotionally drained?

If your response is in the affirmative in more than three of these questions, there is a high likelihood though not guaranteed that you could be an empath. Self-awareness will enable you to be more in touch with your feelings. You can use your empathic abilities positively and choose a career path that resonates with your personality. Knowing your empathic nature enables you to practice effective emotional care. If the test score and the descriptions define you, then you are probably an empath. These tips will allow you to manage as an empath without feeling drained.

- **Set Boundaries**

You can become a fulfilled empath if you learn to set boundaries. Empaths struggle with saying no because they are naturally caring. Constant commitment to people's issues can be emotionally draining. Learn to cut off negative people and say no when necessary.

- **Self-Compassion**

Often, empaths are compassionate towards everyone else except themselves. Befriend yourself and practice being kind to yourself. It might take time, but with time, the self-love will pay off.

- **Get Rid of Self-Critical Thoughts**

Empaths usually have inner voices that border on self-criticisms. With the high sensitivity, wallowing in such thoughts is collective among empaths. It is essential to learn these criticisms and diminish them once they attack. Feeling your mind with positive thoughts about yourself can reduce emotional drains.

- **Meditate**

Empaths have a high affinity for their surroundings. If you don't set a quiet meditation time, you can experience overwhelming thoughts. Meditation enables you to reconnect to your inner self. During meditation, take deep and long depths and focus exclusively on your emotions.

- **Enjoy Nature**

The healing effects of nature are useful, whether you are a geomantic or an intuitive empath. Spending time in nature enables you to relax and rejuvenate. You can sit in a park, hike in the woods, or stroll through the beach.

- **Understand your Empathic Needs**

Once you understand what makes you comfortable or distressed, you will know the strategies to adopt to remain sane. If socializing for more than three hours leaves you exhausted, have an exit plan when your comfort level is over. You can get a private space within your home to have a quiet time when the need arises. For empaths who wallow in binge eating following emotional fatigue, have reminders for meditation, and stock healthy snacks. The coping strategies will make you feel safer as an empath and allow you to blossom in this impressive personality trait. You can reinvent the coping mechanisms to match your interests, such as cycling. Whatever you opt, ensure that it allows you to focus on yourself. Empathy manifests in different spectrums based on an individual. Being an empath can be satisfying; befriending an empath is even more fulfilling. Identifying and expressing emotions is a challenge for many people. Once you understand the pros of being an empath, you can embrace it and enjoy your personality while at it.

In the current modern world, we can feel the biting need for more empathy in our universe. Most definitely, the urge may be evident in the eyes of a counselor who attempts to fix an unfixable bleeding heart. Therefore, it may also be apparent when a grounded teen slams her bedroom door in utter disrespect. This is not knowing her crying mother knows best. These are but a few examples of what truly happens in the twenty-first century. Billions of contributing factors have made the world a nice niche for people who'd need to be empathized with. Empathy can be defined as the ability to put oneself in another's place. The same occurs even if that person is of a different culture, sexuality or gender. Empathy occurs broadly to foster trust in a therapeutic relationship, for understanding and self-exploration.

A significant portion of our global society has morphed into a numb, non-caring population on the planet. Some factors, take social media, for instance, has made people response less sensitively to other people's pain than they were twenty years ago. People coming across horrifying and disturbing images and shared videos of others suffering, daily, would automatically make the viewer "get used to" seeing people suffer. This will, in turn, cause a gradual loss of empathy or instead make one set standards of what level of situations would make one eligible for their (the viewer's) understanding. It's a sad, gripping reality that is creeping into our world without notice. There's a great deal of effort required from us as game changers if we really are interested in turning around. This implies the need to change how humanity is addressed. It also refers to the way we casually view people's pain and lows. In order for us to nullify whatever situation the world is in, we have to understand what we are dealing with. It requires a certain measure of empathy and actually helps to make a worrying fellow go over the moon, happy again. Empathy is a whole lot of topic that though is somewhat neglected, requires genuine effort and time to understand. In a nutshell, empathy is feeling someone's emotions and walking in their shoes.

This is especially when you're capable of acting as nothing happened and walking away like a pro, but, what if the recipient doesn't let you?! What if your recipient has significant differences in comparison to you in terms of background, personality, or even religion? Many factors stand as blocking blocks in the way of administration of empathy. Putting your mind and ambition in showing it is a beginning. Both major and minor factors that hinder the full administration of compassion have the same relative effect over such situations; nothing will be solved!

When our differences step from the background into our reality, nothing is usually solved, but even worse results may end up occurring. *Well, what difference am I referring to? The world's population of seven billion people is outstanding. They consist of Tom, Dick, and Harry in every mannerism, every character, and every quality. What I'm trying to put out is, of the seven billion people, none whatsoever, although even the slightest similarities are precisely equal to another. One beauty of humankind is that nobody whatsoever, on the face of the planet is similar. Everyone is vested with an absolute inborn uniqueness that is the fabric that the skills, experiences, and acquired traits found on. Take, for instance, a clean sheet of writing paper. The piece of paper comes already lined. The lines represent the undesired or default traits that are! The pen represents the factor or situation responsible for the acquired trait. As one writes on the sheet, moving from line to line and leaving words in every passed line represent the acquired traits. The same might be educationally, socially, or psychologically. Educational differences may come about from the gap in educational levels, academic achievements, or even the differences in the quality of education both parties underwent. Cultural differences may be brought by a gap in the party's social class; wealthy, middle class or poor. It may also be margined into religious beliefs or professionalism status. Last of the mentioned differences would, at this point, be the psychological differences.

When it comes to both sympathizing and empathizing, psychological differences play a significant role. The key discussion in this is to understand these differences that hold the cards by determining if your goodwill would be productive and successful. Why is this so?! There are a couple of factors that make the simple act of showing empathy to seem like an unbeatable milestone.

309

Such elements radiate from you as a counselor/template or the person who is to be empathized with. Therefore, as the recipient, the immediate environment also plays a significant role in healing or hurting you. The counselor-recipient clash may paint in when or if the differences of nature between the two parties aren't laid down at agreeable terms before the whole process kicks in. On infrequent occasions, would you find both being of the same traits and interests? However, I presumed that empathy is born in the heart, and this beats any differences. To understand vast energies, a psychological approach towards the matter gives you a grip over as much power as possible.

Factors That Psychologically Influence the Empathy Process

Several factors, as mentioned, affect the empathy process for better or for worse. I will cover five elements in this article: - structural factor, initiative, setting (physical), client's trait and the template (empathizer)

Fundamental Factor

At times, both the recipient and template have different perceptions and views about the nature and aim of empathizing. Most recipients do not understand what to expect from the sessions other than feeling very vulnerable. Having been likely to have sought aid and advice from familiar people, such as peers, friends, and family. This can make them hesitate and not want to open up to you.

There's a natural fear of the unknown that is evident when opening up more about yourself, let alone opening up to a stranger. Without a mutual agreement between the recipient and the template concerning the procedures, confidentiality, and parameters, nothing much would be attained. The structural factor creates a client-template relationship to ensure the success of a session. Psychology plays a significant role in this. Therefore, some time would be adequate for an open meeting. It's advisable to take up to 30 minutes in total. In general, the structural factor promotes growth in an empathy scenario by creating a framework in which the process can start and be conducted successfully. Recipients seek empathy because they are in a static behavioral state, all by themselves. Meaning they are left stagnant in a pool of fears and emotions without a bearing. This is most definitely a hard experience to be lonely in. To help them get a new bearing and a fresh start in life, the template needs to council the recipient following their personalities and energy. Despite trying to understand their strength, it is essential not to get to their sensitive side, go easy. It is beneficial to note that flexibility should be highly considered, and negotiation with the recipient should be paramount.

Initiative

It is presumed that empathy is always fruitful because of one's selflessness to stand up for another. Other subjects are, however, more reserved about being empathized with. When a template meets such, he or she often doesn't know what to do. They may also not know what to say. The result may cause bouts of impatience and irritation, and eventually, they may decide to give up on such. They may also blame others even though it's entirely not their fault.

Some templates may end up blaming themselves, thinking that they may or may not have done enough. To avoid such, one is asked to research which he/she is going to come across in terms of a short history summation.

A Setting

Though empathy can be expressed pretty much anywhere, it is majorly important to consider how and where you are showing it. Some settings promote the process way better than others. A physical environment can either make or break the process. Going for a calm, less-noisy location to talk is nerve-calming. This setting can be a quick remedy if the situation might have been getting out of hand, i.e., in the instance of a tantrum or suicidal thoughts. Certain features of a one-on-one setting can be of great benefit by appealing the general appearance and keep them from unnecessary distractions. Such features include soft colors (gray), chilled atmosphere, quiet lightning with toned artifacts. *recipient qualities*Presentations and first impressions are primary key take-homes during any session in the modern world. The way that a recipient and a template view one another is crucial for the establishment of a fruitful and productive relationship.

As stated earlier, recipients come in all sizes, shapes, forms of battering from society, energies, and personality characteristics, to mention but a few. Some people are hence definitely to get stronger after the process than others. Most people, however, tend to judge or rather perceive the people who stand in owe of their empathy in a different way, in most cases as weak, vulnerable, and at times helpless. It is promising to work with a person of evidential growth.

Some also tend to be non-verbal; a recipient reporting that all is going well but looks down at the ground and frowns while so is most probably indicating just the total opposite. One must be keen to check body gestures, facial expressions, eye contact in an empathy relationship. Different people also express different energies.

This brings us to the discussion

why we need to understand different types of human energy

As much as empathy comes in three distinct phases, human energy is relatively demonstrated in vast differences. There are cases of polar ends being display in the scale of understanding. For instance, person A naturally shows all three types of empathy, whereas person B is totally "cold " and uncaring. Is it unnatural of person B to act in such a style? Is it a nature-nature factor to be considered? There are different human energies and personalities vested in each person, making them equally unique in their way. These differences, depending on how they are expressed and taken, play a significant role in interactions and orients if the interaction's results would be positive or negative. People are different according to their energies. Energies are mostly defined hand in hand with a person's character traits. Warm or positive energy is usually associated with a cheerful gay character, a life surrounded by joy and happiness to the fullest despite obstacles. Negative energy is painted out by an imagination of bitterness in one's heart. Pain and despair are also feelings used to describe negative energies. According to religion, though, energies can be attached to nature and the supernatural world. Some cultures consider it a flow of balance called chakra.

313

One's energy, in all forms of explanations, should be balanced by oneself and understood by the people around the carrier. Energies can be modeled and brought up in a certain way as desired, but cannot be tamed. It is taming in the sense of trying to make it go against its nature to be of one likes. Religiously, yenning would be done, but modernity demands training, rebuking, and punishing. The question is, does it work? Correction (by the use of punishment) on some middle-aged teenagers may have drawbacks. It may not undo undesirable behavior. However, for some, it may suppress it. For others, it may be offensive. It might also stirrup negative feelings in the person who is punished or inadvertently provide a fit of aggressive behavior. So how then, do we get to understand the energies? Nothing works better than proactively connecting and relating to others, regardless of their personalities, energy differences, and other unmentioned barriers. As cognitive empathy states, understanding how one feels and having a mutual connection with them over their ongoing situation gives you a chance (as an empathizer), to feel the person's pain. At this point, however, it is beneficial to provide the recipient with the benefit of the doubt. It is also important to note that different personalities would express different responses when shown even the slightest form of empathy.

The next step is going beyond the connection, into the second phase comes empathy type, emotional empathy. At this point, the other party's emotions are deeply engraved in you that you'd hurt and cry with them. It is the stage where the true essence of empathy if felt; walking in the shoes of the hurting. It requires a lot of patience and perseverance because, you, are deliberately throwing yourself in the deeper end to be with the second person. Study shows that persons with INFJ personality energy would suite this task quickly.

The IN-Feeler/Judger energy trait bearers are sensitive and of secure bonding connections to the emotions of others. I mentioned, though, that everyone is equally strong and unique, so I believe you can do it regardless of your personality type. At this stage, the cliché "introvert-extrovert" differences are lifted, and the energies work together for common ground. Though introverts are presumed to be of the "about me" trait and extroverts to be of the "about others" trait, these titles are dropped off, and together, they both gain a mutual stand both mentally and emotionally. This stage of empathy may equally be the easiest or hardest to go about since the benefit of doubt evidently stands strong. Trust issues may also be displayed by the recipient(s), majorly if they are of different energies to the empathizer. This connection is a makeshift model of the unison you are creating with your recipient. As much as the first person would be trying to understand the second one, he is actually also opening a window and leasing a benefit of the doubt, just to let the second person have a chance of understanding him too. The third step of understanding any energy different from yours is taking action. Taking action cements the imagination and connection to one's situation, as I mentioned earlier. When you proactively take action to counter one's worries, it solidifies your interest in them, your good intentions and purpose you have for them are brought to life. The recipient should, at this point, be able to see that you are investing your time, your effort, and probably your resources in them, to see them smile. Note that at this point, the empathizer is going out of their way, putting aside all differences, whether in terms of social class, personality differences, and maybe even an interactive experience they shared in the past (i.e., ex-lovers).

This is the stage where trust is at its fullest because one person is deliberately taking up another's burden, walking with the other through pain in their shoes. Accurate empathy on all three levels is discovered when you see your clients' world from his point of view. Later on, you can connect and communicate with them. The significant factors stressed are realizing that feelings and emotions do not exist. Secondly, you need to be flexible to venture into the world of the other person. Understand their needs and fix all the issues they have. Remember to communicate a basic understanding of what the client is feeling. This lets you have a relationship, get open, gather data. A maximum understanding of energy also requires assertiveness, convincing, and perceptiveness. You can significantly add to the recipients' perceptions' emotionally or using a self-evaluation, behavioral pattern, or a stimulus. Empathy is determined by the reaction of the one seeking it. Therefore, it is of importance that you, as a counselor, integrate the modes used in response of clients seeking help without empathy in tough situations, the chances that hostility builds up is undisputedly high. This alien hostility can be gassed up by the many silent struggles one undergoes, internally and personally. The resentment can also be fumed up either voluntarily or knowingly as a form of defense from the society as a whole or involuntarily as a psychological reflex to avoid what caused it in the first place. It is advisable to understand one's situation before emphasizing empathy because a wrong move can make everything crumble down. No problems would be solved, but rather, more issues and bitterness would pile up.

Like how a water body with several inlets but not a single outlet would, in turn, become salty. Different energies need to be understood, and this knowledge is the fabric of handling any energy.

Chapter 5: Building Self Protection – How to Protect Yourself from Manipulative People

Psychological manipulation is the exertion of excessive and unwarranted emotional influence over others while putting the victim at a disadvantage.

It is emotional exploitation that leads to mental distortion and loss of emotional intelligence and independence.

The victim becomes emotionally dependent on the manipulator who, in return, derives satisfaction from the control and privileges that come with the lopsided relationship. Unlike healthy social relationships that are constructive and rewarding for both parties, psychological manipulation is founded on parasitism. The victim's energy and their essence of being are sucked by the manipulator; an energy vampire. Psychological manipulators are driven to a wide range of complex issues ranging from their own personal experiences to mental distortion. In some cases, such individuals have been conditioned by the environment especially family settings. Without proper intervention, children who grow up in emotionally abusive environments tend to normalize such behaviors as adults. They, in turn, become manipulative. Moreover, living in an emotionally toxic environment makes individuals vulnerable to accept emotional abuse from manipulators. However, the problem is usually deep-seated, and their manipulative behaviors are indicators of how deep the problem goes.

Humans are emotional beings – we tend to seek emotional validation from friends, families, and even in some extreme cases, total strangers. Whether good or bad, these emotions are important when it comes to establishing and fostering social relationships at home, school, or workplace. However, such a mighty power of emotions can be easily exploited by manipulative individuals. Such individuals are adept at manipulating people emotionally for their own gain while concealing their ulterior motives. They use emotive situations to control an emotionally vulnerable individual while masking their true intentions with a destructive hammer disguised as a helping hand. Manipulative individuals have psychopathic tendencies such as lack of empathy and impulsivity.

They draw gratification and validation from manipulating and holding others back from outgrowing their cycle of influence. With almost genius-level mastery of the art of flip flopping on issues, emotionally manipulative people are cunning individuals who also find a way of adapting to new scenarios to suit their needs. Therefore, ditching them can be a Herculean task, especially for empaths who are emotionally sensitive and prone to emotional manipulation.

Emotionally controlling individuals easily pounce on the naturally giving character of empaths to redirect attention to themselves at the opportune moment. Therefore, it is imperative for empaths to build self-protection against manipulative people.

The first step towards building self-protection against chronically manipulative people is identifying such individuals through their characteristics. Individuals who thrive on negative psychological influence are distinguished by their ability to detect other people's weaknesses, especially emotional vulnerabilities. They are skillful at identifying individuals who are more likely to fall into their well-laid trap. Manipulative people are predatory; they target the seemingly weak prey within the larger social community. Whether within the family, workplace, or any social and professional gathering, individuals with chronic manipulative tendencies have the cunning ability to offer support and help for individuals who are emotionally distressed. After zeroing in on their target, the psychological violation and exploitation begin. The terrible scheme hatched by manipulative people is aimed at convincing their victims that they are the bad guys. They create and nurture the notion that their victims are on the wrong side. Words will be twisted and actions tailored towards their vile agenda.

Being on the receiving end of such well-calculated emotional aggression can be overwhelming and outright confusing for many people. But such onslaught is aimed at cracking an individual's will and perseverance. When not stopped, the victim will surrender the controls to the manipulator with the hopes of finding reprieve. Psychologically manipulative individuals herd their victims towards an emotional island. They then create a sense that the only two inhabitants of the island are the victim and the manipulator. Therefore, the victim readily accepts the deadly tentacles disguised as help. The helping hand offered progressively transforms into a deadly python-like grip. They will relentless squeeze the victim and drain them emotionally. In some cases, the victim is unaware that life is being snuffed out of them by such an individual. However, handing over the reins of control is the beginning of a downward spiral whose nadir is emotional desolation. Such lack of awareness is common among empaths whose emotional vulnerability disadvantages them when it comes to dealing with chronically manipulative individuals. Attuned to absorbing emotions of different kinds from others, empaths are capable of bottling even extreme emotions without necessarily seeking for an emotional outlet. They take in even extreme negative emotions. Moreover, they are introverts and would rarely share their experiences with others. They limit their social circles to small groups of people. Empaths also tend to minimize the time they spend on social gatherings. These characteristics attract energy vampires like manipulative people. Chronically manipulative individuals are shrewd are developing machinations for feeding on the weaknesses of their victims. They use such weaknesses as a weapon against the emotionally vulnerable individuals to their advantage. The primary objective of such machinations to redirecting a victim's energies towards the manipulative individual's self-centered interests.

The victims losses their self-worth and sense of self-esteem. Serving the self-centered interests of the manipulator is the sole target of emotional exploitation and abuse by chronically manipulative individuals. Success to them is measured by close their victims are driven over the edge. They derive power, pleasure, and authority when their victims are hanging on the edge or writhing down in the valley below. When left unchallenged and unchecked, manipulators turn their victims into their puppets and can drive them self-harm. It is not uncommon for individuals who have emotionally abused to entertain suicidal thoughts, especially when they discover that they have been under a manipulative spell. Self-injuries such as slitting or wrist may precede even more ominous problematic and compulsive behaviors such as substance abuse, alcoholism, and even suicide. With introverted inclinations, empaths may resort even to even greater degrees of social and physical exclusion.

Self-Protection Against Sneaky Psychologically Manipulative People

After successfully understanding how chronic manipulative people operate, including their characteristics and their sole objective, it is imperative to learn how to build effective self-protection against such individuals. The key to building a successful self-protection wall around you as an empath understands two fundamental issues. First, chronically manipulative individuals thrive in the chaos created by negative emotions.

They feed on such situations and derive happiness, power, and authority from them. They function by spinning the wheels of psychological manipulation. Therefore, they have well-crafted machinations to identify their victims and adapt their behaviors to lure emotionally vulnerable individuals.

Secondly, the problem is not your emotional vulnerability and sensitivity. The problem lies with the psychotic behaviors of manipulative wheel spinners. However, manipulative individuals would readily and incessantly convince you that the problem is you. It is the first step towards turning someone into an emotional puppet devoid of self-worth. They deconstruct an individual's sense of being and wire a hot stream of doubt through their spine. They become emotionally dependent on their would-be emotional tormentor. After turning their victims into empty shells, manipulative people fill the created void with baseless ideas aimed at promoting their self-centered agenda. Psychological manipulation is essentially slavery of the mind where the manipulator is the master, and the victim becomes the slave.

The victim is deprived of peace, love, and harmony which are essential recipes for self-determination and enjoyment of the abundance of life. The process of becoming an emotional puppet begins with subtle inroads. The first step towards protecting yourself against manipulative people is identifying these traps and avoiding them. To get under your skin and toy with your emotions, manipulative people deploy a wide range of cunning tactics. Ordinary and seemingly harmless questions and comments can be tailored to lure you into the trap. Manipulative people also use confusion to snare their unsuspecting victims. In some cases, they play with the mindset of their victims by guilt-tripping them. Blaming an emotionally vulnerable individual for a mishap can destabilize them psychologically. Consequently, they become easy pickings for calculating manipulator. On the surface, some of these tactics seem well-intentioned. An unsuspecting empath would readily give in to the interrogations and in some cases, accept reasonability for a mishap. However, hidden beneath the mundaneness of these actions are vile intentions aimed at micromanaging the emotional status of the victim leading to emotional submission and subjugation.

Avoid these emotional traps; it is advisable to understand your fundamental rights as a fully functional human being. Psychologically manipulative people pounce on self-doubt and inability of the victims to recognize when their fundamental rights are trampled upon by others. Forfeiture of these rights, for any particular reason, creates a vacuum that manipulators always seek to fill with their ill-motive ideas. Therefore, recognize and defend your right to hold and express a different opinion. This will give you a high sense of control and safeguard against being guilt-tripped by manipulators. Avoid the temptation of trooping with the masses in the hope that it would make you less weird. Holding a divergent opinion is the hallmark of self-determination.

It will set you apart yet wholesome. Expressing your opinion especially as an empath, will rebuff the manipulators who find individuals too strong-willed to manipulate psychologically. Upholding and safeguarding other individual fundamental rights such as the right to be respected and prior setting can keep off the unwanted attention by manipulators. Individuals who understand their need to be respected and can set their priorities can easily turn down the unwanted overtures from chronic manipulators. They stand by their 'no' decisions and answers and do not budge even when enticed by the energy vampires out to drain them emotionally. Moreover, they readily recognize tell-tale signs of mental, physical, or emotional abuse and exploitation. Being on the lookout for such threats discourages emotion puppeteers who prey upon the vulnerabilities and gullibility of others. By safeguarding these liberties, a would-be victim establishes a boundary that keeps out manipulators. Boundaries give an individual to self-appoint themselves leadership supremacy in their lives. Having the moral authority and power to shape your emotions and the general direction of your life is one of the surest ways of keeping manipulative people at bay. Self-assuredness eliminates doubts which manipulators use to cause confusion in the lives of their victims. Individuals who are self-assured are masters of their emotions and have moral authority in deciding the direction of their lives. You can easily set off the emotional traps laid by the manipulators without necessarily getting trapped when you have control over your life.

Secondly, many people fall into the chocking grasp of manipulators because of indecision and passive-aggression. The inability to stand firm against manipulative people is partly due to the flip flopping behaviors of manipulators.

Psychologically manipulative people have perfected the skill of tinkering on the extremes leading to confusion among their victims. Blowing hot and cold on issues ensures that they keep their victims dazed long enough to trap them. It is not uncommon for a manipulator to show heart-warming kindness and politeness to one individual and still be unsympathetic to the plight of another. Manipulators habitually flow by the popular emotional waves. They can be aggressive or passive and helpless, depending on the situation and audience. All these tactics are aimed at entrapping emotionally vulnerable and sensitive individuals.

Sometimes all you may need is a writing pad and pen to note down key points of your conversation to keep track of their wavering opinions, statements, and actions. This is especially advisable once you notice their habitual oscillation between being sympathetic and unsympathetic. From seemingly plausible excuses and justifications to erratic behaviors and viewpoints, identify the patterns in their behaviors and actions. When you constantly remind them of their original stands and statements, manipulators will find you difficult as prey and shy away. Keeping track of manipulators' views and actions not only discouragement but also acts as a shield against falling into their traps. The surest way to set off a trap from a safe distance is by identifying it first.

Therefore, avoid being passive-aggressive when dealing with manipulators. Call them out forthwith once you realize their actions and words are ill-intentioned. As soon as you spot manipulators, actively deal with them, and they will flee from you. Even though they are masters of arm-twisting people emotionally and psychologically, even manipulators feel discouraged when their manipulative feelers are rebuffed or knocked back by their intended victims.

Being actively aggressive in calling out manipulative people can prevent you from becoming their emotional toys. Standing up for the truth even when you are met with their wrath including denying their behaviors, will ensure that you rest easy knowing that you kept an emotional puppeteer at bay. Even when they turn the situation back on you and paint you as the bad person, do not flinch; hold fast to the truth, and they will finally give up. The immediate feeling of discomfort that they create by turning the situation back at you or even denying the whole incident will fade after a short time. However, the joy of protecting yourself will last for a very long time. It might even encourage others to stand up against such manipulative individuals especially at home, workplace or even within the community. And most importantly, pretending that what they are doing to is okay is dangerous. It might set a precedent for others who may fall victim to manipulators.

Manipulators stalk their victims with the view of identifying any signs of weakness. When they detect any weaknesses, they manipulate the situation either by blowing it out of proportion or turning it against their victims. The key to successful emotional manipulation by manipulative people is to make their intended victims feel bad about themselves. By planting seeds of doubt in the minds of their victims, manipulators will go to a great length to nurture and water the seeds to sprout and grow into full-blown self-hatred. An individual wallowing in self-pity and self-blame will feel inadequate and becomes emotionally dependent on others for validation. In most cases, manipulators will present themselves as the safest pair of hands to help them during such times. Buoyed by the false sense of care exhibited by the manipulator, the emotionally susceptible and scarred victim will more likely surrender their free will, freedoms, and power to manipulators.

Whether a conscious or unconscious decision, the move will take the victim down a path of destruction. Therefore, understanding yourself beforehand will ensure that you avoid the temptation to turn to self-blame and personalization of issues whenever something goes wrong. As a self-protection strategy, understanding yourself extends beyond knowing your fundamental rights. It encompasses trusting yourself and establishing moral boundaries. When you understand yourself, you will realize that emotions, whether negative or positive, are necessarily not bad. Additionally, you will get to understand that emotions stem from an unconscious place, including our past experiences. We have little to no control over. Their fizzling is involuntary, but the most important thing is our ability to deal with them. Let no one convince you that you should feel miserable because of your emotions especially in the case of empaths who are emotionally sensitive. The problem does not lie with you or your emotional sensitivities; rather, the problem is with the manipulators who want to blow your emotions out of proportion and make your despondent.

In every situation where you encounter an emotional manipulator, self-protect yourself by gauging whether how you are being treated meets your respect threshold. Examine the expectations and demands that the manipulator requires of you. If you feel, based on your understanding of self, that they are unbecoming and demeaning and inclined towards serving the self-centered interests of the manipulator, firmly and politely reject them. Set the standards of what is a reasonable expectation and curl the perpetrators of unreasonable expectations and block them from influencing you. Additionally, scrutinize the direction in which the relationship with any individual will take. Manipulators thrive on developing one-way relationships with all the benefits going to them.

When employing the self-understanding strategy to self-protect yourself against psychologically manipulative individuals, it is imperative that you always understand the direction of the relationship. How you feel about the relationship is the key to measuring how well it suits your standards and moral compass. While such may be a difficult task for empaths to undertake considering their ability to absorb negative emotions from others, having a go at self-understanding have multiple rewards that extend beyond dealing with manipulative individuals. The fourth self-protection strategy is leveraging time. Manipulators always ensnare emotionally vulnerable people by pressurizing them into making decisions. They prefer on-the-spot decisions since they are rushed and not carefully considered. Knowing that their victims are under great pressure due to their emotionally draining situation, manipulators always seek to push decisions to be made without much thought. Decisions made during the spur of the moment primarily stem from emotions. Such decisions are rarely the product of rational thinking. The emotional wounds are still raw and fresh. At this point, the victim is emotionally vulnerable and more likely to self-blame and personalize the problem. A rushed decision is the manipulator's way of bringing their victims into their immediate influence. Like salesmen, manipulators will seek to seal the deal immediately. Om some cases, they prefer catching their victims off-guard. It is not uncommon for an emotional manipulator to give short deadlines or notices for their victims to accomplish an important and time-consuming task. Failure to abide by the notice or deadline can lead to criticism and manipulation. An emotional manipulator may also seek to gain an advantage over you by picking the wrong moment to ask important questions. Your lack of preparedness in such a situation is the chink in the armor that manipulators are looking for.

Leverage time by asking the manipulator to give you time to consider the request or question. This will give you time to think rationally and critically before making a decision. You can only understand the benefits and shortcomings of a relationship when you give your time to think objectively. Emotions tend to cloud judgment. Exercise leadership over your thought processes and mental faculties by postponing making critical decisions when under emotional pressure. Having time to think will help you in bargaining for equal respect and benefits in any relationship. Giving yourself time is also a great way to create separation from any form of influence he or she might have established from the onset. Manipulators thrive in a momentary lapse in rational thinking. When told to wait, they tend to impatient and shy off. They fear that by asking for time to think about their suggestions or questions, the victims will rationalize everything. This works to their disadvantage. Once you request time to think, keep a safe distance from them. This is because manipulators can easily explain themselves back into the picture. They have ideas at their fingertips to explain things away. If you do not fully detach yourself from them after leveraging time, they can easily convince you to reconsider your stance. They can expertly excuse and justify even the most unfathomable of actions as long as their objective of putting you under their influence is achieved. For empaths who are renowned for their kind and forgiving hearts, they can easily find themselves at crossroads. They may absorb such excuses and justifications and be tempted to give in. However, their rational minds may tell them otherwise. The fifth tip to consider when dealing with chronically emotionally manipulative people is founded on the concept of self-preservation. Prevent being trapped into the toxic web of manipulation by diplomatically and firmly confronting them.

Concisely and effectively articulate your stand, priorities, and opinion without damaging the existing relationships with the manipulator. In most cases, manipulators are people close to us, either as workmates, family members, and friends. These are individuals we interact with frequently and avoiding physical contact with them can be challenging. Even emotionally manipulative workmates are important members of workplace teams. Keeping peace with these individuals may be a necessity due to circumstances. When met with low resistance, a firmly and tactfully said 'no' can foster a great understanding between the manipulator and would-be victim. It can also inspire others who have fallen victim to manipulation within the same environment to stand up and defend their rights and priorities without being guilt-tripped by manipulators. In the end, you end up preserving your peace while also enjoying greater emotional freedom.

Additionally, diplomacy while standing your ground will ensure that you handle manipulative people who become bullies safely. A physically confrontational situation pitying an emotionally sensitive and vulnerable victim against bully manipulators can easily turn ugly. Bullies are emotionally insecure and in most cases, are victims of bullying. Turning in bullying is one of the ways through which psychological manipulators try to make up or avenge their own sufferings. Therefore, bullying becomes a way of pulling others down to their level. When they cut you down emotionally, such individuals will feel a false and deranged sense of tallness and supremacy. Whether in the office, at home, or in the schoolyard, develop a spine and defend yourself against such bullies whose aim is to exert emotional control over you. However, even as you stand for your fundamental rights, consider your safety first. Safety first is a pearl of old-age wisdom whose importance must be emphasized whenever one encounters a manipulator who is a bully.

Ensuring your safety can be achieved by simple acts such as picking the right moment to stand up against a manipulator. Having people as a witness may deter the bully from becoming physically confrontational. Documenting incidences of bullying can also discourage bullies. A paper trail can provide enough evidence to have enough people in your corner to defend you, especially in work settings. You will realize that you are not alone in the fight. There is a wide range of professionals including law enforcement officers and counselors who can support you. By documenting and reporting any form of abuse to the concerned parties, you are standing up for yourself and calling out manipulators.

Another self-protection approach that requires tact and firmness is destabilizing their source of manipulative power. Manipulators exert influence because of the power they perceive they have over others. In work and domestic settings, such power manifests in the form of superior position or seniority, academic qualification, or possession of certain skills considered rare within the setting at the time. Additionally, manipulators who have control over certain resources within the workplace, home, or even community may draw their manipulative power from such a scenario. Others may even draw power from their social and professional connections. This may include co-workers, teammates, siblings, subordinates, influential leaders, and even friends. They will feel that people are beholden to them and, therefore, should bend to their will. In extreme cases, such manipulators may resort to physical and verbal abuse or bullying. They may feel untouchable because of the power they have over others. The sources of power become the center of gravity of these people. Destabilizing this source of stability can tip the balance of power in favor of would-be victims and render manipulators powerless.

To avoid confrontations while also being diplomatic, identify and strive to take away these centers of gravity. If your workmate is manipulating you because of a special skill they possess, take your time and learn the skill if possible. It will free you from having to operate within their circles of influence.

Alternatively, scout for individuals with such skills and let them join the company. If necessary, make inroads into the manipulator's social circles without tipping him or her off. Having common allies will tone down their power. By taking their prized possession and the leverage they have over others, you will diminish their influence. Cut from their power source, manipulators refocus their energies away from trying to controlling others. Siphon power from manipulators is not only strategic; it also throws them off balance. It is a reality check for emotional puppeteers to realize that their would-be victims can match their hyped power and might.

Sometimes power is not derived from such associations and possessions. Manipulators are capable of exercising their dominance in physical places where they own or feel comfortable in. Such spaces can be their offices or even public spaces, including parks where they are familiar with. Such familiarity or ownership will give the manipulator an upper hand during conversations and negotiations. You are likely to feel less comfortable in physical spaces where a manipulator is bound to dominate mentally. Any transactions carried in such environments are inherently lopsided and favors the manipulator. To avoid finding yourself in such a situation of imbalanced power especially during negotiations and meetings, opt for neutral spaces. Home turf will give the manipulator the home advantage over you. However, negotiating or conversing in the manipulator's home turf is sometimes unavoidable.

In case you find yourself in such a scenario, it is advisable to reset your bearings using icebreakers. These can be simple actions such as diversionary small talks or sharing a cup of coffee. Other people get their bearings by taking in their environment. A simple yet engaging talk on wall photos, paintings or hangings can take off the pressure on your shoulders. This can set the stage for a more balanced interaction instead of being controlled and manipulated. Emotional manipulators are cunning characters who prey upon the vulnerabilities of their victims. Any emotional cracks, even the tiniest ones, are exploited and aggravated and turned into diabetic wounds. While such cracks are sometimes unavoidable, developing strategies to keep off toxicities from manipulators can prevent them from becoming diabetic. When emotionally charged, as sometimes is the case for empaths, engage in activities that will enable you to develop inner peace. Consider meditation to calm your nerves. Meditating will help you connect with higher realms and develop positive thoughts. A positive outlook of life keeps away manipulators who thrive in negativity. Emptiness attracts manipulators who will seek to feel the empty space with negative emotions to their own benefit. Meditation will help you make sense of the chaos that unfolds around and find calmness and purpose even in the most difficult situations. Meditation teaches a higher sense of loving kindness even in the face of hostility, which is a great way of avoiding physical confrontations with the manipulator. In most cases where the manipulator is driven by their dark past, resulting in compassion will disarm them. Your loving kindness can transform a manipulator into a genuinely kind and loving individual.

If you have not mastered the art of meditation, consider other options such as reading, exercising, or writing. These activities will enable you to release pent up emotions while also allowing you to zone out manipulators and negative thoughts. The benefits of these activities are manifold. Reading and writing are also a great way of learning new ideas, skills or even art to occupy your time. You develop professionally and personally while also keeping manipulators at bay. If your co-worker, sibling, or friend is always seeking to manipulate you because of a skill they possess; reading to ground yourself can be a great way to offset their power source and center of gravity. In addition to the health and physical benefits of exercising, you also stand to enjoy an improved mental status. Moreover, you get to meet new people, especially in gyms or parks. Group exercises might be a ticket to meeting new allies who will help you built a better social network. This will come in handy when a manipulator's power source is his or her friends.

While grounding yourself and zoning out unnecessary distractions can be an effective self-protection strategy against manipulators, it is always advisable to engage in constructive activities. Avoid the temptation of filling your time and emptiness with destructive activities such as gossiping and binging on television, food, or both. When emotionally hurt, filling up your brain with wild ideas and information propagated on television and social media can lead you to a path whose end is despair and feeling miserable. These are pointless activities that will make even more vulnerable to manipulation. Such information and activities will consume your time, leaving you purposeless and at the mercy of manipulators. They will distract you from your destiny and create a false sense of belonging. Always strive to keep in touch with reality.

Individuals who are staked down to one opportunity are easy pickings for manipulators.

Emotionally vulnerable and sensitive people are easily boxed into staying in unproductive situations. From stale relationships to dead-end jobs, they may find such situations familiar and comfortable. They become emotionally attached to these jobs and relationships and even individuals. They lose their independence and become overly reliant on people, workplaces, and relationships. Upon the urging of other people, they develop a phobia of the unknown. Emotional manipulators easily identify individuals who are emotionally attached to their jobs, relationships or even places. In case the manipulator is your partner or workmate, they are more likely to steamroll over your emotions and use your attachment to confuse and exert undue influence and control over you.

By studying behavior patterns and understanding your fundamentals, assess how genuinely you are respected and treated in any relationship.

When you realize that your emotions are ignored, manipulated, and steamrolled over, break away. However, be tactful and avoid confrontations. Remain cordial but emphasize that you value your emotional well-being; something that the current relationship setup is not currently offering. In some cases, it is advisable to cut off links with such manipulative individuals especially when they resort to physical, verbal or emotional abuse. Such individuals are incapable of sustaining a civil relationship founded on mutual respect. Be cautious from the onset of any relationship. Investing too much at the onset of a relationship is ill-advised. Psychological manipulators will always try to convince you that depending on a single opportunity is attractive. They detest ambition. They champion for contentment; having all your eggs in one seemingly safe basket. However, the safety of this single basket has been set by them. They will gladly justify its safety by all means while trying to tear down any objections you raise.

To them, it is normal and prudent to live in one location or work in the same job and position. Wanting anything else is risky, awkward, and even selfish. They will argue you're your actions are driven by pride. Phrases and questions like 'why fix it when it is working' become commonplace. In reality, they are afraid that your mind will awaken, and you will no longer fall within their circle of influence. Therefore, continuously seek new opportunities to better your life. Create new experiences by taking new jobs, fostering new relationships or even moving to new locations. You will become emotionally independent and happier. Be adventurous and witness manipulators flee from you. Finally, psychologically manipulators always target people with baby mentality. If you are constantly letting people walk over you and later complain, you are a prime target for manipulators.

Remember, manipulators are always seeking for the opportunity to get into your head and mess up with your thinking. Whether you blame them later for your troubles is of little consequence to them. They can readily deny your accusations or turn them against you. You can easily become a bad person when dealing with a manipulator. In some cases, they may resort to physical confrontation or bullying. Repeatedly over-trusting people and getting hurt is babyish. When you are fooled more than once, then you ought to be ashamed of yourself. Despite the existence of manipulative people, the burden of self-protection falls on you. You do not have the free pass to fall victim to manipulators just because they exist and are cunning. It is not the fault of the psychological manipulator for toying with your emotions; it is your responsibility to prevent them from turning you into a puppet. You take full credit for all your successes and failures; they define you.

People will always try to outthink you. They will come up with crafty ways to over-strategize you.

Getting one over you is the primary goal of manipulators. If, upon assessment, you realize that an individual is habitually slippery and flip flopping on issues, do not hesitate to delete them from your life. Giving such individuals second chances is inviting trouble to your backyard. Be bold and cut loose people who you feel are trying to manipulate you emotionally. Having self-respect will ensure that you guard your dignity with jealousy.

Always bet on yourself, including your capabilities and intuition. If you have second thoughts about other's intentions, pull out or tread carefully. Hold yourself to higher standards. Make decisions based on both internal and external factors. And the most important internal factor and the only one you can control is yourself. External factors are beyond your control.

337

Therefore, giving prominence to external factors will only leave you susceptible to manipulation. Shun empty promises. Challenge the status quo and carved out a life for yourself. Stop manipulators on their track by setting consequences for their actions. Babies have a nascent and gullible mentality. When you stop being a baby, you develop a strong mentality accompanied by a high sense of self-worth. Your capacity to take in negative emotions from manipulators without being affected will increase.

Chapter 6: Practical Exercises for Different Empaths

Empaths are capable of assimilating the energy in their surroundings. When placed in an environment characterized by positive energy and emotions, empaths tend to flourish mentally and materially. They operate with a greater sense of purpose. However, this does not diminish their sponge-like ability to absorb negative energies from others. Though an exhausting undertaking, sucking in negative energies, including emotions, heightens the empaths' ability to relate to other people's feelings. This emotional sensitivity and vulnerability is the trademark for identifying empaths. They go beyond sympathizing with others and wear other people's shoes. They connect with the individual at a personal level both emotionally and physically. They sense these energies and feelings without being told and embody them. As a gift, emotional sensitivity and vulnerability can be overwhelming. In contrast to the impulsively controlling nature of many people, empaths handle situations subtly and delicately. And this is their soft underbelly that many manipulative people always target in their bid to enslave them emotionally. How empaths perceive and deal with this onslaught is dependent on their different gifts and skills.

Types of Empaths

One of the commonest types of empaths is emotional empathy. Also known in psychology as affective empathy, emotional empathy allows an empath to connect with others emotionally. They the emotions of others, including those hidden unconsciously or consciously. In advanced cases, this emotional awareness can transform into emotional oneness characterized by sharing emotions. An emotional empath will readily feel another individual's emotions. Such individuals will pick up and manifest these emotions from their environment. It is emotional ownership and transference that takes place in the unconscious and non-physical realm. For example, an emotional empath will show sadness or worry on their faces as those were his or her emotions despite picking them from the environment. Therefore, emotional empaths are capable of channeling two emotions from different sources in a parallel manner. That is, they can channel both their emotions and those they pick from the environment. In some cases, empaths are capable of attuning themselves spiritually to others. Such spiritual empathy is characterized by the ability to feel another person's connections with spiritual realms, including divinity, God, and other objects they consider as divine. When they connect with others spiritually, spiritual empaths are capable of sharing other people's spiritual experiences. When they become one spiritual, the two can express the same feelings and emotions that come with the spiritual moment. This may include the individual's spiritual experience when singing including how the tunes and harmonies of songs and spiritual teachings affect them. When an empath is spiritually attuned to an individual who believes in other spiritual objects such as spiritual beings and spirits of the dead, an empath may become mediums through which emotions from both realms are manifested.

As mediums, they may possess psychic abilities such as communication and expression of emotions. However, it is imperative to draw a distinction between serving as a psychic between different worlds through training and skill acquisition and being an empath. An empath is inborn; not a product of training. In some communities such as Native Americans, spiritual empaths are considered as go-betweens that connect the physical world with the spiritual realm. Such individuals are held in high esteem due to their position between the two realms. It is considered a special power that elevates an individual above the mundaneness of human existence.

In contrast, geomantic empath show elevated levels of attunement to the environments or even a place. They can sense energies in a given physical environment, not only by touching the physical objects within the place; sometimes, all they need is to be present in the place. Therefore, it is not uncommon for geomantic empaths to show exceptional levels of happiness and comfort in some places and feel repelled and uncomfortable in others. When comfortable, empaths are drawn by the positive energies in such places. Physical places awash with negative energies such as sadness and fear may discomfort them. Alternatively, they may express and feel these emotions as they were his or her own. In some cases, the connection that some geomantic empaths have with the earth enables them to predict natural disasters with some degree of accuracy. In some cases, places with dark histories can bring up negative emotions for geomantic empaths by just touching the objects within the place. Components of physical landscapes such as groves and sacred places such as churches and shrines can reconnect a geomantic empath with past events. While he or she may not relive the exact moments of these past events, the energy and emotions that accompanied them may radiate through the empath.

They can glean over information about past events that took place in the location by touching these objects. They are easily moved to tears when they connect with such negative emotions. For plant empaths, seemingly mundane events such as cutting of plants trigger a deep sense of loss, sadness, and grief among. Their attunement with the plants enables them to feel the events as if they were the plants being damaged. Sometimes described as floral empaths, such individuals connect with the energies of the plants. They are tender and caring towards plants due to such connections. Sometimes such connection and affection may be directed towards a specific plant. The plight of these plants, especially those being damaged, can overwhelm them leading to tears. When they absorb positive emotions about the plants, plant empaths visibly express such emotions too.

Other empaths have a special connection with animals. They have a heightened sense of what it feels like to be an animal, and in some cases; they are more attuned to receiving and projecting the feelings and emotions of specific animals. The unique connection with these animals enables them to interact with them on a different and extraordinary level. They can detect changes in the energies of these animals. This telepathic connection may translate in devotion and care for the specific animal.

In the case of cognizant empaths, a strong connection with an individual manifests in the form of a heightened sense of knowledge about others without any physical contact. They get a detailed insight into others by looking at them. They can sense a wide range of issues, including thoughts, lies, secrets, and even overt and covert intents. It is a precognitive capability that may sometimes manifest in the form of dreams. These dreams usually come to pass. The telepathic connection between a claircognizant empath is founded on intuition.

Therefore, they are sometimes referred to as intuitive empaths. They sense and tap into the energetic fields or sensations given out by others around them. They then use these sensations to connect with them thereby gaining a deeper knowledge of others. However, intuitive empaths are distinct from emotional empaths. While emotional empaths attune to feelings and emotions of others, claircognizant empaths tap into the state of mind and personality.

Medical empaths operate in a different realm of empathy. They are receptive to one's health status, including pains and illnesses without having the information beforehand. By picking the energy from other people's bodies, they can use their intuition to identify the source of the ailment. Such sources usually manifest in the form of blocked energies which medical empaths can detect. In some cases, medical empaths can project the symptoms of the ailment especially when a high level of oneness is established between the two individuals. This has seen many medical empaths become trained healers in different healthcare settings.

In some cases, people are blessed with unnatural levels of compassion for others. The feelings of others drive them to act even if it may endanger their lives. They will drop everything they do and refocus their energies on helping others. Compassionate empaths are selfless, which some people may find repulsive. Taking empathy, a little too far can pose challenges to others as some beneficiaries of their compassion may reject their helping hands. When rejected, the emotional trauma may devastate empaths leaving them dejected and drained. It is not uncommon for such individuals to feel confused and exasperated. While some of these types of empaths have a clear distinction in terms of ability and object of emotional connection, some of them also show significant overlaps.

Both intuitive and emotional empaths build a connection with other people that extends into the core of their being. Emotions and personality are sometimes intertwined, and unfurling untangling may call for connecting at both levels. Similarly, floral, animal, and environmental, geomantic empaths may also overlap in how they connect with the objects of their specialty. Animals and plants are parts of the physical environment. Their sensations may be detected by geomantic empaths. However, the intensity of the connection may vary.

Practical Exercises for Different Empaths

The gift of being empowered with sensitivity can be overwhelming for many unskilled empaths. As a talent, empathy does not come with a manual of how to handle different situations that can be draining and exhausting emotionally. It is overwhelming to share and project other people's emotions and feelings without letting them overshadow yours. Empaths run the danger of having their emotions overrun other people's feelings. Some people's emotions can be overpowering and draining. If not dealt with carefully, empaths are at risk of sacrificing their emotions and feelings for the sake of others. Emotional numbness may set, leading to social, mental, and physical health issues. This can lead to breakdowns in social relations. They may become disoriented and confused when the different energies they receive from their surroundings are not properly processed and channeled.

While empathy is a rare talent, its rawness needs refinement into a skill that serves the common good for both the empaths and the people they interact with. The following practical exercises can help different empaths harness their full potential. For emotional empaths, the primary challenge is how to effectively manage two emotional streams: yours and others'. The deep emotional connection with others can confusing and overpowering. The key to mastering your gift of emotional sensitivity is by engaging in exercises aimed at strengthening you emotionally. Achieving emotional control through mediation, stimulating conversations or discussions, and physical exercise will elevate your sense of being and ensure that you are in touch with your emotions. These exercises will ensure that you have a greater sense of yourself, including your personality and how you may react in different scenarios. You will become emotionally stable because, in addition, to create a synergy between mind and body; these exercises will act as emotional outlets. You will have the chance to enjoy the refreshing feeling of emotional release. Empaths with pent up emotions are caught in the crossroads of understanding whether their current emotional state emanates from their current or past experiences or whether they manifestations of emotions they have picked up from the environment.

With emotional stability comes a better level of clarity and alertness to one's own feelings and emotions. An emotional empath who is in control of his or her emotional becomes emotional intelligent and can detect lies and truths from individuals they connect with. And most importantly, they are able to separate their emotions from those they collect from their surroundings. When attained, this level of emotional intelligence is the key to avoiding the danger of becoming dissociated from your emotions and, consequently, your social life.

Helping others will transform into an emotionally fulfilling undertaking. Geomantic or environmental empaths are easily perceived as individuals whose hearts readily bleed for Mother Nature. Destruction of nature overwhelms them emotionally. A practical exercise that such empaths to live a more rewarding life is engagement in nature conservation exercises such as tree planting and restoration of historical artifacts. If you are a geomantic empath, consider having a garden where you can plant new seedlings, flowers, and herbs and nurture them. This will give you a sense of fulfillment. The key to horning and harnessing your skills and talents is keeping in touch with nature. Whether emotionally drained after witnessing nature being destroyed, engaging in a nurturing natural landscape can recharge your emotional batteries. A beautiful environment creates a calming harmony that is emotionally beneficial. Whether gardening or working on the farm, you will experience satisfied with your efforts to preserve something you hold dear to your heart.

Additionally, consider participating in environmental projects aimed at restoration and beautification. Moreover, having ported plants within your home will fill you with positive emotions. The seemingly ordinary watering and pruning of these plants will give a greater sense of satisfaction and emotional stability. Consider going for nature walks in pristine environments. You will have reflective moments in such environments. While these exercises may be replicated in the case of animal and floral empaths, it is recommended that specific animal or plant is identified and a connection established. By sitting under the special tree, a plant empath will telepathically identify the energies of the plant and communicate with it. Nurturing the plant can also bring an elevated sense of inner peace. Studying the plant to a greater detail can also help in fine-tuning your empathy for the plant and other vegetation.

346

These exercises can also help animals empaths in realizing emotional stability even as they attune themselves to animals. Refining your gift by studying the biology of the animal. In the case of animals, your ability to connect with energies of the animals can also prove to be helpful healing. When combined with animal physiology and healing, you can enjoy a greater experience in your relationship with the animal. You might become a professional in your community by refocusing your talent to become an animal healer.

The telepathic ability of claircognizant or intuitive empaths to read and connect with people's thoughts can be befuddling. When not channeled properly, the line between your thoughts and those of others can be hazy. Intuitive empaths run the risk of being bombarded by a barrage of thoughts. The resulting confusing can lead to a mix-up in your thought process. You may find yourself acting on the thoughts of others. You may also be tempted to call out others for lying. Reading people's thoughts and personalities can be off-putting to others who may find you weird. Others may even give you a wide berth knowing that you will read their minds.

Like in the case of emotional empaths, the key to refining your gift as an intuitive empath is achieving a balance between your thoughts and those of others. Master your stream of thoughts and distinguish from those you collect from your surroundings. In addition to mediating and exercising, consider redefining your social circle. When you find individuals who you are compatible with in terms of thoughts and emotions, you stand a better chance of channeling your thoughts positively. Such individuals will act as bearings for your thought process and stream. This is because you have something in common. They will act as your reference point in case you feel bombarded by other people's thoughts. Your energetic field will grow stronger.

Medical empaths have the unique to experience something that is beyond human imagination. Understanding someone's ailments without being having firsthand information can be sometimes thrilling. They can even exhibit symptoms of these ailments even though they are medically okay. Medical empaths can read through the energies of others and pinpoint the problem. Successful harnessing these energy fields from others without causing harm to yourself physically and emotionally requires training yourself on how to detach yourself from these energies. Once you have identified the source of these medical conditions, disengage from the energy field. This can be achieved by mastering your emotions and thought the process of meditation and physical exercises. These activities will help you achieve self-awareness required to maintain a healthy balance between your life and those of others.

Medical empaths can also opt to further their understanding of ailments through studying. Mind-body healing is a long-practice profession whose place in the medical world is well-established. Whether in conventional or traditional medicine setting, body-mind healing is founded on empathy. If you are gifted with the ability to pick and project the energies from other people's bodies and identify their ailments, going for training on healing and medicine, in general, can help you further hone your skills. Such training should also include mind and body exercises aimed at strengthening your energy fields. This will improve your ability to project and identify causes of pains and ailments including their specific locations. Exercises such as yoga, meditation, and even physical exercises will leave you refreshed and energetic while also giving you inner peace. To avoid the pitfall of being rejected or considered overbearing, compassionate empaths should control their emotions by connecting to higher realms of power.

Through meditation and exercising, compassionate empaths will learn to balance between their innate desire to help and respecting other people's boundaries. By defining these boundaries, compassionate empaths will minimize incidences of rejection or being labeled a weirdo. Exercises such as self-reflection can help in reigning on their compulsive desire to overly help others.

Additionally, such exercises can help in dealing with rejection and exasperation. They help in training the mind of a compassionate empath to judge situations rationally and come up with a more acceptable help that does not border on overbearing.

Practical exercises aimed to help different empaths to harness their abilities and strengths primarily target the challenges they face in their lives. With the ability to make other people's emotions their own, empaths experience elevated levels of emotional distress and fatigue. Because of their caring and nurturing nature, they are bound to fall victim to manipulation. They get abused and violated by manipulators because they are vulnerable. The frequency of coming across such manipulators is high because they are emotional magnets and intolerant to interpersonal conflicts. These exercises will ensure that they build on their strengths.

Exercises such as meditation, yoga, and physical activities cut across various empaths because of their well-documented physical, mental and cognitive benefits. They ensure that empaths have emotional outlets to release emotional tensions that are common with absorbing other people's thoughts, emotions and feelings. It also helps them in widening social circles to overcome the frequent urge to opt for solitude when faced with challenges.

Chapter 7: What Are the Abilities of Empaths? What Are Some of Their Exceptional Insight?

Empaths are endowed with innate abilities that set them apart from others. From good listening to emotional sensitivity and the ability to absorb extremes of emotions, empaths have unique abilities that may sometimes put them at a great disadvantage emotionally. When they overcome the various issues that disrupt them on a daily basis, empaths are capable of tapping these abilities to the common of all. These disruptions include emotional wounds that hinder them from erecting effective emotional boundaries needed for productive functioning.

Abilities of Empaths

One of the abilities of empaths that give them exceptional insight into issues is their effective listening skills. Empaths not only listen with their ears; they also use their hearts. They detect even the slightest changes in energy vibrations emanating from other people. They listen telepathically and connect with other people and objects in a different realm that borders the supernatural. For plant, environmental, and animal empaths, attuning even to the most subtle energy sensations from these objects occupies a significant part of their day. They absorb these energies and establish a deep connection with their environment and others.

It is a listening founded on attunement to these objects and mirroring their energies that set empaths apart. Empaths listen to act. Driven by compassion, they go out of their way to act upon the message they hear. They do not discriminate what information and energy they absorb. Whether it is extreme anger, angst, joy, or pain, empaths will take it all in. They will bottle in these emotions and feelings. In the case of compassionate empaths, the desire to help can border obsession and overbearing. However, it is a manifestation of the resounding message they hear from the energy vibrations from others who need help.

The good listening ability of empaths has seen them elevated to higher standings in many communities all over the world where traditional spiritual practices are still practiced. Some empaths have the ability to listen to messages from both the physical and spiritual worlds. Known as spiritual empaths, they are endowed with the gift of communicating with spiritual objects in the spiritual world, including divinities and even the dead. In such communities, they are considered as spiritual leaders and spiritual healers. In the case of medical or physical empaths, listening as an ability comes in handy when listening to energies of pain and ailments. They have the capacity to listen to unique energy vibrations from the human body parts under distress. When honed effectively, such ability becomes a useful skill in mind and body healing; a century-old practice in medicine.

Human beings have intuition; a gut feeling that works as a sixth sense. However, empaths have a heightened intuition. The gut instincts of empaths are capable of sensing both positive and negative emotions in the environment. Whether it is emanating from physical objects, plants, animals or human beings, empaths intuitively detect these emotions, thoughts, and feelings.

351

It is a heightened sense of danger, a survival intuition, aimed at picking out the danger. Empaths are innately alert to these dangers that may harm them or others. Whether in the form of temperaments or actions, an empath's gut feeling will pick the sensations and interpret them. In the case of compassionate empaths, being alive to danger can translate into a strong desire to help others even at the detriment of their personal well-being. This intuitive ability works when geomantic, animal and plant empaths connect to physical objects and landscapes that their energies are synchronized or attuned with. Empaths have an elaborate intuitive capability that allows them to internalize other people's feelings. Empaths also have psychic abilities that extend beyond human connections. They establish telepathic connections with their environments, including human beings, plants, animals, and objects. It is a psychic connection that allows them to read and interpret overt and hidden emotions without having prior knowledge. They can also project and replicate these emotions and feelings through their bodies. It is a natural ability that is inborn. Psychic ability also enables empaths to read emotional imprints of other people, plants and animals. These emotions and thoughts are usually left behind on a wide range of objects including stones, buildings, and trees. In some cases, empaths can detect, interpret, and project traces of emotions by just being physically present in an environment that was once occupied by other people. This is how geomantic empaths are able to read, understand display emotions of people who lived a thousand years by visiting historical sites or touching artifacts they once used. Psychic abilities are sometimes specific to objects and distinguish different types of empaths. The ability of a geomantic, floral, animal and even medical empaths to detect these different energies is based on psychic connection. This psychic ability enables medical empaths to heal others.

352

People suffering from emotional traumas can learn to heal when medical empathy uses his or her psychic abilities to attuned their energies and transmute positive energies to them. Such energies from empaths can also help in healing others with physical medical conditions. It stimulates positive thinking, which is critical in body and mind healing. Healing of the heart is an important step towards healing the body. Empaths are visionary beings capable of discerning hidden messages in scenarios and objects that other people would perceive as ordinary. They see beyond the naked eye and perceive things with extraordinary insight. They draw deeper meaning from events and occurrences by understanding their symbolic meanings. And most importantly, they dissect the human body emotionally to get a bird's view of situations. This visionary ability of empaths is based on their ability to understand the events, situations, and bodies in more than just one dimension: the physical one. They peel the layers and understand the sensations and auras surrounding our bodies and other objects and interpret the hidden messages, emotions and feelings. This gift of discernment enables empaths to react to situations based on priorities; a hallmark of a visionary being. The emotional swells that confound compassionate empaths compel them to go out of their way to help others at all costs is based on vision. The distresses signals they read from others drive them to act in order to avert any danger. The visionary ability of empaths works in tandem with their survival intuition or gut feeling. Empaths have visions of others' sufferings and emotional issues by tapping into their auras. In some cases, such premonitions come in the form of dreams. It is a precognitive capability that allows empaths to operate in the realms of spirituality and the physical world. When empaths project other people's feelings, emotions, and even disease symptoms, it is a manifestation of how they envisioned the events, ailment, pain, or emotions.

The visionary ability of empaths also highlights their creativity. Emotions, feelings, pains, or fear are intangible things. Empaths discern them from the energies of others. Some of these emotions and feelings are hidden. However, empaths have the ability to process them into tangible things by projecting them on their bodies. Transforming energy vibrations from another person's ailment into visible symptoms that project on your body requires unnatural creativity. Nurturing this creative ability can turn empaths into leading professionals in different fields including medicine. Connecting with objects and people emotionally and reading their auras require an unparalleled level of emotional alertness and sensitivity. It is an ability that distinguishes empaths from other people driven by sympathy. Empaths are emotional sinkholes. They capture and take in emotions of different kinds. Their senses are highly tuned and can detect minute vibrations of auras that characterize their surroundings. When they establish a telepathic connection with their environments and objects, they are able to suck in fear, anger, and happiness. They can even lay bare deepest and darkest secrets hidden by stacks of emotions. Some empaths are known to have the ability to detect lies. The ability to unravel and bring to the fore someone's hidden emotions and lies has endeared them to different professions such as psychology and law enforcement.

Such sensitivity also comes with a big heart. They readily relieve the pains of others even when it may pose a psychological and physical danger to them. They are not worried about their well-being. Rather, they are moved by the plight of others. Once they receive negative emotions from others, empaths especially those who are compassionately and emotionally inclined will go the extra mile to alleviate the problem. Empaths may set aside their own problems and refocus their energies on other people's issues.

They shelve their emotions and let other individual's feelings and needs to take precedence in their lives. Empaths' sensitivity and ability to soak in emotions of different kinds has spiritual connotations. They are spiritually open to all kinds of people and rarely set emotional boundaries. It is an ability that is both a weakness and a strength. As a strong point, it enables empaths to walk in the shoes of others. However, their big-hearted and sensitivity nature make them prime targets of energy vampires. These vampires will drain them emotionally by playing the victim or resorting to melodrama to snare empaths. Once they clutch onto their victims, these vampires physically and emotionally drain them to satisfy their narcissistic desires.

Exceptional Insights of Empaths

To experience the level of empathy that empaths are known is to operate in a special realm that borders divinity. Being an empathy is a special experience that interweaves both natural and unnatural worlds. Empaths have exceptional insights on issues and experiences, past and present, that bare traces of spirituality. That they are still considered as spiritual beings or mediums in today's science and technology- driven world shows how exceptional their abilities are. With advanced technologies capable of mind-reading, technical disease diagnosis and treatment, and predictions of weather events and patterns, empaths' continued coexistence with modernization is a testament to their unique abilities. They have continued to cement their places in our societies through their intriguing perception and discerning of issues, events, and emotions in ways that no modern machine can match.

Even before the emergence of these technologies, ancient kingdoms relied on the telepathic connections empaths had with Mother Nature to predict the seasons and weather patterns. Before Christianity became a widely practiced religion, many communities the world over-relied on spiritual empaths to anchor their spiritual lives. Mind and body healing practiced across many healthcare settings in the world borrows heavily from empathy; harnessing the power of telepathic connections and energies to heal both the both and mind.

Even today, spiritual empaths are revered across the globe, not only by communities that are considered untouched by civilization; they are also common in civilized societies. They are the psychics and mediums of these civilized communities that many people, celebrities, leaders and ordinary citizens alike, troop to in their thousands in a quest for spiritual and divine answers. Psychic and medium are a multibillion dollar industry that is popular in civilized countries including the United States and the United Kingdom. In the U.S., in particular, the industry's success is fueled by the many celebrities who frequently seek help from psychics and mediums. They have turned the psychics and mediums into rich celebrities with television programs and huge followings on social medium platforms such as Facebook, Twitter, and YouTube.

One of the exceptional insights that empaths have is emotional awareness. Empaths have unmatched emotional insight due to their intuitive and effective listening abilities. As highly sensitive beings, empaths have a personal understanding of different types of emotions as they are able to internalize all emotions they pick from their environment. They have an intimate and intricate understanding of what it feels like to be angry, sad, happy, or fearful. They have firsthand experience of what it feels like to be hopeless and hopeful.

Their lives are marked by having both sides of the same coin almost on a daily basis because they can take both extremes of human emotions. They have experienced the emotional undercurrents associated with anxiety, betrayal, and victory. As emotional sponges, their perception and sucking of emotions border divinity.

Empaths own the emotions that they receive from the objects they are attuned to. These emotions become personalized and manifest through their bodies or actions. When a floral empath is moved to tears or horrified by the sight of a cut tree, it is because they perceive the pain the tree felt as if it were his or her own. The same applies to animal empaths; the experiences of the animal becomes ingrained into the core of their being. When an emotional empath perceives an aura laden with anxiety from an individual, they become restless. Butterflies start flying in their stomachs even though, in reality, they have no issue to be anxious about. A sacred stone or monuments of sufferings in a forgone era may sadden geomantic empath. A sudden upwelling of emotions may overwhelm when they touch a broken down slave ship or visit a scene of gruesome murder unknowingly. They are moved not because they had information beforehand are now becoming sentient; their emotions are manifestations of the traces of emotions left behind that they picked up.

Empaths have such exceptional emotional insights because they listen with their bodies and soul. They listen with their hearts. They translate auditory stimuli into sensations that they interpret to discern underlying emotions. Empaths also use their intuition to read non-verbal messages. They use their intuition to read and understand the non-visual messages from other people. Their heightened enables them to be alert to changes in energies around people. Therefore, they are emotionally alert.

357

Moreover, they are emotional magnates because of their emotional vulnerability and receptiveness. People who are emotionally burdened find it easier to connect with empaths because they have a connection.

Empaths also have exceptional insights into the human condition. From suffering to happiness and dejection, empaths have the ability to perceive it all without necessarily going the situations personally.

As individuals who are highly tuned to their senses and ability to take in a seemingly endless stream of emotions, empaths are rich reservoirs of human experiences and their corresponding emotions. They have insights on what it feels like to lose a job, a family, or a home. They also understand the experience of winning a lottery. Their minds oscillate between different experiences of human conditions. Empaths have experienced physical pains as a result of a medical condition or accident without getting involved in any of these activities in person. Ideally, they experience these events that mark the human condition by proxy. They are more like bystanders who are not necessarily engaged in these actions but witness them firsthand. Empaths are witnesses to these events that define humanity. However, they are different kinds of eyewitnesses. They participate in these activities and events with their minds and in a different realm. They feel pain without any physical harm. They are saddened by losing a job even though they never really lost any job. It is this ability to project other people's experiences and superimpose on their own bodies that give them exceptional insight into human experiences.

However, such capabilities are not confined to current events. Empaths are capable of relaying to the rest of us experiences of people in the past. They can relay the human experiences of the dead by reading and interpreting their traces of emotions.

Mediums and psychics have been known to use their abilities to relay emotions and messages from the dead. Similarly, geomantic empaths have the ability to relay the experiences of people in the past, including those who lived during ancient times by reconnecting with their emotions. These are powerful insights with divine profoundness and spiritual implications. Their use and importance transcend spiritual and cultural inclinations. Such insights have been used for centuries for spiritual and cultural purposes. In today's world, such insight has been popularized by both widespread usage and propagation through popular media such as television and films. Empaths' great understanding of human experiences also stems from their own personal afflictions. Bottling in other people's emotions calls for a disadvantageous emotional vulnerability. Empaths are afflicted by the physically and emotionally draining nature of their abilities. They experience a myriad of emotions that are reflective of human experiences. However, a greater proportion of their personal insight into human experience stems from emotional abuse and violation, especially by psychological manipulators. Empaths readily give due to their big-hearts. They are nurturers who are driven by the need to help others. It is these qualities that manipulators take advantage of. Without training and a mastery of their skills and talents, empaths may fall victim to ill-intentioned individuals. They may be betrayed, abused and violated. They may also experience moments of victory and happiness. The heart of an empath is a mixed bag of emotions as a result of personal experiences. Personal experiences reinforce their understanding and insight into life in general. Empaths have the inside scoop on life and the human condition from two different perspectives: theirs and others'.

However, their exceptional insight into the life and the human condition is not confined to humans only. In a world where humans are increasingly becoming insensitive, their environment, floral, animal, and geomantic empathies are the closest we can ever be to having a spiritual, divine, and physical understanding of the plight of our ecosystems. This is because empaths have a greater connection to our ecosystems and nature. They are moved by their destruction, which has increased over the past decades. Empaths can internalize the issues and experiences of nature at a deeper level than ordinary people.

When combined with their emotional connection with humans, it can provide a wholesome understanding of nature. A deep and wholesome approach to nature preservation and care can only stem from such an exceptional insight into their plight and importance to humanity.

One of the most dumbfounding abilities of empaths is a telepathic or psychic connection. Empaths attune to people and objects in an inexplicable manner. Some may find the ability of a stranger to read their emotions and unfurl their hidden intentions and feelings overwhelmingly bizarre. Others may even doubt the existence of such abilities, while others may view it with skepticism. However, spiritually inclined individuals may perceive it as a manifestation of divine powers. All these reactions would be justified because the connection that characterizes empathy is not physical. It can only be felt primarily by one party, but in cases of spiritual healing, both the healer and patient can experience it. For many religious and atheists alike, an encounter with an empath may the closest they have will ever come to perceiving a paranormal activity or a manifestation of spirituality and divinity.

Therefore, it is safe to say that empaths have exceptional insights on divinity and spirituality. This insight comes in two folds. First, the big heart that characterizes an empath can only be paralleled to spirituality and divinity. Their ability to accommodate both extremes of emotions and everything in between is uncommon among any species of living things and especially among beings of higher brain functioning. Their instinct and intuition that urge them on whenever they detect negative auras are exceptional and unique to only human beings with such talents. Their selflessness, even in the face of personal challenges, is born out of a high sense of divinity and spirituality. Empaths act in spite of their limitations and danger to their well-being.

Their high levels of emotional sensitivity and vulnerability and compassion point to divine providence. Empaths set a higher standard of purpose for themselves that many people would find too burdensome. The lengths empaths can go in service to others is not mundane; it extraordinary and spiritually inclined.

Secondly, the telepathic and psychic connections that empaths develop with others and their surroundings have spiritual and divine inferences. Reading and interpreting someone's emotions, feelings, and thoughts without prior information by connecting to their auras is a divine and spiritual experience. They understand how such a higher realm works. They do not rely on physical contact. It is a mind-to-mind understanding that defies common practice and belief. How else would one explain how a geomantic empathy can connect with people long gone by touching an artifact they left? Without invoking divine powers, how would a human being feel the pain of plants or animals?

To contextualize the divinity and spirituality of the whole concept of empathy, one only needs to observe the popularity of spiritual healers, psychics, and mediums.

361

Spiritual empaths have the ability to experience a spiritual awakening when they connect with spiritual objects. Shuttling messages back and forth between the physical and spiritual worlds calls for spiritual connection. With massive pervasion of advanced technologies that would have successfully challenged the existence of such divine and spiritual experiences, it is no wonder that empathy has continued to thrive. Science, trusted for its use of evidence to prove or disapprove phenomena, is increasingly aggregating towards recognizing the power of telepathic and psychic connections as that occurs in higher realms. Empaths also have a heightened insight into the concept of emotional tolerance. Unlike other ordinary beings, empaths are accommodative of varied emotions. This is the trademark of being an empath. No emotion too extreme for an empath. They understand what it means to walk with the burden of carrying someone's secrets and feelings. Even when such emotions may overshadow theirs, they will tolerate them. In some cases, they may become drained emotionally and physically. They may become confused and disoriented by discerning people's inner thoughts. The danger of being manipulated does not deter them from being accommodative emotionally. It is their emotional tolerance that spurs compassionate empaths to act. Problems that come with such intolerance like emotional disorientation can be mitigated by engaging in emotional awareness and control exercises such as meditation.

In a world constantly battling with emotional intolerance manifesting in the form of civil wars and confrontations, empaths' have the ability to offer a refreshing perspective into the issue. Their unrivaled insight into human emotions can help in putting human actions into perspective. They can crystallize issues and situations because they are able to connect with others beyond the physical world.

While not all humans are capable of becoming emotional sinkholes, the emotional tolerance of empaths can be used as models to emulate. While it is easy to view empaths are super-humans, their seemingly tough emotional exterior can be misleading. Underneath this emotional shield that they put up, empaths battle with emotional issues beyond the visible emotional exhaustion. Like all humans, they have emotions that can be hurt. Even though they may battle with the problem of defining and distinguishing their emotions from those of others, they have their own insecurities.

However, they have mastered the art of masking their emotions. Empaths are introverts who prefer solitude and silence that comes with it. Alone time is therapeutic and helps them to replenish their energies. Empaths easily deal with their emotional overload by spending time in secluded places. If they were interacting with other people, they prefer small groups. Meeting in quiet places gives them a sense of inner peace.

However, these tendencies to seek solace in solitude should not be misconstrued to mean that empaths do not others around them. Like humans, they need encouragement and constructive relationships that build them. When they absorb positive energy, empaths are known to thrive both emotionally and materially. Therefore, creating a positive environment can help in harnessing their abilities to the fullest. The onus is also on empaths to cultivate a healthy emotional environment around them. Empaths should surround themselves with like-minded individuals capable of stabilizing them emotionally. Sometimes all an empath needs to unburden themselves from emotional overload is a walk in a serene nature trail.

Chapter 8: Top Traits of Empaths

By now, you have gotten a good sense of what being an empath is like. You have seen what characterizes them, and most importantly, what does characterize them. As such, being an empath is not just a catch phrase that you can use to refer to a generally nice person. It is an attitude that permeates every aspect of an empath's lifestyle.

That is why we now turn out attention to the traits that define an empath. Just like the signs in chapter two, these traits are what make a true empath stand out from any other type of person out there.

Moreover, being an empath is a lifestyle that you embrace at all times; it isn't just something which you can turn on and off to suit the occasion. So, let's take a look at the fundamental traits of an empath.

They have a high level of sensitivity

To say that empaths are sensitive is an understatement. Indeed, empaths have such a high level of sensitivity that they instinctively pick up on what others are feeling. It almost seems as if empaths can read the minds of others. Earlier, we highlighted how empaths have a low tolerance level for violence on television and in film. While graphic depictions or real-life violence certainly upset empaths, it gets a lot worse for them when they are faced with the real deal.

For instance, social workers who have a high degree of empathy may find it hard to keep their emotions in check while dealing with folks in distress. Nevertheless, there is no one more qualified than an empath for this type of work.

In fact, empaths are great people to have in any kind of field. Yet, they shine in a good where they come into contact with people. Empaths make great doctors, teachers, nurses, firefighters, police officers, military, and salespeople, among others.

On the flipside, empaths should take great care to get the emotional support they need in order to cope with the situations they face on a daily basis. Often, having someone to talk to is a great way of relieving the burden that comes with helping others on a consistent basis.

Perhaps the most important thing that empaths need to keep in mind is that they cannot be of much help if they can't focus on helping others. Many times, it is easy to get caught up in others' feelings. But that doesn't mean that you need to carry them around as your own. Doing that can make life incredibly hard to deal with. So, it is important to know when you need to drop that load and when you need to help others bear their own burden.

They are emotion absorbers

This particular trait is basically a no-brainer when it comes to empaths. Now, absorbing emotions go back to the previous point about taking on someone else's emotional burden. Often, empaths feel that they need to take the load off others' shoulders in order to help them cope with their circumstances. Still, empaths are the perfect remedy that allows people to relieve their emotional distress. Given the fact that empaths make great listeners, folks under stress can find the perfect listener in an empath. As such, an empath can help anyone in need to find comfort and solace. However, the true role of an empath is to help others find their way of dealing with their emotions. In that sense, an empath can not only lend a friendly ear and a shoulder to lean on, but also a friendly word of advice and comfort. That is why most often empaths need to hang back and listen. Once a person is ready for advice, they will ask for it. That is when an empath can provide a comforting but also an impartial perspective on what's going on in the other person's life. In essence, an empath ought to be friendly and caring but not get directly involved in trying to solve the other person's issues.

While that may be tempting for an empath who is very practical and process oriented, it may lead the other party feeling like they are being scolded. As an empath, you will naturally feel compelled to help others. So, the best way to help others is to let them vent their feelings and offer words of encouragement as needed. Then, when your interlocutor is ready for your words of wisdom, you can help them go down the road that will lead them to gain a deeper understanding of their own feelings and emotions.

They are introverted

Introverts are often confused with shy and withdrawn individuals. The fact of the matter is that an introvert is perfectly capable of being sociable and outgoing. The difference is that an introvert is generally reflexive and thoughtful. This leads them to have a deeper understanding of their own emotions. Introverts also have a better understanding with regard to the source of their feelings. As a result, empaths who are deeply introverted need time along to process their emotions and sort out their feelings. Don't be surprised if going for a walk or a run is exactly what you need to get your head in order. Also, don't be feel bad if you would rather stay home and chill rather go out and paint the town.

Also, empaths can be highly extroverted. For empaths who show signs of extroversion, they can become really fun people to hang around. However, the reason why introversion is much more common than extroversion in empaths lies in the fact that extroverts tend to depend much more on emotional support than introverts.

What this means is that extroverts need to be constantly surrounded by people in order to help them deal with their own feelings. In fact, don't be surprised in a highly extroverted individual seeks the counsel and support of an introverted empath when in times of emotional distress. If you resonate with the description of an introvert, then make as much time as you can for quiet thought and reflection. Often, taking time out and looking back at the way things have gone down will help you gain a deeper perspective on your feelings and those of others. Moreover, introverted empaths are known to take that quiet time to reflect on the feelings of others. This reflection time allows an empath to figure out ways to help others while getting a handle on their own feelings. Lastly, don't be afraid to spend time alone. While we all seek companionship, being able to sit quietly on your own will help you deflect a lot of the feelings that you have accumulated over time. Nevertheless, if you need some social contact, then by all means get out there and hang out with your favorite people. Often, the vibe that comes off from other folks can certainly create a refreshing feedback loop.

They are intuitive

If there is one thing empaths are known for is being intuitive. By "intuitive" we mean that empaths are able to pick up on what others are feeling without them actually saying anything. This is a trait allows empaths to get a quick grasp of what others are feeling without having to dig too deep. In fact, intuition is a trait that empaths aren't necessarily born with but do develop it over time. Naturally, it takes practice to hone such skills.

But what makes empaths so adept at developing their intuition is their ability to pick up on non-verbal clues that come from their interlocutors. So, the next time you are dealing with someone, try to pick up on what they are saying with their facial gestures, with their eyes, their body or their hands rather than focusing solely on their words. As you become more and more intuitive, you will know exactly what to do even before your interlocutor has gotten around to saying what they need from you.

They are loners

We mean this in a good way. This specific trait ties into empaths being introverted. While this doesn't mean that all empaths rather spend time on their own, empaths generally like spending time on their own, away from what can be considered to be emotional overload.

Look at it this way: empaths cannot simply turn off their empathetic nature. So, spending time away from people is a means of recovery from what can be an overwhelming experience at times. The more empaths deal with people on a consistent basis, the more time they need to recover from such interactions.

So, don't be surprised if you find yourself needing some time away from the hustle and bustle of your daily life. Often, this will be your way of recharging energies for the next phase in your day to day life.

They are intense

Empaths tend to have very intense personal relationships. When an empath in engaged in a romantic relationship, they can get pretty intense. The reason for this is that empaths learn to anticipate their partner's needs and reactions. At some point, an empath will use their intuition to determine what their partner needs and when they need it. In terms of friendships, empaths become the go-to friend when things get rough. That type of emotional connection leads to very close relationships. Often, the recipient of an empath's attention may feel "lost" when they are not with their trusted friend.

They are affected by energy vampires

Energy vampires are the people who thrive on literally sucking the life out of others. They drain the people around them of their emotional energy. These vampires generally come in the form of troublesome folks who demand a great deal of attention. Also, they tend to be highly selfish and demand more and more of other people's time and energy. When an empath gets sucked into a relationship with an energy vampire, empaths tend to end up exhausted after interacting with them. In these cases, empaths need to get away from these folks. The sooner an empath is able to identify an energy vampire, the sooner they need to get away. Of course, there are times when energy vampires are in need of help, so it pretty much goes against an empath's nature to move away from a person in distress.

But the fact of the matter is that if an empath decided to go along with an energy vampire's spiel, the empath had better be ready for a long and drawn out battle.

They are nature lovers

Earlier, we mentioned that empaths have a soft spot for children and animals. The same can be said about nature. Empaths are concerned with protecting the environment and nature around them. They are always focused on finding ways to help Mother Earth feel better. However, an empaths connection to nature goes deeper than a genuine concern with ensuring sustainability. Empaths have an intuitive connection with the natural world surrounding them. As an empath, you find a calming and soothing effect while being in natural surroundings. Moreover, you find that there in an unspoken connection between you and all things green. Empaths often make great gardeners. Since they are in tune with Mother Earth, plant life seems to respond to them quite well. So, if you are an empath, your roses might just look better than everyone else's.

They have finely tuned senses

Perception is one of the classic traits of empaths. Often, empaths are called "lie detectors" because they can quickly pick up on someone who is being insincere. This is generally derived from their highly tuned sense toward other people's needs.

As such, they can see through others when they are attempting to be something they are not. By the same token, empaths are able to detect sincerity from others. They are able to see when someone is in genuine need. However, this sense is not something that empaths are born with. As a matter of fact, it might be getting burned a few times by ill-meaning folks before these senses can be honed it all the way. Once an empath has calibrated their senses, they are able to avoid being taken advantage of. Other times, an empath's intuitive nature allows them to sense when something isn't quite right even if they can't pinpoint what it is. Ultimately, empaths cut their teeth as a result of the time spent interacting with others. They recognize when something is off and act on it. That is how they can become so intuitive when it comes to the needs of others.

They are generous

A common trait of empaths is generosity. This is especially true when they have been through hardships themselves. You can tell what an empath has been through by the types of causes they defend. While they will try to champion any and all causes, the ones that they most firmly believe in are the ones that truly resonate with their life experience. For instance, if an empath has experience poverty, they will champion causes and organizations which look to feed the hungry and provide support to homeless people. Sure, they will support any cause that means to help anyone in need, but such causes will always be high on their radar. Additionally, don't be surprised if to see empaths rallying others to support causes they believe in.

Empaths are always out there creating awareness for a specific cause or raising funds to support people. They are usually active on college campuses, churches and other social organizations.

They mirror the pain of others

This is another point we touched on earlier. Empaths are known to actually feel physical discomfort when they interact with someone who is in physical distress. As an empath, if you find yourself mirror someone else's pain, you might want to take a step back. While we don't mean to bail on someone in need, it is important for you to regroup. Otherwise, it might be very difficult for you to help someone else if you find yourself upset or in discomfort. One of the best ways to help with mirroring others' pain is to remind yourself that you need to be in the best shape you can be or else it will be very difficult for you to be of any help. While it might sound selfish to take care of yourself even when someone is in clear need of your attention, it is important to also be in tune with your own needs.

They are healers

Empaths are known to have both a soothing and healing effect on others. For instance, doctors and nurses who are empaths have an immediate calming effect on patients. This helps patients relax on focus on their treatments.

Often, these healers are the kind of doctors and nurses that patients claim to have "supernatural healing powers". But, you don't have to be a doctor or nurse to have this effect on someone. You can have a healing effect on your family and friends due to one simple reason: others know you care. Since they know you actually care about them, this predisposes their minds to heal. As such, any course of treatment will fare much better.

They tend to be outspoken

Even though most empaths are introverted (but not shy) they do tend to be outspoken for the causes they truly believe in. Moreover, they will stand up against injustice and pointless suffering. These are the folks who are not afraid to stand up and protest against issues that are causing harm. A lot of empaths become environmentalists, human rights activists and champions for organizations. Empaths are also fundraisers and organizers. Also, empaths try to change the world from their own corner of it. If they believe that they are contributing, in any way, to harming people or the environment, they will immediately change their behavior in order to avoid harm. A great example of this can be seen in folks who become vegetarian in order to protest against animal cruelty.

They tend to have health issues

Most health issues in empaths aren't necessarily related to physical causes but to emotional ones.

As such, empaths will have psycho-somatic effects when they are having a hard time processing their emotions. This ties back to mirroring the pain of others. When an empath suddenly becomes overwhelmed, they may tend to have an adverse physical reaction to the onslaught of emotion. If you are an empath and you feel such discomfort when you are overwhelmed, it is vital that you have an escape valve for those emotions. Exercise often helps as do hobbies and social activities. Whatever the name of your game is, you must have an outlet for your emotions. Otherwise, you may find yourself suffering from long-term health issues.

They are laidback and easygoing

Since empaths can pick up on the feelings and needs of others, they tend to be very easy to get along with. Also, the fact that empaths put others ahead of themselves means that they are always aiming to please others. This is why empaths make such good friends and co-workers. The dark side of this trait is that empaths may try to become people pleasers. When this happens, empaths may find themselves emotionally shattered when they see that they are incapable of pleasing everyone. Moreover, they may attempt to live up to others' standards and expectations thereby creating unnecessary emotional distress. This is why empaths must learn that it is impossible to please everyone and that there must be a balance between the needs of others and the needs of the empath. When an empath strikes this balance, dealing with others becomes a lot easier.

They tend to be naïve

Lastly, empaths tend to be naïve. This is due to their good nature. Since empaths are loath to harm others, they tend to believe that others also have good intentions. While this is generally true, there are a few people out there who have a hidden agenda. As such, good-natured empaths may get burned quite a few times before "learning their lesson".

So, it is important for empaths to take these lumps and hone their senses. But, they must also take care to ground themselves and avoid becoming bitter and resentful. If empaths allow the misdeeds of others to get the better of them, they will suffer a great deal of emotional pain simply because they will leave in fear of being hurt again. The traits that we have outlined in this chapter are the ones that define the classic nature of an empath. While there are all sorts of nuances out there, it is important for you, as an empath, to find a balance at all times. That way, you can save yourself a great deal of pain and suffering while staying on top of your game. In that sense, you will be able to help others whenever you are able to do so.

Conclusion

It is my pleasure and greatest hope that you have read the entire book. It is also my hope that you have found this book to be highly informative and educative, especially when it's being reflected on the day to day feelings. The book, "Empath Healing" talks much on several ways in which the contributions of empaths can actually be realized. With the correct introduction and definition from previous chapters, I do believe that you have actually gained a lot and this knowledge will help you in many ways.

This book might have many roles in our daily lives, as has been seen in many chapters, but the main objective here is to help us understand how best we can live as empaths and what we should do. It also cautions us when to stop giving our helping hand since we might end up being vulnerable, exhausted and degenerated. It will now be my greatest pleasure if you take your precious time to look at the chapters dealing with character traits of empathy. Another main objective of this book is to help you understand when and how you can be easily manipulated since empaths are just a soft spot for manipulators. It's because of this need that we have actually come up with this book so as to be in good condition to fight for your rights and the rights of others, especially if you are an empath.

Even though this book might have many objectives, but it is better to note that only objectives dealing with how to emotionally help people within the society should top the list. It is my humble advice that you will have your time in reading these chapters that have stinging issues such as the types of empathy and how they react or rather respond to the people around them.

The book, Empath Healing, is a gate through which you need to pass so as to understand how easily you can tell if at all, you are an empath or not. It has clearly shown chapters dealing or concentrating on different attributes or rather different ways on how to tell if someone is really an empath. It is with much hope that you will consider this too. The book will also help you to understand the different energies of empaths and how these energies can be used effectively to help each one within the society.

This book is, therefore, initiating you into the world of self-protection. This is because, within this book, you will come across some important chapters that concentrate much on the different ways of handling manipulative people. Manipulators have the tendency to take advantage of the empaths causing their lives more vulnerable and emotionally painful. This kind of condition results in exhaustion and drainage of empaths. It is now my humble request that you use this book to regain back your happiness if, at all, you are empathetic. This happiness leads to a perfect life after all. Who doesn't want a perfect life? I guess you do care too, and for you to achieve this, then you should use this book as your daily and future reference. This implies that you will have to dwell much on areas touching issues like practical exercises performed by empaths, how to prevent manipulators from taking advantage of you, and much more.

I know reading this book can be easier; it is its application and implementation that might bring some sorts of headaches. It is now my wish that you try as hard as possible to have a look at this book once more since it contains several ways to avoid being extremely endangered as an empath. This will help you to live a life free from harm and pains. Think of a life that empaths exist without pain.

Think of a life that manipulators can actually fail to take advantage of you if you are an empath.

Think of a situation that being an empath will not lead to distress situations. Think about how happy life will be in the absence of all those. It is, therefore, my urge that you read this book so as to help yourself with skills that will eventually help you to avoid stress and achieve this kind of happiness. Without this book, then you are somehow doomed.

All in all, I hope you have actually appreciated this book as it has been helpful. It is my humble request that you may make reviews on other sites. Your remarks and reviews will be highly honored.

Anger Management

A Step-by-Step Guide to Take Control of Your Emotions in Every Situation and Grow Your Self-Help

By: Adam Goleman

Introduction

Anger is a strong feeling of annoyance, displeasure, or hostility towards someone or something. Anger usually occurs as a natural response to feeling attacked, frustrated, or even being humiliated. It is human nature to get angry. The fury, therefore, is not a bad feeling per se because, at times, it can prove to be very useful. How is this even possible? Anger can open one's mind and help them identify their problems which could drive one to get motivated to make a change and help in molding their lives.

When is anger a problem? Anger, as we have just seen, is normal in life. The problem only comes in when one cannot manage their anger, and it causes harm to people around them or even themselves. How does one notice when their anger is becoming harmful? When one starts expressing anger through unhelpful or destructive behavior, or even when one's mental and physical health starts deteriorating. That's when one knows that the situation is getting out of hand. It is the way a person behaves that determines whether or not they have problems with their anger. If the way they act affects their life or relationships, then there is a problem, and they should think about getting some support or treatment.

What is unhelpful angry behavior? Anger may be familiar to everyone, but people usually express their rage in entirely different ways. How one behaves when they are angry depends on how much control they have over their feelings. People who have less control over their emotions tend to have some unhelpful angry behaviors.

These are behaviors that cause damage to themselves or even damage to people or things around them. They include:

Noticeable aggression and viciousness

This is where one aims his or her anger towards individuals or things nearby them. Some of the actions here may consist of yelling at people, being aggressive to people, banging doors, hitting or tossing things, or being orally abusive. These kinds of actions can be very worrisome and unsafe for people around, particularly children. They can cause spartan consequences similar to the loss of a career or even hurting a precious one or just essentially anyone around.

Inward aggression

This is where one directs their anger towards themselves. Some of the behaviors here may include telling oneself that they hate themselves, denying themselves, or even cutting themselves off the world.

Non-violent or passive aggression

In this case, one does not direct their anger anywhere; rather they stick with the feeling in them. Some of the behaviors here may include ignoring people, refusing to speak to people, refusing to do tasks, or even deliberately doing chores poorly or late. These types of behaviors are usually the worst ways to approach such situations.

They may seem less destructive and harmful, but they do not relieve one of the heavy burdens that are causing them to be angry.

Preparation

Weigh your options - In life, many things may be out of one's control. These things vary from the weather, the past, other people, intrusive thoughts, physical sensations, and one's own emotions. Despite all these, the power to choose is always disposable to any human. Even though one might not be able to control the weather, one can decide whether or not to wear heavy clothing. One can also choose how to respond to other people. The first step, therefore, in dealing with anger is to recognize a choice.

Thank you for having this book.

Chapter 1: Understand the signs of your anger

Role of Anger

Getting angry usually relays an important message meant for good, but others may feel offended. Often, we get angry in an effort to be heard only to destroy relationships in the process. In intelligent communication, any form of aggression corrodes your true intent. Communicating with passive aggression is worse as opposed to popular belief. Passive aggression may seem innocent from your words, but they are vicious. Most people opt for passive aggression, but it breaks connections. Therefore, you should consider a better strategy for a better understanding of people. Lately, people are taking to Twitter more and more for those indirect jabs.

Immediate Anger Expression Is Exceptional

Often, we find ourselves mad but can't remember how those feelings started. That is why it is advisable to express your feelings as they come; it helps the negativity go away faster. Extinguish the fire immediately you see smoke; waiting for the inferno doesn't do you any good. Same for your feelings—handle them as they emerge.

Reasons for You to Express Emotions Immediately

They become more intense when you wait. Contemplating your emotions magnifies their intensity. Getting rid of these emotions immediately saves you from more stress. It's easier to handle things before they blow up. People give advice on waiting when you're angry so that you don't regret it later. You regret actions and not feelings. Never be afraid to express what you feel. There is a better understanding. Sharing your feelings immediately removes ambiguity over what made you mad or who did what. It just happened. Bottling up your emotions finds you being set off by minor issues. Confusion over the source of the sudden emotions only creates new conflict.

It's an opportunity for clarification in case of a misunderstanding. Most times, being angry with someone emanates from a misunderstanding. You may have interpreted them the wrong way. A simple explanation over the issue clears out the air. It's unlikely to be fixed unless something is said. The receiving party and everyone else around you do not mind readers. They could never know how you feel unless you tell them. They may be part of the solution; there is no point in holding back. You don't have to fake it. It's draining to hide your emotions with your actions. Being true to yourself is important for both your emotional health and a healthy state of mind.

You don't have to bottle your emotions. Avoiding your emotions doesn't make them disappear. On the contrary, stuffed-up emotions have been linked to several physiological ailments. They include depression, asthma, anger, high blood pressure, and infections.

You are more comfortable with your feelings. When you are aware of your emotions and are able to express them, you become comfortable enough to obtain information crucial in decision making. Your feelings change. The best way to get rid of negative emotions is to get over them. You only get over them by recognizing them and expressing them in a healthy way. Psychologists agree that talking your heart out completely although angry manifests positive feelings. I mean you always feel better if you talk to a friend. You create stronger bonds. People avoid their emotions in fear of being rejected. Ironically, being honest and vulnerable provide a strong base for good relationships. You know the other person better with them expressing themselves. You also get to know how your actions affect the other. Your family and friends start doing the same. People close to you follow your lead if you express your feelings freely. With the same benefits, they become emotionally healthier. This makes you closer to them.

Chapter 2: How anger affects relationships

Expressing Your Anger While Conserving Relationships

In the event you are angry, neither passive aggression nor the extreme direct approach is advised. They destroy your relationships. Instead, follow the guides below:

Become self-aware

Never be too quick to express your frustration. Instead, take a minute for cooler heads to prevail. When our emotions are running high, we are never thinking straight. Be conscious of what's really going on for more effective communication. Take a walk, exercise, meditate or pray for you to regain your composure for a better perspective on the whole situation.

Understand your emotions

Often, we confuse hurt and sadness with anger, which might be easier to express. Frustration could well be pain, sorrow, or rejection. Pinpoint on the real emotion you feel in order to communicate with honesty, hence more effectively.

Be on the lookout for misplaced blame

Always find the root of your anger. You may just be hungry, going through stuff, exhausted, or lacking sleep. Don't dish it out to the next innocent person that crosses your path. Sometimes, it's easier to assign blame as we find it taxing than to think of the real reason behind our frustrations. However, it only drives people we care about away. Nothing is resolved until the real burning issue is tackled.

Be curious

Curiosity helps us see the bigger picture. In our frustrations, we forget there is the other person's perspective only thinking of yourself. Try moving away from being self-centered and ask why the other person made you mad. It couldn't have been intentional. Confronting them doesn't get you real reasons. Care a little as they might be going through something you can help. Try understanding that the other person doesn't aim to hurt you on purpose. You may even get over your anger so easily with a little understanding.

Be compassionate

Don't be quick to assume the worst of people. Try to understand what they're going through along with their point of view. Always show respect for people's feelings, and understand why they act in a certain way. This opens up for effective communication. With compassion and empathy, your relationships get deeper. Aggressive communication makes people angry and defensive in return. Giving people an opportunity to share their perspective makes them respect yours even more.

Communicate with skill

In effective communication, skills like compassion, curiosity, and compromise go a long way. Don't just stop at sharing your feelings, or you'll be self-centered. Go a step further and ask the other party to share it with you. Show interest and be ready to compromise. Never accuse someone without their side of the story.

How to Deal with Passive-Aggressive People

Call them out

Never give anyone a pass for showing aggression in any way. You might as well ask how they meant with their words. People don't expect to be called out when they are passive-aggressive. Ask more questions to get to the root of what bothers them. A grown-up conversation over how they feel would be one way to show them another way.

Ignore them

Even though the other party is trying to get the point across, you shouldn't be drawn into their hostile attitude. Soon as you engage, you enter the same state of mind, which is unhealthy. You live happier by letting such situations go.

Show forgiveness and a little compassion

Tension and frustration cause one to show aggression either directly or passively. Don't be so hard on such a person; they are already getting it bad. Just set boundaries for your own sake, but forgive them and wish them good vibes.

Invite them to share their own feelings and perspective

Show the other party that there is a better way of handling your aggression. Leading by example works best.

When you express your negative emotions, ask them to do the same. Soon they move away from passive-aggressive tactics that only worsen their situations.

In conclusion, it's okay to be mad and frustrated

The important matter is to express it in a healthy way. Proper expression of your negative emotions can leave you feeling better. Funny enough, it might as well be a misunderstanding needing clarification. It's not healthy to be playing okay but you're not. Bottled emotions can make you sick emotionally and physically, too. You see the benefits as soon as you learn to communicate emotions effectively.

While it is important to express your feelings as they emerge, bear in mind you have relationships to conserve. It's not worth it losing friends because you got mad. Apply communication skills. Don't be self-centered. Inquire and be ready to listen and understand the other person's perspective. As you realize, communicating truly has advantages; your family and friends follow suit and reap the same benefits. It is therefore important to notice people with aggressive communication and show them a better way, or just avoid their interactions.

Chapter 3: "How to" Transforming the energy of anger

Run the Stress Off

Running is a great way of combating stress. It is one of the easiest and beneficial physical exercises anyone can engage in.

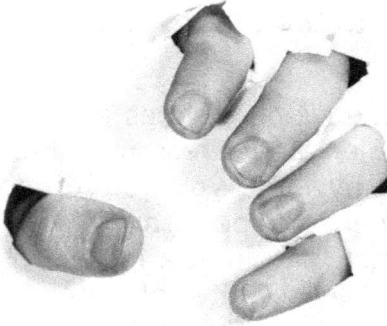

If you are feeling beat down by the rigors of life, take a run down your street or get to the nearest field and run a few laps. There are several benefits that you will experience if you run regularly:

- Running is an aerobic exercise that increases the heart rate and makes you sweat, hence activating chemicals known as endorphins in the body which are responsible for making us feel good, leaving your brain elated and making you happy.

- You will shed calories which will help with lowering your blood pressure and keeping your arteries in good shape.
- Running slows the aging process and reduces bone and muscle loss by building strength and flexibility. It keeps you active and improves your overall health.
- When running, you have all the time to yourself which allows you to process your thoughts. You may use the time to aid you with sorting out some issues that you may be facing or to think through a problem.
- Researchers have found out that people who are regular runners lead a happier, more stress-free life and are generally fitter than those who do not. Your concentration and alertness are also enhanced.

Now, put on those running shoes and hit the road for a healthier, happier, and stress-free life. Running can be done almost anywhere you go, you do not have to worry about where to perform this exercise. It is recommended that you drink a lot of water if you are a runner; drink at least a liter of water an hour to two hours before your run. This helps with hydration of the body and you are unlikely to suffer dehydration. You will not regret your decision as the benefits that will accrue to you are many.

Take a Hike

Hiking is a relaxing walk through a natural surrounding usually at a nature trail, a park, or a forest. Much like running, hiking is a great exercise for stress relief though less vigorous. Hiking combines the benefits of an effective aerobic exercise, natural serene surrounding, and the chance and time to relax and think freely.

The following are ways by which hiking helps the body to deal with stress:

Brain exercising

A hike will afford you the silence and time to think profoundly about things that are important to you. Aerobic exercise coupled with deep thinking will effectively enhance the body's stress management capabilities.

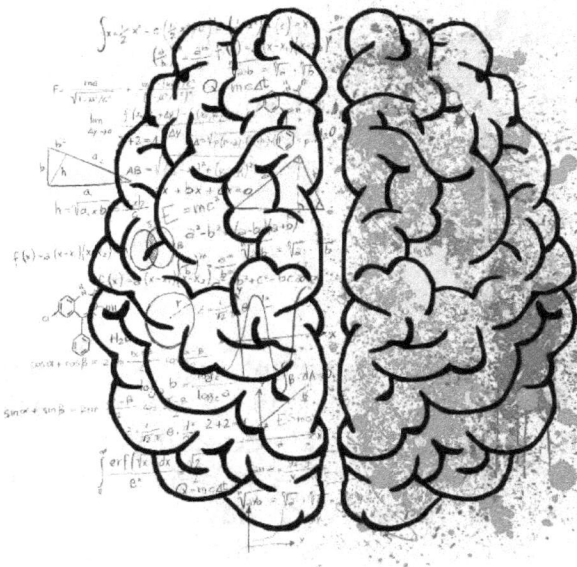

Mental relaxation

Hiking provides the time and opportunity for mind relaxation by getting you up close to nature. Nature has been proven as a catalyst for mental relaxation by giving you the experience and wonders of natural surroundings.

Energizing the Body

Hiking, being an aerobic exercise, invigorates the body and helps with the regulation of stress chemicals. People who hike regularly have higher levels of feel-good hormones like endorphins which reduce stress considerably.

Emotional wellbeing

When you are stressed, you are a prisoner of negative emotions like sadness, anger, nervousness, etc. Hiking will activate positive energy in your body which will, in turn, boost your emotions to make you feel better and happier.

Spiritual nourishment

Being in a natural environment with the wonderful serenity offers the body a chance to get spiritually fulfilled. Your nerves will be calmed and you will get the opportunity for mental clarity and relaxation that you would normally not have every day. Hiking is a great exercise for anger and stress relief and you ought to prepare in advance before you go on a hike. Pack a first aid kit, drinking water, and a phone in case you may be confronted with an accident.

Come on, why don't you start hiking for a change? It may just be the answer to dealing with the stress you have been under lately. So, book an appointment with nature for exercise, mental and spiritual fulfillment, and say goodbye to stress and anger.

Pedal the Stress Away

Do you remember how happy you were riding your bicycle when you were young? I remember my experience and I could give anything to feel the same way again. Exciting, happy, and a sense of unbridled freedom. It was just a great time without a care in the world. Well, you do not have to look back to your childhood with such nostalgia because you can readily bring back those feel-good moments you had on your bicycle to the present to replace all the anger and worries you are facing now!

Don't you want to?

Cycling is another form of aerobic exercise that is great for stress relief, fitness, and general well-being. When you are overwhelmed by life's pressures, simply hop on a bike and start pedaling for stress relief. Being on the bike will take your mind off the problems that are bothering you. Pump some feel-good chemicals into your bloodstream. Pace your heart to leave you feeling refreshed and emotionally elated.

You can cycle after work, on weekends, or your day off or even to work and while doing this, employ the meditative technique of mantra by chanting a positive phrase or word to the rhythm of your pedaling. I assure you that you will be surprised at how fast your mind will be cleared off the negativity and stress that you are facing.

Cycling is not an expensive endeavor; just buy a bicycle and you may start. It is not vigorous if done for leisure or exercise and can be taken up by people of all ages. Cycling will keep you fit and work out your heart for better health and emotional balance.

It helps with the management of chronic conditions like diabetes, cardiovascular problems, and high blood pressure. The healthier and better you feel, the less likely you are to be stressed. Get on your bike and enjoy the stress-relieving benefits you have been missing.

Reading for Stress Relief

Reading is cathartic and is a great reliever of stress for people who are facing everyday pressures and adversity by relaxing the brain and managing the thought process. When you read, your mind travels away from the pressures you are facing. You sink into the story where you will find yourself in faraway worlds. In the duration of your reading, you shall be transported away from your troubles and this helps in balancing your emotional wellbeing.

Reading is a great mental exercise that stimulates brain activity thereby improving mental concentration and alertness. Stress fighting chemicals that give you a happy feeling are released into the brain. An active mind is strong and more likely to cope with daily pressures. You will also fight stress from the motivation and hope you derive from reading biographies and motivational books. Books and other literature are sources of information that enables you to learn more and aid in problem solving. A book will divert your thoughts from the lingering problems or worries that are stressing you out. Set aside a few hours in your day to read and you will experience how fulfilling it can be in your efforts at dealing with stress. When you clear your mind of negativity even for a few hours, you will make huge strides in mental relaxation. With a relaxed mind, you should be able to be more creative and relaxed enabling you to cope with stress.

An active mind also slows down the aging process leaving you feeling younger physically and mentally. A strong healthy body is less prone to stress. If the last time you read was for an exam or for a school assignment, make a hot cup of tea, make yourself comfortable on your favorite seat, and immerse yourself into a book. The benefits for your life and health are great, you need to try it. Get literature that appeals to you, a book, magazine, or newspaper and make it a habit to read regularly for a less-stress life every day.

Be a Positive Thinker

Have you heard of positive thinking? Well, the world works in a very simple way in that whatever you think is what will be manifested in your life. You attract what you think! It may seem simplistic or difficult to accept but take the time to mull it over and you realize that it is true. If you want to get that new job you applied to or want to get promoted, it begins by you want it, then believing that you can get it without having a shred of doubt. Self-belief is a powerful stress reliever. To always be positive and to be ever optimistic. The power of positive thinking is incredible. If you look forward to good things, you will have a happier, less stressful life. Positive thinking is a state where you look forward to favorable outcomes in whatever you do. Positive thinking, therefore, involves actively training your mind to have creative thoughts that transform energy into reality. Avoid dwelling on your failures and concentrate on the successes; use the disappointments as lessons for the future. Studies show that positive thinking leads to a longer and healthier life since you are less prone to stress. You become a positive thinker by identifying the negative aspects of your thinking and avoid them while constantly evaluating your thoughts to make sure you stay on the positive.

Do not be too hard on yourself. Allow yourself joyous moments and take time to have fun. Surround yourself with like-minded people who will help you build the habit of positive thinking. When you are optimistic, you become less critical and are instead more creative and hopeful. An optimistic mindset is able to deal with stress at work more easily and constructively. Positive thinking is a powerful tool for fighting stress and anger. Try it and you are sure of great benefits and happy relaxed life.

Time Management

If you are always late and short of time, then you are most likely leading a stressed and anxious life. There is nothing as stressful as the struggle to always meet a deadline or catch up with something you forgot about. Using the little time we have properly will help you cope with stress. Time management involves methods aimed at using time efficiently to perform all the tasks we have within a given time and involves prioritizing, scheduling, and organizing.

You must assess the tasks on your plate and put them in order of importance and urgency to avoid confusion, conflicts, and unnecessary time pressures.

Plan things in advance to avoid last-minute scrambling in an effort to get something that skipped your mind done. Good time management makes you a more productive person. You will do more within a short time thus gaining more control of your life.

Create a schedule and stick to it. You will have enough free time to engage in fun things that you have been missing. You will have time to go to the movies, play a game, or any other fun activity which serves to boost health and wellbeing. Good time management means that you have enough time for work, family, and friends. These moments with loved ones are the most fulfilling and stress relieving.

It does not take much to be a good time manager. All you need is to start and commit to it. Well managed time leads to a more comfortable and happy life. Benefits of time management for a less stressful life are:

> ➢ Doing more with less time.
> ➢ Getting more free time which allows time to relax.
> ➢ Stress is reduced since you do not worry about pending deadlines etc.
> ➢ Higher productivity since you are fresh mentally, physically and highly motivated.
> ➢ Time management is good because you will be happier, more successful, more productive, and live a fuller and stress-free life. Why don't you start managing your time better and enjoy the benefits?

Get Enough Sleep

Are you sleeping enough? Lack of adequate sleep is a big contributor to the incidences of stress and anger. Getting sufficient sleep is essential in your effort to deal with stress. During sleep, your body gets the chance to rest, to heal, and to be rejuvenated. When you do not get enough sleep, you are left susceptible to stress and other health problems because you are emotionally imbalanced.

Therefore, it is imperative to have a sleeping schedule and follow it so that you condition your body into a routine for sufficient rest. In fact, sleep deficiency is a great source of stress and anger since you are tired, irritable, and have weakened creativity. Between work and your personal affairs, you probably end up not getting enough sleep. It is recommended that you sleep for at least six hours for optimal rest. However, many of us do not meet this target as studies show that most of us sleep for as little as two hours and a maximum of four hours in a 24-hour cycle!

We do not get sufficient sleep because of our poor bedtime habits that end up interfering with our sleep. To sleep better and longer, try the following:

 - ➢ Set a sleeping schedule. You will sleep better if your bedtime is predictable. Your body will adapt and you will rest more.
 - ➢ Do not indulge in a heavy meal during dinner. Have a light meal at least two hours before you retire to bed.
 - ➢ Physical exercise is a great sleep inducer. Work out three to four hours before you sleep.
 - ➢ Do not take caffeinated drinks close to your bedtime. Your last caffeine drink should be averagely six hours or more before you lay down.

➢ Keep away from alcohol four to six hours before your bedtime. It will disrupt your sleep.
➢ Sleep well for emotional balance. You will wake up refreshed, well-rested, and energized. When your body has this balance, it can easily manage or ward off stress.

Listening To Soothing Music

Music is very relaxing and has the ability to change moods positively by acting on our minds to avert stress. It acts quickly, is available, and will relieve you of stress and anger. The calming effect of music has a distinctive relationship to our emotions and is an effective way to cope with stress. Slow classical music is extremely peaceful and has a positive effect on our bodies and minds. This kind of music has its advantages. It slows the heart and pulse rates, reduces the production of stress hormones and blood pressure.

Music engrosses our thoughts to distract us from whatever worries may be lingering in our minds. Most times, when you are stressed and anxious, your mind tends to wander off causing you to think of the things that cause you more anger. However, music acts as a cushion and helps your mind to relax and better concentrate.

For years, music has been proven to treat ailments and restore coherence and balance between your body and mind. Furthermore, research has it that music is therapeutic in the following ways:

➢ Some music compositions can help disabled people by boosting harmonization and communication and improve their life.

403

- The use of headphones when listening to music can lessen anger and stress especially when one is about to go for surgery and after the surgery.
- During extreme pain or post-surgery, music has been known to ease and numb the pain.
- Music is also known to alleviate depression and enhance self-esteem in older people.
- Soothing music has been proven to improve mood and reduce burnout.
- Music is therapeutic especially for cancer patients as it improves the quality of life and reduces emotional trauma.
- Music is food for the soul. The next time you are facing adversity or are feeling down from mental fatigue or some other worries, turn on your favorite music. Enjoy the relaxing and positive vibes that will be provided by the music.

Share your Problems by Talking to Someone

A problem shared is a problem solved or half solved. How insightful this is. Sharing our problems is therapeutic and a quick fix to stress. Putting a lid on your suffering and keeping it to yourself is an emotional burden and is very unhealthy. Many of us are fiercely independent and would want to solve our problems on our own. However, there is a point where you are better off talking to someone about what you are going through.

Pent up emotions and suffering will turn you into a very stressed and imbalanced person. Reach out to someone you trust, a friend or relative, for a listening ear and realize the great positive impact it will have on you.

Talking to someone has the following benefits:

➢ Sharing your problems will help you get rid of bad emotions like worries, anger, etc. You will feel better after since you will have let go of the emotional burden.
➢ Your pain is reduced since you will have someone sharing your problem and empathizing with you.
➢ Solutions to your problems are easier to come by, as you will be readily advised by the listener.
➢ By sharing, you lead a healthier life since you negate the effects of emotional distress caused by pent up emotional turmoil.
➢ You will simply feel better and happier at having talked about whatever is bothering you.

By sharing, we get the load off our chests leaving us emotionally boosted, relaxed, and stronger. It also prevents the situation from deteriorating to a much deeper problem like depression or emotional breakdown. With a relaxed and more stable mental state, you have the clarity and strength to handle your problem, and will easily embark on problem solving for a stress-free life. From now on, if you find yourself in a tight place emotionally and are feeling stressed, seek someone you can share your problem with and enjoy the quick stress relief that comes with it.

You Should Laugh More

The benefits of laughter in coping with stress and for a healthier life are numerous. It is proven that humor is a powerful tool for stress relief. Try and laugh and be cheerful despite the tough times.

Laughter has a way of rubbing off on others, so if you are happy, those around you will follow and you will be surrounded by happiness. A happy life is a stress-free life. Laughter enhances oxygen intake and stimulates the functioning of body organs like the heart, brain, and lungs. Your heart rate is also improved for better blood flow and cardiovascular wellbeing. By laughing your way through life, you benefit from muscle relaxation and tension relief. Your immunity will be enhanced through the release of stress-fighting chemicals in the body. All the pain you are suffering emotionally and even physically is reduced by laughter which triggers the production of the body's natural pain-killing hormones.

A happy person is a magnet, attracting people for improved social life and emotional state. So, when you are downcast, just smile through it; you will feel better. In any case, the difficulties will soon pass and with a positive and happy approach, you will survive it. Laughter subdues toxic stress attracting thoughts, help you forget your worries, and enables you to concentrate and work on the tasks at hand. Be happy and grateful for the good things that you have been blessed with. Think about them when you are stressed. Laugh and smile as you recollect and be assured of a stress-free life.

A good sense of humor is not a panacea but it is sure to improve your outlook at life, your health, and your social standing. A good laugh will do you a lot of good smiles and laugh more; laughter is indeed the best medicine.

Eat Healthy Foods

Food is the fuel and the source of nourishment for the body; an integral part of our general wellbeing and good health. It is important that we eat the right foods and eat well for us to stay healthy. A healthy body is able to fend off the side effects of stress with ease.

Food and stress are uniquely interwoven. When faced with adversity, some people have a sudden craving for food while others will lose their appetite. It is, therefore, necessary that we know the right foods to eat, especially when we are under some sort of stress. When we encounter stress, we crave comfort foods such as fats and sugars. These foods are not healthy and cause harm to us and will cause us more stress.

To stay healthy and manage stress, we have to avoid:

> ➤ Consumption of a lot of fast foods because they are unhealthy and more expensive than cooking for yourself, in the long run.
> ➤ Skipping meals because it is a catalyst for stress. If you miss meals, you are likely to be fatigued and less nourished thus susceptible to stress.
> ➤ Too much caffeinated drinks which interfere with your sleep and deny you adequate rest.
> ➤ Eating the wrong food types. Eat a balanced diet and resist the temptation of eating too much of foods rich in fats and sugars. These foods only lead to weight gain and cardiovascular problems.

A poor diet will leave you with problems of hormonal imbalance and weight problems – either loss or too much gain. You will develop a weak immune system and are likely to be susceptible to illnesses. Unhealthy eating will also lead to an imbalance of the blood sugar which may lead to diabetes. Stress makes your body burn nutrients you consume much faster than normal that is why you should be on a healthy diet. It is wise that you replenish these nutrients to help cope with stress.

Balancing Between Your Life and Work

Continually working without getting a break does not only make you less productive but you easily get bored with your work. You will also become boring to your colleagues. You need to have some time away from your job to have fun and engage in things that excite you and pump your blood. Most adults who are stressed can trace the source to their work because we spend a lot of time on the job.

It is, therefore, important to balance the time we spend working and time for ourselves for a healthier lifestyle. Work-life balance is about dividing your time effectively and adequately between work and your private life. If you let work consume most of your time and neglect or shortchange your personal needs, you will end up stressed. When your personal life is in order, you are less likely to be stressed since you will worry less. Your mind will not be stretched from being divided between what you need to do at work and the personal matters awaiting your attention. Spend time with family and friends. It is relaxing and healthy for you. When was the last time you went cycling or shopping with your children? These mundane activities are the foundation of a well-balanced healthy life devoid of stress. If your private life brings you happiness, you will able to face pressures that come your way. After spending time with your loved ones, you need to set aside personal time for things that are self-gratifying. Go for a massage or run a few laps at the neighborhood field, volunteer your services for a worthy cause, etc. Such acts are great for boosting your emotional wellbeing. If you embrace a healthy work-life balance, you will reap the many benefits. Personal nourishment and care are important for overall health. Balance your private and professional life for a stress-free healthy life where you are happier and revitalized.

Write, Pick Up Your Pen and Paper

Another technique of dealing with stress is writing. It is especially encouraged when one is so stressed or depressed. Putting down your experience, feelings, and thoughts in a journal is very therapeutic for recovery and for defeating stress.

Writing works by clarifying your mind and thoughts and it is a form of therapy in the sense that it compels you to recall events and thoughts of the day on paper to give you a better avenue to analyze and understand what happened. It is also meditative. It slows down your heart as you focus on your writing to stream out your thoughts to paper. Writing sharpens and stimulates brain functioning and activity to improve your mental acuity and concentration as well as improving your vocabulary. You are, therefore, better equipped to handle stressful situations. When you write regularly, the stress triggers in your head are disrupted allowing you to better relax and sleep better. You get up well-rested and energized. Writing also fights anger by removing the thoughts from your mind to the writing pad, essentially offering you a platform to vent it out. When you write down your worries and problems it is easier to solve them. Writing allows you to identify what the problem is, think it through overtime, and most likely, come up with a great unrushed solution and avert the stress that you may have. Having a to-do list or schedule helps you focus and get organized. You are able to plan in advance to avoid last-minute rushes or procrastination that will only serve to make your life stressful. Writing will boost your immune system. By slowing your breathing, you are able to breathe in more oxygen to better nourish the brain and blood leading to faster healing and an enhanced ability to fight pathogens. Better breathing also strengthens the lungs, which has a positive effect in fighting respiratory conditions like asthma. To reap the benefits of writing for better health and stress relief, it does not matter what you write, the main thing is to be able to jot down your thoughts and review them. You do not have to be a John Grisham! Write down what is on your mind because the healing power lies in you letting out the negative thoughts that are weighing on your mind.

Chapter 4: Don't Fall into Provocations

Anger Triggers

Individuals that suffer from anger are not affected by the indications which may be present in situations that they encounter socially. Whenever they feel confident about the people they are interacting with who may include their peers, work colleagues, their sisters/brothers, the inner circle of friends, their family members including extended, chances are there will be a failure to exhibit any manifestation of anger in any way. They are also confident while speaking to a large audience concerning a topic they are well conversant with.

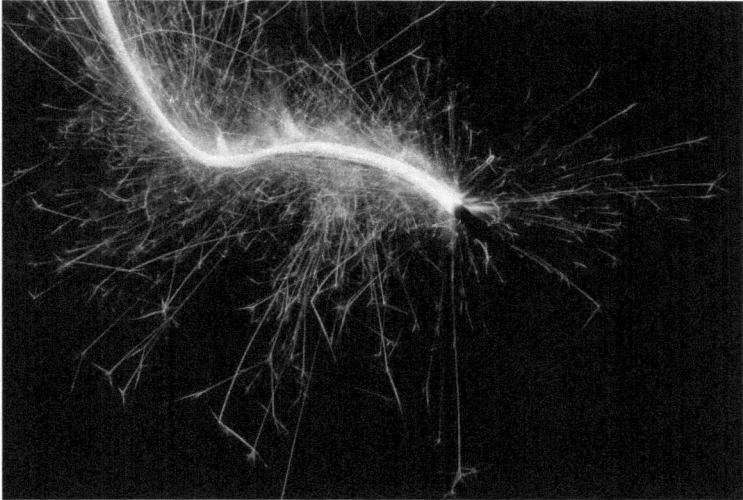

However, several circumstances can lead to agony and anger. Although, the anger expressed may not seem to bother or threaten a large group of people. A number of the commonly known and studied motivators for anger patients are:

> Abuse in terms of language
> Disrespect
> Invasion of personal space
> Injustice
> Shaming
> Lies
> Threats, mostly physically
> Being teased or kidded.

People with anger disorder, most of the time, conclude that being made fun of is something personal. They do this by:

> Feeling uneasy when someone is looking at them while they perform a task they are not familiar with
> Lack of self-control
> Relationship wrangles

A lot of people with an anger problem have more than three circumstances that make them react in an anxious and overwhelming manner. They usually do their best to get away from such causes as much as possible. Although there may be other instances that these circumstances occur, the signals of anger may be less extreme but the end results end up making life hard and strenuous.

Tackling an Anger Problem

When anger is not diagnosed and consequently not treated, it is very devastating and eventually affects how one functions daily. After an individual realizes they have an anger problem, they may not have the strength to seek help. They keep away from therapists, making sure not to interact with them in any way. Truth be told, treatment for anger problems is highly effective and the results achieved in a short or long time are commendable.

Though doctor prescribes medicine to curb depression and anger, going through psychotherapy is highly recommended. Treatment that helps with cognition and behavior (CBT) is mostly recommended by doctors who have patients with an anger disorder. These treatments are offered on an outpatient basis. Nonetheless, individuals who have had anger struggles over the years benefit greatly when they are admitted so that they can concentrate on recovering. Under the programs are residential, CBT, and other services that are essential. They are also offered but in an atmosphere that centers solely on the patient. In these programs, they may interact with their peers who are facing a similar challenge and they get to know ways of overcoming the challenges they have.

Although anger is not an easy experience, by using specialists and medication, it's controllable. Anger can frustrate and fascinate when the individual experiences it, they might seek to know, "What lead to anger? Why do I have to cope with this?" Curiosity can occur even when you, as an individual, is not a victim. You may have a close friend or family member having an anger problem or you get to explore deeper on the deeper issues concerning. No matter the reasons, getting to know the causes is important.

These will enable you to be in a better position to empathize with the millions of people who cope with an anger disorder. If you keep on giving yourself restrictions, and even in the process of tiring someone, then getting to know the causes is the first step.

The main causes of anger that are widely known are seven. They cause anger that is within. These are:

> Past encounters and environments as well as impacts associated with parenting style, trauma, and so on.
> Behaviors that are maladaptive and behaviors that have a negative effect.
> The temperament that is negatively affected by behavior and a style that not securely connected.
> Anger that is genetically passed down generations.
> A neurological disorder which is associated with overactivity in specific areas of the brain linked to anger
> The adverse effects of technology where individuals do not take time to converse face to face and they also do not have time for themselves.
> Physical causes such as being in situations and events that will make men and women be anxious, hence set in motion the characteristic which accompanies anger.

These factors influence each other in certain ways. Going through experience, being in an environment which is linked to interactions socially result in men and women developing bad beliefs and maladaptive behaviors. These beliefs and behaviors may cause and nurture interpersonal anger. The cognitive results then change brain construction and functioning.

414

Anger that is passed down genetically, through character and being attached, is more likely to result in anger disorder. When individuals panic socially, then a number of triggers are set off thereby opening them up to various anger signs. These include setting themselves apart and being agitated. In order to familiarize ourselves with the above, let us go to the next topic.

Overcoming anger

Earlier on, I talked about the nature and frequency of anger. When you find yourself reserved and nervous in a diversity of social circumstances such as talking in front of a group of people, meeting new individuals, using communal closets or rest places, or even drinking in public, you may fear that certain individuals will realize your fear and get humiliated. This might show you that you're suffering from anger disorder. A lot of folks with this problem will decide to avoid circumstances where they forestall being nervous or they might take alcohol or else drugs to self-medicate before entering these circumstances. Personal anger is related to amplified risk for alcoholic drinks abuse, unhappiness, loneliness, abridged occupational, progression, and the augmented likelihood of hanging around single.

Cognitive behavioral counselors make great advances for a drug-free approach to dealing with these problems. Right now, there is considerable proof that Cognitive Behavior Therapy is an efficient treatment for anger. This particular remedy focuses on your behavior and what you are thinking about. So, let's take a closer take look at how this approach can help you overcome your social panic.

The particular behavioral problem for those with anger is the tendency to avoid anger-provoking situations. When the socially anxious individual anticipates heading to a celebration, he or she becomes quite anxious. However, when he chooses not to go, the anger immediately subsides. This reduction of panic with the decision to avoid the party, or to leave a party, strengthens avoidance or escape. This simple reward for avoidance confirms the concern of negative social examination even when the individual really does not experience humiliation. For example, if I feel stressed thinking of approaching someone and then I decide to avoid talking with him or her, my panic immediately subsides. This immediate decrease in anger dictates that for me to feel less anxious, I should just avoid interacting with other people.

A significant issue of CBT is to aid the person to practice imminent social situations and sojourn in them so as to know that nothing is really bad will perhaps transpire and that their anger will decrease. An individual also learns that he can do it and the simple willingness to confront his fears is empowering. You start realizing that you are not the sort of person who can actually try this kind of thing. The first step in helping people with anger is to identify the situations that they are avoiding. You can make a listing of the types of situations that you feel anxious in or avoid. For instance, one person realized that using a public toilet where he was worried that individuals would observe him, meeting people at a party, speaking up at a meeting, and talking to a woman for the first time were some of his anger triggers. What are the situations that provoke your anger? What are you likely to avoid? Make a listing.

Setting up a hierarchy of fear

For every situation, you can identify how the situation could be rated in terms of how much anger that you would experience. You can rate each anticipated response on a scale of 0 to 10 depending on the level of anger that you might expect. One would mean there is no anger while 10 would signify a panic attack. For instance, a young man with the fear of meeting people at a party experienced the following stages of fear, from the lowest to the highest. Thinking of going to the party rates at three, going to the party is at five, walking into the room ranked at six, seeing people in the room is also number six, deciding to begin a conversation rests at number eight, and talking with a stylish woman. It's important to write down your predictions so as to be able to find a way of discovering how nervous you really are as you go. Most of the time, folks realize that they're not as apprehensive as they expected they would appear.

Test your Expectations

We often fail to recall the fact that we deal healthier than we assumed it we would. This is an inordinate chance to examine your exact predictions. As I stated above, you can write down how worried you think you'll be for anything that you do. What's the level of the rage that you anticipate? How far will you stay anxious? Precisely, what is your prediction? This is how you can examine your disastrous fortune-telling. For example, a middle-aged man who was informally anxious foretold that he might have a level of rage at nine for the whole extent of speaking with a lady at a party. He projected that his brains would go blank and that he'd be so nervous that he would want to leave.

417

As a result, he was very concerned when he started a conversation, but when he was into the conversation, his anger decreased to level three. He did not walk away and, in fact, he got the impression that the lady he was talking to actually adored him. As a result, be clear of what you're predicting so you can find out if you're antedating more than what actually occurs. Maintain a constant record of your expectations.

Determine your behaviors and eradicate them

A lot of people are anxious about irrational behaviors that they consider to led them to safety or more likely to embarrass themselves. These safety 'manners' consist of self-medicating with intoxicating drinks or drugs, making yourself very stiff, evading attention contact, holding a mug tightly so that folks will not realize your hands are trembling, wiping your hands so as people won't notice you are perspiring, rehearsing precise what accurately you'll say, and speaking very fast. The problem with defensive behaviors is that they're like the training tires on a bicycle and they allow you to believe the only way you can get over this knowledge is to use the exercise wheels.

Chapter 5: Anger Management Advice

The optimistic part of the handling 'behavioral and cognitive' side of anger has resulted in an extraordinary result. Evidence that is proven in a clinical and research methodology concludes that therapy offered comprehensively in a behavioral and cognitive way has a positive lasting effect on individuals.

Through being persistent and consistent, anger can be brought under control and eventually eradicated. Each and every individual can progress positively when given the right treatment. In several centers that deal with anger, behavioral and cognitive therapy is referred to as comprehensive, hence separating it from the concepts that cognitive therapy is simplistic and only uses a number of strategies.

A program that will have sufficiently solved anger difficulties should address all the scholarly methods, procedures, and important factors that give room for the mind to drastically revolutionize. The mind is continually learning. Illogical thoughts and standards can change, therefore, this needs a cognitive procedure. The perfect response should disclose the events they're used to.

Looking for Anger Solutions

Anger, together with other anger challenges, can be treated successfully. In line with looking for a solution, you should also visit a specialist.

Consult a person who:

- knows this problem well
- Handle it through experience

Arm yourself with information as a customer by asking questions. One way to inform yourself is seeking to know whether the counselor perceives your self-consciousness which is caused by being looked at by others and them having an unpleasant opinion about you. Or are they not paying much attention to what you are saying and answering in the negative, suggesting you are fine. What you are feeling is an exaggeration.

Though the feeling of being looked at or judged increases our self-consciousness. If your therapist does not understand this, then he/she does not have the capability of helping you. Hence, keep in mind that the professional should always welcome your questions. A therapist should be kind and accommodative, enabling you to speak out what is bothering you freely. If they do not have these qualities in the foreground, then they are suitable.

Individuals who are on the way to recovery from anger and its effects need to be supported, encouraged, and be in a friendly atmosphere so as to enhance the healing process. An atmosphere that is calm helps in learning the habits that need to be acquired so as to tackle the various effects of anger in our lives and eventually anger itself. This has a ripple effect on every area of the individual.

There are words that a therapist should not use. Like, you should tackle your fears head-on and they will eventually disappear. Anyone who has undergone social panic has tried to tackle their fears and these statements are not helpful at all. It is imperative to get a therapist who will help you through the process of healing from anger adequately. Although learning how to handle anger and eventually overcoming is not a one-off thing, it can be done in a consistent and systematic manner. When most people are tackling with anger problems, they may feel overwhelmed and may not be willing to go through the healing process. That is why a qualified therapist will encourage and lead the individual on the right path to healing.

The following are special aspects involved in anger management:

- A clear perception of the underlying issues.

- Being dedicated to following through the treatment which may seem repetitive

- Finding ways of practicing and exercising what you have learned so that these cognitive methods become habitual and automated

- Be part of a team. Here you can activate fully and slowly tackle the triggers and the various aspects of anger in your life.

For example, if you cannot gather the strength to stand before an audience and read out loudly, then there are ways that one can use to tackle your fear/situation. The therapist can also form groups where an individual's role play in various tasks, for example, an interview before a panel of judges to enable each individual to reach their intended goal.

Groups

Anger behavior treatment groups should not push or persuade individuals to engage in group activities if they are not interested. Each individual should be left to freely choose whether they want to participate or not. This does not mean the treatment they are undergoing is not working. Each individual has a variety of anger issues that should be handled in a different manner. For some groups, a session is not the way to go, so they should not be coerced into participating in any activity they do not want. There should be motivation and positive undertakings in the group which will, in turn, enable the participants to reciprocate. When this is achieved, they are able to positively progress towards tackling what is ailing them socially. For all this to take place, the therapist must now what methods to use so as to achieve the desired results. Nowadays, the treatment of behaviors and cognitive can handle the stress that is in the social sphere. This therapy does not dwell on the past by bringing it to the foreground. Rather, the day-to-day challenges are handled using various techniques that do away with thoughts on anger, including what we believe and feel.

Some individuals start worrying when they know they have attended an event. This may take place many days before the event. Then, they now worry about how they conducted themselves and what others thought about them. In general, there is no single reason why people suffer from anger disorder. Having the same genes i.e. family members can be responsible. People from the same family who have suffered from a social phobia may pass on the genes to their kin. Inter-personal panic attacks usually start when an individual is at the onset of teenagehood (Thirteen). In most cases, there is a connection with their past where bullying abuse and teasing can be traced back.

A child who is shy may end up becoming uneasy in their social life in their adult life which is also similar to children from parents who are domineering. There are also conditions which may happen in regard to our health. They may make our voices and appearances to be noted. This can also be a trigger for someone with an anger problem. Lots of people with anger also exhibit a number of issues concerning their health. This may include depression, generalized panic attacks, or disorders of the dimorphic in the body.

When to get help for anger

Taking a step to go to your specialist when you feel your anger is getting the better part of you is a wise decision. Being overwhelmed by anger is not an out-of-place problem but has beneficial therapies that work. Though you may find it difficult to reach out and seek help, you will be surprised that it's a challenge that more than the average number of people have. Your therapist, if experienced, knows many people have an anger problem and thus will attempt to ease down your anxiety. He or she will ask several questions such as, how you feel when angry, what makes you angry, is there a place you go and do you begin to feel angry? All these questions are geared towards determining the magnitude of your anger. If they think you could have anger issues, you'll be referred to a mental health specialist to have a full assessment and weigh the treatment options. Moreover, you can also recommend yourself directly for mental therapies without seeing your doctor.

How you can overcome social stress

Anger is very tasking to handle even though some steps and actions that you take can lead you to the initiative to try. Furthermore, there is also a wide variety of medical options and treatments as well as support groups that are quite beneficial.

Things you can try

Individually helping yourself may not, in most cases, remedy anger. The anger may subside and it is equally a major step towards finding more helpful ways. Let us see what other steps we can undertake:

- By first analyzing what you think about before you get angry and the action you take after gives you a clear view of what challenges you are facing.
- At the time, you may feel a certain situation did not happen as planned. Be reasonable about it and you may conclude what you had planned was impractical.

- Get the attention away from your mind and yourself. Focus it on other people. You will realize the social challenges you are having are not apparent.

- Start involving yourself in what you would naturally keep off. You can do it in small doses, then progress as you feel comfortable about it.

Remedies to cure panic socially

Some primary examples include:

1. Through a professional therapist who uses a remedy that is both behavioral and cognitive. This remedy is helpful in enabling you to recognize behaviors and patterns that have a negative impact on your behavior.

2. Using individual help. By using a course downloaded from the internet or through a workbook and sufficient one-on-one help from a professional therapist.

3. Anti-depressant medicine. This is a type of medicine called a picky serotonin reuptake inhibitor or SSRI. The commonly known options are escitalopram or sertraline.

CBT is thought to be the best option for treatment, even though other modes of treatment are effective in case it does not give the desired results or you are not keen to undergo the therapy. Other individuals, however, respond well when several treatments are combined.

How is anger treated?

First of all, visit your general physician or healthcare specialist about how you feel. Your practitioner will carry out a test and ask questions regarding your health over the past period. This is done to rule out any other problem that may not be responsible for your current mental health status. Then they will refer you to either a doctor who specializes in mental health or a counselor. They will get to understand the underlying factors that lead to your current mental issues.

Anger is usually treated with psychotherapy, which is at times referred to as "talk" or face-to-face therapy, whereby medicine can be added or not. It's important to openly discuss with your doctor what treatment is fit for you and any adverse reactions you should expect.

Support Groups

A number of individuals prefer being with like-minded or with people facing similar challenges as what they are facing. In these groups, they find support and are given feedback to any questions that have without being judged wrongly. In these groups, they also get to hear how other people handle their anxieties in a social setting and may be inclined to try out. In doing so, they feel they are not the only ones going through that challenge, and hence, motivated to keep on achieving good and better results through their effort.

Psychotherapy

There is a category of psychiatric therapy that is both behavioral and cognitive and is very helpful in the treatment of anger. It has a variety of ways that one can think, act, and react to circumstances that make you end up feeling less worried and at ease. It also enables you to enhance your skills in your social life. When this therapy is done in a group setting, the results are remarkable.

Medicine Used

The medicines used to treat disorders that are as a result of stress socially are only three, namely:

- Anti-anger medications
- Antidepressants
- Beta-blockers

Anti-anger medications work in a powerful way and have an immediate effect on reducing feelings of uneasiness. Nonetheless, such medicine is not recommended for use for long periods. This is because as patients get used to them, they may require excessive dosages so as to get the preferred effect. In order to keep away from such problems, doctors prefer giving it for a short length and older patients are mostly preferred for these dosages.

Anti-depressants. Though they mainly work for individuals who are depressed, they also do well in tackling anger symptoms. Unlike anti-anger medicines, depressants take a number of weeks before they work. They also have various side effects such as sleeping difficulty, headache, and nausea.

Although these effects are not severe for individuals whose dosage is gradually increased, it is always important to contact your health provider in case of any undesirable drug outcome.

Beta-blockers medications enable the prevention of a number of signs that occur physically. These include body tremors, an increase in heart rate, and perspiration. Beta-blockers are mostly used for the "performance anger" which is also a category of anger. By working closely with your medical caregiver, you will find the most suitable medicine for you. A larger part of the population finds out that they get better results when different medications and other psychotherapies are used. As you discuss the dosage and length of treatment, bear in mind it might take a bit longer, so be prepared psychologically for the long haul. This helps in not giving up on treatment. Remember to not only rely on the medications but check how healthy your lifestyle is and make any positive changes that need to be made. For example, if you do not exercise, get some time and start and let it be regular. Getting adequate sleep and reaching out to your family and friends when you need someone to talk or support you will give you positive results in the long run.

Treatment Options

There are various treatments for anger difficulties though they may affect each individual differently. While a few may require a single option, others do well when various options are combined.

Your general healthcare physician will refer you to a mental care provider if they deem so and in regard to your symptoms and treatment needed. The various treatment alternatives include:

Cognitive Behavioral Therapy

This therapy is useful as it enables one to have control over their thoughts when angry via taking in short breaths and generally relaxing. The thoughts are geared towards being positive hence the anger is controlled.

Exposure therapy

When using this therapy, you gradually gain the courage to face situations in your social life that you avoided or felt coerced to be involved..

Group therapy

This therapy is for people who need to feel at ease in social gatherings, as they acquire the skills and techniques needed to be able to socialize and interact with others. Being a participant in a group opens you to the reality of not being alone in tackling anger issues. You also get a chance to showcase what you have learned before going out and meeting different people in different settings.

Treatments that one can do at home include:

1. Staying away from coffee

Caffeine drinks, as well as chocolate, are body stimulants and they may trigger anger. Soft drinks are also not recommended.

2. Having a lot of sleep

When individuals do not get enough sleep, their irritation levels heighten and they might not be very pleasant to be around. Getting enough sleep preferably for eight hours is highly commendable.

Just like many other mental health conditions, anger condition is also likely to arise from the interaction of various factors which include both environmental and natural.

These causes are:

➢ Qualities may be inherited down generations and in some cases, anger issues stand out. Although this observation is not fully clear as to what degree people inherit anger genes or is the anger they portray learned from childhood.

➢ A feature in the brain. Amygdala is a part of the brain that is responsible for how we respond to various circumstances. Individuals whose amygdala is highly active may be easily triggered into anger.

➢ Anger learned from our surroundings. Some individuals grow up in homes where there are heightened anger levels, so they learn what it is to be angry and how to react. There may be a connection between domineering parents and anger issues in children.

The Dangers

Anger can be encouraged through the following factors:

- **Background.** You have higher chances of developing anger in case your birth parents and siblings had the same issues.

- **Unfavorable encounter.** Individuals who are teased, bullied, rejected, ridiculed, or humiliated may be more vulnerable to anger. Additionally, other undesired occasions such as conflicts between family members, abuse, or trauma are anger linked.

- **Temperament.** Kids who are withdrawn in different and unfamiliar circumstances are highly vulnerable.

- **Demands made by changing social life and work.** Signs of anger basically kick in during teenagehood, although being in unfamiliar territory like reading a speech for the first time in public may provoke anger signs.

Complications

If left untreated, anger can ruin your life. Anger disorders can interrupt one's personal relationships, work, and school or other joys of anger. Anger is also responsible for:

- ➤ Shallow self-assurance
- ➤ Problem with being confident and firm.
- ➤ Talk about oneself negatively

- ➢ Very sensitive to any kind of criticism

- ➢ Inadequate competence socially

- ➢ Solitude including lack of skills to engage with peers

- ➢ Below average in work and academic achievements.

- ➢ Abusing of alcohol and alcohol-related products.

- ➢ Have a tendency of trying to commit suicide.

How to avoid the above complications:

There are various ways to help us cope, and hopefully, avoid the above complications. In doing the following, we will also be keeping away from having anger-related problems.

- Getting help earlier. Procrastination is one of the greatest enemies of dealing with anger issues. This is because as anger continues to affect your mental health, other areas of your life also suffer certain effects.

- Keeping record. Tracking your daily reactions in different circumstances and places will help you have a clear record as to how you can handle anger issues in your life.

- Get your priorities organized and be mentally prepared to follow through. This will enable you to feel in control and you are also able to engage and use your energy in what you enjoy. Thus anger issues will stay at bay.

Avoid anything that is addictive and harmful to your health. These include alcoholic drinks, drugs, nicotine, and caffeine. Though quitting may not be easy, you can consult with your health provider or even join a similar support group that will help you.

Chapter 6: Anger Management and Emotional Intelligence

What is Nonviolent Communication?

Human beings cannot live in isolation. We are a social species, and we need interaction and communication with other human beings for our sustenance. For us, connections with other human beings are not just a convenience but essentiality for survival. Communication is the most basic need of any social group including animals. Every animal species has its way of communicating and talking with each other.

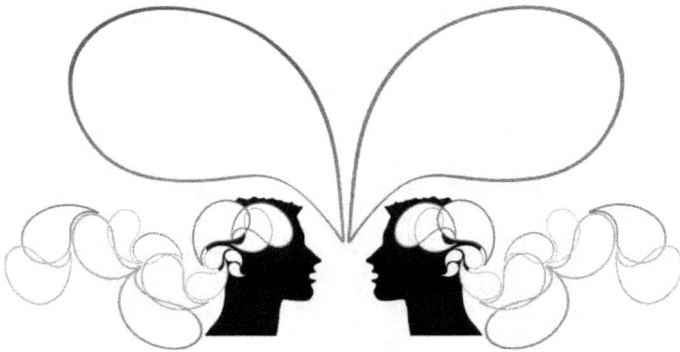

Therefore, communication is a two-way process by which thoughts, ideas, and emotions are exchanged meaningfully. Talking to people gives us happiness and joy. Talking to people also makes us feel sad, angry, and resentful. What is the difference between the two types of talking? What is it in the process of communication that affects how we feel?

Violent Vs. Nonviolent Communication

What kinds of communication make us happy and joyful and what kinds make us sad, angry, and hurt? Violent communication creates sadness and hurtful feelings whereas nonviolent communication creates joy and happiness for everyone involved in the discussion. Violent communication can include a range of elements including:

> ➢ Judging and criticizing people, deciding good/bad behavior, right/wrong people and situations
> ➢ Having prejudicial views based on race, gender, caste, creed, nationality, or anything else
> ➢ Discriminatory behavior
> ➢ Finger-pointing and blaming
> ➢ Talking without listening
> ➢ Reacting negatively when angry
> ➢ Name-calling
> ➢ Using rhetoric
> ➢ Being defensive

Any conversation or interaction with one or more of the elements mentioned in the above list is bound to result in violent communication.

So, what is nonviolent communication (NVC)? It is a form of empathetic communication that is based on the belief that every human being is capable of compassion. Nonviolent communication is deeply rooted in compassion. Marshall B. Rosenberg, the founder of the Center of Nonviolent Communication (CNVC), believed that being compassionate is the natural state of being for all humans. It is natural to find joy and happiness in giving and receiving from the heart. If this is true, what is it that disconnects us from our natural state of compassion and makes us behave exploitatively and violently?

Also, what is it that helps us remain in this natural state of compassion even in worst-case scenarios? One of the biggest factors that affect our compassionate nature is language and communication. Many times, even if we don't appear to talk violently in the physical sense, our choice of words can make an interaction violent inasmuch it causes pain and hurt to others, and that is referred to as violent communication, too.

Why do we indulge in this kind of communication style? Dr. Marshall Rosenberg said that this is because we are trained to perceive and speak judgmentally, labeling elements as right or wrong, and evaluating things in ways that disconnect us from our natural compassionate nature. Nonviolent communication is an approach that teaches us to give and receive from our hearts so that we are reconnected to our natural state of compassion.

NVC helps us to overcome automatic, habitual reactions, and responses and choose to express ourselves objectively and non-judgmentally by being conscious of our behaviors, feelings, and choice of words. NVC helps us to express ourselves honestly and clearly even, as we listen and pay attention to others' emotions and opinions empathetically and respectfully. In any interaction based on nonviolent communication, not only are we aware of our deep needs and desires but also conscious of other people's needs and desires. By careful observations, we are able to specify external conditions and internal thoughts and emotions that are affecting our behaviors, and then make appropriate changes to our communication style that facilitates compassion and understanding for ourselves and fellow human beings. Nonviolent communication is a combination of four elements or components including consciousness, language, communication skills, and means of influence. Let us look at each of these four elements of nonviolent communication in detail.

Consciousness – An individual who displays consciousness in his or her communication holds four human values high in their life; collaboration, compassion, authenticity, and courage.

Language – A nonviolent communicator is one who understands the importance and value of words and how they can increase or decrease distances and connections between people.

Communication skills – Nonviolent communicators have excellent communication skills. Such people:

➤ Know how to ask for what they want
➤ Know how to listen to others even in disagreements
➤ Know who to collaborate with and find solutions that work well for all stakeholders

Means of influence – Nonviolent communicators accept and acknowledge the importance of 'sharing power' instead of 'using power over others.' Nonviolent communication helps us to live with deep connections with people and sensible choices based on facts enabling you to live a meaningful and happy life.

Marshall B. Rosenberg said, *"Human beings are powerhouses of joy and happiness, and each one of us is capable of enriching lives through our words and interactions with other people. We can have great support. We can nurture. We can contribute and participate in other people's enjoyment.*

On the other hand, we also have the power to make people miserable through our words and actions. It is up to us to make the right choice of learning the various aspects of nonviolent communication to enrich our lives and those of others."

How is NVC different from other self-help, communication, and conflict management tools? - The uniqueness of nonviolent communication can be found in the following elements:

Assumptions of NVC are unique – The start of NVC itself is beautiful and unique. This communication self-help tool assumes that every human being is capable of compassion and love. We are all nonviolent by nature, and violence is a learned behavior supported by or taught by external circumstances, including but not limited to the prevailing culture and norm. Another important assumption of NVC is that all human beings have the same primary needs, and all our actions, reactions, and responses are used to meet these basic human needs.

The NVC tool is simple to learn and use – The process involved in using the NVC tool is simple to learn and master and equally simple to implement in our daily lives. The crucial thing about NVC is that it is not merely a communication tool. NVC techniques teach us how to stay connected with our life energy. It improves our consciousness by making us focus on how our thinking and communication impacts our daily conversations.

NVC can be applied effectively for a wide variety of purposes and needs – The use of NVC techniques is not restricted to any one or two communication needs. You can effectively use NVC techniques on a wide range of needs ranging from personal, professional, business, interpersonal, family, parenting, sibling, and more. It also helps to overcome social issues such as alcoholism, substance abuse, recovery from trauma, and prisoner rehabilitation.

NVC promises amazing results – NVC techniques can transform destructive attitudes such as anger, resentment, and more. It helps you break destructive habits and convert them into life-serving and peaceful behaviors. NVC has been used all over the world to reduce conflicts in families and business organizations, increase trust, and foster deep emotional connections to benefit all stakeholders.

Benefits of Learning Non-violent Communication

Learning the skills of nonviolent communication helps you with the following:

Conflict resolution

Nonviolent communication methods teach you to resolve all kinds of conflicts amicably. You will be able to get to the root of the dispute quickly, and effectively help you find solutions.

With nonviolent communication, you will learn to improve your listening skills significantly which allows you to get enhanced levels of cooperation from the different people you deal with. Nonviolent communication skills help you convert criticism and blame into a compassionate understanding of the other person's point of view. With the help of all these conflict resolution skills, your ability to reduce misunderstandings and prevent pain from similar mistakes both for yourself and the people around will improve considerably.

Improved personal relationships

NVC is great for personal relationships. Being skilled in nonviolent communication helps you deepen your emotional connections with other people. Your improved listening skills will increase cooperative interactions with your family and friends. You will find ways to get what you want without the use of guilt or shame.

Improved family relationship

With NVC, you will reduce sibling rivalry and family conflicts and you will be able to help people in your family to go beyond power struggles towards an attitude of cooperation and trust. NVC teaches you the power of using unconditional love to bring a family together. As a parent, you will be able to nurture your children without stepping on their sense of autonomy and freedom. NVC skills teach you to motivate by sharing power with loved ones rather than using power over them.

The improved education system and better students

NVC helps us to optimize the potential of each student and strengthen their passion, interest, dedication, and connection to learning and development. NVC skills help to improve connection and trust in the classroom and empower them to feel safe and secure. NVC helps to improve efficiency and cooperation among students and enhance teamwork in the classroom while strengthening the power of parent-teacher relationships; a key ingredient in the overall development of a student.

Self-healing and personal growth

NVC empowers you to change guilt and shame into learning elements. It helps you heal old, festering pains and also facilitates the elimination of old, limiting habits and thoughts. NVC helps you to remain connected with your desires, preferences, and needs. It teaches you how to cultivate the habit of eating by choice and not by habit; a crucial item for physical health.

Organizational effectiveness

NVC improves the productivity and effectiveness of meetings. Also, employees will feel an increased sense of morale, confidence, and team spirit, helping them improve their productivity for organizational effectiveness and development. NVC helps you optimize the quality of work and also the social benefits of your company to the community and society.

Anger management

NVC helps you redirect your anger productively before it can drive damaging behavior. NVC enables you to identify and understand the needs of your anger, the triggers that drive angry behavior both for yourself and others. NVC helps you overcome the challenges of anger and facilitates solution-driven proactive behavior instead of regretful reactions. With nonviolent communication, you will find ways to express your anger without harming anyone.

Business relationships

NVC helps in building employee loyalty and morale by helping them achieve their optimum potential. With NVC, you will find ways to resolve workplace conflicts effectively and with little or no residual damage. It reduces absenteeism and stress in the workplace. It helps in improved customer relationships by understanding and preempting their needs and requirements.

Spirituality

NVC helps you connect to your inner being. You will find that with NVC you are able to align your actions with your spiritual values and moral principles helping you lead a wholesome and meaningful life. NVC helps you overcome conditioned harmful behavior developed from your cultural background and connect with the whole of humanity. NVC helps you understand that identifying and satisfying your own needs is the first step to building compassion for others.

You can also reap all these benefits and more by learning and implementing NVC techniques in your life.

The Four-Step Nonviolent Communication Process

To reiterate one part of what was already said in the introduction chapter, the primary premise on which Nonviolent communication (NVC) works is that all human beings have the same basic needs. One of the most important human need is the sense that they are being listened to, understood, respected, and valued. NVC techniques are all designed to have meaningful conversations that connect to everyone's needs, and not to 'win' or 'lose'. The four-step communication process of NVC includes:

Observations

A neutral way of observing what is happening inside and outside of you is the first and foremost step in the NVC four-step process. In a conversation, this is best done by recapping what has been said by others without attaching any emotion to it. When you recap or summarize a person's conversation, it is imperative not to be judgmental about the 'story'. Recapping what the other person is saying helps in the following ways:

- It slows down the conversation giving everyone time to rethink and reconsider their understanding and interpretations. The person whose idea you are recapping feels that he or she is being listened to and understood; one of the most important human needs.

443

- Recapping helps people to enhance their memory about the conversation helping them recall it better in the future.
- It helps to catch and correct errors. When we are talking fast and without a stop, it is natural for all of us to make mistakes in the form of misplaced words or phrases that mean something quite different from what we actually wanted to say. Recapping helps in catching and correcting these mistakes. Recapping acts like an editing process of what was spoken earlier.

Recapping works extremely well when you use the first person. Instead of starting with 'You said that,' it would be better starting with, 'I hear what you are saying….' Here are some examples of recapping:

Suppose your husband walks in and says, "Oh God! These immigrants have come into our country and are taking our jobs away." Your response would be, "Did something happen in the office today that is making you feel insecure about your job? Would you want to talk about that incidence?"

Notice, by recapping what your husband said, not only did you let him know that you were listening to what he was saying but also catch the underlying fears about something that happened in the office that day. Your recapping of his statements has made him think about what he said which, in turn, will slow down his speed of thoughts giving him the necessary time to really comprehend his emotions and feelings. He is forced to reflect on what he said, and clarify his stance. Moreover, he feels a sense of connection with you, and he is ready to discuss the issue without letting the fears affect his judgment.

Feelings

The next step in the NVC four-step process is to describe and focus on the emotions and feelings, and not the situation. If you want to be heard, then you must describe your feelings and emotions, and not just what is happening because everyone can easily see what it is. What they cannot see are your feelings and emotions which makes it important that you reveal them through words. The crucial aspect of expressing your emotions is to ensure not to make it feel like you are blaming someone or something. For example, if you say, "I feel misunderstood...' it could translate to someone not making an effort to understand you resulting in transferring or laying blame on others.

"I feel good about what happened," or "I feel bad about what happened," is talking about your feelings. Similarly, asking someone, 'How do you feel about what happened?' instead of simply asking, 'What happened?' will shift the focus from the situation to the person's feelings and interpretation. This makes people feel like they are being heard, and their concerns are being addressed.

Needs and Requests

The third step in the NVC four-step process is to identify the need behind the feelings or emotions. This approach is based on one of the assumptions of NVC which is that we all experience emotions because of an underlying need. So, the next step after identifying the feeling is to discern and identify it. Human beings feel a sense of dissatisfaction leading to anger and resentment when we have unmet needs.

Interestingly, the founder of NVC, Marshall B. Rosenberg noticed that nearly all human needs could fit into a small list of categories including honesty, connection, and peace, a sense of purpose, physical well-being, and autonomy. Identifying needs is the turning point in conflict resolution. You can ask questions that will bring the underlying need of the other person's emotions to the surface. For example, you can say, 'Can you tell me exactly what your concerns are and from where do these concerns arise?'

Similarly, when you are talking about your unmet need, you must explicitly express the problem. For example, in that husband-wife conversation, if the husband had said something like this, 'I am worried about job security if people are allowed to migrate without restriction,' would have immediately reflected the unmet human need of peace and well-being. In any conversation, if two people are talking without understanding the drive and motivation of the other person, then the resultant conversation will look like two overflowing glasses of water with no space to hold anything more. In order to understand any person's perspective, you must first empty your mind so that there is space for what the other individual is trying to put in.

The Importance of Unlearning Old Lessons

Here is a beautiful Zen Buddhist story that illustrates the need to empty our biases to understand and appreciate someone else's point of view. A highly learned professor went to a master to learn Zen. As the master was filling the professor's teacup, the professor was continuously talking about what he knew and had heard about the subject.

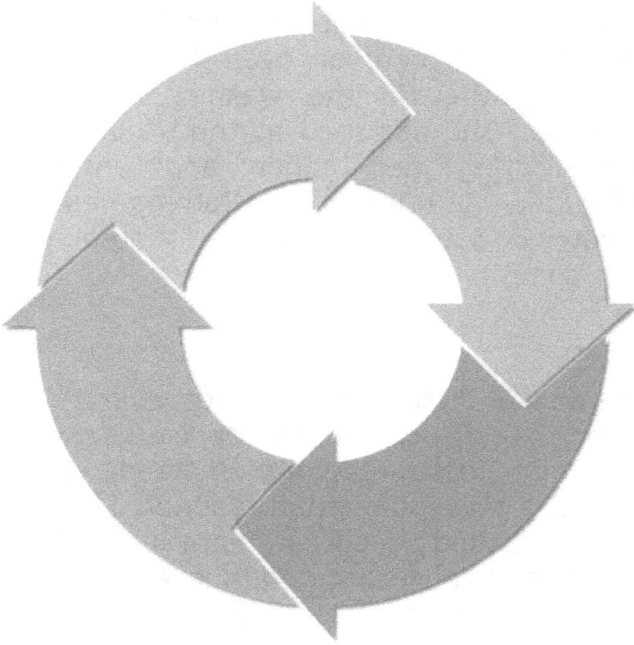

The master listened without saying a word and poured tea into the professor's cup until it reaches the brim. However, the master did not stop here. He continued to pour the liquid resulting in the cup overflowing. The professor watched this strange action for some time, and then abruptly stopped talking about Zen, and told the master, 'Stop pouring. The cup cannot hold anything more.'

The Zen master replied, 'You are like the teacup. Unless you empty your cup, how will I fill it with what I know of Zen?' So, first, empty your mind, and only then are you ready to receive more. Every situation can be seen through this four-step process which can then be used to improve your communication style effectively. Here is an example that explains the use of the 4-step nonviolent communication.

Sharon's mother, Denise, is feeling quite frustrated with her daughter's annoying habit of bundling her socks into balls and throwing them all over the house instead of putting them either in the washing machine or the laundry basket. She has tried all the traditional methods of communicating her anger and annoyance; by screaming, cajoling, bribing, etc. Nothing has worked. So, Denise now decided to use the 4-step process of nonviolent communication.

Observations – First, she observes everything around her and the external conditions. Denise keeps out words like 'annoying,' 'frustrated,' etc. Instead, she observes everything in a non-judgmental manner. She notices the mess that the balled-up socks create in the living room, kitchen, etc. and these are common areas in the home used by other members of the family too.

Feelings – Next, she looks at how she is feeling and recognizes and identifies some of the top emotions she is experiencing. Denise is frustrated, angry, and feels helpless.

Needs – Denise then looks at her underlying need in this entire situation. She needs the common spaces to look clean at all times so that everyone in the house can get together without any feeling of discomfort brought about by the odor of smelly socks.

Requests – After following the three steps, she words her communication like this: Sharon, I can see three balls of socks under the dining table, and two balls of rolled-up socks under the settee in the living room. It angers me to see these lying around in the common area of the home because this space needs more order than your bedroom as everyone in the family accesses and uses it. Can I request you to put your used socks either in the laundry basket or the washing machine from now onwards?

The last sentence is the request part of the NVC process that has to be delivered so that others can clearly and unequivocally understand our needs. These needs are the ones that enrich our lives, and nonviolent communication is the way that helps each of us achieve our needs using our natural feeling of compassion to give and receive from the depths of our hearts.

Chapter 7: Mental Disorder, the Origin of Problems

What is mental health?

According to WHO (World Health Organization), health, which includes mental health, involves a state of entire mental, physical, and social well-being, which means it's not just about the absence of a disease or condition.

The same definition applies to proper mental health, which implies it's not just about the presence or absence of mental disorders such as anxiety and depression, or bipolar disorders, amongst others. If one is mentally healthy, then it means they are aware of their own capabilities, can cope with life's normal dramas, and will work effectively in a bid to make a mark on his or her community. We can, therefore, say that good mental health is the core of the effectiveness of an individual and the community around him or her.

In the name of good mental health

CBT has done a great job of making people realize themselves and be able to get back on track. It has been used to treat several conditions (you can refer to the Introduction to see what CBT can be used to address). On the other hand, mental health involves more than one strategy if we need to make sure that positivity stays in us on a long-term basis. Promoting good mental health involves utilizing strategies and prepared programs that generate an enabling environment that has the right living conditions for people to abide by and be able to maintain healthy conditions.

There is no particular program aimed at mental health, and that is why it will involve more than CBT. The range of programs available should be thanked by those who have benefited, since one specific measure may not suit your troubled neighbor. They all give us a chance to enjoy the fruits of staying positive by allowing the mind to adjust the way it thinks.

What determines your state of mental health?

Mental health has a range of factors that influence it, which is the same as physical health. The factors are also interactive, and they include psychological, biological, and social aspects. Research has shown that the evidence is well portrayed in poverty, low or improper education, low income earning, or poor housing and sanitation. The declining socioeconomic status that has more disadvantages will force individuals to succumb to mental disorders. Those who are more vulnerable involve the less fortunate or disadvantaged and within a community prone to mental disorders. If other additional factors such as insecurity, hopelessness, poor body health, increased risks of violence, and rapid social change are also around, that also partially explains why we may be having improper mental health.

Ways that you can use to promote overall psychological wellbeing

Here are some things to consider as you look forward to reinstating good mental health.

Look for what is affecting you

Since we aren't the same, it is crucial that you investigate your individual causes of ill mental health. On the other hand, some shared causes may be becoming stressed, or depressed, finding difficulty in coping or quit something, or generally upset. There are life events that may affect our mental health.

They include:

> - Being lonely
> - Loss of someone close to you
> - Illicit relationships
> - Financial issues
> - Work-related problems

NB: loneliness, insomnia, stress, and inactivity are all forms of negativity when it comes to mental wellbeing. At times, it is almost impossible to determine why we experience mental disorders. While it is a cause to worry, there are other factors that will lead to such feelings. They maybe happened or occurred in the past.

They may involve the following:

> - Neglect, child abuse, or violence
> - Homelessness, especially for those who have experienced foster care
> - Social discrimination
> - Terminal illness in us or in the family
> - Loss of a job or unemployment
> - Poverty and debt
> - Trauma associated with life experiences such as high-level crime, military issues, or being involved in major tragedies such as bomb attacks

Regardless of the cause, what you need to remember is that you have a right to feel great and there is a protocol for you to achieve that.

Building relationships that can help you

Getting involved in social groups or having a friend will give you a sense of belonging if it's not yet there. It will help you cope with difficulty if you manage to do the following:

Connect with loved ones: Always keep in touch with your friends and relatives with the convenient method available. You can plan to visit, call them, or leave them messages.

Joining social groups: What do you like to do? Some of us like playing instruments, others drawing, swimming, and the list is endless.

Talk about your feelings: If you have someone that you can trust with your personal issues, it's a good idea to open up to them. It also shows that you are aware of what is happening to you, so explaining it to someone actually helps. At times, it is hard to explain it to our friends, but you can do that to a person who has a similar experience. If you have a chance, please utilize it. There are online groups that one can join in expressing and try to solve mental matters.

Make time for yourself

It can appear selfish to set time for yourself, but it is vital to your overall wellbeing and can help you spring out from mental difficulty.

Mindfulness: Having your presence helps you to realize oneself and be able to manage what we feel. The goal here is to enjoy life again and accept what is around you. We will cover this in detail in the next chapter.

Acquire a new skill: If you learn something that you have been longing for, or will help you later, it gives you the confidence and the joy of achievement. You could sign up for a class or try a new language. Whatever it is, it doesn't have to be big.

Relaxing techniques: Do something that soothes your mind such as having a bath, listening to music, or going for a jog. All these and more will help you cope with stress and mental disorders.

Examine your mental health status

If you are already aware of your mental condition or difficulty, take the appropriate steps to make sure that you are improving.

Talk about what will help you: If there is a strategy that worked on you before, tell the one helping you out. Let those close to you know what can support you better such as listening to your troubles or making you aware of your issues.

Stay alert for warning signs: If you can be aware of how you feel and are able to spot signs that depict you are unwell, that is much better. Being aware of such signs will help you when it becomes hectic, and it will also form the base guidance to those who are directing and supporting you.

Use a mood diary: Just like we track our daily activities, we can also record our moods, and we have seen that is possible in the previous chapters.
Have a way to record your moods, the negative issues that you think of, and ways to help you stay positive. If you have no idea how to write one, there are online sources to help you with that such as moodscope.com

Upgrade your self-esteem: It is one of the major steps in making yourself ready to challenge your mental issues.

Physical health is vital to mental wellbeing

Look after your body and what you are subjecting it to. Here are a few recommended things:

Eating healthy

- ➢ Invest in a well-balanced diet
- ➢ Eat regularly so that your energy levels are constant, and the body can regulate sugar levels
- ➢ Have fruits and vegetables aplenty
- ➢ Avoid alcohol and other drugs that ruin the mental ability

Moving it

Engage in exercise to keep the juices flowing, which will also help you get rid of negativity. Some activities include:

> - A walk
> - Bike riding
> - Swimming
> - Yoga
> - Football
> - Martial arts

Have enough sleep

Tiredness brings in more worry and stress. Doctors' orders direct you to sleep 8 hours per day.

> - Have a bedtime routine, such as drinking milk or hot water before sleeping. Later, you can read a book or listen to music that helps you sleep.
> - Sleep and wake up at the same time every day.
> - Do not drink anything caffeinated after lunch.

As we wrap up this chapter, it is important to consider other methods that will help you gain better mental health as you continue with CBT. That way, you will have more tools to conquer what you need to get rid of.

Chapter 8: How to Increase your Self-Awareness

Self-Awareness and Emotional Intelligence

Let us assume a situation that is happening in your professional life. You own a small website-building firm that is doing reasonably good business. You have five employees working for you, and your professional life is well on its path to becoming a big success.

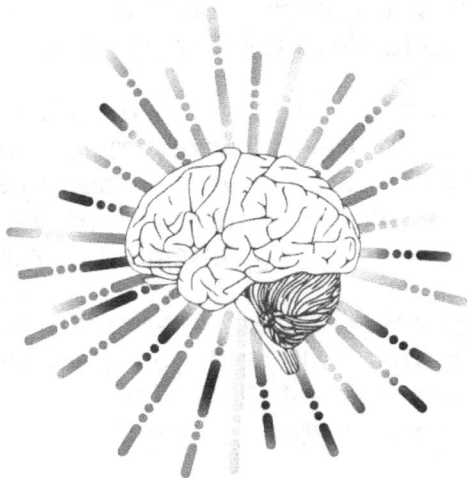

It is a clear Monday morning; sunny skies and all your employees have turned out. Your accountant prints out last week's sales figures and you are happy with the numbers. The present week also promises to bring in some good business. Everything seems hunky-dory, and you are feeling happy and good. There are no major strong emotions in your system currently.

Suddenly, your phone rings and one of your topmost clients; one who contributes to nearly 20% of your business is on the line.

He is furious because his website has stopped working, and he has lost a lot of business because of this, and he blames you for it and threatens to take away his business unless you find a way to correct the mistakes right away. In that spur of a moment, you become acutely aware of the following:

- Your heart is beating fast.
- Your hands are all clammy with sweat.
- You are unable even to form words of apology.
- You almost drop your phone.

You become aware that you are now anxious and the calm feeling you had a couple of minutes ago has gone! This is the most basic form of self-awareness which is a simple phrase to explain a complex network of information and data about your feelings, your thoughts, and all the things happening to you. Self-awareness is a measure of how well you know yourself at different levels including the senses of your physical body, emotions, intentions, preferences, goals and desires, how you are perceived by other people, and more. The higher your level of self-awareness, the easier it is to find ways to adapt yourself to different situations and requirements. And the better we can adapt our responses and reactions to the people in our lives, the more satisfying our relationships will be. We are constantly bombarded by messages from all over the globe, and yet we know so little about our own selves. We don't know how to set up a conversation with ourselves and build our self-awareness. And when we don't know ourselves well, we fall short of understanding other people too.

Our inability to recognize and identify our emotions reduces our ability to respond appropriately and in ways that meet everyone's needs.

Therefore, increasing your self-awareness is a crucial element to improving emotional intelligence. All emotions and feelings are nothing but bytes of data made up of energy. All types of emotions are giving us information of some sort. Even unpleasant emotions give us valuable information. Therefore, emotions are always positive when it comes to how much we can learn from them. The more we tune in to our emotions, the healthier we become by leveraging the power of the data provided by the feelings.

Being Aware Of Your Emotions AND Expressing Them

Yes, expressing your emotions is quite a different matter from being aware of them. How we express our emotions, or even whether we express them at all, is our deliberate choice. However, making the right choice regarding emotional expressions first requires you to be aware of them, to know they exist, and the physical and mental feelings they bring with them. Once we become aware of our emotions, then an entire gamut of how we can express them opens up, and you can choose what suits you the best at that particular point in time.

Reacting to emotions without being aware of them are automatic, and are neither guided by intuition nor by reason. Suppose you start your day with some negative experience.

The unpleasantness of that bitter experience will invariably spill on to the day, and you will show your unhappiness and negative behavior right through the day without even knowing that these negativities are the residual effects of the morning unpleasantness. Then, someone who cares for you and knows you well walk into your cabin and reminds you of your irritable state of mind right from the morning. That is the first time you are made aware of your feelings and emotions and their root cause. We are, in effect, startled into a state of awareness. Once we 'experience' our emotions, then our brains are wired into this experience, and it uses this new data to find ways to overcome your negativity. This new information gained by our brain through our awareness of the feelings is used to look at things from a positive perspective which was not visible before we became 'aware' of that nasty emotion.

The lack of self-awareness also can be damaging because you could have reached the brink, and if you still are not aware, then wittingly or not someone is going to push you over the brink. This situation happens because a limbic memory (something beyond our control) has been triggered, and we end up using responses learned earlier during our childhood days such as shrinking from our boss when he or she shouts at us just like how we behaved during our childhood days when some strict elder in the house or teacher in school screamed at us for some wrongdoing.

The lack of self-awareness results in the loss of self-control. Therefore, self-awareness is the first step to get back control of your life and empower yourself to react and respond appropriately. This self-control and the freedom to behave as you wish are the pillars that hold up the power of empathy and genuine concern for fellow-beings.

461

Most of the time, we are unaware of our emotions until such time they become very strong. It is important to know that just like how we are always thinking something (our thoughts never stop), we are always feeling something. Just like how we have to become acutely aware of our thoughts to be more intelligent, we have to become acutely aware of our emotions to become emotionally intelligent. We should learn to feel and experience our emotions.

Self-Awareness and Nonviolent Communication

Let us look at the four components of nonviolent communication through the lens of self-awareness and understand the connection between the two. The four pillars of nonviolent communication include observation, feelings, needs, and requests.

Observations and Self-Awareness

What is observation? It is our ability to discern the various stimuli that are driving our reactions and responses. The sight of a cute baby gurgling with laughter brings a smile to our faces. The sight of an image depicting a starving child in a remote famine-ridden place fills our heart with sadness, and many times, such powerful images can involuntarily bring tears in our eyes. Observation is what we see, hear, feel, and sense the different stimuli within us and in our surroundings. The purpose of self-awareness is to be accurately aware and describe what we are reacting to or responding to.

The trick in self-awareness is to be aware of everything that is taking place at any point in time neutrally and objectively. You must be like a video camera that is merely capturing everything that is happening at the point in time without judging. What we observe neutrally and specifically gives us the context for our reactions, responses, and the expressions of emotions and needs. The key element in building good observational skills is to be able to separate your own opinions and judgments from the description of the stimuli, and this attitude and approach are what will help in creating and maintaining nonviolent communication with everyone around us.

For instance, if we said, 'You were rude to me,' to someone, that person is quite likely to disagree with us. However, if we said, 'When you walked into the room, I noticed that you did not greet me,' they are more likely to agree with you because your description of the observation was accurate, objective, and did not include your own interpretation. When we describe our observation in this way without mixing up our feelings in the description, the person you are speaking to is quite likely to involve himself or herself in this first stage of the conversation without reacting negatively, and more willing to move towards the feelings and needs aspect of the communication process.

Therefore, by becoming more self-aware, you learn to translate your own opinions, interpretations, and judgments into an objective observational language. This approach helps to move away from our feelings of right/wrong. Consequently, we will find it easy to take responsibility for our actions because this objective outlook will direct our attention to the fact that our feelings are a result of our needs, and does not have anything to do with the other person(s).

Therefore, building observation skills helps us develop increased self-awareness, helping us get closer to our true selves. Increased self-awareness builds our relationships and connections with other people as well, and our overall consciousness will shift towards becoming more authentic than before.

Feelings and Self-Awareness

What are the feelings? They represent our collective physical sensations and emotional experiences connected to our met and/or unmet needs. Self-awareness is our ability to identify and label these feelings, again without judgment. It is important to focus on words that express the feeling and emotion instead of focusing on words that express our interpretations and opinions on the actions of other people. Here is an example to illustrate the above point; telling your partner 'I feel lonely,' describes your feeling. However, if you said, 'I feel that you don't like me anymore,' is a description of your interpretation of your partner's behavior. Expressing your feelings is continuing to take responsibility for your actions and your experiences.

Here is another example to illustrate how increased self-awareness about your feelings and emotions can help you manage difficult situations. Suppose your new team member goofed up big time on a very important project that is due in a week. It is true that you are angry with him or she for the mistake committed. However, if you include your own feeling of anxiety about completing the project well and on time, then your reaction to the person's faults will be more wholesome, and you will be in a better frame of mind to help the new person to correct the errors and still meet the deadline.

Consequently, the listener gets to hear about your feelings without the burden of having to take blame, criticism, or responsibility for your experiences. This kind of situation enhances the chances of the outcome of the communication process to meet the needs of everyone concerned. Identifying and labeling emotions is a critical step to building self-awareness, improving your nonviolent communication capabilities, and increasing your emotional intelligence. Remember, there are no good or bad emotions; there are only emotions. Yes, some of the feelings may appear to be more pleasant to experience than others. However, every emotion is giving you valuable information, and self-awareness helps you discern this valuable information.

Also, feelings need not always accurately reflect the situation. It is possible for you to feel guilty even when you know you have done no wrong or feel a sense of panic when there is really nothing to fear or a sense of joy even in a toxic relationship. Even misplaced emotions are communicating something important to you.

For example, if you are feeling unduly guilty, then maybe it is time for you to start creating boundaries for yourself and reducing other people's expectations from you. Feelings of misplaced fear could be an indication that this is new territory for you, and you will benefit from the learning. All this can happen only when you become increasingly aware of your feelings, and delve deep into your psyche to try and analyze them, and see whether or not they fit into the situation that created them in the first place. Here are some feelings and what they might convey to you. Remember, this list is only a guideline to get you started on increasing your self-awareness about your feelings. You could build your own set of guidelines as you become increasingly aware of how your emotions play out. Also, remember the intensity of the emotions is telling you something.

465

Love – Love could be telling you that something (or everything) about a particular relationship or situation is going well.

Grief – Sadness or grief is an indication that you need love and succor from others. It is important to listen to this emotion and reach out for help because unresolved grief can lead to disastrous outcomes.

Guilt – Guilt is typically an indicator of some mistake we have done. You can use guilt to correct mistakes. Undue guilt could be an indication that you have let others raise their expectations from you excessively.

Shame – Perhaps, one of the most unpleasant emotions to go through, shame also has a purpose. The biggest disadvantage of feeling shame is that it makes us feel inadequate and flawed, and these negative feelings could drive us to go into hiding which is counterproductive to solving problems. For example, if you are ashamed of being overweight, then not being socially active could be a way of hiding this feeling. Identifying and labeling this emotion is the first step to correcting such faulty beliefs, and finding ways to overcome challenges that are creating the feeling of shame in you.

Anger – This is a powerful emotion that tells us that we have been wronged. The most basic reaction would be to either confront the person who is the cause of your anger or simply speak to someone you trust and express your anger openly.

Accumulating anger is one of the most debilitating ways of handling this potent feeling. You can channelize anger into productive work.

Anxiety – There are two types of anxiety namely productive and non-productive. The productive anxiety is giving you mature advice to remain on your guard and alert to get the best outcome for yourself to achieve all your dreams and desires. Non-productive anxiety, on the other hand, is debilitating to the point of not allowing you to do your regular daily tasks. It increases stress and reduces your ability to get things done effectively and efficiently.

Happiness – Like love, the feeling of true happiness is an indication that something is going right. Happiness can be felt even during difficult phases of your life. For example, if you have not had enough money to take your children out for a fancy Christmas dinner but have managed to cook up some amazing food for them at home, and they have that grateful smile on their faces despite their disappointment, you will feel happiness.

Needs and Self-Awareness

All human beings share critical survival needs including food, sleep, shelter, rest, and a desire to connect with other human beings. Other than these basic needs, we have other needs that we share. These needs are experienced by different people at varying degrees of intensity.

Some of us need the feeling of connection more than others while some might have an increased need for self-esteem. Moreover, in different situations, our needs could be different. For example, when at home, one individual might need the attention of his or her spouse more than anything else while at the workplace, the same person might not need the attention of other people. Self-awareness is to be totally aware of these deep longings that form the foundation of our life purposes. When we are deeply aware of these longings, then we are able to connect to ourselves in a much better way than before which in turn helps us build better relationships with other people. Being aware of our needs helps us behave and act in ways that meet everyone's needs.

Most often, we express our wants and needs through a strategy of asking for something from someone. For example, 'Please come to my birthday party,' is a specific strategy that reflects your need for love and companionship on that special day. Once you shift your focus from the strategy to the underlying need, then you liberate yourself from finding having to limit the ways of meeting that need. You are ready to explore other alternatives. Moreover, when you become aware of the fact that everything you do or say reflects an underlying need, then you will also learn to understand that the same holds good for others as well.

When needs are met or unmet, feelings arise. Feelings are triggered by our experience associated with the unmet or met needs; positive if met and negative if unmet. When we connect our feelings to our needs, we take responsibility for our emotions resulting in blame-free and criticism-free relationships with others.

Requests and Self-Awareness

Requests represent strategies that help us meet our needs. Identifying and accepting this deep connection between requests and needs will enhance our self-awareness. Quite often, in any given moment in time, the responses of other people to our requests are based on our connection with them. For example, if you ask someone, 'What do you think of this?" their response to your question is dependent on your connection with them then. The most important element of creating strategies through requests is to be ready to take 'no' for an answer and continue to seek out alternative solutions either on your own or with the help of others. A critical difference between a demand and a request lies in our response to a situation when the other person denies our request/demand. In the case of demand, a denial typically leads to conflict or some other sort of punitive consequence whereas a denied request usually leads to further dialogue.

In a requested scenario, a 'no' is nothing but an expression of some unmet need for the other person which is preventing him or her from saying 'yes'. Increased self-awareness will alert you to the fact that saying 'yes' to your request is proving very costly for the other person, and a bit of negotiation is in order to make sure that both your needs are met. Here is a classic example of how to discern between an undoable demand and a doable request that meets the needs of everyone concerned. Suppose you have an employee who has a problem with coming late. One way of ensuring discipline is by saying, 'I want you to be on time to the office consistently.'

However, this is undoable because obviously, there is some his of need that is being unmet which is why he is not able to come on time.

469

Moreover, he is bound to come up with some excuse each day even after promising to be on time due to other unmet needs that were not resolved with your undoable demand. Instead, if you told him, 'Can you spare me 15 minutes so that we can discuss how we can help each other to make sure you don't come late to the office every day?' Now, this request is doable because not only is your need for time discipline met but also the employee's needs of confidence, connection, trust, respect, responsibility, etc. This willingness to work together to meet everyone's needs is a sign of high emotional intelligence and a key differentiator of a highly self-aware individual.

Tips to Build Self-Awareness

So, how can you build your level of self-awareness to develop your emotional intelligence and nonviolent communication skills?

Here are some tips for that:

See yourself objectively – When you see yourself objectively, it is easier to come to terms with your weaknesses and feel proud of your strengths without bordering on arrogance. For example, think of your current situation, and write down your thoughts. Here are some prompts:

- What are you good at?
- What do you need to improve on?
- What are the accomplishments are you proud of?
- What are the things that could you have done better?

470

- What are the happy memories of your childhood? What has changed since then, and why?

Seek out people whom you trust and ask for honest feedback – Knowing yourself also means knowing how other people perceive you. This can be quite a challenge because most people find it difficult to give honest feedback. The ones who dislike you will be critical of your every effort, and those who like you might not want to hurt you by giving criticisms. It is only those who truly love and care for you will give you honest, upfront feedback; using which you can progress in your self-awareness journey. Keep track of such people, and always keep them in your life.

Maintain a journal – Write down your thoughts in a journal as often as you can. Doing it every day before you go to bed is the most effective way of looking back on your day objectively, as you note down the events and your accompanying thoughts and feelings. However, sometimes, during highly emotional periods, you might want to write down your intense emotions immediately. Don't hesitate to make a note in little chits of paper. This action of transferring your thoughts into a written form is a great way to release the emotion-driven stress from your system. Make sure you write down both the good and bad things that took place during the day.

Also, write down your needs, plans, goals, and priorities. Thoughts are nebulous and putting them down into words and saving them on paper is the best way to read and learn from your experiences later on.

Allocate some time for self-reflection – Increasing self-awareness means you have to be with yourself for some time. Use this alone time for self-reflection. Don't skim the surfaces of your emotions. Dig deep and ask yourself why you are so happy. Don't feel ashamed to face your jealousy and other weaknesses. There is nothing wrong with having flaws. What is wrong is not finding the courage to fight them and overcome them.

Focus on your breath – Get away from the hustle and bustle of your daily life for at least 15 minutes each day. Choose any convenient time. Find a quiet, undisturbed, and comfortable spot. Sit down, and close your eyes. Now, observe how you breathe. Don't try and control it. Simply observe the inhalation and exhalation process. Your thoughts are bound to wander away. Bring your mind gently to focus on your breath. Initially, 15 minutes will seem like a long time. However, soon you will find that you feel more connected to yourself than before. You are comfortable being alone with your thoughts. You like solitude.

Practice mindfulness – Mindfulness is the science of 'living in the moment' so that you experience and engage with life fully. Immerse yourself in every action you are performing. Focusing on your breath is a deliberate mindfulness exercise. Here are some more. For example, when you eat your meals, the current trend is to watch TV or carry on a conversation with other people. For your next meal, focus only on eating your meal. Take small bites. Chew at least 20 times before swallowing. Focus and feel the flavor, texture, and taste of the food. Don't focus on whether you like it or not. Simply focus on the sensations in your mouth and tongue.

When you are walking, focus on the sensations on your legs, how the calf muscles, ankles, and other parts of your legs are moving. Focus on your breathing. Is it very fast or is it slow? Don't try to control it. Simply observe all your feelings and sensations. Slowly, with practice, you will find yourself becoming increasingly productive and efficient because your entire being is focused on this one act. You will find yourself being able to recognize every feeling your body senses as you eat, sleep, walk, wash dishes, breathe, etc. These are some of the most basic methods of developing self-awareness. The more self-aware you are, the better control you have over how you choose to react and respond to your emotions.

Chapter 9: Mindfulness, Use Mindfulness Techniques when you are Angry

Alertness is to purposefully mind about an occurrence as it unfolds. These happen as we watch but without us imposing any of our comments and not having a vague idea of how it should turn out. It is a healthy way which enables us to respond to what we are experiencing. In addition, we able to conquer the tendencies of our mind that are not intended and hence protects us from feeling we did not get what we wanted.

 The practice of meditation is a fundamental technique for the development of mindfulness. Meditating has its own mental and physical effects which enable our ability to naturally become aware of the eternity in us. It is also a transparency of our persona to face what is real without being biased. When alertness and meditating are faced through this vain, then letting go of former expectations, ideas, and opinions we may have formed about this subject. These happen in both the physical and metaphysical areas.

Over time, two moral standards of discipline that is empathy and wisdom are built up. When we able to see clearly the fundamental reality of nature then that is wisdom.

We can practice being alert. Any individual can use these techniques to perform the simple areas of life such as talking sensing, feeling, breathing, and even driving.

Mindfulness in Practice

If like most people, you get upset and annoyed with yourself for feeling disturbed, edgy, or panicky and in response to your frustrations, you try to resist these feelings, you'll soon realize that you are only strengthening these negative emotions and making them worse than they already are. What you should do instead of resisting your feelings is just to allow yourself to feel the way you are feeling. Learning to accept this will help a great deal and it will eventually settle down and pass.

Here are three fundamental and brief mindfulness techniques that you can apply to help you find a release from worry, anxiety, and a panic attack before it escalates.

Anchoring

One of the best ways to quiet yourself down is to ground yourself. Yes, ground yourself. In other words "anchor yourself." You can achieve this by channeling the totality of your thoughts and attention into the lower half of your body.

> ➤ To begin, focus your attention on your feet. Concentrate on how they feel inside your socks or shoes. Pay attention to the hardness of the ground against them.
> ➤ Now that you have a complete focus on your feet, allow that focus to move from your lower legs and gradually through your upper legs. Savor the sensation. How does it feel? Dense or feathery? Toasty or chilly? Exited or paralyzed?
> ➤ To conclude the process, feel yourself inhale, exhale, and relax as you continue the breathing process.

This is an extraordinary method of anchoring yourself. It is something you can practice at any time, having your eyes open or closed, in a seated position or even while moving around. It is easy: anchor yourself and then breathes.

Breathe Counting

The mind is always busy, recounting stories, translating our experience by filling in missing snippets of information, and afterward, ruminating over the stories it has created, whether they are actually true or false.

This method can either be utilized in conjunction with anchoring or utilized alone.

➢ The first step is anchoring. Count up to "6", as you inhale deeply the next time you breathe in.
➢ Then count up to "10" as you exhale.

This strategy has the impact of protracting both the in-breath and the out-breath, thereby slowing down your breathing. It additionally lengthens the out-breath more than the in-breath, driving you to discharge more carbon dioxide, slowing your pulse, calming you down, and re-establishing emotional equilibrium.

Ensure you fit the numbers to your breath and not the other way around. On the off chance that 6 and 10 don't work for you, discover another proportion that works, provided that the out-breath is longer than the in-breath with a minimum of two counts. You can count for one full breath, then take one normal breath and count the next one if it becomes too difficult to continue breathing at the same time as counting.

In the event that you can't manage counting because you feel panicked, then as you breathe in, say to yourself, "in" and as you breathe out, say, "out" completely, endeavoring to extend the out-breath. Repeat the process for at least one minute, or you can go for whatever length of time that you require. This method can be cast-off very effectively to charge off approaching panic outbreaks at night.

'Finger Breathing'

This is another version of 'breathe counting.'

The following are the procedures of the above subject:

> Bring one of your hands in front of you with the palm facing towards you.
> Trail up the outer length of your thumb by the index finger of your extra hand whereas you breathe in. Break at the peak point of your thumb and now dash it quickly on the other on the side while you breathe out. That's a single breath.
> Keep an eye on up the side of the ensuing finger while you draw in. Recess at the top and, later, trace down the extra side of that finger as you respire. Those are now two breaths.
> Continue outlining along every finger as you tally every breath. Move back up the preceding finger after the accomplishment of the end of the finger and reprise the practice in reverse.

This exercise is extremely valuable when there is a lot going on around you, and you find it difficult to close your eyes and focus inwards. It gives you something visual to focus on, something kinesthetic to do with your hands, and it also helps you focus on counting and your breathing. This is a very simple procedure to teach young people and children.

Doodling

Doodling is an incredible tool to activate your celestial creative self. When combined with the power of Mandala, it can help you access profound parts of your brain through these steps.

- ➤ Draw a dot at the center of your canvas /paper. This dot represents the seed of an idea you want to expand on and get innovative with. Everything creative started with a basic seed. It's like the Big Bang.
- ➤ Next, you develop your idea and your creativity by drawing 4 lines out from the dot, each line pointing toward north, south, east, and west, respectively.
- ➤ Continue expanding your idea by drawing the next 4 lines out from the dot, which will look like lines extending NE, SE, SW, and NW.
- ➤ Draw a petal on each line. The petals represent your personal, creative development.
- ➤ Draw a heart in the middle of each petal and a circle around the lines.
- ➤ Then, again, draw a heart in between every two petals
- ➤ Now draw a circle around the entire center. This speaks to advance creativity and growth within the circles you have made with the networks and connections you have framed.
- ➤ Draw a dot that connects each line with the circle, then, on the circle, draw 8 dots. This depicts co-creation within your connections and networks and planting seeds of growth along the way.
- ➤ Draw the image for the lotus petal, joining each dot.
- ➤ Inside each lotus petal, make a sketch of any preferred symbol (the symbol must be similar). Make a sketch of a symbol that represents something significant to you, such as a flower, a

479

musical note, or maybe a football, inside the lotus flower. What you doodle doesn't matter. Make a doodle of anything that comes to your mind. That's your mandala!

There is no restriction on how big or how much you draw so you can keep expanding out and including details Bear in mind, however, that it won't be perfect, but it will be lovely!

Coloring

This is similar to doodling

➢ Keep it artless. Start with a blank page and a color.

➢ Start with a figure that you find stress-free to draw. For instance, a loop. Remember to retain it simple.

➢ Draw form after form, and believe your instinct. Perhaps make a bunch of rounds together.

➢ If you think there should be limited lines, go forward and do it. Make those outlines. Get silly.

➢ Give yourself the approval to put whatever you want on the page. You can fill the sheet as far as conceivable, or halt when you have a longing for faltering. Simply keep up with it till you feel done.

➢ Get your day feeling revitalized. The simple turn of sketching on a page can do miracles.

The most vibrant thing is to quiet your thoughts. On the occasion that you discover yourself being tense and distressing that you are not doing it correctly, simply grasp a deep gasp and let that self-deprecation go. The goal is to attain a nice of Zen state, where you're only giving your hand an opportunity to make scripts, and your brain to have contemplation without verdict while you're not really thinking about no matter what in precise.

These mindfulness techniques are not new. They have been utilized by many psychologists and counselors for years. The fact that we can all benefit from these techniques and the fact that they are effective for everyday experiences is a relatively new discovery. Try them and notice what happens.

Chapter 10: Cognitive Behavioral Therapy

What is Cognitive Behavioral Therapy (CBT)?

Mental health is paramount in the way we conduct ourselves. That is why CBT (Cognitive Behavioral Therapy) takes a step to change how we think, the beliefs that hold us back knowingly or unknowingly, our attitude towards various issues affecting our lives, and how we behave when facing challenging situations, not forgetting to strive to achieve our set objectives. Adjusting your negative thoughts using this form of therapy does not need to take your whole lifetime. Those who receive it from their therapists know that it takes utmost, ten months with 50-60 minutes per session once a week. While we can view it as a hands-on approach that requires you and the professional to be available, sometimes it's overwhelming to see you juggle your mind in front of someone who is continuously looking at their watch.

That is why we give you a solution that you can use while at home.

This does not mean that you should ignore professional help when presented. If you can read and are able to identify what is troubling your mind, therapists may not be necessary after going to that quiet spot a few times a week just like in therapy.

A Little History about Cognitive Behavioral Therapy

Aaron Beck is the name behind this form of therapy. In the '60s, this man was busy working on psychoanalysis on his patients. During the analysis, he noted something strange and unusual. They seemed to have an *inner dialogue* going on in their minds as if they had someone else talking to them in there or were merely talking to themselves internally. When Beck enquired about their thinking status, the patients only produced a portion of the total information. To give an example, the patient in his office was probably thinking, "The therapist is super quiet today. Am I boring him or does he have a lot on his mind to ponder?" The first sentence of thought triggered the second one, and this is how such an internal dialogue starts. After some time, the client would think, "Maybe my issues are not that important to this high-end figure." At this point, he or she will not adequately communicate their real feelings. That is when Beck came to know that something connected one's feelings and thoughts. He went ahead to come up with the phrase *automatic thoughts* to signify the ideas overwhelmed by emotions that come abruptly to mind without the knowledge of the victim. While it may not be possible for the client to know what is happening in their brain, there is a way to identify them and report when they occur.

By identifying such thinking modes, the client would then be able to understand what is happening to them and eventually overcome the hurdles in life.

That is when Cognitive Behavioral Therapy was born. The primary purpose was to place the importance of thinking about the forefront of solving our problems. The terms cognitive and behavior are joined together since apart from the mind, behavioral techniques also need to be addressed. A balance between the two varies depending on other forms of therapy using CBT as the main basis, but they are all defined under this form of treatment. Today, it has undergone various professional trials all over the world in a bid to solve mind and behavior-related problems.

Cognitive Behavioral Therapy in Depth

Cognitive Behavioral Therapy represents a goal-oriented psychological therapy treatment whose hands-on approach drives towards problem-solving. The objective here is to change our thinking patterns or the behavioral aspects that bring about the difficulties which will eventually replace the focus of our feelings. If you looked at the introduction, there are many problems that this form of therapy can address, from sleeping troubles to anxiety, depression, and drug abuse. Using CBT means finding a way to change the patient's attitude and how they respond to situations by shedding light on the beliefs, images, and thoughts held in the cognitive process. In that way, the victim can focus and be able to deal with emotional situations.

Think of it as a combination of behavioral therapy and psychotherapy. The latter focuses on the meaning we use on what we come across in our lives and how the thinking pattern started when we were little. Behavioral therapy, on the other hand, digs into the relationship available between our thoughts and problems and how we behave. The following diagram will show you how the things mentioned above are interconnected. We will then focus on it by applying various life situations that will pick the same pattern as depicted below.

SCENARIO

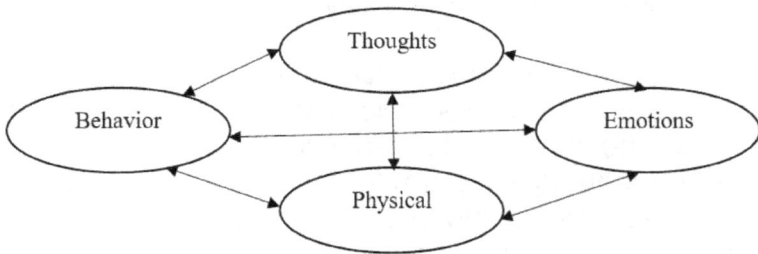

CBT Principles

Since it includes learning essential skills that will help us manage what makes us feel down, you will possess new methods of behaving and thinking as you look forward to controlling your situation in the future. Here are a few things you need to understand when using CBT.

This form of therapy focuses on the present

We must dig into the past to get the cause of what is happening to us. On the other hand, CBT treatment will focus on the symptoms that are currently driving you in the wrong direction and not where it all began. So, for example, if you are dealing with anxiety, knowing where it all started is not enough to help you cope.

Homework is essential

Whether it comes from a therapist or this self-help book, homework is vital. Doing the assignments given means that you will have something to do every week and you need to practice what you learn by applying the skills daily? Since it is homework, you need to keep using what you have gained until it sticks in your mind.

Necessitating the need for practice is not enough, so you need something more than motivation. Unless you learn to practice the things you have learned, what is most likely to happen is that you'll forget after some time. When you are later facing your problem, it will be hard to remember how to utilize the skills.

Learning the new methods can be compared to gaining a new habit, healthy to be precise. If you need to start jogging in the morning, it might appear hard in the first few days, but after a few trials, it will become part of your routine. CBT applies the same notion. If you make it a habit to practice what will make you change the way you think and act, you'll soon get used to it. So, the more you are into it, the easier it gets.

Are There Pros And Cons In CBT?

While it is as effective as the medication used when treating valid mental disorders, one man's meat is another man's poison, so it may not suit every psychologically-driven behavior. The advantages include:

- ➢ Time taken can be relatively shorter than other forms of therapy consume.
- ➢ It can be the only solution where medication is not working.
- ➢ There are many ways of presenting it, which include using a therapist, getting self-help books, or using apps.
- ➢ The skills taught are practical when applied in everyday life even after therapy.

The disadvantages include:

- ➢ There is a need for more cooperation and commitment since it is a long process.
- ➢ Much time consumption especially if it involves a therapist and extra work to be done.
- ➢ There is a confrontation of emotions and thoughts here so, during the beginning, one is bound to experience some uncomfortable form of anxiety.
- ➢ Complex mental issues may need further assistance and treatment. At such a point, CBT may not be of good use.

This Is What You Need To Remember

➢ CBT is research-based, so there is proof that it works.
➢ CBT teaches us new thinking and behaving ways. This is a self-help book that can help you with that.
➢ What we think, feel, and behave are all in a cycle, so they are interconnected. Changing one means affecting the rest.

Chapter 11: Meditation Techniques

The Power of Meditation and Relaxation to Ease Anger

The word meditation originates from the Latin word 'meditatio' and means to think, ponder or contemplate. Meditation is a way of transforming the mind and body through techniques that enhance and develop concentration and positivity. It is a method of deep relaxation that rests the mind and in turn the body.

Simply put, meditation is the peace of mind!

The aim of meditation is to achieve self-regulation of the mind by using the various meditation techniques for relaxation, mental clarity and building positive internal energy. It is this end that helps to manage health problems like anger, depression and high blood pressure.

The body is nourished and healed through rest. Deep rest and relaxation achieved through meditation are, therefore, great for rejuvenating the body to leave you well and mentally serene. Research has shown that the degree of rest achieved when one is meditating is greater than that harnessed from sleep. The findings are incredible. 20 minutes of deep meditation has been equated to 7 hours of sleep!

The desired goal of mental clarity, positivity, and peace are reached through a regular practice of meditative techniques. For maximum harvest of the benefits, be committed to this art. In the course of time, your body will get into a rhythm and in tune for inner peace.

Types or Techniques of Meditation

There are many different types and techniques of meditation that we shall not be able to cover everything. Meditative techniques are in the hundreds but are all linked by the common thread of aiming at achieving inner peace for the practitioner.

First and foremost, all meditative practices engage in mind control techniques as a way to achieve relaxation and peace. Secondly, there are postures and body movements that are found in all forms of meditation. These two traits are evident in all meditative practices pointing to a common goal for all of them.

Meditation helps to relieve our bodies and minds of the toxic effects of stress, relaxes us and brings the peace of mind that we all yearn for. Before you pick up one form of meditation or another, it is important to do your research and learn as much as you can about them.

Interrogate yourself, find out and decide what your meditative goals are or would be to help you pick up the right technique for you. In some cases, you will need to get a teacher or join a meditation school for the right advice, coaching, and mentorship in taking up meditation. There are types of meditative practices that cannot be performed by beginners, people with certain conditions or illnesses or older people for example. Seeking the right information will guide you to the right technique. It is also important to remember to take on a meditative practice that will fit your lifestyle. Meditation requires consistency, regularity, discipline, and high commitment for one to realize the desired fruits. With the many types of meditation in existence, we can generally categorize meditation as follows:

1. Concentrative Meditation

In concentrative meditation, the mind is directed to a particular object, chant/mantra, sound, or sensation. The practitioner will focus their mind and energy on a focal point of their choosing that best works for them in an effort to clear and calm their minds and bodies. These types of meditations are good for beginners.

2. Mindfulness Meditation

This type of meditation does not rely on focusing the mind on an object but relies on feelings, sensations, emotions and thought patterns to achieve a meditative state. These are more advanced types of meditation that are not for everyone especially beginners.

3. Effortless Transcending

This is another form of reflection that is referred to as "effortless". This is because no effort is needed to perform it mentally. It is also called "pure being", "transcendental". This form seeks to calm you as you meditate inwards and empty yourself of any hindrance. This enables the practitioner to recognize their true essence by emptying or eliminating all their thoughts.

With consistent practice, our souls are an open space that allows for relaxation. It has been compared to massaging the brain. The transcendental process will help the practitioner be in a silent zone where they are aware of their deepest state of being conscious. Individuals who practice this type of alertness testify of finding the great feelings in the experience. Below are various reflections

4. Buddhist meditation

a) Zen Meditation (Zazen)

Zazen is Japanese meaning "seated Zen" or "seated meditation"- referring to the form of Zen meditation practiced while sitting. Zazen originates from Chinese Zen Buddhism. It is done while seated on the floor usually on a mat with crossed legs and was traditionally done in the lotus or half-lotus position.

For the mind, Zazen employs two techniques:

- Focus on breathing. The practitioner will pay attention to inhalation and exhalation will silently counting down with every breath and back.

492

- Shikantanza. Here, there is no specific object of meditation. One remains in the moment being aware of what goes through their mind and what passes around.

b) Vipassana Meditation

Vipassana means clear seeing or insight and is a Buddhist type of meditation. It is ideal for mental discovery and awareness. It starts with mindfulness of breath to stabilize and focus the mind –focused mind meditation. Then it moves to develop clarity of awareness of bodily sensations and mental phenomena. Sit on the floor legs crossed with a straight back.

5. Mindfulness Meditation

Mindfulness meditation combines practices from various Buddhist meditation practices. It is widely employed in hospitals and other health benefits as a form of treatment. Here, the practitioner will focus on the moment while not losing awareness of thoughts and emotions experienced.

6. Religious/Spiritual Meditation

These are meditative practices that are practiced among different religions. Remember that spirituality is one avenue for achieving peace of mind and relaxation. Here, meditation and prayer are combined to achieve spiritual development by the reflection of God's word.

Meditation is a communion with the self with the aim of spiritual development or divinity. Meditation in religion is practiced for peace of mind by steadying and focusing it on giving the practitioner the ability for divine insight. A practitioner of Christian meditation said that God is sought through the study of scripture but through meditation, he is found. There are forms of meditative practices in almost all religions which prove the close link between spirituality and meditation. Sufism meditative practices are some of the most elaborate of religious meditation. Practitioners get into a rhythm of chanting and movement that eventually transports participants into a spiritual realm. In Christianity, there are examples with the Catholics and Orthodox sects that have mantras or repetitive prayers.

7. Metta Meditation

It is also referred to as loving-kindness meditation and has its roots in Tibet. This meditative form enhances empathy and compassion to make one more loving to self and others. The practitioner will sit and close their eyes, then generate feelings of kindness and compassion in their mind towards themselves then progress to others. Just like the name suggests, this type of meditation aims at creating harmony with one's surroundings. Treat all things with kindness and the rewards are happiness and compassion for you. You emit happiness and the world bounces it back to you.

8. Hindu Meditations

Vedic and Yogic forms of meditation are Hindu forms and are classified as follows:

Mantra Meditation- Mantra involves the repetition of a word or phrase to focus on one's mind.

Transcendental Meditation- Transcendental techniques aim at opening the mind.

Yoga Meditation- Yoga means union and there are many types. Yoga combines mind relaxing and focusing on practices with stretching movements and postures. Of all the meditative practices, yoga is the most popular of the secular forms of meditation and has the most following for non-religious or spiritual meditation. You will find that most people who meditate are practicing one form of yoga or another. How then do we use these techniques for self-improvement and relaxation? Let us first know the benefits of meditation.

Benefits of Meditation

There are several benefits apart from the ones we have discussed in the preceding sections. It is no wonder then that meditation is being promoted as an alternative to clinical treatment for cure and management of several health conditions and for general wellbeing. Meditation leads the body to undergo a change. Cells in the body are injected with more energy resulting in peace, happiness and motivation as the energy levels in the body are boosted

The benefits of meditative practices are:

> Meditation reverses or reduces the production of stress hormones (adrenaline) by creating calmness and eradicating anger to prevent chronic stress. With controlled or regulated stress hormones, the body is more relaxed.

> It is good for managing blood pressure and other heart diseases or conditions since the heart rate and breathing is slowed down. When we are not stressed, worried or anxious, the heart rate is slow therefore the blood pressure is also low. Meditation can help greatly with conditions like high blood pressure since it works to create calmness and relaxation.

> Boosts the immune system and slows aging as a result of less production of adrenaline by the body. The immune system is boosted since one ends up being healthier as a result of the suppression of destructive stress chemicals.

> Meditation brings clarity to the mind and creativity is enhanced. With a relaxed mind, one is sure to be more creative and productive.

> Meditative techniques advocate for a pure life and in fact, the aim of meditation is to attain purity akin to the higher being, so practitioners find themselves quitting poisonous habits like smoking, drug abuse, and alcohol consumption.

> Brain functioning is greatly improved through the boosting of psychological creativity, better memory, and a settled relaxed mind.

➢ Meditation makes you happier since your mind and body feel better. A relaxed person has no worries and will be a happier person.

➢ You will sleep better since you are relaxed, enabling you to have more rest and better rest to face the day and tasks that you are faced with.

➢ Reduces how fast we age through mental and physical exercise. People who meditate have a slower aging process. Stress hormones hasten aging while meditation is known to halt or significantly reduce their production.

➢ Meditation reduces or eliminates stress. A meditation practitioner is a calm and happy individual who is essentially immune to the effects of stress.

➢ A relaxed and happier person has the benefit of a better functioning body. Immunity is boosted and diseases are kept at bay.

➢ When one embraces meditation with all its tenets and understands it, they hold life to a greater value since they learn the true meaning and purpose of living.

➢ Meditative exercises improve metabolism and help regulate weight by fighting obesity.

➢ Meditation helps you feel more connected and in tune with yourself.

➢ Meditation brings emotional balance and harmony.

➢ Personal transformation is inevitable with meditation. You end up being a new person.

It is recommended that you meditate at least once in a day for optimal results –dawn meditation is highly recommended usually between 3 am to 6 am. Dawn meditation is considered more beneficial as you tend to be more alert and well-rested after your sleep. The environment is also quiet and ideal for meditation. In the next part, we shall learn how to use meditation to reduce stress in your life.

How to reduce Stress by Meditating

So, what is stress? Stress is basically the body's way of responding to pressure that may be exerted on it physically or psychologically. Stress is caused when the body releases stress chemicals usually adrenaline into the blood in an effort to combat whatever pressure it is confronted with. Stress can be classified as follows:

> ➢ Survival stress. This is stress that we face when we are confronted by dangerous situations where you feel that physical harm is imminent. It is here where we have a fight-and-flight response to fight stress.

> ➢ Internal stress. This is stress caused by worries over things that are out of your control. Simply put, internal stress is self-imposed stress that can be avoided by not giving yourself so much pressure over things that are beyond you.

> ➢ Environmental stress. This is stress caused by factors in your surroundings like noise etc. Stay away from environmental stress triggers and you have a happy life.

498

➤ Tiredness. This type of stress is caused by fatigue which usually accumulates over a long period of time due to such things as overworking.

Stress is an inescapable part of life and sooner or later we experience it. What we need to do is learn how to manage it so that it does not overwhelm us and take over our lives. Stress is not an entirely bad thing as it can enhance our alertness and concentration. However, in excess, it is very unhealthy.

Symptoms of stress

How do you know if you are stressed? The following are some signs that will let you know if you are stressed:

Cognitive symptoms

➤ Problems remembering things

➤ Low concentration

➤ High anger

➤ Constant worry

Emotional symptoms

➤ Being moody

➤ Highly irritable and angry

➤ Loneliness and reclusion

➤ Sadness

Physical symptoms

- Low libido
- Aches and pain
- High heart rate
- Dizziness

Behavioral symptoms

- Eating disorders. Bingeing or self-starving
- Lack of sleep
- Substance abuse
- Nervousness

Causes of stress

External causes

- Major life changes. Divorce, chronic illness, the death of a loved one
- Work burden
- Financial problems
- Trauma

Internal causes

- Constant worry
- Negativity and pessimism
- Fear and anger
- Unrealistic expectations

Stress can cause serious health and social problems if it is not dealt with immediately and well. Some of the side effects of stress are:

- Mental disorders like depression and anger
- Cardiovascular problems. High blood pressure, heart disease, stroke, etc.
- Weight problems such as obesity
- Problems with menstrual cycles
- Skin and hair problems such as acne, hair loss, etc.
- Sexual dysfunction
- Gastrointestinal problems like ulcers

Meditation and Stress Management

Meditation has been proven as a stress reliever and is being embraced by many for relaxation. Stress relief needs both mental and physical relaxation and meditation provides that.

To understand why meditation is so helpful in reducing stress, we should know what it takes to relax:

Deep breathing

Deep breathing is a quick and sure way of deflating stress from your system; a simple technique with far-reaching positive consequences in keeping stress in check.

Balancing the nervous system

For the body to function optimally, the nervous system must be at equilibrium- you must be at peace mentally. Stress destabilizes this balance and the only way to stead your system is by relaxation. A state of profound serenity of the nervous system which is the counter to stress.

Using Meditation to achieve Relaxation

Relaxation is a state of mental and physical calmness and serenity where one is free from tension and anger. Meditation practices reduce muscle tension, lower blood pressure, calm the mind and eliminate stress in general. A response christened 'relaxation response' is elicited when the one is relaxed. It is the opposite of stress response experienced when one is under pressure. Meditation is one sure way of generating the relaxation response.

Regular meditation will regularly generate the relaxation response giving you more control of your body for a stress-free life. The following are the most used relaxation techniques:

- **_Progressive muscle relaxation_**

This technique is used for relaxing deep muscle tension. Tension in the muscles increases anger and this technique will reduce muscle tension and lower the heart rate and blood pressure. It can be practiced while lying on your back or seated. You tense each muscle group for a few seconds and relaxed. This is repeated until the whole body relaxes.

- **_Deep breathing_**

Deep breathing emphasizes breath control and focuses on your breathing to achieve a relaxed state. Take deep breathes from the stomach, breathing in enough air into your lungs. Deep breathes mean more oxygen into your system. More oxygen means less tension and anger. Deep breathing is simple but a powerful relaxation technique that is easily learned by all and can be done almost anywhere. It offers a quick fix for managing stress levels. Remember that deep breathing is the basis of other relaxation techniques and can be applied together with other relaxation tools like aromatherapy and music. You can use the following routine for your deep breathing meditative technique:

➢ Sit with your back straight, a hand on your chest, and the other hand placed on your stomach. The hands should guide you through the breathing routine.

- Breathe in using your nose. The hand placed on your tummy will be pushed up while the other on your chest will move very little.
- Breathe out from your mouth, releasing the most air you can manage while constricting your stomach muscles. The hand placed on your stomach will move inwards as you breathe out while they will hardly move.
- Continue breathing in using your nose and exhaling through your mouth. Breathe in sufficient air so that your lower tummy rises and drops.
- Count down slowly as you breathe out.
- If breathing from your abdomen is a problem while you are seated, lie on a flat surface - the floor is ideal.
- Place a light visible object on your tummy to act as a guide and then breathe so that the object rises as you breathe in and falls as you breathe out.

Tense/Relax method - This technique is similar to progressive relaxation where you tense and relax muscles for relaxation.

Autogenic method- The autogenic method is also about muscle control to make one calmer and relaxed.

Guided imagery or visualization method - This can be used in conjunction with progressive relaxation or by itself. After you have relaxed your muscles you can get into the visualization method and use mental imagery to relax your mind. Visualization method is a variation on traditional forms of meditation techniques that require that you use all senses; visual sense, of the palate, feel/touch, hearing, and smell. Visualization method entails the creation of an image in your mind which leaves you feeling at peace and free to release all tension and anger.

504

Self-hypnosis - Hypnotizing oneself is a form of meditation that is guided and participants listen to a recorded song or sound. By doing this, they are able to access and reach a state of deep relaxation as soon as possible. In this state, you are more open to suggestions giving the hypnotherapist the opportunity to target and improve a particular aspect of thought.

Standard meditation – Primarily, these are reflections that have particular guidance. They seek for particular aims and purposes. They are not similar to each other so you ought to know what you are using and where it is guiding you to.

Body scan - This is a reflection where the practitioner is guided on which part of their body to concentrate on. Then they are asked if they can identify anything. The practitioner has to be comfortable since it may take up to an hour even though shorter versions are available.

Brainwave meditation - This type of reflection targets brain waves for stress relief and relaxation. Brain wave meditations start out with a guiding voice, which is usually just relaxing sounds of music. Their aim is to keep the mind focused on the tunes.

Affirmation meditation - This meditative technique uses assurances to plant certain thoughts then generate particular feelings into a practitioner's mind. The practitioner's mind becomes at ease and they can be easily led to be more willing when in this state.

Every time you want to embark on a relaxation technique, do the following:

> Find a quiet spot where you will not be disturbed.

505

- Get into a comfortable position. Sitting or lying down.

- Loosen your clothes and free your arms and legs

- Dim your lights

Mastering these relaxation techniques will take time. Over time, your body will be in tune with the sequence of the relaxation techniques. With this mastery, you will be able to get deeper relaxation. Make these practices part of your lifestyle and do them daily. As much as it may be difficult to find exclusive time for meditation, these techniques can be put into practice as you engage in doing other things.

It is possible to meditate on a bus or while commuting for concentrative meditation. Mindfulness techniques can be put into play while walking or exercising your pet or while taking a lunch break at the park, etc. Nonetheless, if you can designate a daily time for relaxation, do so for predictability and ease. Do not try these relaxation techniques while sleepy, as you will fall asleep and miss out on your target for relaxation. Relaxation requires maximum concentration and alertness.

No one is perfect, especially at the beginning. Do not pinch yourself for missing some sessions. The main goal is to build momentum so that after a while, you can get into a rhythm and routine.

Peace of mind

Peace of mind is the key to true life. Happiness, good health, and success is something that should be accessed by every one of us. Meditation is one of the ways that you can attain the mental peace that will give you a wholesome life. When we look at the many benefits of meditative practices listed earlier, they refer to or are a testament to a state where one's body is in total control and fully functional.

Bad habits are jettisoned for a purer health-conscious one. Mental strength and brain functioning are greatly improved and nurtured. Immunity is boosted leading to fewer or no diseases affecting us. We are less stressed and a lot happier when we meditate regularly. This happiness and well-being are what spawns peace of mind. One becomes aware and in tune with themselves. Full self-awareness is achieved and with that comes the peace. When your mind is peaceful, you will be more productive and you will relate better with people around you.

Your family, friends, colleagues at work and strangers that you bump into will notice the difference in how you relate. You become more likable, as the happiness and peace you exude rubs off onto others.

Meditation indeed leads to peace of mind. Take up meditation, won't you?

Quick and Simple Techniques for a Beginner's Practice

Now that you have all the basic knowledge you need, it is time to delve into the practice itself. There are many kinds of meditation techniques that you can get acquainted with, and this chapter will aim to give you as many options as possible to help you start strong.

Fast and Simple: Techniques on the Go

There are just too many people out there who don't have enough time in their hands but still want to practice meditation. Although meditation can be done anywhere and in almost any circumstance, it is important that you start with some beginner-friendly practices that won't take up too much time. All the exercises in this section can be done within 10 minutes, but you can make it last longer if you want. When you are using certain techniques to fit a certain time frame, you have to put all thought of time constraints out of your head. It would be best if you chose a short time after you wake up or just before you go to bed. Keep in mind that making your mind be still is not easily accomplished, especially for a beginner. But also know that this can become simpler and easier as you go along, so don't let yourself be discouraged by any short-term setbacks.

Basic Meditation with Affirmation

This basic meditation technique is a great way to start your practice. This starts off with the basics and you can add visualizations or added stillness later on.

> ➤ Sit on the floor or on a chair and keep your back as straight as possible without straining yourself. Make sure that you are comfortable

508

and can hold the position for at least five minutes. Choose a place where you won't be disturbed.

➤ Breathe deeply and relax your body as you breathe. As this is probably your first time, it might be wise to keep your eyes closed throughout the process.

➤ Choose a phrase that you would like to affirm in your life. Try and use the first person and make sure it's something meaningful to you. Examples can include "There is peace inside me," "I am worthy of love," or "God watches over me."

➤ Take slow measured breaths. Make your breathing as easy and relaxed as possible and empty your mind of other thoughts.

➤ Now repeat the affirmation to yourself quietly. Try and focus only on the affirmation. If you do get distracted by random thoughts, allow the thought to pass rather than suppress it. Simply return your attention to the affirmation gently.

➤ If you find it difficult to focus on a purely mental effort, you can try and whisper the words to yourself, moving your tongue without really speaking a word. Join your breathing with your affirmation and repeat the phrase as you breathe out.

Continue this exercise for at least five minutes. Remember not to get frustrated, as your body will end up tensing rather than relaxing. Notice how you felt during the exercise. Was focusing your attention on affirmations and breathing difficult for you? What kinds of thoughts did you find popping into your head?

Focused Breathing

When you can manage to stay focused on affirmations, it is time you focus solely on the breath. This is a great way to develop focused awareness, concentration, and stillness of the mind. Don't expect to have a quiet mind right away. This is all normal and will improve as you continue your practice.

> ➢ Sit comfortably with your back straight in a place where you won't be disturbed.

> ➢ Breathe deeply and relax your body. You can choose to close your eyes or keep them open. However, if you find that your thoughts still have a tendency to race around you, keeping your eyes closed will help keep distractions at the minimal.

> ➢ Turn your attention towards the sensation of your breath. This is a good time to practice the beginner's mind. Experience your breathing as if for the first time. Feel your chest rise and fall as you breathe. Listen intently to the sound of each breath and feel the air enter and leave your body.

> ➢ Continue this meditation for at least five minutes. Since you are focusing solely on your breathing, you might find yourself easily distracted by random thoughts and emotions. Don't be alarmed or critical of yourself when this happens. Simply acknowledge the thought or emotion without judgment, then let it go. Gently direct your focus back to your breathing.

It would be beneficial for you to continue practicing these techniques before you move on to more complex practices.

As the basic core of almost all of the meditation practices involves awareness of the breath and concentration, these techniques are great if you simply want to stay with the basics or if you want to move on and deepen your practice.

Conclusion

Thank you for coming this far. If there is anything in life that everyone yearns for, it is great. The good thing is usually not just enough. You will always want to be great in everything you do. Be it coding, playing football, playing the violin, or even in writing. The key to being great at something is usually very simple—practicing. The practice is the habitual art of repeatedly exercising an activity so as to acquire perfection in it. Practicing the right way can really mean the difference between good and great. Let's look first at the quantity of practice time. You might ask yourself, for how long should you practice something for you to perfect it? You might know some top athletes, footballers, or even musicians. They always have one thing in common. They usually put in lots of hours per day in perfecting their skills. The measure of perfection, therefore, is usually measured by how much time you put into the practice. However, as much as practicing is all about repeatedly exercising an activity, taking too much time on an activity can lead to boredom. So, what is the upper limit to how much quantity of practice time is good? Many are the times when more is not better if it becomes too much. You should, therefore, be aware of the number of hours you need to practice activity so that you can acquire its perfection. The upper limits, therefore, for the hours that you should practice in a day as an adult professional are four to five hours a day. These hours should be divided into sessions lasting not more than sixty to ninety minutes. Taking more time than this can lead to boredom, burn-out, and even lack of focus. Kids, however, reach their upper limits of focused practice much faster. In general, though, more practice usually means better perfection. A person who practices for a whole hour will attain perfection faster than the one who practices for just around fifteen minutes.

The thing to note, however, is that the practice should be mindful, and you should be focused when practicing. Now, let's look at the quality of how someone practices. For you to get great at something, you need to take into consideration the quality of practice that you undertake. Focused practice will tend to yield much better results. The main reason for practicing is usually to perfect something. For this to be achieved, you must be mindful of every repetition that you undertake. You must always visualize ahead before any repetition and identify the achievement that you would want to achieve at the end of the practice. Moreover, you must always try to review the achievements made at the end of a repetition. By doing this, you are sure that you will gain better performance at the activity being practiced. In addition to this continual post and pre-analysis, a focused and effective practice also includes breaking down complex components into small components. For example, when you are learning how to play the piano, you do not just start by jumping into the piano itself. You first have to learn the different keys and master their locations. After breaking down the complex components into simple components, you will later gradually put these small components together and achieve longer sequences.

Mindless Practice

You might have seen an athlete or even a musician engaged in the practice. There is usually a designated pattern that they usually follow. You might have noticed this if you were keen. Some of these distinct patterns include the following:

- **Broken-record method**: In this case, you will only repeat the same thing over and over again. Be it repeating the same key on a piano, the same drills in football, or even the same tennis serve. From a distance, one might view this as practice; however, it is merely just a mindless practice.

- **Autopilot method**: In this case, you will just be on the autopilot system and coast. This means that you will not have a specific goal to achieve at the end of the practice. This is like when you just get to the field and just play aimlessly for the whole time.

- **Hybrid method**: This right here is a combined approach. For example, when you are practicing how to play football, you will play continuously until you reach a point when you do not perform a particular skill right. At this point, you should repeat the skill over and over again until you perfect it.

Three Problems

Mindless practice, however, usually has some setbacks. Here are the three problems that are usually associated with this type of practice:

1. ***It's a waste of time.*** Why is this so? To start with, this practicing method does not really lead to any perfection. This is the reason as to why you might practice for almost a whole day and still not improve all that much at something. In fact, this model of practicing just tends to make you perfect on undesirable habits and errors. This, therefore, increases the likelihood of inconsistent performances. Once these unwanted habits have been attained, you'll find it rigid to let go off these bad behaviors as you move on.

2. ***It makes you less confident.*** Mindless practice makes you less confident. Why is this? They say that you can lie to everyone else, but you cannot lie to yourself. When practicing mindless practice, a part of you will always be aware that you are not practicing in the right way. For this matter, you will always have a sense of uncertainty deep down that just won't go away. This is amid the fact that you are making great progress in what you are doing.

3. ***It's mind-baffling dismal.*** Practicing senselessly is typically like a chore. The measure of achievement, in this situation, is usually signified by the number of times you exercise. This, though, shouldn't be the circumstance. You should've some customary goals that you'd achieve at the conclusion of the training sessions. For instance, when you're practicing on how to play football, you'd set objectives like, "I should be capable of achieving the skill flawlessly by the end of the training session."

How to Accelerate Skill Development

Practicing can be a very complex task to undertake. This is because it requires one to be fully committed and cautious about many things.

However, it can be made much easier by just following these five principles:

1. *Focus is everything.* Focused practice tends to yield many more results. Therefore, you should keep your practice sessions as short as possible so as to remain focused. This duration may be as short as ten to twenty minutes and as long as forty-five to sixty minutes.

2. *Timing is everything.* For the practice to be effective, you must choose to do it when you are most active. This can be like in the mornings. Practicing during your most productive times will help you think clearly and stay focused when practicing.

3. *Don't trust your memory.* For any effective practice, you have to carry out an analysis of your progress and goals. What do you want to achieve by the end of the session? What have you achieved at the end of the session? These signs of progress should be noted down on a practice notebook. You should not try to memorize all your progress. Noting down helps a lot because you will be able to keep track of all activities.

4. *Smarter, not harder.* "Work smart" is a phrase that you are aware of. This phrase also applies during practice. You should always go out of your way and try to come up with simpler ways to achieve perfection in anything that you do.

These simple ways will tend to occur naturally when doing an activity because you are the one who has come up with them.

5. *Stay on target with a problem-solving model.* As humans, it is only normal to lose focus when trying to pursue something. It is for this reason that you should keep yourself on task so as to avoid the mindless practice. To help with this, here is a six-step problem-solving model:

Step 1

Define the problem. In this stage, you should ask yourself questions like "What result did I get?" "How would I like the result to sound like?"

Step 2

Analyze the problem. In this stage, you should ask yourself questions like "Where did I go wrong?" "Why does the result occur as it is occurring?"

Step 3

Identify potential solutions. In this stage, you should ask yourself questions like "What can I do to change the result to what you wanted?"

Step 4

Test the potential solutions and select the most effective one. In this stage, you should take into consideration all possible solutions, and choose the best one. This is by asking yourself a question like "Which solution can really yield the best results?"

Step 5

Implement the best solution. At this stage, you should now implement the best solution so as to make the changes permanent.

Step 6

Monitor implementation. After implementing the solution, you should continuously reinforce these solutions so that you can continue producing the result you want.

Maintain your gains at all times

Before we conclude, it is essential to address the reason why you need to maintain your achievements. Achieving the gains is easy but we cannot say the same about maintaining them. It is common to think that once you have acquired what you are looking for, the benefits will stick in you magically and forever. From experience, thinking that way will make you fall back on what you solved sooner than you thought.

Therefore, the question you should ask yourself is this: how do you intend to keep the progress that you have developed so far? How many sessions do you need or how many times do you need to revisit the techniques offered in order to guarantee the longevity of what you have learned?

Have a message that helps you stick to your values, such as 'Use it to live happier and less worried.' Such messages will help you every time you need to troubleshoot future events.

As We Conclude

Practice really does make perfect. This is only achieved through a few contributing factors. These factors can really help one in achieving perfection when followed. Practice, however, should be carried out mindfully. You should be focused and should have a clear mind when practicing. Mindless practicing can lead to perfection in undesired habits and errors rather than perfection in the skills. Therefore, learn to practice mindfully and incorporate it into your daily routine so as to achieve perfection.

Good luck.

Memory Improvement

Gain Accelerated Learning Capabilities to Increase Concentration and Memory and Remember More

By: Adam Goleman

Introduction

Congratulations on purchasing your copy of the book Memory Improvement: Gain Accelerated Learning Capabilities Increasing *your Concentration and Memory to Remember More* and thank you for doing so.

The following chapters will discuss the intricate world where thoughts reside, memories are built, and cognition rejuvenates. Your mind is a whole universe compacted in a small area. The nature of nervous paths interconnecting the brain regions define the way you behave, think, act, and memorize. The traces left by the passage of bio-electric signals on this path make up your memory structures. The more the similar path is visited or revisited, the more defined and prominent the traces will be and the stronger your memories will become. However, the theory suggests that these traces tend to fade away over time due to one or many reasons. There may be a lack of proper brain diet and workout, or inadequate sleep, or perhaps a lack of reconnections and regular revisions. Lost focus, will power, and concentration can also be the reason for memory decline so that it can be the weakened state of biochemical energy inside the body. Let us explore these reasons and their solutions in the upcoming chapters. Are you eager to know some of the most effective techniques for memory improvement and accelerated learning? Embark on this exciting reading ride to review these strategies and be aware of how to maintain your mental health properly.

Books about the subject are aplenty in the market, we appreciate that you picked this one! Every energy spent on creating this book was focused on giving as much useful information as entertaining. Have a happy reading!

Chapter 1: Memory in Our Mind

Humans are thinking animals. The more we see and observe, the more experiences we gain, and thus more memories are made in our minds. But the question is, what actually is considered as memory?

What is Memory?

Being a part of a social environment, we are living numerous experiences on a day to day basis. Think of them as packets or blocks of raw data that enter the cognitive arena and get decoded by the mind. Now this decoded information, once comprehended, becomes a sensible memory and is stored in a file inside the brain to access at a later stage.

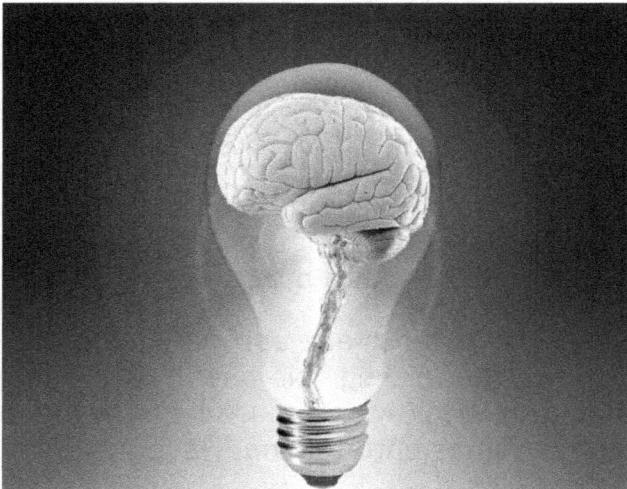

The Brain as a Memory Storage

Consider our brain; it is a powerhouse of several processes running cognitively, including perception, listening, thinking, and talking. Among these processes, memory analysis is also a very important intellectual process. By saving memories as imaginary files organized according to the priority level and retrieval redundancy, our mind works systematically. How are memories triggered? It depends on a kind of familiar environment or a certain object to which a person is exposed. As we try to recall, our mind accesses the respective memory file in the virtual storage cabinets and retrieves it so that a particular scenario or event is refreshed in mind.

Structure of the Mind: Synapses or Wiring Connections

The mind has special areas dedicated to processing special functions. Each area or region has some wired connections or synapses that are formed through an ongoing process. It is known that at the time of birth, the human brain is an immature organ, i.e. not fully developed at that time. The development of the brain continues even after birth as the synaptic connections are made and remade. A synapse of a synaptic connection is basically a linkage between neurons through which sensory impulses are passed to conduct a message to the brain center of that region. If these links or channels are frequently used, the connections sustain. However, if the frequency of action is absent, the synaptic connection is weakened, broken, or *pruned.* This ability of the brain to shape and reshape is subjected to the nature of usage and frequency of an action.

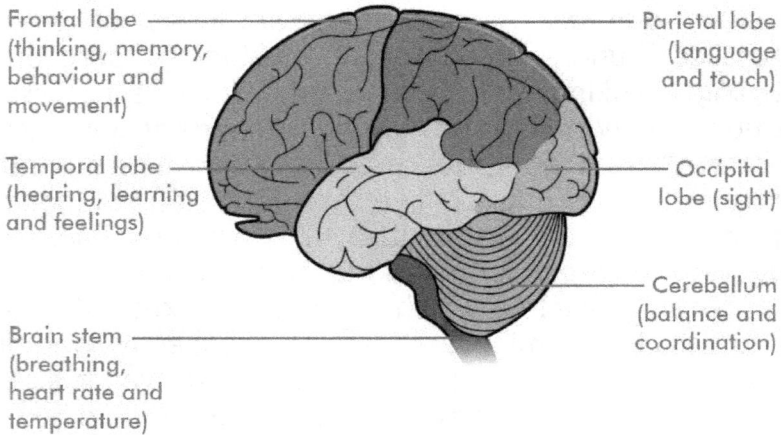

Frontal lobe (thinking, memory, behaviour and movement)

Temporal lobe (hearing, learning and feelings)

Brain stem (breathing, heart rate and temperature)

Parietal lobe (language and touch)

Occipital lobe (sight)

Cerebellum (balance and coordination)

Consider an example of a hearing experience that a person gained earlier. He heard a word; "comprehension". He learned it by hearing as the neurons in the hearing region transmitted the message to the brain through a synapse. Now, if this person frequently hears this word in daily conversations, he will be able to recognize it instantly because the connection is still wired in the brain. But if he doesn't hear or use it for a long time, the connection will be broken. So, the next time he hears that particular word, he wouldn't be able to recognize it instantly as new wiring of connection will have to be formed then. That is why learning new languages become easier through frequent practice and speech.

According to neurologists, the brain has a massive number of wired connections and even though the neurons or brain cells are in a fixed number (i.e. approximately 100 billion neurons), every single neuron is connected to another neuron by numerous synaptic links.

The plentitude of synaptic connections, however, doesn't guarantee the brainpower. Instead, the lack of practice and stimulation can easily weaken these connections. The wiring of the brain is actually a network of pathways that should have active signals in order to strengthen the roads or else they could be eliminated. If all the connections are used purposefully, frequently, and systematically, a sort of functional coordination occurs where each action of a person is in sync with the other.

To understand this, consider another example of the facet of language and proficiency i.e. listening, writing, reading, and speaking. If you are listening to a particular story or conversation, your brain cells or neurons will need a pathway to transmit chemical messages or impulses that are carried by sensory messengers called neurotransmitters. They reside in the narrow pathways or passages called synapses which enable the neurons to link together and communicate.

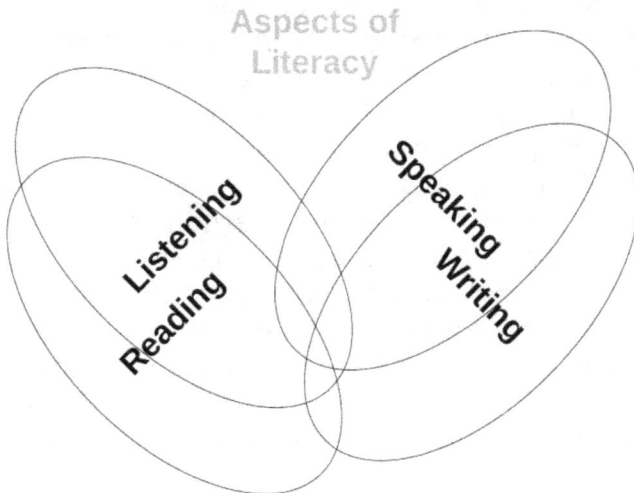

Aspects of Literacy

Listening

Reading

Speaking

Writing

Now, this communication helps in sending the message to the brain and stimulating the desired response, which in this case is the comprehension of the conversation heard. As there is a difference between hearing and listening, the latter requires comprehending the words as well. So, when you have understood what you have heard, listening is completed. But the connection remains there unless a long gap occurs without repeating the action of listening to a similar story or conversation. If you proceed systematically while involving all aspects of literacy learning, you will be able to speak what you have listened and when you do so, a new connection is formed as the neurons involved in the speech region of the brain pass the electrical signals or sensory impulses to it, and this stimulates an utterance or speech in response. While you speak the same words you have listened to, the connections are coordinated, and the response is much faster due to the easy availability of interlinked pathways of synaptic connections.

Afterward, when you start reading the things you have listened to and spoken of, yet another network of wired pathways are generated to transmit the new knowledge to the brain and process it. As the information has already been processed before in the alternative forms of listening and speaking, the reading becomes more familiar and previous knowledge is easier to recall through old connections. Similarly, when you begin to write about what you have learned so far through different aspects of language and literacy i.e. listening, speaking, and reading, you gain a stronger grip on your memory, comprehension, and depth of knowledge due to the good coordination of the miraculous network of wiring present inside your ordinary-looking brain. Therefore, it can be deduced that no one has a good or bad, strong or weak memory.

Instead, it goes down to the very fact that how the connections inside our brain are arranged and how with some determined practice, systematic conditioning, and strategic mindfulness, they can be rearranged.

Memory as a Cognitive Process

Among the most intriguing cognitive research debates is the concept of memory as a part of analytical processes running in the human mind. How the mind receives information, processes it and stores it is an intricate, speedy work that may seem ordinary at a superficial glance. However, the mysteries of the brain suggests having a closer look at the whole process to understand it further. How we learn things depends primarily on our memory. The way we act, the way we behave and exhibit emotions, are all linked to the past memories we have accumulated inside our cognition as indicators or models of future behavior. As Rick Warren quoted: "Your self is created by your memories, and your memories are created by your mental habits." So, our actions can reflect our memories. Hence the importance of improving the memory to improve the present actions and comprehend experiences.

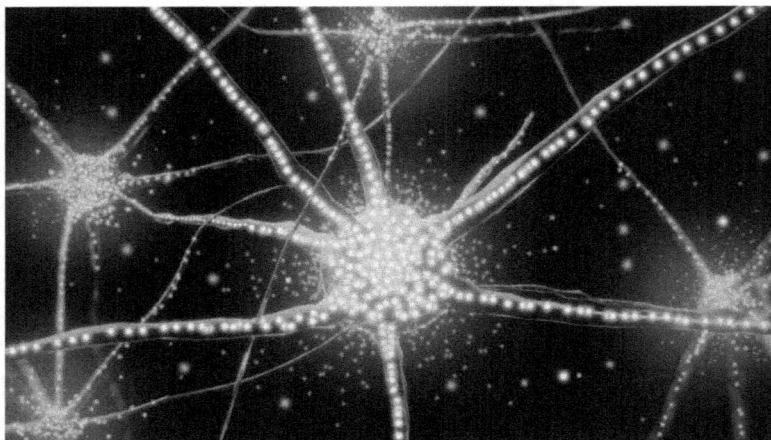

Research shows that in the early years the ability of the brain to learn and relearn i.e. its plasticity is more evident. Young ones are quick to catch new vocabulary, recall words and incidents, and relive past experiences. However, adults too, through practical methods and proven strategies, can clearly improve their memory power and brain performance. These learning strategies and accelerated memory techniques will be further explored in the upcoming chapters.

Surely, you would have often heard a phrase; *"food for thought"*. This could be taken in quite a literal sense as we speak of brain development and memory. In later chapters, you will come to know how our mind needs concentration, purpose and positive experiences to feed on. Just like our body needs vital nutrition and memory-boosting ingredients to gain strength. All of these factors influence our overall performance.

Four Stages of Memory Process

Considering the human mind as an input processing or computing device, the following stages of the memory process can be analyzed comprehensively.

1. Attention: At this stage, the person is paying attention to the surroundings or a particular object, event, word, action of interest. This is an observational stage, i.e. perceiving and exploring in detail.

2. Encoding: At this stage, the observed facts are taken as input data to be processed in mind. This is a stage of knowledge acquisition. Gaining insights, increasing the intellect and learning new things.

3. Storage: Here the processed information is retained. Storing the encoded experiences helps enables the mind to recall it whenever needed. Therefore this stage is also very important in ensuring the ability of a brain to sustain and prolong learning and comprehension.

4. Retrieval: After the brain has stored the specific information in the respective compartment or functional region, it recovers it when the need for recall arises.

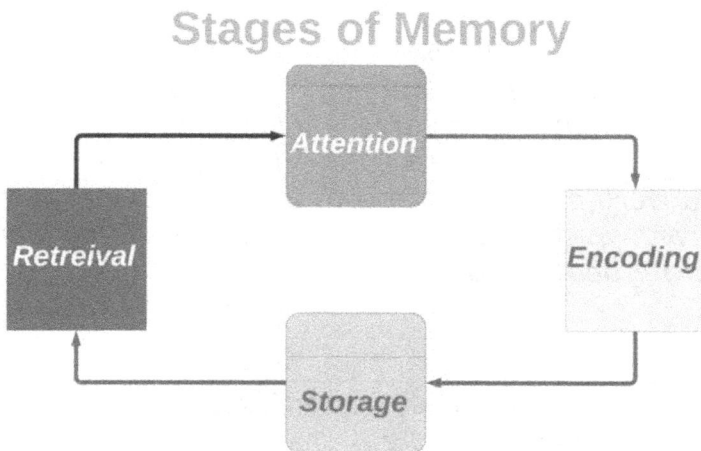

Stages of Memory

Attention

Retreival

Encoding

Storage

All these four stages of the memory process are equally important. However, the early practices and research studies focused more on storage and retrieval than on the former two i.e. Attention and Encoding. The modern findings in cognitive research emphasize the need for conscious concentration and focused attention in order to receive information. This is essential for increasing the chances of retention for an extended period of time.

For occasions like these, if a person doing a picture description activity pays close attention to the picture of a park that is shown to him, he is likely to encode the details and objects depicted in the park more effectively.

When he is assessed later, upon being asked comprehensive questions such as; *"What objects would you normally find in a park?"* or, *"What game were the two children in the picture playing?"* or, *"Where was the cat sitting in the park?"*

He is able to recall with more clarity and can answer confidently such as; *"You would normally find benches, play equipment, grassy area, hedges, fences, a fountain, and trees, etc. in a park."* or, *"The two children in the picture were playing catch with a green colored ball."* or, *"The cat, which was black in color, was sitting beneath the corner bench in the park."*

"To observe attentively is to remember distinctively." - Edgar Allen Poe

---

How our memory works, how it is retained, and how it is recalled or recovered, can be greatly influenced by the information-processing theories and models that we are following and implementing. In some models or theories, the linkage between the sensory processes of attention and memory retention is so strong that it has been declared as a key to powerful learning and accelerated improvement in the memory retrieval process.

The major details and workings of memory retention and storage will be discussed extensively in the next chapter under the topic; types of memory.

Chapter 2: Types of Memory and Memory Loss

The human memory, more appropriately perceived as a process rather than a thing, has 3 distinctive types, which in turn, can be further classified into subtypes. These three types are *sensory memory, short term or working memory, and long-term memory.*

Most often what we refer to as memory in routine life is long term memory. The interesting fact is that the other types of memory like sensory memory and short term or working memory are referred more in terms of their weakness called forgetfulness. However, all these types of memories and their capacity range are important indicators or measures of a person's overall intelligence.

The Sensory Memory

The sensory memory is an instantaneous memory retained or less than a second. Shortest of the three, the sensory memory is used by our senses or sensory organs such as eye, nose, ear, tongue, hands, etc., to take in information from the surrounding environment. The information quickly transferred to the short-term memory registers after being input by the sensory receptors.

There are several things we see, hear, taste, touch, or smell in our daily life, such as a bus passing, a bird flying, smell of coffee brewing, smell of roses while passing by a rose garden, hearing students' chatter while passing by a school building, experiencing roughness upon touching a scrub, tasting bitterness when swallowing medicine.

These instances are retained for a short period. The types of sensory memory include visual (iconic) and echoic (audio) memory. Sensory memory teaches us that information must be coming in small bits in a steady pattern to be manageable and easily transferrable to the short-term memory. Also called sensory register, the sensory memory lays the foundation for short term and long-term memory as without the presence of the former the latter two cannot be formed. That is the main reason senses are called *windows to the mind.* Remember that sensory memory requires paying attention in order to make productive use of your senses. If during a lecture, you are looking outside the class, observing the school grounds. You are exhausting your sensory receptors of both the visual and auditory senses by trying to focus on two directions simultaneously. Now, whichever thing interests you more, or you pay attention to it more, will win a place in the sensory register and you will lose focus on the lecture or tune it out.

Short Term Memory

Being labeled as working memory, it is the part of the memory process where the recently encoded information stays for a short while to be actively used while working presently. All the information processing occurs here, it is a temporary container or notepad for holding the information you are currently working on. It is, therefore, also called primary or active memory. You can perceive short term memory as *RAM* of the mind. In order to retain short term memory, repetitions are needed. You can remember a particular sentence that you have just read for less than a minute before it vanishes from your mind unless you repeat it again.

533

Memory Consolidation

Memory consolidation is the technique that lets us retain short term memories or prolonged duration. It is the method that basically transforms the short-term memory into long term memory by means of reinforcement and systematic revisions.

Long Term Memory

Long term memory is where our major life experiences are stored in and retrieved from. The storage does not occur in the short-term memory because of its volatile nature. The information in long term memory, however, can be retained for an indefinite duration and can be managed or manipulated. The experiences that you have encountered days before, you can easily recall due to your long-term memory. Major unconscious and conscious decisions in your life are made based on your long-term memory content. The long-term memory can be divided into two important subtypes; *explicit, and implicit memory.*

Explicit Memory

Also called, a conscious memory or declarative memory, an explicit memory type is an objective type of memory that recalls conscious events that are more tangible in nature. These events can either be *episodic* in nature such as past incidents or experiences that you have observed or felt, or *semantic* in nature such as science concepts learned in the class or general world facts that you know of.

Implicit Memory

Implicit memory is more subtle in nature, sort of unconscious. You can recall some procedures without deliberate effort, by way of unconsciously following what you already know.

For example, some tasks and procedures are so strongly engraved in your mind that you can follow the steps even with your eyes closed, such as washing dishes, operating a TV remote while your eyes are on the screen, opening your door lock, etc. You perform these tasks daily; these procedures have become familiar patterns of information in your mind and can be recalled unconsciously or automatically. Implicit memory is also called procedural memory.

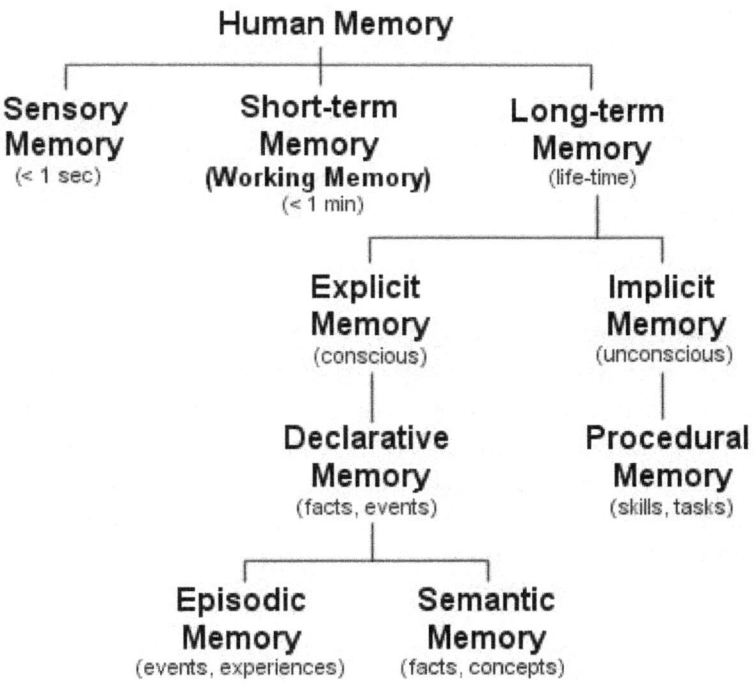

Human Memory

- **Sensory Memory** (< 1 sec)
- **Short-term Memory (Working Memory)** (< 1 min)
- **Long-term Memory** (life-time)
  - **Explicit Memory** (conscious)
    - **Declarative Memory** (facts, events)
      - **Episodic Memory** (events, experiences)
      - **Semantic Memory** (facts, concepts)
  - **Implicit Memory** (unconscious)
    - **Procedural Memory** (skills, tasks)

Types of Memory Loss

Memory loss also referred to as *amnesia,* is the neurological phenomena of either an inability to remember or retrieve the information that was stored previously inside the brain or an inability to store new information inside the brain.

Certain drug maltreatment, or traumatic experiences, or brain injury or infarction, or extreme seizures due to stress, or excessive alcohol intake, etc. can cause memory loss. Memory loss or amnesia has three major types:

1. Retrograde Amnesia: This type of memory loss causes an inability to remember pre-accident incidents and facts while the person is able to store and recall current memories after the accident.

2. Anterograde Amnesia: This type of amnesia causes the lack of ability to formulate memories of new incidents that have been occurring after the memory loss event i.e. post amnesic incidents. The person suffering from this type of memory loss can remember the past memories though. Alzheimer's, a neurological disease, falls under this category.

3. Global Amnesia: It is a transient or temporary state of memory loss. It is a combined form of the other two types of amnesia. This is mostly caused by severe stress or sudden shock or concussion. Although quicker to be recovered, it may disrupt the short-term memory for a while. A person should gain adequate rest, relaxation, mental and physical training, to avoid the risk of possible amnesic episodes.

What is Dementia?

To put it in simpler terms, Dementia is an umbrella term for loss of cognitive skills such as thinking, memorizing, comprehending, analyzing, etc. Dementia is often caused by the death of healthy brain cells, due to which normal functioning of the brain is affected. Often it is seen in old-age people who lose even the basic brain functionality in a severe case of the disorder and become dependent on others. Sometimes it is genetic too.

The Decay Theory

The decay theory suggests that memory will fade out with the passage of time. The word decay is supposed to imply that like every tangible matter on earth, time leaves its effect on the memory too, decaying it after a period of time. In an intangible sense, we can say that if left unattended, memory can become replaceable. The explanation of leaving the memory unattended is that memory must be either recalled and remembered from time to time or it gets buried under heaps, and heaps of other relatively new memories. This burial can cause it to decay just like any other matter on earth. Contrastingly, the interference theory of forgetting states that an interfering thought about a thing can make us lose focus and forget the other things. The decay theory doesn't present the memories to be dependent on each other, instead, it makes them individually dependent on the frequency of recall function.

Chapter 3: Mind as a Stack

In a literal sense, a stack is a collection of some items organized one after the other. According to the computer science concept, a stack is a dynamic data structure used to store information in a linear sequence. The stack is so-called because of its resemblance to the stack of plates being added or removed, sequentially starting from the very top going linearly down. The action of *push* and *pop* demonstrates the addition or removal of an element in the stack. It is called dynamic data structure due to its ability to keep changing each time the new information is added or retrieved. The stack works on the principle of *last in first out (LIFO).* This means that the topmost information is the last one to be added but the first one to be removed due to the specific structural nature of the stack data.

There can be a striking resemblance to our mental structure with the stack data structure. The fact that memories in our minds are organized in compartments or cabinets is actually an explanation of the stack concept. The memory cabinets are like filing systems labeled and organized as data structures. Each time a new memory is added, it is pushed upon an existing pile of memories. Each time the same or another memory has to be retrieved, it is removed from the pile linearly.

However, our mind can work both ways i.e. *LIFO (last in first out) as well as FIFO (first in first out).* The first method may be possible if the present working memory is weaker than the long-term old memories. As happens with most patients suffering from dementia. The recent memories are unable to be retained but the old memories are permanently stored and easily retrieved. The second method suggests that the short-term memory is stronger and can retain the newly added information effortlessly to ensure instantaneous retrieval without going to comb through the stacking memories linearly.

The chaos may occur when some of the disturbing memories don't get a proper filing place in the cabinets due to weak memory consolidation or decreased focus during encoding and processing. This has to be programmed systematically. Repeated practice is needed using techniques involving dedicated concentration for memory retention. Before discussing the memory retention and memory improvement techniques or methods, let us first explore the subtle yet important differences between these two targets set by most people for achieving brainpower.

Memory Retention v/s Memory Improvement

Consider the case of Sam, a young man who shares his experience and thoughts on the subject of memory. He says that he believes himself to have an average memory and needs to understand the reason why compared to his peers, he needs a longer time span to memorize things. He also seems worried about his upcoming competitive exam and would like to ensure that he remember things for a longer time period. Sam says that forgetfulness would be a major concern in the exam. So, what is happening? What made him think that he has a weaker memory than his peers? What could the reason behind the *inability to quickly recall recently learned information* and the reason behind the *inability to learn things quickly?*

Memory Retention: Ability to *continue remembering* things that were already learned for a longer time period i.e. *retaining it.*

Memory Improvement: Ability to *quickly memorize things* while learning them.

Coming back to Sam's thoughts, he thinks that the reason why he is unable to memorize things quickly is his lack of belief in his own memory ability. He also cannot recall things as fast as his peers because of his lack of confidence that *he can do it if he wants to do it.* He finds himself doubting the learned facts at the time of quizzes and thus his mind also loses focus and confidence in recalling the things. Experts say that Sam can have an improved memory when he becomes well-focused. If a person can feel himself to be more confident or rather more focused because of a good memory, he can also have a good memory due to increased confidence.

The concept of confidence here is used interchangeably with mental focus.

Memory Reconstruction

This phenomenon suggests that memory can be recalled by way of formulating old experiences on the newer incidents. Many factors such as mental schemas, time, learning attitude, mental inclination, etc., can help alter our memories or reconstruct them. This idea indicates that memory retrieval is often not accurate and can be manipulated. The possibility of a reconstructive memory gives an answer to the questions regarding memory distortion and lack of memory retention. Reliving the past events require a repetition of various mental processes in the brain's working memory. Perception, reasoning, thinking, analysis, etc. The reconstruction process often involves the supplementation of a past memory by using similar experiences and practices that aid in recalling the past memory. These supplementary incidents initiate a cohesive thinking process that enables successful recall. Several memory-strengthening methods are used to ensure memory errors such as *confabulation* during a recall can be avoided. A confabulated memory can be a falsely fabricated memory without a conscious realization. This normally happens due to a lack of clarity at the time of encoding the information, thus blurring out the events stored with the passage of time. This cognitive dysfunction can be avoided by systematic remembrance of stored information inside the brain. The hippocampus, a small yet essential organ present inside the brain's medial temporal lobe, is the key function center for memory encoding and recall.

Experts claim that the hippocampal memory retrieval can transition from recall to reconstruction as more time passes as lack of revision causes the original traces to fade away. Without further ado, let's study some of the most effective memory improvement techniques that can help encode, store, retain, and recall the learned information better, and yes, exactly in that particular order.

Chapter 4: Memory Improvement Techniques

Cognitive/Strategic techniques for memory power and enhancement

- ***Memory Palace or Magnetic Memory Method***

    Also called the method of loci, the memory palace is an amazing tool to increase spatial awareness and visualization power which, in turn, help improve the memory power. As early as the time of Greek civilization, a long history of neurological improvement methods shows the successful use of this method by ancient people.

    The method involves the use of imagination and visual creativity. It has been used by popular authors as an interesting plot device in their mystery thrillers as well. To apply this method;

    ✓ *Suppose an imaginary place inside your mind.*
    ✓ *The more familiar the place, the better. For example, your childhood playground, or your treehouse, or your old town library, or your current home's lounge.*
    ✓ *The chosen place should be spacious enough to let you store sufficient information. Its details should be clear enough to you in order to visualize with clarity.*
    ✓ *Decide a specific way of entering and walking through the place. Fix a route or track. Keep that in mind.*

✓ Now the most important step is to locate the areas or corners of the place where information storage could be possible in your imagination.

✓ Consider the data you have to memorize and recall, according to the size of the data, select locations and allocate specific bits of information to them.

✓ The spots allocated should be unique and distinguishable, so that information stored wouldn't get mixed up causing unnecessary confusion.

✓ Attempt to sketch out your imagined memory palace on a paper to match with your visualization in a more concrete form. Try to get each detail straight.

✓ Select the order for memory allocation, and recall. Recite that order until you get it straight.

✓ Both room or a road can be imagined as a memory palace, use noticeable pieces of furniture, bookshelves, and wall hangings as data allocation spots in case of the former. Whereas, in the case of the latter, select signposts or symbolic landmarks for specific data storage spots.

✓ Distribute your information in small chunks, allocating them to specific locations.

✓ The allocation should be in the order in which you would later retrieve them.

✓ The multiple interesting ways in which the data allocation can be done in your memory palace will be discussed in some subtopics below.

✓ Experts recommend dedicating some time to your memory palace daily. Visualize the place, walk through it, associate the important chunks you need to remember with the specific locations present in your memory place.

✓ The most satisfying aspect of this technique is the ability to practice visualizing the memory bits with your eyes closed, anytime, anywhere.

544

Another brilliant tip for long term usage is the regular cleaning of the memory palace. This method is reusable over and over again. Your memory palace is quite dynamic and alterable. Use it again by deleting the previous data that is no longer needed for memorization (for instance, after an exam), and reallocate newer information inside the same place. The memory palaces can be used extensively in a variety of subject areas to memorize and retain key information. Memorizing the physics equations and laws, chemical elements, historical years and facts, numbers and symbols, character sketches, personality traits, verses, speeches, vocabulary, etc., all sorts of data can be stored inside your memory palace. You just have to find an appropriate way to convert the data into manageable chunks and then store it. For example, you cannot feed an entire 1000 words essay to the imaginary place. You have to extract key points in the introduction, body, and conclusion of the essay. By making small headings or symbolic phrases representing the subsequent information under that heading can compress the extended information in a comprehensive manner. This makes it easier to store the information in the locations present in the memory palace and visualize the information too.

- **Mnemonics**
  The *mnemonics* are memory tools. Any method or learning technique that helps us to remember and retain the learned information is called a mnemonic device. The ancient Greek etymology of the word mnemonic suggests *memory* or *relating to memory.* By encoding the intended information in a specific way through imagery, symbols, acronyms, certain cues, hand gestures, infographics or lists, etc., the brain

inputs the targeted information efficiently and quite symbolically. This increases the chances of successful retrieval of information at a later stage. The success of mnemonics involves an underlying principle that the human mind gets more influenced by the symbolic data instead of abstract information.

A famous example of mnemonics can be the use of hands' knuckles to remember the number of days in a month.

The mnemonics technique was used in ancient history as well to help in remembrance of important data. This method evolved to be popularized as the *art of memory.* The significance of using the various techniques involving mnemonics made it an art unto itself. The principles of this art include *visualization, order, manageable data, association, effect, and repetition.* The *association principle* may involve the semantic priming method where the association between two words may enable memorization easily. That is where the concept of analogies came from. Grouping the relatable information into a single chunk makes it more logical for the brain to encode and remember. For example, remembering a phrase containing relatable words such as *a teacher and a student* is easier than the phrase *a teacher and a patient.*

The *effect principle* is quite an interesting aspect of the mnemonic technique. The fact that our brain encodes the information emotionally is understandable when we realize how a particular incident is remembered due to an element of surprise, pain or happiness attached to it. How often a particular memory is triggered by a similar emotion experienced in the present time.

The *repetition principle* suggests the iterative philosophy of learning by constant revision. Most of the following techniques listed below are the variants of the mnemonic method and are included in the arts of memory.

- **Narrative Storytelling & Link Method**
  The human mind is interested in incidental happenings. A twist on an otherwise regular routine, a surprise element, a romanticized turn of events, and a dramatic affair. These factors make an interesting stimulation for the emotional brain. Memory can be served as a plot device in the story of your life. A climax or anti-climax related to incidental scenes in the storybook of which you are a character. When learning new things or memorizing several pieces of information together in a serialized manner, the storytelling method proves to be quite useful. The narration of events or things makes them more systematic and easier to remember. The linking of important events or objects by means of associating them with a narrative image makes them relatable and memorable. For example, your toddler child has a collection of miscellaneous toys you want him to remember the names of, along with getting familiarized with the shape and functional purpose of each toy.

The list of targeted toys includes:

bed (miniature)
wallet
shopping basket
car
potted plant
broom

dustpan
glass
fence

Suppose you know about the link method and implement it by telling you child story by linking the toys together being narrated in a logical manner:

*"Hannah is a little girl. She loves plants. On a Sunday morning, she woke up early in the morning and her mother gave her a **glass** of milk as breakfast. Then her father told her that they would go shopping. She took the **shopping basket** from her mother. Her father and she sat in the **car**. They went to the local nursery to buy a **potted plant**. The nursery gate was surrounded by a white **fence**. The nursery was full of trees, small plants, and grass. She saw a worker collecting dry leaves in a **dustpan** with the help of a **broom**. The gardener gave them the **potted plant**. Her father gave him the money from his wallet. Hannah carried the **potted plant** in the **shopping basket**. They returned home in the **car**. Hannah was very happy. She entered her mother's room. She saw her sitting on her **bed**. Hannah showed her the **potted plant** which they had bought. She liked it very much."*

The story can be demonstrated by the respective toy objects, appropriate facial expressions, and hand gestures. This way the names of objects and their usage can be engraved in the listening child's mind.

- **Letter Patters**

This strategy is not very common but can be effective in learning a specific text. Memorizing the lengthy text can be challenging, however, making use of letter patterns can make it easier. By making up a combination of short sentences describing the keynote of a portion of the text is what letter patterns do. Originally used for memorization of alphabetical letters formation in preschools, it has slowly become useful for adults as well. An example could be a description for a lengthy tutorial about computer processing:

"Input data as instruction, process information and display output by the control unit, store temporarily in RAM, optional permanent storage in the hard disk."

Another example could be of describing the shape formation to a beginner:

How an ellipse is formed?

"Make a horizontal line, make a vertical line in the middle to make a plus sign, join the ends of lines curvaceously."

This should be recited, following the actions to draw the shape in reality, making a lasting impression on the learner so that he can recall the catchphrase/mantra/chant, etc., the next time he draws.

- **External Memory Devices**

You may have heard about the external memory of a computer. Flash drives, memory cards, hard disks, compact disks, etc., are all secondary/removable/external devices for storage. Are you wondering why we are mentioning the computer's external devices here?

Of course, to give you an example of how easily possible it is to leverage your memory instances by storing them in your journals, recording clips, thought wall, log files, etc. These are more like sources or tools instead of techniques for memory improvement but here we are mentioning it nevertheless because of the importance of this method to externalize your internal thoughts. Memories when externalized, become tangible pieces of important information that the brain feels consciously connected to. The conscious, repeated habit of making use of these tools to record past experiences, memory notes, and things to do, acts as a constant reminder to make the brain more active and present-minded even with respect to past events.

- **Mind or Concept Maps**

This technique is very productive to conceptualize the complex and detailed topics in a very comprehensive and concise manner. Often students are presented with concept maps at the beginning and end of a lesson to introduce and summarize the chapter respectively. The mapping of important information graphically makes it systematically classified in a logical way to understand and recall. For example, the following map represents the complex, full-length chapter about atomic structure:

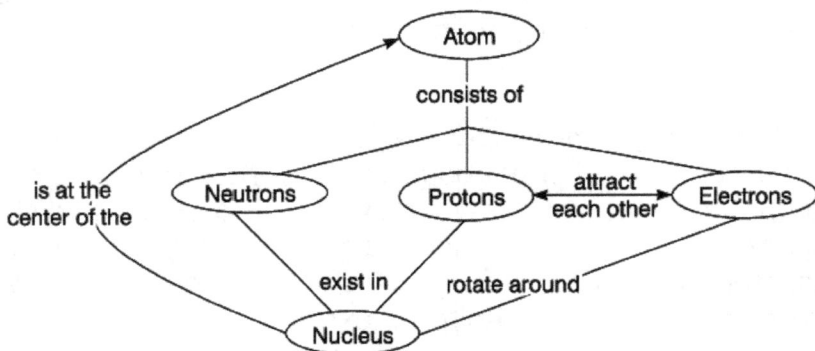

You can see how concise the data has become after being sketched out like this. The mind doesn't need to remember long definitions and textual explanations, yet it would still be able to describe the overall central idea, if an effectively displayed concept is used intelligently, like in mind mapping or concept mapping. Research shows the positive effects of this method in all sorts of ages, especially the youngsters as their analytical skills are sharper and could be used constructively here. Memory improvement training sessions involve the use of a textual explanation of an incident followed by a concept map blank template to be filled by the attendees. They can project their memories and thoughts into action on the map sheet, in order to revitalize their cognitive skills.

- **Graphic Organizers**
Graphical representation of information can be strikingly familiar and retainable for a long time in contrast to the textual one. There are numerous variants of graphic organizers used to depict the relational model between the combination of facts and ideas.

Originally it is used as an umbrella term for all sorts of infographics and knowledge maps. However, as it is also called cognitive organizer, we will mention some subtle nuances that make a real difference.

Unlike other mind maps, mostly the graphical template blocks or flowcharts have question prompts to trigger the thought process. Creative thinking and reasoning skills can be enhanced exponentially using this technique. In reading comprehension, graphic organizers can be very constructive.

For instance, suppose you have read a particular novel in your English class and now you want to revise important details and memorize the plot well prior to attempting the exam.

What you can do is, make out a template, organizing facts and outlining key questions like *What are the plot devices used in the opening chapter? Who are the most important characters? List down the physical traits of the protagonist. Summarize the anticlimactic scene at the end.*

Following graphic organizer template sourced from *dailyteachingtools.com* is an ideal example of usual graphic organizers used in high school classrooms for reading comprehension. The after-lesson practice of filling this organizer form can increase the memory retention of the learned concepts comprising the lesson or the novel previously taught in the class.

Characterization

Directions: There are four ways in which an author develops characters. Write one of your character's names in the center circle. Then, give an example of each characterization method in the appropriate outer circles.

Physical Description
Of the Character

What the Character
Says

Character

What the Character
Does

What Others Say
about the Character

- ## Legend Lists

This technique is a self improvised method for listing down pieces of data. The vertical lists are basically simple, linear stacking method for compiling the memory cabinet. The legend symbolism gives an opportunity to add meaningful tags in order to classify groups of similar tasks, objects, or facts.

If you have a collection of miscellaneous tasks to be carried out or a list of diverse objects to be shopped from various locations. Try making a list of these assorted objects to be shopped for, using a specified legend system. Consider the example below:

- ☐ tea leaves
- ☐ cereals
- ☐ rice
- ☐ lentils
- ☐ coffee
- ☐ cake mix
- ☐ sugar
- ☐ juice
- ☐ salt
- ☐ medicine
- ☐ maple syrup
- ☐ cottage cheese

At a glance, we can deduce that the above items are either liquids or solids. Allocate red (or any color of your choice) to liquids while blue (or any color of your choice) to solids. Make small colored squares in front of these items according to them belonging to either solids' group or liquids' group. Make a legend key at the top or bottom of the list in a prominent position depicting the color code.

• **Doodles / Graffiti**

If you have heard about a thought all before, hear it again in more detail here. Our mind's creative instincts once triggered, can keep generating ideas that swarm in mind making it abuzz. It needs an outlet to project them on a surface. If not given a chance for proper expression, it can cause frustration, over anticipation, and loss of focus resulting in hindered cognitive processes.

The thought wall can be used not only for free self-expression but also to reinforce elemental ideas and previously learned facts. Enabling the expansive external display of one's internal thoughts can broaden the cognitive spectrum in a purposeful manner. Doodling or graffiti is an informal, candid recording or projection of ideas on the easily available surface. Mostly it serves as a therapeutic activity to release inner conflicts, memory struggles, and random; swarming notions in mind. In a way, it helps clean up the mind from trifling matters to let it regain lost focus. A person can also get a flashback of past instances of memory by reviewing his creative doodling on the idea-wall or in the memory journals.

• **Chunking**

The cognitive memory process can be accelerated by dividing information that is to be encoded, into chunks or individual data sets and then grouped together as larger sets. According to various researches made in cognitive psychology, it has been proven that chunking was the method of making productive use of working or short-term memory by means of holding few manageable chunks of information at a time. Chunking laid the foundation of several different memory concepts. The research also established the fact that a limited range of short-term memory to hold large pieces of data at a time causes people to be unable to retain information for long or memorize more things in a short time span.

Chunking involves the following basics:

- ✓ Know your mind by reviewing your prerequisite knowledge.
- ✓ Know the chunking principle; "Each skill or knowledge concept is made up of smaller chunks of interlinked concepts that are grouped in an integrated whole".

555

✓ As the capacity of your working memory is limited, mastering one small, individual chunk at a time makes you able to increase the range of both the short-term memory and the memorable information.
✓ The practiced, repeated chunking technique can make you capable of memorizing the smaller to the larger data set unconsciously. This way your memory will show considerable improvement.
✓ The chunking process can be subdivided into three main steps or phases:
  ▪ Searching the chunk-able information pattern in a given data group.
  ▪ Breaking down the large data into smaller chunks and memorizing them.
  ▪ Then using these smaller chunks in active practice.
  o The conscious phase is the first one where working memory focuses on analytical searching of the data to convert it into smaller chunks. After that, the process is almost an unconscious effort.

• **Crosswords, puzzles, and Sudoku**

Games such as crossword, hangman, anagram, puzzle, scrabble, chess, and Sudoku are quite a memory booster and external cognitive catalyst. They motivate the brain activity and accelerate the thinking skills.

Experts believe that attempting a crossword activity on a daily basis can enhance memory. What happens is that your brain needs to think in all directions, combing through already known knowledge as well as opening sensory windows to accept newer, spontaneous ideas to solve these brain-teasing activities. It is a proven strategy that these brainers can help people with Alzheimer's too. People starting to show signs of memory decline should make some time for indulging in these games to give your brain some time for working out as these mini challenges can extend the mind power.

Scrabble, anagram, and hangman is a good choice for fun-filled brain exercise and memory recall or reconstruction. Especially these games can help in achieving high literacy and increases the power of speculation. Accelerating the numerical learning process through logical games like Sudoku also helps in unleashing that latent mental potential or energy that is said to store in our medulla oblongata or vertebral column. Similarly, the jigsaw puzzles actually help in piecing together our random memories, converging them on a focal point that increases the mental concentration. When a missing piece gets fit in the puzzle, it makes our mind more driven towards a single goal, exercising it to the fullest. Several research studies show that as piecing together a jigsaw puzzle involves both the creativity and intuition of the right brain and logical reasoning of the left brain, this activity can stimulate the dual potential of the mind.

- **Customized brain-teasing games (memory games)**

Memory Game is a Montessori inspired innovative game to memorize numbers or words. It works on the principle of association, either by associating numbers with corresponding symbols or words with respective pictures or objects. It can be played in a group where a fixed number of people are present. There is a huge box having compartments equal to the number of people present. There are a couple of smaller boxes present in front of a group of people. One contains pictures of

557

objects in the same number as the people present, while others contain the corresponding words' chits to be memorized.

- ✓ The conductor of the game, a memory trainer, will tell the members of the group that he will be telling them which picture to get.
- ✓ He will distribute the paper scraps or slips on which different words are written, one by one to each member.
- ✓ He will tell them not to show anyone their slip.
- ✓ Each group member will then be instructed to go and take out the picture corresponding to the word written on their slip, from the box and put it inside their compartment in the larger box.
- ✓ The instructor will ask everyone to carefully look and guess which word the person got.
- ✓ Then each person will do the same for their paper slip.

This game can be an interesting grouped exercise for recalling the previously learned vocabulary. It is a twofold revision technique as the person associating the word with the picture is testing his own memory, while others who don't know which word he got, are testing their own memories by guessing as they watch him take out the corresponding picture and put it inside his compartment in the larger box.

- **First and last letter association with link method**

Almost similar to acronyms (another mnemonic strategy) with a subtle difference that acronyms are pronounceable, word- letter association is an intelligent technique of memorizing quickly by making logical associations with the first or last letter of a word.

By fixating a significant word as a full form for each word of a long sentence can make it quite easy to learn and remember. For example,

Great minds think alike is an idiomatic phrase, if you want to memorize it quickly you may review that it can associatively be distributed to become:

"G M T A"

Similarly, the last letter association technique where the last letter of a word could be associated with a concept or image to help remember a related thought. The link method in the same context can help you to memorize things better still. For example, if you want to remember the sentence:

"The computer is a processing device."

Write each word in a vertical column separately, as individual units. See this sequence:

The
Computer
Processes
Information

Now, take each word's initial letter to write together like this:

TCPI

When you later need to remember this sentence, you simply have to recall this combination of initial letters.

This technique also helps in taking a snapshot of the available information in such visual prominence that the mind can clearly retrieve the intended information due to the flashes of these snapshots at the time of recall.

• **Alphanumerical Associative Combinations**

Sometimes, to enhance the memory efficiency to recall numbers systems and numeric sequences. Each chunk of numbers contains a limited number of numeric symbols that can be associated with alphabets or words. Many aptitude tests and analytical reasoning exercises involve this technique to decode or decrypt information. For example, to memorize the number set:

$$2\ 3\ 4\ 1\ 5\ 3\ 6\ 2$$

Associate with each number, its corresponding alphabet in the sequence of its place of order. Such as 1 represents A, 2 represents B, and so on.

• **Treasure Hunt for Words or Objects**

Muscular memory is a type of memory that helps familiarize the muscles of the body with a particular environment, structure, or place by means of exploring it with the tactile sense (sense of touch), often done with closed eyes, it can be done with opened eyes as well. While playing a treasure hunt, sensory reception is sharpened due to touch and search. The treasure hunt for words can be an interesting stimulator for a curious search for information not only physically but mentally too. Objects to be memorized are hidden inside certain places in a room preferably with shelves. Each hidden object is searched by following a trail of innovative cues found in various nooks and corners. A person searching, if follows the clues accordingly, will be ultimately led to the hidden object, triggering his analytical and memory skills along the way.

- ## Spotlight Method

This famous method is a proven strategical method for memorizing information in flashes. The spot-light or flashbulb uses a beam of focused light projected on a particular area of information (for e.g. selected textual paragraph). The room should be in complete darkness while the only light emitting from the spot-bulb or flashlight illuminates the selected information to be memorized. This method helps the brain to encode the text as images that can deeply be implanted in the brain through the retina. This is also called the military method due to its resemblance to some of the similar techniques used by them. The flashlight can be turned on and off more than a couple of times to repeatedly imprint the textual image in mind. The technique can be applied for memorization of maps, pictures, graphs, etc., as well.

- ## Color Coding

The color coding is a popular trend to set up an organized system in any particular environment. Be it the arrangement of spices in the kitchen, orderly display of clothes and shoes in the dressing room, or the classification of jewelry in your vanity closet. The objects when coded in a pre-determined format based on a color legend, can be easily retrievable. For e.g. blue studs and pendant along with other blue trinkets are put in a blue-colored box, red in red, yellow in yellow and so on. Some objects if not colored can still be color-coded by customization. For e.g. in your filing cabinet, all the files that you have are brown in color. You can place a color identifier or legend on the spines of the file on the region where it can be shown as soon as the cabinet is opened to retrieve any file. Draw a legend key describing each color code, with a respective group of files and topics, on the cabinet door to refer to it each time you need to search a particular group.

When this orderly format is followed, it brings peace of mind and internal satisfaction is achieved due to the avoidance of chaos.

- **Group Discussions, Memory Portals or Forums, and Blogging**
  Humans tend to open newer doors of knowledge and learning through interaction and socialization. Brainstorming ideas, revising old concepts, and sharing past experiences can bring considerable improvement in mind power and idea restoration or generation.

- **Songs, Parodies, & Poems**
  This particular technique is an absolute favorite of many people having a creative mind and humorous disposition. Learning recipes, authors' names, historical events, chemical elements, significant dates and years, main essay headings, idioms, etc., all sorts of information can be memorized by verification technique. You just need to put the concepts into a rhyme or poem format or making an informative yet humorous parody of an already famous song, all this so that you can revise and recall things effortlessly., For e.g., you need to memorize the function of pineal gland in neuroscience.

You can make a parody of famous children's poem and incorporate the intended concept in it to make the memorization easier:

(Parody of twinkle twinkle, little star)

Pineal, pineal, little gland you are,
your other tasks are still bizarre,
though you bring some sleep to the eye,
secreting melatonin when night stops by!

The following picture shows another rhyming memory technique called pegging system:

Visual Mnemonics: Peg-word system

* Technique used to memorise lists of words

* Learn basic organisational structure......

One is a bun
Two is a shoe
Three is a tree
Four is a door
Five is a hive
Six are sticks
Seven is heaven
Eight is a gate
Nine is a line
Ten is a hen

- **Willpower & Conscious Effort**

Though familiar incidents, memory devices like patterns and pegging, visual linkages, and other environmental stimuli do activate the memory and accelerate the learning process, it can still be less effective if not accompanied by a constant inner will to achieve improvement. As mentioned earlier, the increase in confidence level can consequently increase the brainpower improvement levels. Humans are a wonderful creation of God. They have the potential to achieve amazing things if they put their mind to it. As the old saying goes, determination breeds success, you can improvise a little and update it a little according to the *mind over matter principle:*

"Man breeds determination in his mind, which materializes as success in his life."

Your vigor of mind and mental thought process will determine your strength of the memory. There is an optimistic thought, even if you think you may have a below-average memory, realize that you do tend to know and try to remember what's important to you. At the end of the day, cling to this positive notion and improve your memory by practicing these techniques.

Chapter 5: What is a Photographic Memory?

Also sometimes referred to as Eidetic memory, the photographic memory is an enabling capacity of the brain to recall images, text, graphical symbols, etc. with shocking clarity after being exposed to them for a short span of time, in some cases only seconds or instances. Generally, it is seen that people are more inclined towards visual patterns and can memorize them easily. However, the people with eidetic memory can literally take a snapshot of the information and save them exactly as it is in their mind without having to use any sort of specific mnemonic or memory improvement technique. Sounds great, doesn't it?

Imagine yourself carrying a natural medium-sized camera in place of your head and another tiny one in place of your eyes, all the information in the world could be captured in the blink of an eye and within a passing impulse inside the mind.

How wonderful is that! All the memories could become a scrapbook or photo album in your head, stored in the respective compartments. Whenever a particular memory is needed to be accessed, you could just skim through the album to retrieve the particular photo. However, here comes the catch, not everyone is born with a naturally gifted Eidetic or photographic memory.

Photographic Memory in Early Years

Research shows that it is rare to witness a truly eidetic memory in adults, however, in early years children often go through a phase where they tend to develop a sort of memory which enables them to observe objects for a short span of time and recall them afterward in vivid detail. This mostly happens when a child is exploring his environment, his young mind is like an absorbing sponge, taking in all the impressions and exposed details of the surroundings and memorizing them exactly as they are. There are also several sensitive periods of development at work in the early years. Children accumulate all the available knowledge consciously or unconsciously and language acquisition also occurs at that time.

Educationists suggest that the symbols or flashcards used in preschool setups are actually a tool to enhance the child's photographic memory and make use of his visual sense in order to speed up the learning and memorization of sight words and sounds. Similarly, many activities in the early years' classroom are planned to facilitate learning through visual charts and pictures.

Sometimes children are even asked to touch the objects and feel them in order to remember the shape and recall it later. Many irregular words that cannot be read phonetically i.e. sound by sound are often listed under puzzle words and are taught to the child as a visual image.

In this way, the child's photographic memory is triggered and he is able to memorize them with ease. The word becomes a complete picture in front of his eyes and he quickly saves it in his mind without having to break the word into sound letters to read it. Statistics show that after growing up, many adults who had a good photographic memory at some stage in their childhood, tend to find difficulty in memorizing things. So, what is the mystery behind photographic memory? Can it be acquired at a later stage in life? Can it be lost forever or strengthened further with practice? Let's explore these inevitable questions below.

Photographic Memory in Adults

Brain experts claim that what we generally see nowadays is only a small part of what a photographic memory could really be. Some adults may be able to distinctly remember the images or text that they saw only for a few seconds, however, a completely advance photographic memory may not exist in our world as there is no actual evidence seen to date, of someone possessing it in its entirety. What we can do though is, practice some strategies to acquire something close to it. A strong memory that can help us remember things vividly. To be honest, we actually don't need a photographic memory as it can be chaotic at times.

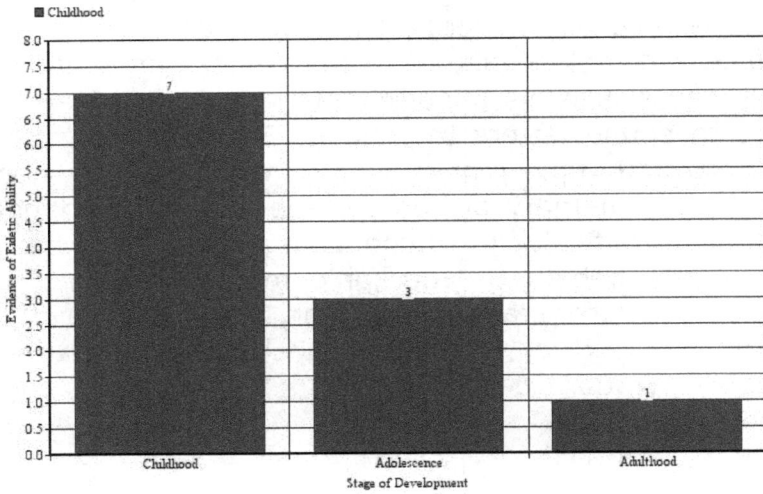

Cognitive psychologists agree that if an adult person was to have a photographic memory, due to his vast exposure, socialization, numerous daily experiences, he would have stored so many memories in his mind that even recalling them would become a chore, albeit organizing them. As compared to an adult, a child is more likely to be happy with a photographic memory. His limited experiences and exposure would enable him to store the information with clarity and recall them instantly too without having to go through thousands of stored virtual images every now and then. Instead, concentration is the key as our goal is not to distract our mind due to irrelevant images, but making it focus more on the task at hand.

Actionable Tips to Memorize Photographically

There was a game we used to play as a kid. One of us would place a series of objects upon a desk in a particular sequence. Then he would ask us to glance at the desk momentarily to perceive the displayed setting before closing our eyes. Now he will ask us one by one, what did we see on the desk. Everyone would try to describe in great detail, all the objects that they saw along with a description of the order in which they were placed. The description would, of course, be according to their perception and observation. Here the individual power of our memory would become evident. If we miss out on the details, the points will get deducted from our scorecard. Similarly, if someone would succeed in getting all the details correct, they would get to win the *"brilliant picture memory"* badge. Recalling and replaying this game, we can relive those experiences and revitalize our memories.

So, are you ready to learn those 10 universally actionable tips that we have hand-picked for you to be practiced along with different memory improvement techniques? These tips are like maxims that lay a foundation for improved memory. Once the ground is laid and a mechanism forms, you can start seeing the results soon.

1. Observation:

This is an incredible tool to master the art of knowledge acquisition. Observation is basically a gateway to learning new things. A sort of microscope through which even the minutest details can be recorded. Those who practice the art of observation are often the ones who successfully improve their memory power in the long run. Things are always angular. Every other glance at them will reveal a newer angle to the keen eye.

A good observer not only observes the details but absorbs it too. This trait can be very helpful in developing the ability to memorize things photographically. How would you find that you can become a good observer? It's simple. First, try to check if you have got those telling signs in you. Do you often tend to look around while waiting for a flight in a departure lounge? Are you keen to stand in the balcony and glance at the passerby when you have nothing else to do? Do you often find yourself as part of an audience rather than on stage, in action? Be rest assured, you have got it in you. You can do this!

The AFDOC principle of observation and its elements:

- Be Attentive:

One of the most important open secrets of a good observation is the ability to pay attention to the slightest of details. You can never be too attentive when it comes to observing a scenario. When practicing the drill, you will get to know how often we miss the most obvious details due to a lack of proper attention. Haven't you encountered at times, the trouble of forgetting the easiest things in daily life? Yes, it sucks but it can be cured. Keep reading to find out.

- Be Determined:

This is actually the driving force behind every success story. Determination, stemming from a constant need to prove yourself and succeed. A sizeable bout of determination can push you in the right direction. As an observer, you have to persevere and collect the information keenly. Don't give up, practice daily. It is not a one-time deal. It is a continuous process of making the brain get used to the idea of clear-headed perception and detailed observation.

- Be Hasty:

  Yes, you read it right. Careful haste is something that you have to develop in order to absorb every detail in a given timeframe. Being slow and lazy will not work for you here. By being quick, you will stimulate your brain to accelerate the functional processes of perception, hearing, and listening, etc. This way you will gain speed and push your potential to the optimum. Several of the unused connections of the brain can be alternatively used to speed up the processes, hence fueling the neurotransmitters and oiling the pathways that were corroded due to lack of use.

- Be Objective:

  Being accurate, unbiased, and objective is the key to an honest observation. Always remember to feed a perfect memory to your brain, the original incident should be clear and accurate. Or else the memory would be hazy as the facts become jumbled up with your own opinions and overshadowed by your personal judgments. Until when the time comes to recall it, you would be confused by the very fact that whether what you recall actually happened or at least a part of it is only a figment of your imagination.

- Be Curious:
  Remember that the person not *willing* to learn new things can *never* learn. Remember that the person not *interested* in improving his memory can *never* improve it. If you are observing something, try to take a deliberate interest in it.

571

Try to be curious about the details that are visible. Try to explore the possible angles that are not so obvious at first glance but can become apparent at a second or third glance. Curiosity may have killed the cat, but here the case is quite different. Lack of curiosity may kill your interest and willingness to learn and memorize, hence killing the chances of improvement.

2. Concentration:

Concentration not only makes a person focused but also levelheaded. Once you decide to converge your energies on a targeted focal point, you can even burn the lens if you want i.e. hitting the target successfully. Never set yourself aboard an unrealistic goal. Trying to practice all sorts of techniques and memorizing numerous things simultaneously can diverge your energies until they burn out, instead of converging them on a common goal point. The brain hangs up and tends to shut down like an exhausted computer if instructed to perform a multitude of heavy tasks at a time. All of us have experienced a load of learning material to revise prior to the exam. How much the mind diverts while memorizing a particular topic when a pile of other topics is beside you, begging to be revised. Naturally, you have to prioritize and organize in order to avoid losing your concentration. Just like that, if you don't select a setting to be observed priorly, you may glance at other things during the observation outside your selected frame which may result in lost focus, missed details and an overall decline in the level of concentration. Memorizing photographically needs you to concentrate on the task at hand. Stop being distracted by random thoughts.

They say that thinking meaningfully is the only way to think because thinking without meaning or purpose is basically overthinking which is quite exhaustive in nature and detrimental to your memory. When so many thoughts are accumulated in the brain, the old gold ones become older and are get buried under random pebbles. Digging becomes a cumbersome task and they become long forgotten, while the mind becomes full of meaningless trash.

3. Order:

Order is a word which itself is very orderly. Just look at how it smoothly rolls off the tongue when articulated. Precise and collected, it should be inculcated in your daily memory drills. As the mind senses order, it becomes calm. This way it is able to collect and recollect incidents and experiences clearly. Bring order in your study notes, kitchen cabinets, workspace, clothing closets, nightstand, and even your bric-a-brac section. You would have heard about people being able to walk in the dark inside their homes, correctly guessing the place of things, position of furniture, and direction of rooms. Some of them even know a particular room should be a certain number of steps farther from their standing point. They can even discover a particular object they are searching for from a drawer of a dressing table or vanity cabinet. All of this is possible because they have arranged things in their life in an orderly manner. You can do that too.
This will not only improve your memory greatly but also enable your brain to function in a systematic manner. On the other hand, chaos will only bring disturbing thoughts and feelings which can damage the brain's will to encode new information or retrieve the older one.

4. Confidence:

Confidence is not just a word, it is an entire system of beliefs. Believing in your ability to move forth. Believing in your need to improve. Believing in your strengths and positive traits. Believing in your determination to succeed. Most importantly,

"believing in your memories."

This may sound strange, but you have to be confident not only at the time of storing the information but also at the time of retrieving it. You are sure that you have memorized something yet you lose confidence in your ability to recall it. How can that be a successful mindset? The brain needs assurance. You provide it with your words when you give your brain a pep talk, and with your actions too, when you are learning new things with a determination to recall it afterward.

5. Clarity:

This is part and parcel of focus and concentration. Even if you have preselected your subject of memorization and are singularly pursuing it, you may encode the intended information along with a lot of fluctuations. Try to clear out those pathways to receive a clear message. A blurred message is encoded when some sort of residual stress or disturbing thoughts are lurking behind the scenes. Make sure you are not falling prey to these grainy thoughts that spoil the whole clarity of a message, thus storing a shady memory.

6. Positivity:

Making yourself influenced by your dark experiences may preoccupy your mind, thus stopping your ability to make room for newer memories. A negative mindset even subdues your zest for regaining mind power or building it anew. Stop dwelling on that one incident where you flunked an exam or lost in a spelling bee contest. Mind you, memories can be rewritten so it can be the past. History may repeat itself, but the repeating pattern is decided by the people themselves. If you have lost in the past, the loss may reoccur but maybe not for you this time. Believe it! Being positive is the way towards accumulating all the right information in your mind. The one which is easily retained and recalled as it is something you want to hold on to. It is something you *want* to happen *again* and *again.* Your mind remembers that it is important to you, healthy for you, thus it cooperates.

7. Compartmentalization:

Now, this is something easier done than said. As the word suggests, this is a method of actionable sorting and management of the brain's junk. Consider your mind as a large walk-in closet. Each set of accessories has a dedicated space allocated for it. The clothes go in the hangers inside the wardrobe space on the right-hand side. The shoes displayed nicely on the left side shoe rack. The jewelry tucked in safely inside a gorgeous vanity case set upon the dressing table, across the frontal wall.

The rule of thumb is:

" A thing for a place and a place for a thing. "

Suppose, you enter the closet, walk through it, you are in a hurry to get ready for work. You grab the wardrobe door, slide it quickly to reveal an array of clothes hanging. Every other set of clothes beckons to you. You rummage through them in a haphazard way, grabbing a few, replacing them again, looking for a particular piece then compromising on another due to lack of time. You quickly change leaving a mismanaged mess in your wake, reassuring yourself you will see to it *later*. Moving towards the dressing table, you pick up a brush, yank through your hair, a couple of things may fall from the table in your haste to search for a bottle of moisturizer or a particular mist or that perfect pair of earrings. Then comes the turn for shoes, each pair is placed in order but for some unknown reason, you can't find those regular black pumps. You hunt through the shoe rack and at the last minute find them actually sitting on the very top shelf, quite obvious to the calm eye. While you put them on, you send a cursory glance to the resulted state of your shoe rack, after what you did in your quest to find the most obvious thing. You push the depressing thought of this messy state of affairs aside, and vow to deal with it *later*. We all know that *later,* soon becomes history.

This sort of sorry story happens inside our brain too. The orderly nature of the brain by default compels it to install each memory in a particular section. Making it organized and easy to retrieve. But when chaos occurs in your life and you are short on schedule, you ransack your brain, hurriedly rummaging through the compartments or sections in search of a particular memory.

This random marauding makes it nearly impossible for your brain to keep compartmentalizing things. What you can do to avoid this is, associate each memory with a particular incident or scenario. Link together similar sorts of experiences in an array or chain of memories that can be triggered one after the other by a particular picture, journal entry, color, or catchphrase, or word. Here we can consider the case of a middle-aged housewife named Sarah. She wants to keep order in her life and maintain her memories and brain activity in an organized manner. By jotting down her notes, recipes and pantry lists in her cooking journal, she maintains a record of her kitchen experiences. She also adds time and again, snapshots of specific moments that she wants to remember. A picture of a perfectly cooked meal perhaps, or an ideal sequence of utensils in the cabinet, or maybe a perfect combination of ingredients for a spur of a moment personally customized recipe. These things keep her kitchen department and its respective mind compartment in order. Now, whenever she needs to remember a certain recipe, she may just flip through a set of pictures depicting the ingredients and all the necessary procedures and relevant steps are recalled in a flash. Similarly, she compartmentalizes her socialization and family gatherings. A particular sitting arrangement and hospitality method for a particular guest can help her recall the previous meeting with the same person. She maintains a meeting log, making sections dedicated to her most frequent guests and social meetings. Through regular log entries such as concise phrases, socio-grams, or a clicked photo to commemorate the event, she can be more spontaneous in her responses while socializing. For her, every passing day becomes as easy to remember as the present day.

People often get surprised and popular comments are:

"Sarah has a very good memory, she even remembers what dress Anna's baby girl wore at the previous annual community dinner"

or

"Sarah always remembers to serve me her delicious coffee in that large black ceramic mug that I love so much"

or

"Sarah is a lady of honor, she remembered what she promised me even after so much time has passed".

The above case shows that compartmentalizing your memories is an effective way to increase your power to retain or retrieve them. To a very busy person, Sarah may seem to have so much extra time at hand to invest in journaling and logging all the time. But the truth is, Not doing so will waste your time more in the long run. Systematic conditioning of the brain is very important to avoid future disruption.

Moreover, once you get the hang of things you master the speed and accuracy at the same time i.e. you may not need to spend as much time on these trivial records in the future as your brain will get used to picking up the important details, distributing them into respective compartments. It will develop an affinity with storing what is needed, discarding what is not, retaining what is always needed, recalling what is occasionally needed.

8. Repetition:

Can you teach a goat something, anything?

Maybe yes, but can you teach it to recite a poem instead of uttering *baa* each time it opens its mouth?

Maybe not! But if *you* want to memorize something like a poem may be, you can by teaching a goat. No kidding. People repeat things in front of their pets as though they are teaching them, talking to them, regardless of what their response is. This constant repetition helps them memorize the subject fast. People are seen repeating and practicing in front of a mirror prior to making a public speech, etc.

Why do they do so?

Because, perhaps the very idea of just facing yourself without interruption or unnecessary criticism appeals to them, calm their nerves don, boost their confidence further. In the case of repeating and memorizing a poem in front of a pet, perhaps the innocence of a pet appears less intimidating, so they can focus more on the words they are reciting without stressful distraction. All in all, the idea of repetition is the crux of memorization. The connections in the brain are improved and strengthened when similar actions are repeated again and again until the brain gets so familiar with certain functions, you can even recall them in sleep. You can recall where you left off a conversation even after hours have passed, you would even be able to utter a sentence in the same tone of voice and with the same gesture and facial expression. That is often seen when people have watched a particular theatrical performance or comedy show multiple times repeatedly, they can mimic the expressions exactly as they saw.

If you want to improve your memory to a nearly photographic level, repetition and revision is a mandatory practice.

9. Implementation:

Several of us have heard the famous hierarchy of educational learning called *the bloom's taxonomy*. It has three domains essentially i.e. cognitive, affective or emotional, psychomotor (relating to the mind and body). The cognitive domain is mostly used in the academic sense. It has six levels or steps that can be implemented in a sequence to ensure effective learning outcomes. These six levels are placed in the pyramid hierarchical model and comprise (from bottom to top): *knowledge, comprehension, application, analysis, evaluation, and synthesis.* Many universities and colleges and even secondary schools follow this model to devise lesson plans, assessments, and research activities. The *application* stage is basically the implementation.

Consider a student Ben, today he has been introduced to a new science topic about light and electricity in his class. The teacher has stated and defined the term electricity and then ask the students to repeat what they learned. Level 1, i.e. knowledge has been achieved. But this is only the start. Ben's brain has gained information and stored it but is he able to understand or comprehend the concept of how light or electricity works? This remains open for discussion.

The next day, his teacher makes him sit in a study group with his peers to *discuss* and *explain* what they understood by the previous day's definition. Ben is able to *recall* some of the words, maybe, but the concept is not that clear. After discussion though, they may be able to explain a little in their own words. Level 2 i.e. *comprehension* would be accomplished after further explanation of the concept by the teacher and the ability of the students to *summarize* that explanation in their own words. The third stage starts when the teacher assigns a project to the students to make a simple circuit or a toy torch to *apply* their *knowledge* and *comprehension* practice. This gives them the chance to implement the learned concepts and the knowledge is retained as the memory improves with repetition and implementation of the same concepts over and over again. This is not where the learning ends though, the higher stages in this taxonomy suggest more abstract thinking and practices that can be glimpsed in the following figure depicting Bloom's cognitive model in great detail:

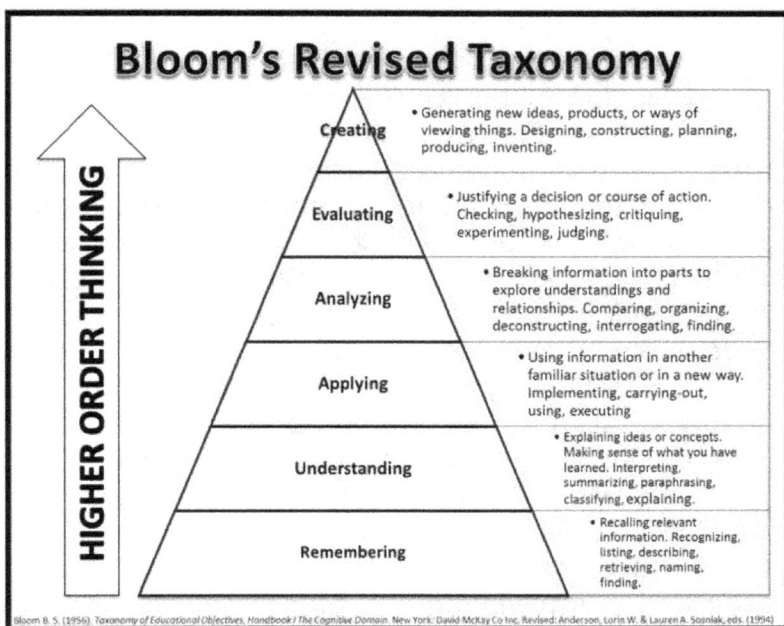

Bloom's Revised Taxonomy

HIGHER ORDER THINKING

Creating • Generating new ideas, products, or ways of viewing things. Designing, constructing, planning, producing, inventing.

Evaluating • Justifying a decision or course of action. Checking, hypothesizing, critiquing, experimenting, judging.

Analyzing • Breaking information into parts to explore understandings and relationships. Comparing, organizing, deconstructing, interrogating, finding.

Applying • Using information in another familiar situation or in a new way. Implementing, carrying-out, using, executing

Understanding • Explaining ideas or concepts. Making sense of what you have learned. Interpreting, summarizing, paraphrasing, classifying, explaining.

Remembering • Recalling relevant information. Recognizing, listing, describing, retrieving, naming, finding.

Bloom B. S. (1956). Taxonomy of Educational Objectives. Handbook I The Cognitive Domain. New York: David McKay Co Inc. Revised: Anderson, Lorin W. & Lauren A. Sosniak, eds. (1994)

In 1956's older version of the bloom's taxonomy placed *synthesis* before the *evaluation* stage. Which puts the concept of assessment or examination of facts and knowledge to create or synthesize newer strategies or ideas, in a wrong sequence. The modernized version came after results gathered from the academic statistics and students' and teachers' experiences. The altered version placed the *evaluation* or assessment stage before the *synthesis.* Therefore, it has been proven that knowledge after it is gained, is retained by understanding, repetition, implementation, evaluation or examination, and finally creating or synthesizing a new whole by putting together miscellaneous parts of previous knowledge. That's how inventions happen in our world!

10. Assessment:

This tip is a nail in the coffin. You lock your important memory by assessing it through various practice tests, quizzes, and questionnaires. You test your brain and condition it to be capable of conjuring the required information with detail the instant you summon it. Why the exams are so important? Why every academic institute create such a hype over admission tests, aptitude exams, and classroom assessments? Because this is the easiest way for them to check if you actually remember what you have learned previously. In order to not waste their time or yours, they need to be sure that knowledge is being invested, not wasted. The brain's rule of thumb or knowledge is, *use it or lose it.* like it or not, it works that way. Your brain has a knack of discarding garbage and it is always on an automated mode when it comes to dumping waste. The brain's standard for measuring whether a particular piece of memory or information is important or not is to check how frequently it is recalled and how *useful* and *used* it is.

Chapter 6: Cramming v/s Spacing v/s Accelerated Learning

Imagine going for a vacation. last-minute packing is remaining. Travel bags are all full to the neck. No space for a couple of extra clothes, that comfy green jumper, or a pair of newly bought sneakers. What do you often do? Tie the sweater around the strap or wear the sneakers yourself instead? or maybe opening the zip wide, pushing the clothes that are already inside, even more inside with a fist, to make a nonexistent space for some last-minute add-ins. This is what cramming is!

Have you tried a napkin dance before? Contesting couples are given a piece of napkin each and are told to dance standing on their respective napkin without stepping outside of the limited space. After every music break, the napkin is folded once. In the first round, the napkin is a single-layered square, then a two-layered rectangle, then 4 layered square again, until the time comes when most of the couples are eliminated due to stepping outside the narrow and congested surface inevitably. This is what cramming is!

Cramming

In a strictly academic sense, students cram when they tend to take in too much information in too little a time. They revise large piles of books in a single night before a particular exam, crowding their brain in the process.

This sort of cramming largely happens when students procrastinate the entire academic year, don't set their priorities straight, and don't allocate appropriate hours for both study and play. The misbalance in sleep, play, socialization, and studies results in a compulsive need to cram every book before an exam, burning the midnight oil. Most students claim that they have aced an exam while preparing only a night before. But if you closely enquire, you will come to know that most of those who actually achieved good grades even after only a night of revision are the ones who paid attention in the class throughout the year or at least attended most of the lectures. If that is not the case then they dedicated some portion of their time to self-studying and covering the missed topics. However, the results are not often satisfactory due to mental stress, lack of sleep, and sluggish brain activity. Think of it as a traffic jam when roads are crammed with vehicles of all sort, honking from every direction, trying to grab attention. It is a nightmare in making or a disaster waiting to happen.

The study is not magic, it is a habit. You work hard, you learn, you revise, you succeed. It is simple. For some of you, the requirement level of hard work may vary but still, it is required by all.

A student who doesn't appear to note down anything during a lecture about the national economy may have absorbed it word by word through attentive listening skills. He may even be discussing the same topic with his peers outside the class context, explaining it, again and again, giving reference to it in daily conversations at home during evening tea, relating it to the real-world examples during shopping for groceries in a supermarket. Whereas a student who has scribbled throughout the lecture, making important notes in his journal, may not even open it at home afterward albeit discussing or revising it until the very night before the exam.

Who, do you think is likely to succeed more in the exam or at least has developed a better level of understanding which is the main aim of studying? Who do you think will be able to readily recall the concepts that were explained in the class, even if not the exact words of the lecture? Of course, the one who has maintained a close connection with the learned concepts in any form throughout the year instead of one who succumbed to cramming as a last resort.

Spacing

Many of us have, consciously or unconsciously, tried a method of revision where you are asked a set of questions by your partner. Whenever you fail to answer a particular one, your partner tells the correct answer and then moves towards the next ones, only to come back later to ask the missed question again. This time you may answer it correctly.

Spaced learning was first introduced by Hermann Ebbinghaus, a psychologist and memory researcher belonging to Germany. He got his inspiration from the work of Gustav Fechner, also a psychologist who wrote a book about his experimental findings on psychophysics. As mentioned above, Ebbinghaus was quite passionate in his quest for examining the mysterious workings of mind and memory. It was this persistence in experimenting everything personally without getting overshadowed by prevalent theories, which led him to discover his famous forgetting curve. You read about memory loss in chapter no. 2. However, here we will relate it with the spaced learning effect.

So, let us first understand what spaced learning really is?

Spaced learning or spacing technique is the method of distributing information over an extended period of time, inserting short intervals of distraction in between. This method is proven to be far more effective than cramming where you try to accumulate a large volume of knowledge in a very short time span. Spaced learning is more systematic and result oriented. Rather than stretching it in a single session, why not spread it over multiple sessions?

Remember,

Stretching brings strain and tension while spreading brings richness in approach and flexibility.

Equally effective in both formal and informal learning contexts, and for both children and adults, people can efficiently learn skills such as vocabulary, numbers, art techniques, culinary skills, etc. by spacing the content that is to be learned and memorized. Even the classroom blocks or periods in a school are scheduled in such a way that learning is mostly preceded by an assembly or physical exercise and proceeded by a game unit or recess. This helps students to release their pent-up frustrations and get distracted in a good way, refreshing them to start memorizing them anew. It also eliminates the possibility of getting the knowledge that was acquired in the previous session mixed up with the one acquired in the next session. So here comes the compartmentalizing.

Each session's information is tucked away safely, labeled and locked, not to be confused with another topic. Thus the order prevails and the performance improves.

Next time you sit for a revision, make sure you set a realistic timeframe and divide the selected content into manageable portions spread across that timeframe with recreational breaks in between. You will understand the art of spaced learning and experience its perks first hand.

How do we forget and remember?

Ebbinghaus observed that the mind can dispose of the unused information with the passage of time. The hypothesis he proposed after his observations and experiments became the beginning of forgetting theory. According to the results of his memory testing over a period of time, he plotted a graph that materialized as a curve showing the diminishing memory as time passes. This curve is called the *forgetting curve*. If it wasn't the case of us forgetting things, no one had to revise anything. The concept of repetition wouldn't have existed. The memory loss and its nature can be defined by the forgetting curve.

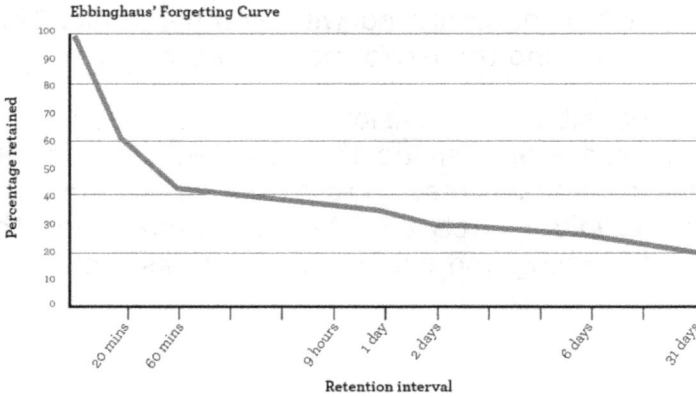

Ebbinghaus' Forgetting Curve

Percentage retained (y-axis: 0, 10, 20, 30, 40, 50, 60, 70, 80, 90, 100)

Retention interval (x-axis: 20 mins, 60 mins, 9 hours, 1 day, 2 days, 6 days, 31 days)

Why do we forget and remember

Why crammed facts soon disappear from the mind is because the curve shows us that information recently acquired is the fastest to lose. The exponential drop occurs within minutes of learning a thing if not given frequent, timely reminders day after day. It is where the role of spaced repetition comes in. The *forgetting curve* can be changed into a *learning curve* or slope by way of spaced memorization technique, also called distributed learning. To slow down the forgetting process, you need to provide your recent memory some robustness and longevity by revisions and repetition over time. Because the content of large length can simply not be memorized in single repetition without enough reminders; no matter how much the concentration or attention is paid. Even the small piece of content needs a couple of revisions to be able to recall exactly.

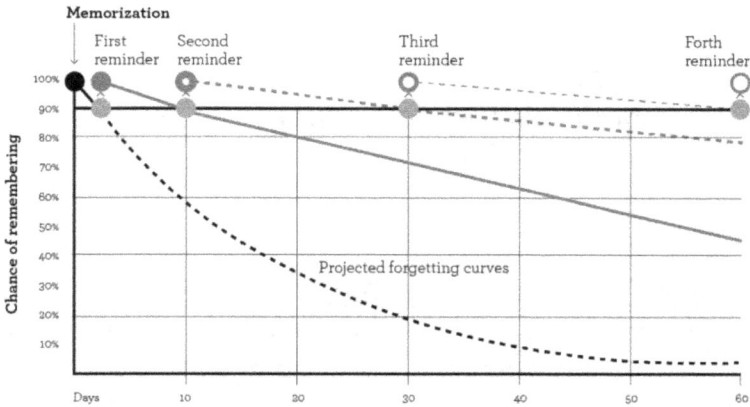

Memorization

| | First reminder | Second reminder | | Third reminder | | Forth reminder |

Chance of remembering

100%, 90%, 80%, 70%, 60%, 50%, 40%, 30%, 20%, 10%

Projected forgetting curves

Days 10 20 30 40 50 60

What do we forget and remember

We, humans, are emotional beings to the extreme. We breathe emotions, talk emotions, and feel emotions. We even think emotionally. We cannot separate the emotions and intensity of some level from our thoughts and responses. What we remember is most of the time attached to our hearts. Some incident that has an emotional story behind it. Some intense moments of self-realization, success, or disappointment. We cannot help stereotyping our memories by labeling them as happy, sad, or hilarious. We even train our brain to be nostalgic about a past incident and thus our brain becomes emotional too. If that is how we tend to function most of the time, why not take it to our advantage?

589

> *"There is no such thing as memorizing. Rather our brains are designed to think and automatically hold onto what's important." -*
> *Gabriel Wyner*

The intensity of the things experienced the first time, help us recall them the second time we feel the same intensity while experiencing other things. We attempt to correlate the experiences of a similar intensity that aroused a similar emotion in us. when something seems worth remembering, just mark it as important and your brain would *feel* the urgency of emotion and its importance. In his text, *"Memory and Forgetting"*, Ebbinghaus described the importance of attention, interest, intensity, and concentration for the retention of memory. Even to be able to reproduce the experiences and tasks, there should be some greater level of intensity of interest attached. Interest or focus alone, while observing someone will not suffice. A shocking incident has an element of surprise in it and is likely to be remembered more than an ordinary one that occurs almost daily.

Suppose, you visit a park daily, you encounter many passersby, you cannot remember all of them. But this morning when you passed the walking track you saw a boy wearing a neon orange jumper suit, yelling at the top of his lungs, chasing after a runaway dog. You were startled for a second due to his screaming. You are likely to remember him or a while may be due to his unusual suit color or his unusual behavior or his runaway pet that gave a bit of a shock. And when you recall the incident, you may also experience the same emotion associated with it.

Accelerated Learning

They say relearning is better than learning and recall is better than identification. It is true. Why are you advised to practice mock tests and quizzes rather than linearly reading through the book? Because most important is to *recall* and *retrieve* your previously learned knowledge. These revision tests are specifically designed to trigger the diminishing memory and highlight the key points enabling you to get a grip on nearly lost information.

This is one of the reasons why a highlighter should always be in your hand while listening to a lecture or reading through a text during self-study. Highlighting the most important details and description during your study will help you at the time of revision. You can just review the highlighted part of the paragraph to be able to remember what was discussed in the whole paragraph.

This way you can not only save time but also increase performance and accelerate the overall learning and relearning process. This, in fact, is one of the several techniques of accelerated learning.

Accelerated learning can be defined as the process of interactive learning that is learner-centered and provides room for learners taking the initiative. It is an activity-based, stimulating method that urges the learner to be involved in the learning process as a whole. Shunning the passive, prolonged methods of conventional teaching, an accelerated learning educator adapts the role of a facilitator rather than an instructor enhancing the cognitive potential of the learner to the optimum. Through various activities, the learner is given a chance to explore and discover things through actively exercising his creativity, memory power, and previous experiential knowledge.

He can implement ideas and make meaningful creations that take him from known to the unknown. The idea of scaffolding and Zone of Proximal Development (ZPD) is taken to the next level here. ZPD suggests an area that ranges between what a learner can do on his own, what he would be able to do if provided some assistance (this assistance or guidance is called *scaffolding*), and what he has yet to achieve.

VISUALIZING THE ZONE OF PROXIMAL DEVELOPMENT

THINGS YOU CAN DO ALL ON YOUR OWN

THINGS YOU CAN DO WITH A BIT OF HELP

THINGS YOU CAN'T YET DO, NO MATTER HOW MUCH SUPPORT YOU GET

VERBALTOVISUAL.COM

The pioneers of accelerated learning call it a must-have 21st-century skill. Our era is that of dynamic change and speed. Every single moment unveils a series of newer skills and opens doors to previously unknown facts. Time is money here, speed is its currency.

Therefore educators of accelerated learning focus on applying multi-faceted learning techniques that involve all the sensory domains of development including cognitive, social, emotional and physical. They target the holistic learning and retention of knowledge. The acquirer of the knowledge through this method is presented with alternative ways to learn the same information, not just relying on a single method of presentation. For example, if he wants to learn the process of gardening and he has opted for the accelerated version of the course. He can learn the process in a couple of months instead of a year-long course.

How? You may ask.

When he enrolls in the accelerated training program, he will be given opportunities to actively participate in learning through presentations, experiments, practical gardening sessions, excursions to the nurseries and local botanical gardens, discussing the pros and cons of a particular seeding method during group discussions, presenting his analysis on a particular research material on tropical plants. He would be able to grasp even the more in-depth topics such as comparing the effects of certain fertilizers on the level of toxicity of the soil, by plotting a statistical graph after studying past data. All this would be possible because, in this program, he would be letting the information come in through various channels, keeping an open mind, and following an integrated approach to learning. Thus strengthening the memory and completing the acquisition of knowledge happens in the shortest time period possible.

Sometimes another term for accelerated learning is used interchangeably, i.e. *mind hacking.* Even though the former is more like a goal to be achieved while the latter is one of the methods to achieve it. Experts state that learning is a part of development and development is not a linear process, it occurs by leaps and bounds. The following graph can show this concept a little more visually.

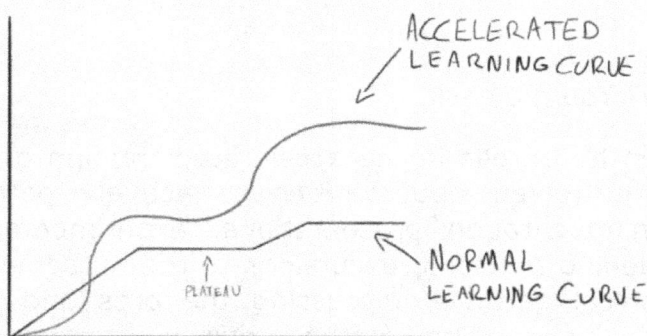

ACCELERATED
LEARNING CURVE

PLATEAU

NORMAL
LEARNING CURVE

DARIUS FOROUX

Learning with acceleration focuses on not only *what* a thing is, but *how* it works too, at the same time. By taking the initiative in learning, the learner develops a *want to* attitude instead of *having to* mindset. Referring back to the term *mind hacking,* one can say that it a process of meta-learning where your brain is literally reprogrammed and reconditioned to function in a certain way. Your brain needs to be aware of the way *you* want it to work instead of the way it functions on an auto-pilot mode.

Multiple Intelligences and your Neural Learning Model

Howard Gardener, a renowned American psychologist of educational and development, proposed his theory about evidence of multiple talents possessed by every human. The tendency of a person to be skilled at multiple things makes the concept of intelligence quite vast. It broadens the possibility of improvement and boosts the confidence of even the most average of students.

A person can be good at wordplay, *or* physical sport, *or* music, *or* creative art, *or* cooking, *or* math, etc. Or he can be a jack of all and these talents can be present in him concurrently. In that case, we can replace those *"or"* with *"and"*, can't we?

Similarly, the neural programming model suggests that a person may be more of a visual nature, or a lingual one, or an audio-visual one, etc. This means that some people are more sensitive to what they perceive graphically rather than what they listen to or speak of. This makes them more visual in nature and a similar approach should be adopted while presenting them with memory improvement techniques or accelerated learning activities.

For example, they would be more interested in watching a short graphical documentary on a particular topic than reviewing an informative but textual article about it in a magazine. A lingual person, however, would be eager to swallow up the whole book in order to learn information on a given topic. But if he was assigned making of an info graph or creating a chart to summarize what he has learned, he may find it a chore. Therefore, assessing yourself to know which sort of behavior model your mind follows, is an important prerequisite to adapting a particular learning strategy or memory boosting method.

Speed Reading

Speed reading is one of the strategies of accelerated learning. It is the ability to quickly scan the printed words visually rather than *sub vocalizing* them in your mind. This means that you are not going to read the text to yourself or mumble them. Instead, you will take the images, quickly run your eyes over them to grasp the full sentence and keep moving forth.

What happens when you subvocalize?

Sub vocalizing means to utter the text in your mind i.e. with your inner voice. The biggest setback to reading quickly is focusing too much on the comprehension. Many people tend to repeat a sentence a couple of times in their mind to understand more while attempting to read quickly too. This contradicts the speed.

What happens is that your brain is working every single nanosecond of the time. It never stops. When you read a word mentally, it is taken as a new task. A message is sent to the brain to encode it, while your eyes are also at work to see the letters that form the word and the phonetic sounds that are combined to articulate that word even if only as an inner voice. A series of messages are sent and received in a short span of time and occupy your mind thus slowing down the reading process. Instead, if you avoid subvocalizing, your brain will directly encode the text as visual images and show you what they are and how they look to help you recognize them quickly. Just like when you *see* a tree, you will *recognize* it as a tree if you have *seen* it before.

An average person can read around 200 words per minute without practicing speed reading skills. But skilled speed-readers tend to accomplish a speed for reading about 400 or more words per minute. Almost double of what an average reader does. Sometimes they even reach 700-1000 wpm range through repeated practice and determination.

The important thing is to understand when you should require speed reading and when you should opt for comprehensive reading. Usually, when you are researching for something you often must go through numerous papers and studies. The speed-reading techniques can prove to be handy here. However, always remember to maintain some semblance of the basic concept or argument being presented in the text that you are speed reading without spending too much time over analysis now. The time for review and analysis would come later when you prepare a critical summary.

We are listing some major points to remember while speed reading a text:

- *Avoid subvocalization:* Don't read to yourself.

- *Avoid visual regression:* Don't let your sight wander around the next page. Compel it to follow the train of the sentence with a finger or a tip of a pencil.

- *Avoid too much focus on comprehension*: Don't be caught up in visualizing the scenario you are reading about. Don't try to analyze it just now. Keep reading. You only have seconds to complete a sentence.

- *Avoid perceiving a certain collection of words as single units*: Try to catch them as augmented groups or phrases. Most words are used together in a group or universal phrase so often that you recognize them in an instant when you spot them on the page.

  For e.g. when you see; "Looking forward to hearing from you", you can read it as a whole quickly. It is also a way to predict text, that is what Google often does while you compose an email. Similarly, the idioms like, "beating around the bush", can be taken as a complete unit too.

- *Avoid reading linearly (line by line)*: Read the first and the last sentence of each paragraph before taking a quick snapshot of the middle. The opening sentence will usually tell you what will be covered in the following paragraph and the last sentence will provide you with the crux.

- *Push yourself to read faster:* Don't settle for less, be ambitious. Push your limits to extend further, aim higher. If you are managing to read at 400 words per minute speed, aim for 450 wpm as your next target. When you start managing 450 wpm, aim for 500 wpm instead. Force your eyes to move quicker than they are moving currently.

Remember, accelerated learning techniques are all about a psycho-emotional mindset. Your emotions, behavior, and intention, they all matter a lot when it comes to achieving improvement in targeted results.

Chapter 7: Mind Programming, an Insight

Programming is basically used in computer science as an act of designing a set of instructions to be executed by a computer. A computer program is a set of instructions which tells the computer what to do and how to process. If it were not for these carefully designed and structured programs, the computer would have been just a physical body of useless hardware without a functional brain. *Mind programming* is usually referred to as an act of structured encoding of information that can be controlled and executed in an organized manner *willfully*.

The above explanation of computer programming can be applied in this context as well. As the mind absorbs information, it needs structured, systematic instructions to process this information. This is where programming is needed. Studies have linked the process of mind programming to both individual and collective settings. Experts state that the mind is not just an individual's tool for thought. It is much more complex than that. The mind can be a medium for communication between individuals. It can be a sponge that absorbs external impressions and environmental vibes along with its own collection of internal thoughts and emotions. It works as an implicit as well as an explicit channel of interaction. However, it should be used to control the chaotic thought process, instead of controlling other people. It should be more about regaining focus on your own responses and behavior, instead of manipulating others' reactions.

Many of you have heard a word being frequently used in wordy speeches and marketed content; *"result-oriented".* Have you ever wondered how the notion started? There is something called thinking backward i.e. top to bottom. Normal, average people may start a task from the bottom, working hard to pass the milestones to achieve the goal. Mind programmers would First jump to the top, imagining the ultimate result of each particular course of action they might take. Then they will travel backward in their thinking to trace the possible pathways that would have led to that result, ultimately reaching the bottom starting point to realize what should be their first course of action to reach the desired goal or result.

Similarly, unleashing the astonishing powers of mind by repeated practices and training sessions, what once can eventually control is the ability to overcome challenging situations and remain steadfast in stormy life weather. He can be unfazed in front of turbulent waves of uncertain circumstances. Mind programming has an innate concept of *mind over matter.* This principle skill suggests that no matter what you encounter in life your mental strength, determination, and stoic ability can make you have the upper hand on the situation and let the *steering wheel of your mind* handle the *vehicle of your body*. Minding something literally means *to "remember and pay attention to."* If you think something is important enough to be noticed, you not only pay extra attention to it but make a conscious effort to remember it as well. Paying attention and making a conscious effort is the key to mind programming. When you hear something like; *By having optimistic thoughts, you will meet positive results.* You might doubt the authenticity of such a statement. However, it can be true because what you *convince* your mind to think is what it eventually compels you to act upon.

Your actions are mostly driven by your ambitions and your outlook on life has a powerful grip on your decision-making mechanism.

"Don't convince your body, convince your mind."

The more you open the windows of your mind, the more open your eyes will be to the secrets of a successful life. Now the question is, are there really windows in your mind? What sort of windows are they?

Actually, in a strictly biological sense, you have those windows as sensory channels through which your sensory organs take in information and your brain processes it so that you may learn about new things. However, by keeping an open mind you let all the possible tracks for making new mental connections or rebuilding the older ones, become traceable.

Sometimes the idea thoughts as invisible beings sound quite daunting but it also makes us capable of possessing something that is only ours. The personal forces inside our brain that can be our treasure alone, easily attainable, and durably appreciable. No one can fight us for possession of this treasure. No one can even see our weapon for winning the battles of our life. This can make us lead an independent, powerful life. Though modern studies have devised quite a few methods to read the mind and unveil its hidden treasures, there is still a long way to go before it becomes a completely transparent container.

Still, thoughts can no longer be considered a matter of abstract reality.

For even your own understanding you must perceive them as manageable packets or blocks of information or intention that can be classified into colors, or images, or objects, or symbols, or letters, or numbers, or even food items! Whatever you choose them to be in order to organize them in clearly defined categories or compartments.

This is what personality modeling or thinking styles classification, an important aspect of mind programming teaches us.

According to some thinking, styles vary according to personality traits. First, you must identify your personality model in order to identify how your thinking processes. There is content galore on the subject of self-help and soft skills mastery. These books explain behavior models and are the tips given in them are often based on the characteristic personality models. For example, modern job interviews and selection screening tests are often designed to contain at least some questions that assess the personality of the candidate by measuring the quotient of his id, ego, superego, as described by the famous psychoanalyst and neurologist, Sigmund Freud. This is because emotional intelligence is considered as much important as academic excellence in the recent era. The *id, ego, and superego* are three structures of personality that can be instrumental in assessing your personality behavior and model. This, in turn, would be helpful in programming your mind. These personality elements determine the nature of your behavior while resolving various conflicts that arise at every stage of life. Id, Ego, and Superego are depicted in the info graph below.

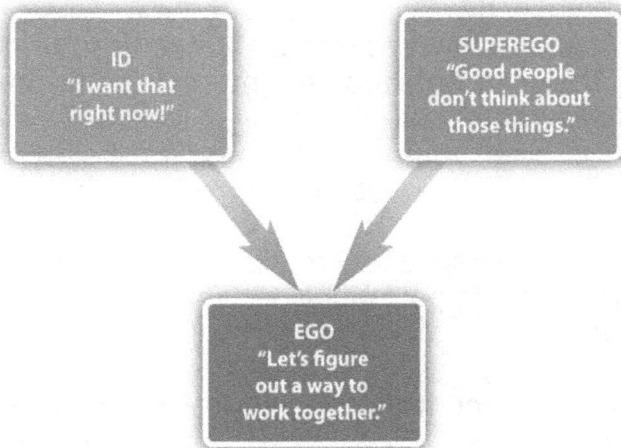

ID "I want that right now!"		SUPEREGO "Good people don't think about those things."
	EGO "Let's figure out a way to work together."	

The focus of this book was not to let *others* understand *your* mind's power, but let *you* gain insight on how to have a mindset that can improve your thinking style and memory capacity. Therefore, we have described mostly about how mind programming works for an individual's personal improvement.

Personality Behavior (Who) ---->

<----Thinking Model or Mindset (How) ---->

<----Intentions and Goals (Thought-driven) (What) ---->

<---- Decisions / Actions ------>

<------ Achievements

The term actively used nowadays with respect to mind programming is *mind hacking* which is actually the shortcut method for the former. While the latter may achieve some progress by accelerated training and, it may not reach the profound mental layers and personality issues, thus being effective for only a short term. While careful mind programming achieves long term results and a complete restructuring of the mental schemas.

604

There is often a concept of classical and operant conditioning involved in these training sessions. *Accommodation* and *adaptation* are also practices to ensure maximum learning and restructuring of mental schemas.

What is schema

In cognitive psychology, a schema refers to a set of information or encrypted code associated with a particular experience. When a person encounters a situation, the way he reacts during it marks an impression in mind and in response to this stimulus a schema is organized. Now if a person reacts the same way again in a similar situation, this schema will be maintained and newer experience will be added as well in the same set of mental structures. However, if that person reacts in a different manner the next time the same situation occurs, the schema will be altered or discarded to be replaced by the new information that is generated for a different response to a particular stimulus. When the old schema is removed to make room for or to *accommodate* a new experience, *accommodation* occurs. Whereas, if the old schema is maintained with little or no changes, and similar experiences are being *added* to just update the existing cognitive structure, *assimilation* occurs. To review these concepts in a little more detail, let us quickly answer the following questions:

What is classical conditioning

Being one of the learning procedures which determine the way our mind works, controlling the way we think and act, classical conditioning is a behavioral psychology phenomenon, presented by Russian physiologist Ivan Pavlov. Also referred to as an automated or associative type of learning, classical conditioning lets the mind learn a certain response or behavior by automatically associating one stimulus with the other with or without any distinctive relationship between the two. For e.g. At the start of a lesson, when you often see your teacher take out an attendance sheet each time she enters the class, you would automatically consider or *assume* any piece of paper in her hand as an attendance sheet expecting your roll call. But maybe the next time she takes out the first paper upon arriving in the class, it could be your recent test report instead of an attendance sheet. What happens is in normal circumstances you may not expect any sheet of paper to be an attendance sheet or if you meet the same teacher after school near the parking you will not expect her to start calling your name for attendance, but if it is the *start of a lesson, and that particular teacher carrying a sheet in her hand*, you would expect it to be the roll call because your mind has become conditioned to produce a similar response each time these two stimuli are presented to you together in a certain setting. Most of the phobias such as fear for fire and emotions of anxiety, anticipation, boredom, nausea, etc. are triggered by associating certain surroundings (stimulus 1) with certain objects or smells (stimulus 2), etc.

A person who was burned by a candle flame in a dark room may start fearing both the candle and the darkness. A person who feels the urge to vomit every time he sees blood in the hospital may have nausea when he sees a hospital room even when there is no apparent display of blood.

However, most of the time these behavior patterns get conditioned only through reinforcement. Therapies in mind training sessions can be conducted to make the previous behavior extinct but extinction is not particularly translated to forgetting a memory, instead, it means that newer experiences replace the older ones, therefore new learning occurs.

What is operant conditioning

A remarkable contribution to the behavioral conditioning theory is the operant conditioning given by B.F. Skinner. It is a type of associative learning that is more controlled than the classical conditioning to achieve the desired outcome. In contrast to the classical conditioning, operant conditioning operates on the principle of conditioning the desired response in a person by revealing the possible consequences of his certain behavior in each situation.

This ensures the achievement of positive learning outcomes through a concept of reward and punishment. For e.g. A learner associates his scoring high in a quiz (desired behavior or response) with getting no-homework pass or best-student badge (reward). So if the teacher wants to improve the student behavior, she conditions them by letting them know the possible consequences of how they respond. Through repetitions or reinforcements, encouragement or discouragement, a particular good or bad behavior can be strengthened or weakened respectively.

What is the accommodation?

Altering the mental environment in order to make a suitable room for new information. Here, the old responses prototyped in the existing mental schema to certain experiences are not consistent with the new ones so they must be replaced by a new schema to accommodate the new information. Mastering the way mental schema is patterned leads us to get the knack of mind programming. The very term called *prototype* in the context of programming means that structuring of mind is indeed what lays at the heart of mind power.

What is assimilation?

Adjusting new information in an existing schema to be in sync with the older experiences. To assimilate is to understand the new information based on past experiences. Assimilation is actually the foundational pillar for experiential learning. It is also the concept through which many sequential forms of academics are taught in schools. The term *prerequisite* is the derivative of this very idea of assimilation that shapes the mental schema or cognitive structure in our mind. This state of mind suggests stability or equilibrium that ensures smooth learning.

However, sometimes accommodation is needed instead of assimilation to let the innovation, creativity, and dynamics enter the static stream of mind.

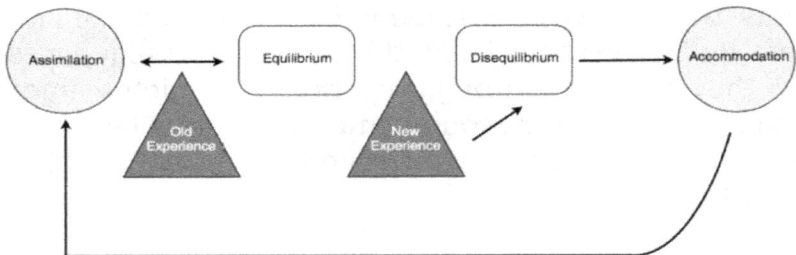

The Law of Attraction in Mind Programming

The dynamics of mind programming include several inspiring concepts and motivational outlook on life obtained through the powers of mind. The law of attraction is one of those extremely inspiring concepts that has a very positive vibe to it.

"The imaginable is achievable"

If you can consider your mind having magnetic power, you can imagine your desired results automatically being attracted to your optimistic thoughts carried by your magnetic mind. What you think is what you become or what becomes of you.

Consider these tips for reference:

- ✓ Avoiding mental laziness and procrastination is one of the keys to unlock successful outcomes.

- ✓ Have a pep talk with your inner self each time you feel negative thoughts swarming in your mind.

- ✓ Reward yourself on your hard work when you perform well. It can be anything from a cheat day incorporated in your diet or a simple compliment to yourself and no, it is not against modesty. Believe that you deserve it.

- ✓ Don't underestimate yourself, don't overestimate too. Set realistic goals but try to expand your potential by positive self-encouragement.

- ✓ Intend moderately but act generously to pursue the unwavering thought.

- ✓ Having confidence in your intentions can make the process of the proceeding actions easier. The mind focuses on the goal post, the body on the playground.

Chapter 8: Life Skills for Memory Improvement

The famous pioneer of the Montessori Method of Education, an Italian Doctor Maria Montessori says:

> *"All victories and all human progress are dependent on the strength that comes from within."*

Progress is most often built on the obvious, existing things that we overlook in our quest for hidden secrets of success. We perceive self-help as an out of the world training, even though it most certainly is an inner motivational concept. Our life is shaped by the way we *live* it. By changing the way of our existing lifestyle, we can improve the living standard exponentially. If you take sufficient sleep, eat healthily, and socialize with nice company, you can achieve a kind of stability in life that helps you relax and let your brain gain more focus.

Nowadays, the concept of life skills is getting all the necessary hype and duly so. Gone are the days when leisure activities were just pass-times and habits just a routine. Eating, sleeping, communicating, socializing, exercising, all these are counted as skills now. They are taught in personality development centers specially dedicated to groom you and organize your mentality to make use of these life skills.

However, you don't specifically need to get enrolled in an institution to learn these skills that aid in increasing your brainpower and improve your memory.

Yoga & Exercise

Muscles are known as *instruments of movement,* so described by Dr. Maria Montessori. She says that the will in our mind is implemented by the muscles in our body. Hence the relationship between mental and physical processes is vital for development. Inactivity and sedentary lifestyle dictate exhaustive mind labor dissociated from the active muscles, eventually increasing the immobility in mind as well. If the body is not trained for physical labor the mind will suffer in correcting the mistakes made by the body and the struggle that it may go through upon encountering any physical challenge. Yoga and exercises such as walking, running, skipping, swimming, etc. not only help to activate the muscular system by increasing the blood flow but also help to alleviate stress and depression. The relaxed mind is, therefore, able to remember more and retain it longer.

The practice of yoga basically originated from India as an orthodox principle school of complementary medicine. Old Indian yogic practices suggest that yoga can be used to increase motion range, core strength, physical flexibility, and mental focus. It can be a perfect mood improvement therapy which can also be an elemental practice in disease prevention.

There is a famous and interesting concept in authentic Indian yogic scriptures which state that the human body has amazing latent energy stored in its core or spinal column. The air that we breathe enhances the recharging power of the electrical potential present in our brain matter.

Even the way we breathe through our left or right nostrils affect the way our internal body heat is increased or decreased. Each time we breathe through the right nostril, energy in the form of oxygen increases the blood flow to the brain and positive charge is produced and stored in the brain cells. A time comes when positive energy reaches a peak level so that we tend to breathe through our left nostril automatically. This time negative charge is produced and stored until it reaches the peak level too. Again the breathing alternates from left nostril to the right nostril. This alternate transition makes a path for the current to pass from positive to negative and vice versa which in turn, produces the electricity that flows along with the blood reaching different parts of the body.

The produced electricity is stored as a latent potential inside the vertebral column because of the presence of some brain matter in the spinal cord, as it is also a major part of our nervous system. When this potent electrical energy is revived or recharged through regular practice and yoga sessions, it passes through the core, reaching the brain and revitalizing the brain cells one by one. The major activation of nervous chips in the computer-like circuitry of our brain opens a series of wondrous revelations for a person. It gives him a new perspective of things, new thoughts, and ideas that can be instrumental in bringing out his optimum potential and improvement in his memory skills. This is ordinary people are stimulated and trained to achieve great things in life.

Meditation and Mindfulness

They say when *no one speaks, the mind does.* Meditation is to the psyche what physical workout is to the body. It is a mind training method to gain focus and concentration. Mindful meditation is a type of meditation where you train your mind to focalize on a singular thought process. This increases the ability to concentrate, avoid unnecessary distractions, and improve memory. When you are focused on life, you achieve bigger things. Reflection is the primary principle of meditation. To meditate as a beginner;

o Select a peaceful environment to sit.
o Make yourself in a comfortable position, relaxing your posture.
o Close your eyes.
o Take a deep breath carefully focusing on your inhalation and exhalation.
o Let your mind speak to you.
o Listen to the thoughts and reflect.
o Open your eyes after an initial 10-15 minutes session.
o Practice daily.

Sleeping well

Sleep is not just a way of going into oblivion, but a way to refuel your brain. Sleep lets your otherwise busy brain to relax and focus on detoxification of the nervous system. Even the metabolism in your body works better during rest periods. The blood flow is better during sleep and the energy level is restored.

Sleep deprivation causes harmful toxin production inside your brain and hinders the mental processes.

The adverse effects of too much wakefulness without adequate sleep, include obesity, memory decline, metabolic imbalance, hypertension, early death risks and several other health concerns due to the weakened immune system. The happy hormone, *serotonin* is said to be a precursor agent in *melatonin* formation, the latter is said to be actively produced in the darkness of night, helping you to regulate your inner biological clock. Melatonin is also responsible for maintaining your sleep-wake cycles. This makes it evident that sleeping at night is very important in organizing your routine. Together, both serotonin and melatonin play an important role in regularizing your appetite, sleep, and behavioral patterns.

Eating Healthy

Healthy nutrition is one of the most important milestones to be achieved in your journey towards memory improvement. Healthy food choices can positively affect your behavior and thought process along with maintaining your body's functionality. For instance, when you are hungry you feel quite cranky and when you eat a lot you feel sluggish or drowsy. Unhealthy patterns of eating should be avoided to gain stability in life. The food supplements to improve your mental capability and contribute to your overall physical health have been discussed in detail at the end of this book.

Smiling and Socializing

Dopamine along with serotonin is released when a person smile. Both neuro transmitting chemicals travel inside the brain letting your nerves know about your smile and the brain becomes happy to see you in a happy mood! The benefits of a smile can be enough to make an encyclopedia out of it. Here we are just relating it to your brain activity as is the purpose of this book.

Socializing is an art of living. Information is the primary subject of your memory and most of it comes from interaction. When you interact, you meet new people, accumulate new ideas, get inspiration to change your outlook, gather various topics in your mind to ponder upon. In short, you gather a wealth of cognitive intelligence through socialization. You gather food for thought. You become used to remembering people, their conversations, their opinions, etc.

Can you imagine a mind becoming powerful and capable of memory enhancement when the person bearing that mind is always alone, isolated from the outer world? Imagine your mind becoming a closed-door room, with closed windows, becoming void of oxygen, filled with the stale smell. It is slow brain death. Smile and socialize to give your mind proper ventilation. Take a breather!

Walking Backwards

Yes, you heard it right! Walking backward is not a play, it is a carefully planned, conscious activity to stimulate mental performance. Apart from its physical benefits, it can also help in getting the attention of your mind due to the unusual movement of the body.

As your body is going against the normal nature of walking, each step is to be taken with mental consciousness. This compels your brain to remain actively attentive. These sorts of unusual practices must be incorporated periodically in your routine exercise or as an early morning brain warm-up activity. It helps ensure the reconstruction of an otherwise usual, routine to avoid monotony. The brain becomes so conditioned at procedural routines that it goes on an auto mode. To jerk it out of that boring, lethargic mode, an unpredictable activity is needed to sharpen and improve the memory focus.

Chapter 9: Alternative Natural Therapies for Memory Improvement

The happiness of enjoying sound health is invaluable. Nothing can replace it. The human body is like a highly functional, busily active working complex. Each department is dedicated to a particular aspect of the business. Every day is full of a hectic schedule, busy with work overflow. There are many floors in this business complex or building. Each floor has a special purpose of serving. There is a food production area or pantry. There is a sewerage maintenance floor. Then there is ventilation or air quality maintenance system as well. One floor has a smooth transport system used is entirely for communication management and logistics between all the other floors. The top floor is higher authority supervisory committee, heading the overall processing of the business.

The simulated example above can provide a clearer picture of how integrated our body is, how hectic the daily work of food energy processing, respiration, excretion, blood circulation can be. How it makes the work of the brain harder, as all the functions are eventually supervised and controlled by the brain. This all integration of working floors needs perfect coordination and control. Brain health must be in a sound position to make the work smoother.

The human body has an active flow of electricity inside it just like batteries have an electric flowing inside them. All the nervous system is coordinated by the smooth transmission of electric impulses or signals from channel to channel, as discussed on some occasions in previous chapters.

The signals once traveled on a particular channel leave a memory trace in their wake. As our brain is composed of both white and gray matter, its shape is quite like the inside of a walnut. This bi-colored matter is a special battery-like structure, conductive for electric signals. Through the proper supply of oxygen and nutrition, the batteries of the brain get recharged. More details of how this electricity in the brain is actually produced and how it gets recharged will be discussed under the topic of *Acupressure* or *Reflexology*.

Acupressure, Acupuncture & Reflexology

Neurological research suggests that brain cells are structured in such a concrete manner that they are quite protected inside the nervous system, recharging them or reviving them takes quite a lot of effort. However, some complementary alternative medicine has provided remedial methods to revive them and prevent them from becoming depleted debris, sometimes referred to as brain-sand. Most of the calcified, hardened debris accumulates in the pineal gland inside the brain. This gland is mostly known for releasing melatonin, the sleep-regulating hormone that is stimulated in darkness. The pineal gland often referred to as *the third eye* in modern spiritual practices, is vital in mental relaxation and stress alleviation. Its detoxification is as important as recharging the depleting brain cells.

CAM (Complimentary Alternative Medicine) experts suggest that most of the disorders are caused by weakened brain cells and an increase in depleted cells' debris. This also weakens the flow in brain electricity which is essential or active functioning of the body. It is exactly like when an electronic toy cannot be operated on a dried-up battery cell and therefore stops functioning. Experts advise consuming charged metal (gold, copper, silver, etc.) water to help recharge the cells in the brain. Even the patients with paralysis, cancer, arthritis, etc. were treated using this water and showed positive improvement. It proves to be an energy tonic for the weakened mental state and anti-aging supplement.

The above details were given to give you an in-depth insight into the importance of the proper flow of electric current in your body and what consequences may result from the inability of brain cells to recharge. Adequate maintenance of the electricity flow can be possible by the Acupressure method. Acupressure is actually an ancient practice found years ago in India. *Devendra Vora* in his book about alternative therapies, *"Health in your hands"*, states that the practice wasn't duly preserved in India and therefore traveled afterward in the form of its variant called *Acupuncture,* from Ceylon to Japan and then China. However Chinese claim that the practice was already prevalent in traditional Chinese medicine.

Acu means, "needle", pressure here indicates the method of applying firmly controlled pressure by fingers and thumb or an unpointed compress, on specific body points called acupoints that reflect certain areas of functionality. Acupuncture method, in contrast, uses piercing objects to treat specific illness points. Both practices are effective as the points on the body targeted to treat the diseases are more or less similar.

The term reflexology is also sometimes used interchangeably with acupressure due to the same underlying principle of treatment though pressure reflexes. Acupuncture is mostly used to reach deep skin to treat the disease as it involves piercing and penetration whereas acupressure uses pressure on the surface to trigger the profound body parts.

The concept of acupressure is governed by bioelectricity. The negative energy or charge is *chen* while the positive energy or charge is chi.

This electricity controls the five body elements known as, earth, space, fire, air, and water. These five elements are said to be represented by our five fingers of the hand. The paths for electric current to pass are called meridian channels that for the right side, go from right-hand fingers' tips to the right foot's toes. Similarly or the left side as well. The fitness depends upon proper current flow in these meridian channels. If due to some disease or toxification, blockage or stagnation occurs in the blood flow, the reflexive pressure technique helps resolve it. Many of the head nerves and brain acupoints are located in your feet and hands. For example, the left and right feet's toes and hands' thumbs are for brain stimulation and control. By applying pressure to these specific points, an electric current can be passed to the respective organ and activate it. The pressure can be accompanied by a sporadic massage technique at the targeted point area to help stabilize the pressure and blood flow.

Meditation & Prithvi Mudras in Acupressure points' combinations:

As mentioned before, the five fingers in our hands represent five basic elements of nature:

Thumb = Sun / Fire

Index = Air

Middle = Space / Sky

Ring = Earth

Small or pinky = Water

By pressing a combination of specific points on these fingers, elemental vibes can be controlled. Many diseases can be prevented and many positive effects on mental and physical health can be achieved. A mudra is a certain hand gesture or symbolic hand position that carries a spiritual meaning significant during meditation and yoga. It uses acupressure or reflexology principles to influence the energy flow. The meditation mudra is simply posed by touching the index finger with the thumb. Do it with both hands while sitting with your back straight, preferably with closed eyes. You may or may not sit in a lotus position, however, the latter is effective for better results. Applying too much pressure is not needed, a subtly focused touch will do the trick.

Effects: It benefits the mind by increasing concentration, memory power, and insomniac tendencies.

The Prithvi Mudra is posed by putting your ring finger i.e. your fourth finger pressed to your thumb. Here also you can sit in a lotus posture to achieve better concentration.

Effects: It benefits the mind and body by regaining the lost strength, increasing the bio-electrical energy inside the body also known as life force or Chetna. This energy can induce a new vigor in an ailing mind-body system. It also helps recollect the peace of mind, enabling increased memory retention power.

These mudras can be practiced daily for 10-15 minutes as a beginner, then extended to half an hour at a later stage.

Cupping Therapy
Many of the people unfamiliar with alternative medicine therapies might not have heard about cupping therapy. However, the truth is that its history dates back to as early as 1550 BC. The people used it in Egypt and China in 5000 or so years ago. It was the most effective practice for treating several different ailments during the time of the Islamic empire. Cupping therapy is also known as *hijama* literally meaning *sucking* in Arabic. It is strongly recommended in Islam as a remedial practice for detoxification and universal healing. It is highly advised instead of fire cauterization methods. Extensively being practiced in the modern era, still, it is quite new to some people. Hijama therapy is advised to be practiced in the second half or third quarter of the month and generally

before summers as monthly and annual detoxification rituals. Hijama should be done on an empty stomach so that the energy is vitalized towards the brain after the toxins are eliminated. That is why fasting is advised on middle specific dates 13th, 14th, and 15th, of every month. What happens is that the body gets concentrated on cleaning up the toxins already inside the body, without having to focus on the additional nutrition process or digestion. Avoiding some meals by fasting in the day and eating by the end of the day (dusk) and before dawn can help metabolize the deposited fat and sugar and lower the cholesterol level. It will also help calm the body's aggression and blood rush that happens during a full moon. Ramadan fasting and another voluntary fasting which Muslims observe, along with being a religious practice is a good detoxification method also followed by various other people around the world.

According to *Islamic tradition,* the lunar calendar i.e. the Islamic calendar system holds an important role in following the cupping practice and fasting. People should know that the moon has instrumental effects on the earth residents and the environment. Being the closest satellite and previously a part of the earth's terrestrial body, moon not only affects the water bodies on the earth but the humans as well. This can be seen during full moon phases. The gravitational force of attraction causes the raising of tides in the water.

Every single thing on earth experiences a rush of energy and a pull towards a higher level. Even the blood in the human body is raised according to some alternative medicine pioneers. They say that the moon does affect human behavior and there is evidence of increased aggressiveness in schizophrenic patients during full moon cycles. The heightened tides coincide with heightened emotions.

While the body's blood rush is at its peak, it waves up and pushes aside the toxic garbage, just like the ocean waves rage towards the beachside then revert back, leaving the flushed out waste in their wake. After the full moon starts waning, the toxins rushed towards the head settle down like sediments, gathered between the shoulder blades and the upper back region.

After that, the cupping is advised in the latter half of the month according to the Islamic healing philosophy specifically on the 17th, 19th, and 21st of each month. This helps the brain to concentrate on the cleaning up, collecting the already accumulated dead cell debris and toxic chemicals inside the body. Several of the hijama cupping therapy points involve the treatment of serious diseases. Hijama is also very effective in improving the memory. There are specific points serve this purpose. After applying subtle incisions, suction is done through appropriate glass or plastic cups or a specialized pressure/suction gun.

Ayurvedic Tips
The Ayurveda is an Indian medical system. It has a wealth of text showing years of research about different types of food items and spices, their respective nutrients and their effects or after-effects on health. There is a general principle stating that:

Heat is life, cold is death. Eat or drink to preserve the fire or heat inside the body to help maintain the digestive system.

The *dosha* concept in Ayurveda explains the mind-body prototype. The person living an appropriate lifestyle according to his *dosha* can maintain a mentally and physically healthy life. The great herb *Gotu Kola* or *Indian Pennywort* used in the Ayurveda tradition is proven to be an effective brain booster. It is shown to increase the intellect, making learning easier and strengthening the memory too. There has been evidence of improvement on both animals and humans. This herb is also called Brahmi literal Hindi translation means; *"giving supreme knowledge"*. You may use it as a memory-enhancing tonic by soaking the leaves overnight and then making a paste by grinding it with nuts, milk, and honey. It is very beneficial for nervous system improvement.

Aroma Therapy

Often called a holistic healing method, aromatherapy is used to treat illnesses by making use of natural extracts derived from plants. Due to its method of using essential oils as healing agents to promote health and wellness, aromatherapy is also called essential oils treatment. Aromatic oils are plant extracts obtained from the flowers, wood, leaves, and fruits, etc. They trigger the mind, body, and soul. Enhancing the senses and lifting the mood, relieving the ailing person from inner conflict and emotional stress.

As essential oils' potency is very high, instead of letting the patient directly smell them, the aromatherapy is done by diffusing the essential oils' aroma in an enclosed, quiet room. Either the diffusion is done by an electric diffuser or a manual one. While the aromatic atmosphere is created the person is prepared to take a massage in the aromatic room.

The soothing fragrances when inhaled, calm the mind and the body and affects the neuro-limbic system. The massage can be a topical aroma-therapeutic method while the same scent can be inhaled internally as well. This region of the brain's nervous system is known to regularize the memory structures, emotional behavior, and endocrine function of the body.

The aromatherapy, although popular for beauty purposes in the modern era, it is in fact, one of the most effective cures for mental stress, anxiety, mood swings, memory decline, and emotional imbalance.

Some of the notable essential oils for mental health are listed below:

Sandalwood: Derived from the sandalwood tree, inhaling this oil can uplift the mood during meditation. It gives off a pleasant woody smell and is perfect for releasing tension. It is a memory improvement agent that helps relax the brain.

Bergamot: It has a citrus-smelling fragrance. It helps decrease the anxiety and depression levels. Hence, improving mental health.

Rosemary: It is an ideal catalyst to sharpen concentration and increase mental activity.

Tea tree oil: It can calm the mind. The soothing nature of the extract makes the inhaling person considerably lighter, more relieved.

Lemon: By boosting the defense mechanism, this citric oil can enhance the energy level and concentration. The heightened senses and increased focus can help prevent memory loss and other mental disorders.

Peppermint: A refreshing fragrance oil, peppermint gives instant energy to the inhaling person. It relieves headaches, nauseous feelings, and stress. Research shows that reasoning power, thinking skills, and attention span can be improved by inhaling the peppermint oil.

Lavender: It has a special calming effect. It can improve the insomniac concerns and help to relax the mind, enhancing the cognitive skills further.

Jasmine: Carrying a sweetly infectious scent, this essential oil can boost the metabolism, libido, and is also helpful in boosting brain activity by reducing anxiety and stress.

Chamomile: chamomile tea is quite famous for its relaxing quality. The chamomile essential oil can alleviate sleep deprivation, anxiety, and a dampened mood.

Art Therapy

Art therapy is a beautifully effective way of self-expression and channelization of inner thoughts, ideas, and conflicts. Leading to a stabilized balance between the brain hemispheres, the integration of emotional externalization and internal mind notions, brings out an encouraging effect on the overall health. The art therapy is proven to be an influential trigger for the activation of dormant memories and lost experiences especially in patients suffering from Alzheimer's. Art therapy is a form of psychotherapeutic remedial process that uses artistic techniques to treat psychological disorders. The creative process not only is explorative self-discovery, but it also increases self-confidence and a sense of purpose in life.

Color Therapy or Chromotherapy

An interesting way of treating health issues, color therapy is done by inducing effects of different colors on the mind and the body. By vibes emitting out of swirling colors in a color therapy session, a holistic remedial approach is adapted to maintain the inner system of the body. To make these sessions a sensory experience, we need to perceive the colors as wavelengths that are interpreted by our brain through the retina, the human eye camera. This makes the experience more enhanced in terms of sensations and perception. The wavelengths in the colors are stimulators for electrifying the nerve impulses responsible for the smooth working of several biochemical processes in the brain.

This therapy can be done in various ways. Sometimes it is combined with aromatic oil diffusion technique to increase the focus while multiple specific colored fabrics are applied on your body. Sometimes different colored lights are illuminated to be reflected across the room where the person is sitting. Sometimes this light projection on the body may be accompanied by a massage on specific body points. Mostly shades of indigo and violets project a peaceful, calming effect. Green is closer to nature, helps purify the toxic nature of the body while red is more energizing if used moderately. The yellow is said to be a noticeable color, stimulating the nervous system. Due to its flashy and highlighted tone, yellow is considered a happy color that relieves the stress and depression. Experts in complementary medicine suggest that a combination of magnet therapy and color therapy on fingers helps in memory improvement. The blue environment in a room can help trigger creative skills in brainstorming tasks while a red-colored environment can boost the potential for memory retrieval.

Although there are some contradictions, still color therapy is reportedly an alternative treatment achieving positive results in many affected people. The right color combination can achieve powerfully instrumental contrast, which enables memory retention and cutthroat thinking skills. However, researches are still being conducted to gain further insight into this unusual but useful practice.

Chapter 10: Effects of Life Experiences on Brain and Memory

John is a healthy child, starting school. His parents are both working to provide him a perfect home and his teachers are trying their best to make the school environment an extension of his home. His family wants to see him growing with sound health and positive memories. Hence they are trying to act as good role models for him, avoiding rows or even verbal sparring in front of him. They are creating a breathable atmosphere for him where he can grow happily, eagerly collecting the pleasant memories and cherishing them well. How john's parents can ensure or expect that their kid will become a happy man once he grows up?

The answer to this question can be deduced as a result of various scientific studies involving brain development. These studies suggest that the way our brain starts developing from childhood and to adulthood and afterward largely depends upon the early life experiences that we have encountered throughout our childhood and youth. These experiences become engraved in our mind's console. Each similar experience or incident can trigger the flashback or an associated feeling of a long-forgotten incident that happened in early childhood. A man who has been bitten by a dog in his early years as a child may demonstrate an abnormal fear for dogs even after he reaches his 60's. A kitchen maid who can work for hours cleaning the countertops, doing dishes, scouring floor tiles, rubbing the stoves, may not be as inclined to light up the stove with a matchstick.

Why? Because she had burnt her hand by a lighter accidentally when she was a toddler. These feelings die hard. Too hard to discard. They remain in the subconscious part of the mind like lurking shadows of the past. Coming back to John's case, his parents are trying to protect his childhood by getting influenced by any sort of neglect or negative experiences. They want him to not only develop physically or academically but socially and emotionally as well. Emotional development is as much an integral part of brain development as cognitive development. That is why modern psychology insists on emotional intelligence as an important personality development trait and essentially a life skill.

It is a known fact that the brain continues to develop even after birth. Development is a phenomenon of overall maturation of the cells of the body including both the size and the function. Some research evidence points to the concept of an increase in brain size during development. However, results of maltreated children neurological tests state a shocking revelation i.e. Children with negative experiences were left with a small size of brain matter, while stress-free children with positive, healthy experiences continued to have increased brain volume.

Scolding, bullying, abuse, and neglect, can cause the brain to focus more on self-protection and expression of basic personal needs. Hence in his quest to getting his needs fulfilled and his basic rights acknowledged, a child may invest too much energy in this aim. His brain may put essential skills such as cognitive development and communication skills at the back burner because it is too busy trying to be able to survive in society first. Not only will the self-esteem of the child suffer in this entire struggle, but he also becomes an introvert, shying away from the world, getting locked in his shell to protect himself from harsh behavior, criticism, and indifferent attitude of adults.

His energies would all be singularly consumed in one basic domain of development and that too, in a limited way. Thus his brain potential for further growth and development in other important domains such as social, cognitive, physical, moral, language, etc. would be crushed. Here we can refer to Maslow's hierarchy of human needs graphically represented by a pyramid where each preceding stage of human needs must be fulfilled for a person to advance to the next level.

MASLOW'S HIERARCHY OF NEEDS

SELF-REALIZATION — Morality, creativity, spontaneity, problem solving, lack of prejudice, acceptance of acts

ESTEEM — Self esteem, confidence, achievement, respect for self and others

BELONGING — Friendship, family, sexual intimacy

SAFETY — Security of body, of employment, of resources, of the family, of health, of property

PHYSIOLOGICAL — Breathing, food, water, sex, sleep, homeostasis, excretion

According to research, genetic expressions are all dependent upon the nature of life experiences one has undergone from infancy to maturity. While positive experiences switch the genes *on,* negative experiences can have an adverse effect on turning the genes *off.* This may result in perfectly normal children growing up becoming abnormal or showing at least some symptoms of mental disorder.

Some of you may argue that people who regardless of going through several hurdles in their early life became eventually able to cope with them later on. Maybe because of therapies or mind training or meditation techniques.

But the truth of the fact is, if we closely look into their background, we might be able to find some strong bonding of love and understanding with at least one character present in their lives which made them cling to the sanity despite various disastrous relationships or experiences. It is very significant that even the most maltreated and traumatized individuals should be considered redeemable because the brain is capable of reconditioning and rewiring.

Neurologists suggest that if can understand the mechanism of wiring and rewiring of the brain's circuitry, we will be able to condition the plasticity of the brain. This will help mind trainers devise strategies and therapies to reconnect the disconnected synaptic links in the brain which act as *windows of opportunity for learning.* This way, even the most deprived person can have an opportunity to relive the missed normal, happy experiences that can still have a positive effect on his life due to these reopened windows of opportunity or rewired neural connections. In terms of brain development and intellectual wealth, lost potential is far too detrimental a risk to be taken lightly. Therefore, stability of mind, memory, and emotions on the part of each member of the society play a vital role in the stability of human behavior, social normalcy, and overall human development index.

Chapter 11: Foods and other Edible Supplements as Brain and Memory Boosters

Do you imagine your brain as a separate living entity? Even if you don't, start doing it now!

Your brain is the driving force behind every action and emotion of yours. Your heart doesn't carry feelings, *your brain does.* Your heart pumps blood, while your brain deals with all your baggage. Stress, loneliness, failure, desperation, boredom, hyperactivity, and several other messy emotions are frequent visitors to your mind. That is the main reason, the subject of psychology is the human mind, not the heart.

What your body needs to relax and energize, your brain needs it double in amount. While you derive your body's vitality from food and nutrition, you tend to forget an important master organ of that body that is the powerhouse of all organs, *your brain.* You must feed those vital nutrients to enhance their performance. Remember, if you have a strong mind, you will ultimately have a strong body due to that mental strength present inside your mind pushing you to be healthy.

✓ Focus on what your diet *lacks* more than what your diet *should have*.

Consuming a healthy diet to vitalize your body is easy when it comes to selecting nutrient-rich vegetables and cereals. But focusing on *how to vitalize your brain too,* often becomes an overlooked concept.
Nature has an interesting way of growing fruits and vegetables that are vital for our body organs.

If we pay attention, we can discover how most of the nutritional fruits and vegetables resemble the shape of our body organs. For instance, Almonds for eyes, Walnut for brain, Apple for heart, Grapes (resembling pulmonary air sacs or alveoli) for lungs, Pears (/ Banana / Peru / similar) for ovaries. Similarly, in the context of our topic, nature has bestowed us with a wealth of edible bounties that possess astonishing potential to improve brain activity and memory retention. For a keen eye and determined mind, the shut doors of the world open up to reveal several brain-boosting herbs and foods that can be a real gamechanger.

As you consume your diet, energy is produced by break down of the complex dietary substances into simpler particles. This energy is required to keep you functioning. Almost a whole quarter of that energy is utilized by your brain to cater to various functional processes while the rest is distributed among the remaining organs. Most of the nutritional energy is needed to enable you to interact with people, keep your emotions in check, and handle your day to day experiences. To facilitate this, your brain cells are always talking with each other.

Many of the *Integrative Nutritionists* suggest that our brain is a network of chemicals (neurotransmitters) flowing around via neural pathways. The level of cognitive power depends on the nature of chemicals' behavior. When you consume something, each morsel in your diet has some sort of chemical energy which can positively or negatively react with the chemicals of your brain. Maximum cognitive performance can be attained by consuming the right chemicals in the right amount. Plant-derived oils and serums, remedial drinks, energy boosters, nutty treats, herbal extracts, etc.

636

They all are a bunch of effective brain-boosting food. Studies prove that most of the ingredients in our food consist of plants and vegetables. Herbs were also a major part of edible medicinal products. This fact inspired a more detailed foray into the nature and composition of plants' bodies. Results show that the chemicals inside a plant react well with the brain chemicals to help increase the efficacy of several brain functions. They complement the chemicals interacting inside your brain, providing a necessary supplement, like leverage, to boost up the process where it slows down.

The Science behind it

During mind processing, neurotransmitters working inside the brain are mostly proteinous amino acids with some exceptions. Amino acids are basically compounds containing nitrogen, hydrogen, oxygen, and carbon. They are founding elements of a protein chain. The proteins are the major factor in repairing the damaged cells, regenerating the dead ones, and control several other body functions. The neurotransmitters or simply the chemical messengers actually pass on the prompted message among the brain cells by bringing that impulse or electrochemical message to the brain cells of a respective brain region through a process called *endocytosis (bringing inside the cell).*

The intricacies involved neurotransmission is actually quite easy to understand when pictured like this: Several milkmen carrying bottles of milk exit the dairy farm. Every milkman has a destination where he must drop the milk by the door. He also has a known path to follow while dropping it off. This way all the bottles are delivered to the respective destinations by each milkman and a network is formed.

This network remains connected with known and repeated parts unless a new client books an order for daily milk delivery or an old client shifts to a new place or cancels the delivery. This way new connections are formed, old ones are discarded, or reconnected in a different pattern. We may call the milk as an electrochemical message, milkman as a neuro transmitting messages carrying the electrochemical message, destination doorstep as a neuron receptor, traveling roads or pathways as synapses.

Back in Chinese ancient medicine, scholars used to research a lot on the effects of toxic food and drugs on the performance of mind and body. That is why detoxifying drinks became so popular. People began to believe in the wonders of chemicals and their effect on the well being of both the mind and the body.
Many unusual methods were devised and many unique remedies were discovered to cure mental illnesses. Some supplements were purely devised to increase immunity and mental power such as Azoth. This universal medication or antidote was considered an invaluable concoction generally afforded by only the rich. Many variable accounts could be found in history describing its mysterious ingredients. It is also a famous element mentioned in alchemical studies.

Knowing your genetic history and the prevalent diseases in the family can also help you identify which foods are going to help you and which of them will have an adverse effect on you. , Moreover, age is not just a number here, it can be a deciding factor as well, so it can be the weight. These things definitely affect how you behave and what will work for you.

Emotions as Biochemicals

Later it was discovered that even our emotions and feelings are the byproduct of biochemical reactions inside our body. To understand this concept, we would need to understand that there are two types of chemical releasing organs in our body called glands. The first type is the glands that secrete chemicals on the medial surface such as lacrimal glands (tears' secreting glands) or the glands that release chemicals on the outer surface such as sebaceous gland (sweat secreting glands). The second type is the glands that secrete chemicals inside the body, directly releasing them in the bloodstream. These sort of glands normally secrete chemical enzymes which have catalytic properties to speed up the biochemical processes happening inside the body systems. an example of these enzyme secreting glands are pancreas and liver that secrete enzymes to help in digestion but they may also secrete chemicals or hormones like insulin and other growth triggering hormones to aid in metabolism. Other hormone-secreting glands are thyroid and pituitary glands which help in releasing the necessary chemicals such as thyroxin and oxytocin to name a few. These hormones travel in the blood, reaching the cells, stimulating the responses needed in several growth and maintenance functions of the body. They also are the reason why we experience responses like happiness, excitement, depression, love, passion, and emotional warmth.

Take *Oxytocin* for instance; known as a culprit behind an urge to cuddle and love, this hormone is released when you intimately socialize with someone and hug your friends or family members. Similarly, when you experience a sudden fear, shock, or rush of excitement, it is actually due to the release of *adrenaline* hormone secreted by adrenaline glands that are part of your nervous system.

639

They produce a sort of urgent response in an emergency situation also known as *flight or fight* response.
Another instance can be considered to review your emotions as biochemicals; you have often heard that eating chocolate makes you happy.

Is it a myth? or a proven fact?

Actually, there is a chemical famously known as being both a neurotransmitter and a hormone called *serotonin.* This wondrous chemical substance is not only a regulating element for sleep, mood balance, social behavior, appetite, and sexual activity, but it also a definite memory enhancer. All the mystery lies in altering its present level in the body. Too much decline in the serotonin levels may cause depression or stress while too much increase may attribute to panic disorders and anxiety. Dark chocolate and bananas are said to be a mood lifter as they help produce serotonin. But too many bananas can induce diarrhea as well, why? Because due to an increase in serotonin, muscle activity in the stomach also increases and over digestion occurs, thus causing diarrhea. We will discuss the issue of dark chocolate, caffeine, and their relation to serotonin in the upcoming pages separately. So, let us commence the detailed listing of major brain-boosting bounties one by one:

1. Omega 3 Sources:

There is a wealth of research available that proves the benefits of consuming food sources that are rich in omega 3. Modern statistical data has shown several positive results in the improvement of memory aspects such as spatial awareness by controlling the intake of Omega 3 supplements.

Omega 3 is the collection of three most important fatty acids i.e. AlA, EPA, and DHA. They control various functions of the body due to their important role in the central nervous system. To explain it more simply, a fatty acid is a molecule of fat or lipid, just like an oil molecule, composed of carbon and hydrogen molecular chains structured in a complex bonding. It is mainly derived from plant oils, animal fat, and is present naturally in our body too as part of lipid composition. These molecules, however, cannot be easily synthesized inside the brain and are generally required to be obtained from nutritional sources and supplements.

Essential sources of Omega 3 include:

✓ *Fish, particularly a fatty one:* Salmon, Anchovy, Sardine, Mackerel, Trout, Tuna, Albacore, Pilchard, etc. are some of the notable examples. Fish is considered to be one of the staples in the brain-food list, it helps in the regeneration of nervous tissues containing brain cells. By boosting brain development, it improves memory and helps in avoiding memory disorders such as Alzheimer or Dementia.

Historical pieces of evidence dating back to 1997, shows the result of an observation spanning three years. A group of old age men in the Netherlands was measured for their cognitive development levels and a significant decline was witnessed in those that used to consume less fish. Further longitudinal studies showed a decisive decline in brainpower for those having a low intake of Omega 3- rich diet.

✓ *Cocoa Butter:* It is a derived fat compound from seeds or beans of the cocoa plant. It is a vegetable oil, rich in omega 3 fatty acids. While the extract of these seeds is utilized as oil or butter, the pulp of the fruit containing these seeds is later used as cocoa or coffee. The cocoa liquor consisting of cocoa butter and finely ground particles of roasted cocoa beans plays a major part in the composition of the chocolate. The presence of cocoa butter in chocolate also helps it in melting easily.

✓ *Shea Butter:* It is a beautiful, ivory-colored oil that remains solid at room temperature. It is extracted from a plant species generally found in Africa called shea tree. Mostly used for beauty purposes, it can sometimes be substituted for cocoa butter if it is of food-grade quality.

✓ *Nuts, especially walnuts, chestnuts, water chestnut, and other:* Containing high content of DHA, one of the three Omega-3 fatty acids, nuts are a healthy food choice when it comes to memory improvement. Much like a computer, your brain's performance depends upon the number of instructions it can process in one cycle of activity. This can be accelerated through increased concentration and speed which is induced by various types of nuts.

✓ *Seeds such as flax seeds, perilla, chia, and other:* Also called the miracle seeds, these healthy seeds can fatty acids, nutritional fiber, and antioxidants that help in digestion, relaxation, and elimination of stress.

Flax seeds are said to be a major help in the reduction of the tumor. The seeds that are rich in ALA, can also decrease the potential risks of a heart attack. Perilla both as a seed and leaf has been used to treat various illnesses in Chinese medicine. It is known for its antidepressant and anti-inflammatory properties.
Some brain training methods use perilla oil for inducing brain power and memory energization, preventing cognitive impairment.

✓ *Eggs:* Eggs are a powerful source of vitamins, minerals, protein, and healthy fats. Choline in the eggs can help in the composition of neurochemicals and enhance brain activity. The protein-rich content can also help in increasing the immunity and boosting the defense mechanism of the body.

✓ *Avocados:* This tasty, fleshy fruit can be a real brain booster due to its richness of caloric fat and fiber content. But watch out the size of portions in which you consume it as a small daily portion could go a long way depending on your requirement. Due to their *good fat* content, Avocados are often known as a superfood.

✓ *Seaweed:* Belonging to one of the various algae groups, seaweed can be a perfect alternative to meat for a vegetarian diet. Rich in proteins, minerals, and omega 3, it is a uniquely healthy choice for both mental and physical health.

✓ *Fish oil such as cod liver oil:* Being a supplement that is derived from codfish, this omega 3- rich oil also contains nutritious vitamins A, and D which help in brain health. The supplement can be consumed as a medicinal capsule too.

✓ *Other vegetable oils such as coconut oil, soybean oil, etc.:* Coconut oil is a major part of a ketogenic diet, the fats in the oil convert to ketones after breaking down and help energize the brain.

For years, it has been used as a head relaxant massage oil also effective in hair growth. Soybean oil can be a good vegan substitute for fish oil.

2. **Sesame seeds:** Although sesame contains a little or no omega-3 fatty acids, they are rich in omega 6. They also contain a high content of iron, calcium, and fiber which give them a nutty, crunchy taste. Memory reconstruction is often said to be one of the many advantages of sesame seeds. People even use sesame oil as a muscular pain relaxant and hair growth supplement. Tyrosine present in the sesame seeds helps in

fighting depression and anxiety, revitalizing the brain activity.

3. **Carrot:** Carrot is always attributed to eyesight sharpener that also aids in strengthening the intellect by activating the cognitive processes. What actually happens is, carrot contains a type of compound that can also be found in some other herbal plants including chamomile, celery, rosemary, etc. This compound namely; *"luteolin"*, is notable for preventing nervous inflammation and memory decline. This compound is also present in olive oil. Earlier research experiments conducted on mice showed the positive effects of luteolin in young species that were subjected to a luteolin-rich diet. They exhibited improved memory and spatial awareness after the decreased risk of brain inflammation. Carrot's nutritional benefits can also be obtained by consuming the roasted carrot seeds as an evening snack.

4. **Bottle Gourd Seeds:** Also known as calabash or long melon, this nutrient-rich food source is considered to be mind-and-heart healthy. Cultivated as a vine and used as a vegetable, it can provide multiple astonishing benefits to its consumers. Its white flesh along with the seeds contain a type of neuro transmitting chemical called choline which can improve the mental functionality. By maintaining the to the brain, it enhances the memorization and recall. It contributes to heart health by maintaining high cholesterol levels and preventing hypertension.

This in result eliminates stress and depressive feelings and helps in regaining the lost focus.

5. **Sunflower seeds:** Being an excellent source of Vitamin B complex, Sunflower seeds are important to nervous health. The mineral content of these seeds includes adequate amounts of magnesium, potassium, calcium, and iron, etc. All of these help in regularizing or boosting the nervous system. Sunflower seeds are also a great serotonin-level enhancer and help in improving the memory.

6. **Licorice:** Licorice root has a sweet, tangy taste. This woody supplement can be greatly beneficial in relieving the throat ache and increasing speech power. The licorice is thought to be a mind-sharpener by some experts due to the presence of a compound called carbenoxolone. This compound was tested on a group of people intent on improving their brain performance. The oral pill containing the compound was given to them as a dietary supplement but they thought it to be a miracle medicine due to the placebo effect. After a month, they showed signs of sharpened vocal skills and articulation. Their communication skills and literal memory also improved considerably. More tests were carried out on diabetic patients as well. They appeared to have developed a noticeable fluency in wordiness and textual remembrance. Licorice is often available at herbal stores in the form of powdered supplement or small wooden sticks which can be suckled on like a lollipop.

7. **Spanish Cherry or Bulletwood:** Botanically called *Mimusops elengi,* Spanish cherries are native to Asia and northern part of Australia. These are edible fruit of an evergreen tree species often used as an effective herbal remedy for various ailments. Its leaves are a popular cure for headache and other mental disorders in Ayurvedic medicine.

8. **Black Pepper:** Most common of the various seasonings and spices, black pepper contains *piperine* which can be a powerful brain booster. Research shows that piperine has a positive effect on the improvement of the immune system and memory skills.

9. **Chickpeas:** Loaded with proteins and minerals such as magnesium, chickpeas can be an energizing supplement for the mind. Accelerating the transfer of signals across nervous pathways, the nutrients in the beans or chickpeas, helps the brain to respond more quickly.

10. **Dark Chocolate:** In recent centuries, the hype about the chocolate and its positive relation to health has been towering. Research after research has been conducted to unveil the mysteries behind chocolate, preferably dark chocolate. People are euphoric about dark chocolate's rich color, flavorful taste, and gratifying aftertaste. Obtained from the cocoa tree as mentioned earlier, the cocoa beans are roasted and ground then a mixture of these ground beans, cocoa butter, and sweetener etc. is

concocted. This way it all transforms into a yummy chocolate bar that is rich in minerals, chemicals like serotonin, and other antioxidants. Unsweetened variety of chocolate, taken in moderate amounts can be a healthier choice. The high percentage of magnesium present in cocoa helps in smooth transmission of nervous impulses or electrochemical messages, thus boosting the brain activity exponentially. About the relation of chocolate ith serotonin, much has been the subject of research an much is still open for debate. As the neurologists suggest that serotonin levels in the brain cannot be altered by serotonin being produced or consumed in the gut, this means that the brain must maintain its own range of serotonin. Chocolate or its parent source; cocoa beans, help in increasing the levels of this neuro transmitting chemical serotonin in the brain. Cocoa also helps in maintaining the blood flow to the brain, hence accelerating the brain activity. Like many other plant-derived foods and supplements including fruits and vegetables, chocolate also contains pigments called flavonoids. These molecular compounds help in detoxification of the brain and the body. They are called antioxidants because they eliminate free oxygen radicals or ions found in the bloodstream which may cause harm to the cells and hindrance to their regular functioning. However, food scientists suggest that flavonoids may surpass ordinary antioxidants in their added benefits such as; their behavior improvement properties and memory enhancement potential.

So now you know, that dark, rich color of your chocolate bar is not just for show!

11. **Coffee:** The main reason why coffee is always promoted as a mood enhancer or memory booster is because of the presence of caffeine in it. According to a neuroscientific research study, caffeine intake during a revision prior to an exam often result in better performance and result outcome. This is due to the discovery that caffeine help maintains and retains the learned information as a long-term memory.
It blocks the sleep stimulating hormone and makes you more active, sharpening your thinking skills. However, it must be consumed in moderate quantity to improve cognition as coffee is also said to be a great help in preventing *MCI i.e. Mild Cognitive Impairment.*

12. **Green tea:** Contrary to black coffee, green tea contains smaller amounts of caffeine. Instead its antioxidant properties, vitamin, and mineral-rich content, and anti-inflammation compounds complement the health further. According to research, all the components of the green tea when consumed together can provide a whole healthy uplifting to the overall body functions. The polyphenols in the green tea when mixed with a little caffeine, can activate the short-term memory or working memory and help prevent cell degeneration.

13. **Ginger:** Consisting of more than 90 nutritional compounds, half of which are antioxidants, ginger easily surpasses many other dietary supplements in providing amazing health benefits. By preventing inflammation in the brain and other body parts, it helps eliminate mental ailments such as Alzheimer's and brain fog. It also possesses anti-aging, anti and anti-depressant characteristics because it helps increase the levels of serotonin. It can help boost up the blood flow and improves the activity of glial cells and vagus nerve that is why it has been used to treat dementia as well. Glial cells are the most common type of brain cells found in the central nervous system. Although not active participants in nervous signal transmission, these supporting cells or cleaning agents play a vital role in the disposal of the dead cells' remains. Whereas thee vagus nerve is the connection between the brain and the body and handles several essential nervous functions. Those having ginger extract as a supplementary medicine have been known to exhibit stronger critical thinking skills and longer attention span.

14. **Ginseng:** Typically, a root of a plant called *Panax ginseng*, this superb herb is an invaluable health supplement. Popularized in traditional medicine as an all-in-one remedy for universal well-being, its cognitive benefits include increased brain activity and strong immunity. Ginseng can be taken as a leafy diet, in powdered form, or brewed as an herbal tea.

It is considered to be a precious part of wild flora, to avoid risking extinction, some countries have strict laws against harvesting it illegally. Some states allow its cultivation and export though. Some apply conditions such as prohibiting the premature harvest and letting it grow for at least five years before collecting the crop. However, you can cultivate it in your own backyard legally and gain long term benefits. Common variants include Korean ginseng, American ginseng, and Chinese ginseng.

15. **Ginko Biloba or Maidenhair Tree:** Due to its ancient history and millions of years of age, this popular tree is lovingly named as a *living fossil*. Its medicinal history dates back to early Chinese medicine. Accounts have been mentioned in renowned traditional medicine scriptures about its effect on preventing memory declination. However, modern studies deny any considerable effect on cognitive improvement. Still, the matter is of contradiction as several users of the herbal extract claim improvement and promoters of alternative medicine continue to present this as a memory-enhancing supplement. Regardless of the debate, no one can disagree with the fact that the herb is rich in antioxidants that eventually complements brain function due to their detoxifying properties.

16. **Turmeric:** Also called lively spice and blood purifier, turmeric is a miraculous kitchen ingredient that can be used to treat various ailments. It contains a compound called *curcumin* that has brilliant anti-oxidation properties, it can

lower the risk of Alzheimer as well. Curcumin extract can be available in separate supplementary form as well which, if taken regularly, can improve the mood and the memory.

17. **Blueberries:** This beautiful, colorful fruit is a treat to the eye. Berries' rich blue color is also due to the plant pigment called Flavonoids. As mentioned before, these antioxidants are not only a detoxifying factor in the biochemical processes of the body but also help in memory improvement.

18. **Broccoli:** This nutrient-rich, leaf green vegetable is widely used across the globe. Revered by the health-conscious people, broccoli contains a high content of vitamin K and is also rich in neuro transmitting chemicals called Choline. Some benefits of Choline has been mentioned before as well. Here we will tell you an important reason for why Choline can be a brain booster. Actually, Choline is an essential factor in producing the neurotransmitter called *acetylcholine.* This chemical is the main stimulator for increased functionality of memory, muscle, and behavior.

19. **Spinach:** Rich in minerals such as magnesium, zinc, iron, and vitamins such as A, C, E, and K, spinach can help prevent memory decline and hypertension. As experts state the reason for low attention span and drowsiness is often due to iron deficiency. As a green vegetable

comprising leafy flesh, it is also rich in dietary fiber that is needed for digestion and overall improved functionality of the body.

20. **Indian Gooseberry or Amla:** Rich in vitamin C, various minerals such as phosphorus and calcium, fiber content, and antioxidants, Amla is a good source of brainpower. Often referred to as a super brain diet, the literal meaning of Amla in Sanskrit is: *"the rejuvenator"*. It can be consumed both as a fruit and juice or energy drink. Even the oil extract from this fruit, applied on the scalp as a massage tonic, works wonders for brain relaxation and hair growth.

Chapter 12: Practical Exercises and Fun Tests

Memory Mnemonics
Required Material for Exercises:

- A paper and a pen.

Exercise # 1:

Objective:

Consider the given information and make a suitable rhyming mnemonic for it to be easily remembered.

Information:

"There are about 118 chemical elements discovered until 2019. The periodic table is a brilliant way to represent these chemical elements and categorize them into groups and periods. This way their properties can be learned easily. The first published periodic table of Mendeleev was recognized in 1869. There are 7 horizontal rows in this tabular display called periods and 18 vertical columns called groups."

Exercise # 2:

Objective:

Read and arrange the following names of certain countries of Asia in order to create an easily memorable acronym mnemonic representing these countries appropriately.

Information:

"China, Pakistan, Bangladesh, Japan, Iran, India, Malaysia, Singapore, Vietnam, Myanmar, Philippines, Thailand, Afghanistan, Bahrain."

Exercise # 3:

Objective:

There are some pieces of information (a, b, c) given below. Using any of the learned effective mnemonic strategies such as legend lists, images, letter patters, concept maps, chunking methods, narration, association, link method, or color-coding, devise a suitable strategy to learn each of the following pieces of information. Note that your choice of mnemonic for each piece of information must correspond to the style of that information in order to facilitate the ease of remembrance and relevance of the memory technique used.

Information (a):

"The book we are discussing contains these concepts and ideas as its main theme. Natural herbs, Benefits of health maintenance, Vegetarian diet, botanical gardens in Asia, Effects of cocoa beans on health, Green tea as a herb, Herbal remedies, and products, etc."

Information (b):

"The traveling bag must include these 5 articles for any journey you are embarking on: 1) Clothes, 2)Dry Food, 3) A Spare Pair of Shoes, 4) Water-Proof Camera, 5) Money / ID Card Wallet."

Information (c):

"Human body's organ systems and each organ's function in detail."

```
*----------------*-------------------*-------------------
*------------------*----------------*
```

Fun Activity: Creating Your Own Memory Palace or Maze

Exercise # 4:

Required:

- A physically real, complex place. Clearly seen and mentally imaginable.
- A piece of information to be remembered.

Information to be Allocated and Stored:

"Answers to the expected questions of an upcoming viva. Such as:

Q1: What is the aim of learning?

Q2: What is meant by gender in Education?

Q3: How do you differentiate between Society and Community?

Q4: What are the different types of educational philosophies?

Q5: Why is learning soft skills more important than academics nowadays?

Q6: What is your opinion regarding the vocational training of the youngsters?

Q7: How can homeschooling lack in social development of a student?
Q8: Why is school considered a mini-society by John Dewey?

Q9: What is meant by Pragmatism in education?

Q10: How do you define the phrase: *Education for Life?*"

Objective & Method:

Select a familiar place to act as your physical memory storage or mind palace. Imagine this place in your mind. You must have seen it clearly beforehand to be able to visualize each nook and corner with clarity and detail. Arrange each answer of the viva questions to be allocated in a particular place in your memory palace. Use the method described in the memory improvement techniques earlier in this book.

--------------------------------*----------------
--------------------------------*

Daily Practice: Creating Your Own Memory Journal

Material:

- A journal or logbook to record daily entries.
- Some, pens, color highlighters, and markers.
- Some bookmarks and sticky notes.

Objective:

This practice is important to be regularly maintained in order to increase your memory retention and refreshing your acquired knowledge and life experiences.

Method:

- Select a time for your daily journaling, usually in the night. Try that this remains the same throughout your daily schedule. i.e. the exactness of the time slot daily will start habituating and alerting your inner clock after a few days. The mind will also start anticipating the refreshment of memories at that particular hour of the day.
- Reflect on the experiences of that day, think about them and recollect them in your mind.
- Make use of mnemonic devices such as word expression mnemonics, outlines, models, graphic organizers, etc. to summarize the

information and devise your own version of a shorthand strategy.

- Use highlighters and bookmarks wherever necessary to emphasize the importance of certain points.
- Use markers or sharpies for bolding and color-coding information in the journal entries.
- Revisit and refer to old entries whenever linkages are necessary or recollection is required. Also revise them on occasions just to keep your memories afresh.

Bonus: Homemade Brain booster Remedy

This amazing homemade recipe has garnered more results than even the most expensive medicinal supplements couldn't. The ingredients used in this brain booster are all easily available in our homes or local herb shop.

Ingredients:

- ✓ Fennel seeds: 1 cup
- ✓ Almonds: 1 cup
- ✓ The famous four seeds combination: 1 cup
  - *(Pumpkin seeds + Musk melon seeds + Watermelon seeds + Cucumber seeds)*
- ✓ Rock brown sugar or *Mishri*: 1/2 cup
- ✓ Roasted chickpeas: 1 & 1/2 cups
- ✓ Cashews, pistachios, and oatmeal: optional
- ✓ Milk: As required
- ✓ Honey: As required

Method of Preparation:

1. Grind together fennel, almonds, *four seeds' combination,* rock sugar, roasted chickpeas, and other nuts or oatmeal (if added), in a grinding machine until finely granulated or powdered.
2. Fill a medium-sized jar with this powdered supplement.
3. To make a serving, take a glass filled warm milk.
4. Add a tablespoon of honey in the milk and stir.

5. Now take a spoonful of the supplement from the jar and mix it with the honeyed milk, stir well.
6. Consume the brain booster this way, twice a day before breakfast in the morning and before sleeping at night time.

Note:

Daily intake of this twice can reveal significant improvement in memory retention and brain activity. It has been quite successful with school and college students and exam attempters. Those who memorize lengthy scriptures also found this recipe quite helpful in stimulating high response and sharpened memory.

Conclusion

Thank you for making it through to the end of *Memory Improvement*, let's hope it was informative and able to provide you with all of the tools you need to achieve your goals whatever they may be.

The next step is to start benefiting from the content presented to you and implementing the useful strategies discussed in this book. Most of us often close the books and along with that, close our *windows of opportunities* too. These windows of opportunities are our memories. Our senses absorb the surrounding impressions and store the knowledge as memories. The book you just read may or may not have increased your knowledge but it sure has emphasized some useful points and concepts. At least you have made some new memories and revived some old ones.

Most of us have experienced that crucial moment when you are about to say something to someone and just as you grab their attention, you forget what you were about to say. These sorts of issues make you all the more eager to learn and implement helpful techniques for memory improvement. The learning has started as you began reading this book or similar books on this topic, now is the time for active practice. The path to actual improvement and implementation starts where the book reading finishes. Now is the time for real work.

Before the final note, we are leaving you with a quick self-question:

Are you a memory decliner, memory retainer or memory improver?

Narcissist Nightmare

Understanding Personality Disorder in Order to Recover From Psychological Abuse and Growing Your Relationships

By: Adam Goleman

665

Introduction

What exactly is narcissism? In a nutshell, it is a distorted sense of ability or importance. A narcissist tends to think in a grandiose way concerning their social value compared to those around them. Such thoughts and behaviors tend to have a long-standing pattern. This means that someone does not just wake up one day and become a narcissist. As you learn more about this, if you have a narcissist in your life, you will be able to see that their behavior is something that has always been present.

Who is a narcissist? The simple answer is it can be anyone in your life. It could be a neighbor, a coworker, a family member, a friend or even your significant other. Just because you have known someone for a long time or have a deep relationship with them does not mean they cannot be a narcissist. This is certainly not easy to confront, but it is imperative that you do if you think you might have a narcissist in your life. Doing this involves learning more about narcissism so that you can identify it.

Narcissism and the Details

In 1898, Havelock Ellis, a British physician and essayist, first identified narcissism. Narcissus, a mythological figure, is who the disorder is named after. In mythology, this figure saw his own reflection and fell in love with it. When you interact with a narcissist, you find a lack of empathy, a deep need for extreme admiration and attention and a highly inflated sense of importance.

However, below the façade lies fragile self-esteem and an extreme lack of confidence. In fact, even the slightest criticism can cause a narcissist to lose their mask completely. Psychologists believe that narcissism develops between six months and six years old. These are among the primary formative years for a child. In personal development, the individuation-separation phase essentially goes wrong, or some outside force interrupts it. The child then uses narcissism as a type of defense mechanism to cope with the inevitable fears and hurt involved.

In child development, narcissism is considered to be a normal stage, according to Sigmund Freud. However, if after puberty, a child is still exhibiting the behaviors and emotions, it then becomes considered a disorder.

There are a number of psychological theories concerning what might contribute to the development of narcissism. One that is widely recognized and has been deeply studied is the theory discussed by Otto Kernberg, an Austrian psychoanalyst. He suggested that this behavior is a type of defense.

According to Kernberg, when a child grows up with parents that are cold and lacking empathy, the child basically becomes emotionally hungry. As a result of parental neglect, the child responds with rage and anger. To prevent this, the child learns to essentially use narcissism to find a refuge from the neglect and the associated negative emotions.

The child seeks out attention and admiration from other people to make up for what he or she is not getting from their parents. Over time, this ultimately results in an inflated and grandiose sense of self. Kernberg concluded that a narcissist is constantly questioning their self-worth and they are vulnerable inside, but outside, they appear grandiose and extremely confident.

The defining behavior of narcissism is grandiosity. This is a sense of superiority that is unrealistic and far more severe than vanity or arrogance. The narcissist truly believes that they are superior or special in some way. They feel that only those with equal superiority can understand them. When it comes to anything ordinary or average, they believe they are too good for it.

Even when it is undeserved, they expect others to recognize them as superior. To try and get this recognition, they will lie or exaggerate their talents and achievements. For example, if they receive a general promotion at work, they will spin a tale that makes it seem as though they now run the company.

Chapter 1: What's Narcissism Means

What is Narcissism

If you've been living with a narcissist, you probably already had a good idea of what narcissism is. Anyway, let's talk about what a narcissist is, what makes them tick, and why they act the way they do. Once you have a better understanding of these aspects of your partner's personality, you will be better prepared to take and stand up for yourself, and help your partner change into a more loving person.

In general, a narcissist is someone who needs people around to admire them. They feel that they are the most important person in the room, or even in the world, and so they expect everyone to act a certain way toward them because of it.

They also have difficulty with empathy and are not able to relate to the fact that others have thoughts, feelings, and ideas independent of them. When this becomes extreme enough, one can be diagnosed with a Narcissistic Personality Disorder, which is generally considered more severe and oftentimes, incurable. But there are ways to deal with narcissism with someone you love, which is the purpose of this book.

Research has shown that there are generally two types of narcissists. The first type has been labeled the **Vulnerable Narcissists**. These people have an outward sense of self-importance, but it is usually hiding some deep vulnerability. They have a weak sense of self and cover this fact up with an inflated sense of importance, and they expect everyone to treat them with devotion and respect in order to feel better about themselves. Generally, these people are easier to change because, as they are able to develop their self-esteem and feel comfortable as a human being, their need for admiration will naturally disappear.

The second type is called the **Grandiose Narcissist**. This type of narcissist acts more confidently yet less sensitively. People with this type of personality don't have a sense of shame and empathy, and they obviously have very high self-esteem.

They believe in their own greatness which caused them to treat other people quite poorly because they believe no one else can measure up to them. They don't feel the need to treat others with dignity and respect. Both types of narcissists treat people crudely. Because of their lack of empathy for others, they have no problem hurting or using them for their own gain. The emotions of others have no meaning to them. Moreover, they tend to use manipulation to get whatever they want in the world and tends toward psychopathology, which means that they have difficulty forming relationships like an antisocial person. Remember that they have no ability to relate with others in a meaningful way, so people end up being tools they use to get their own needs met. They don't see others as separate individuals.

Although the causes of narcissism aren't known positively, there are many theories. Most people with narcissism had a difficult parent-child relationship when they were growing up. They might be surrounded by narcissistic people or might have been abused and abandoned as a child and so they developed a self-inflated sense of self in order to cope with life. It's also possible that their parents have ignored them or have been overly critical so they developed a narcissistic behavior. Another causative factor suggests a genetic link. Having a narcissistic family member provides a higher chance of developing a narcissistic personality.

People easily fall for them because, as a tool of manipulation, they are charming. They like to have a good time and they know how to get others to see their eminence in order for them to fall in love.

If you have fallen with a narcissist, you know exactly what I'm talking about. Although some of their behaviors can be frustrating at times, they seem to be able to make their partner happy in many other ways. That's what makes dealing with a narcissist so tough. There are things you really love about your partner and there are other things that you hate or disgust about their attitude. You may love the excitement your partner provides in your life, how sweet and charming they are at a dinner party, but you may have more difficulty at home when you are alone. Your partner probably treats you very differently than when you are in a public place. Before deciding whether you want to stay and deal with the techniques in this book to try and improve your relationship, you need to make sure of one thing. Is your relationship abusive? Not all narcissists resort to violence to get their way, but some do exercise physical or emotional abuse toward their partner. If you are being abused, you probably won't be able to do the work necessary for helping yourself and your partner in a safe environment. You might be better off finding a way out rather than trying to change yourself and the person you love. It all depends on how the two of you talk, accept, and deal with the problem. If you feel like you can make the necessary changes in a safe environment, then you can continue and move forward. The things to note here is that both of you will need to be willing to make changes to help your relationship and to take care of your partner's narcissistic disorder. In a relationship, it takes two to tango, as they say, and it's important to note that your own behavior may be feeding the narcissist.

You will need to change how you interact with your partner in order to help that person make changes themselves.

Recognizing the Narcissistic Behavior

A narcissistic personality disorder is one of the many types of personality disorders wherein people suffering from such disorder have traits that will cause them to behave in socially distressing ways. They also have limited abilities to function in areas like work, school and life in general. Unlike sociopathy, it is easy to tell whether a person suffers from narcissism because they exhibit signs and symptoms. However, people who have no experience dealing with people suffering from this disorder have no idea about the signs and symptoms. Thus, this section will talk about the different signs and symptoms of narcissistic personality disorder.

Showing an exaggerated sense of self-importance thus they tend to proclaim all of their achievements in order to be acknowledged by others.

- Always expecting to be recognized as superior even if they did not have any achievements that warrant their superiority.
- Exaggeration of talents and achievements.
- Being preoccupied with fantasies related to power, success, beauty and brilliance.
- Always associating themselves to people whom they believe are equally special people or superior like them.
- They require constant admiration in order to become motivated.
- They have a deep sense of entitlement thus they think that they deserve everything good that life has to offer.
- Taking advantage of other people to get what they want thus they are highly manipulative and often resort to using their beguiling charm to deceive others.
- Having the inability to recognize the needs as well as the feelings of other people.
- Being envious of other people and thinking that people also envy them.
- Behaving in both arrogant and haughty manner to people whom they think are below them.
- Inability to commit to serious relationship and intimacy.

- Goes through a relationship that is largely superficial and they are constrained in a relationship because there is a need for personal gain.
- Goes to excessive attempts in order to attract as well as be a focus of the attention of other people.
- Expects positive reinforcement from other people such that they demand praises from people in order to be motivated even if the reinforcements that they demand are out of place.

People who suffer from narcissistic personality disorder are people who are always thinking about themselves and have less empathy towards other people. If you see these signs on people whom you always associate yourself with, know that they are no longer acting normal and that they need help otherwise they might inflict pain not only on themselves but also on other people.

Narcissism Scale

Sadly, we all have that one friend or relation with an ego so big it's a wonder another human being can fit in the room. Now don't me wrong, not every egotistical human being is a narcissist but ever narcissist is egotistical.

So before you start getting dizzy from all that comparison, I'll just go ahead and tell you that narcissists are generally decent, responsible, intelligent and often charming individuals who for some reason, seem to think the world revolves around them; believe they are always right; love having their ego stroked; and aggressively 'punish' any form of opposition.

At first blush, it may not seem like a big deal; just a personality quirk. But in truth, narcissists generally do not know when to stop and if you let them, they can ride rough-shod over you and strip away your confidence and self-esteem bit by vital bit. Whether it's personal or work relationships, being with a narcissist can be anything but easy.

Narcissism is a personality disorder (just in case that nugget slipped your attention) but not every narcissist has had an official diagnosis. This could be because people tend to shy away from what they see as clinical labels. Sometimes knowing you have a problem is one thing but hearing an official confirmation makes it more real right? Well confident as they seem to be, narcissists sometimes do not like to face this hard truth about themselves. On the other hand, most narcissists do not have a problem admitting that they are narcissists; maybe not in so many words though. For instance, they could tell you plainly that they hate being contradicted, they often believe they are better than everyone else and deserve special treatment and you better believe they would often insist on it. It is a form of egocentrism and was in fact at one time referred to as megalomania.

Narcissists are usually preoccupied with personal adequacy, power, vanity, and an inability to see the resultant damage their attitude wrecks on themselves and others. They love being admired but they have no ability whatsoever to feel empathy because in their minds, they are the center of their own universe. To put it simply, they take self-absorption and self-love to a whole new level and the fact that they are often highly outstanding in whatever they do.

Narcissists are often manipulative and quick-tempered. They place themselves so far above everyone else in their own minds that they end up cutting others off and becoming emotionally isolated whilst using people every chance they get. They can often be loud and proud and some others can be quiet and shy.

If you want to watch a Narcissist fly off the handle, dare to criticize him/her. They often do not have a sense of humor, they are often cruel, casual dishonesty, impulsive, stingy, self-contradictory, and they are often envious and competitive.

An ancient Greek myth tells the story of Narcissus known and widely loved for his amazing beauty and physique. Gods, nymphs, maidens and even young men fell madly in love with him but he felt nothing for anyone of them. One day he tried to take a drink of water from a river and became entranced by his own reflection in the water; he fell so madly in love with what he thought was a spirit.

He spent the rest of his days staring at his reflection in the water and died a tragic death when he wasted away from lusting after his own reflection. Given the mythical genesis of narcissism, you could probably be forgiven for expecting that constant absorption with their reflections in an actual mirror would be an obvious sign. Sadly, the looking-glass symbol is more metaphorical than literal; although some narcissists do spend hours doing nothing else but pounding the treadmill and arranging their hair just so. Either way, you could spot narcissists from a mile away, if you know where to look. Thankfully, while most people tend to have some narcissist tendencies, people with a full-blown narcissistic personality disorder are way fewer. Now while I would probably beam like a proud parent if you suddenly develop mad narcissism-spotting skills, after reading this book, I would prefer that you try to avoid paranoia. Not everyone who seems self-absorbed is necessarily a narcissist; nor would it be fair for you to write off your seventy-something old neighbor as a narcissist just because he stopped listening when you started waxing poetic about your love of sky-diving. And despite how much you would like to think otherwise, that ill-mannered woman who cut you off at the line in the grocery store is not necessarily a narcissist just because she was selfish. Narcissism can more accurately be discerned if a lot of the common symptoms pop up in an individual over a long period of time. Narcissistic personality disorder entails a long-term pattern of abnormal thinking, feeling and behavior in different situations.

Many things are beneath a narcissist including everything from simple household chores to the feelings of co-workers, family members and even lovers.

Understanding Your Narcissism

A narcissist is a person who has a personality disorder in which he or she is excessively preoccupied with dominance, power, prestige, and vanity. They do not realize the destruction they cause to themselves and others. A so-called narcissist can do things without noticing the feelings of the people around them. They consider themselves truly superior and they need to be respected. You can call them vain or selfish, those are just some of the common labels used by many towards narcissists. They are involved in feelings, as for them it's only normal to feel hurt. They came up with this narcissist version of themselves so that it can serve as the shock absorber.

However, narcissistic pain is different from other types of emotional pain. People who suffer from narcissism often display attitudes like being snobbish, patronizing or even disdain. For example, he or she may complain about a bartender's rudeness or stupidity or conclude a medical evaluation with a condescending evaluation of the physician.

A personality disorder is a kind of pattern and behavior that deviates from the norm individual's culture. This pattern is seen in the following areas: cognition; interpersonal functioning; impulse control; or affect. The enduring pattern is not exactly flexible and it can also be seen at one's early childhood characteristics. The pattern is stable and is in a long duration. Narcissism is more prevalent in males than females. However, as time passed by and when they suppress all the feelings, this disorder is to decreased and symptoms become lesser at the age of the 40s to 50s. There are things that cause a person to become a narcissist. Researchers today don't exactly know what causes a person to eventually turn into a narcissist. There are many theories, however, only about the possible cause of narcissistic personality disorder. There are actually treatments of this personality disorder, which typically involve long-term psycho treatment or psychotherapy, with a therapist who has a wide experience in treating this kind of personality disorder. Some medications can actually help with specific sets of symptoms. The person with this kind of disorder usually exaggerates things around him, they also tend to have daydreaming about fantasies of beauty, success and power over dominating their thoughts. This type of person is also too sensitive.

They need to be admired in everything they do at all times. If not, they will be hurt deep inside. They also tend to manipulate and take advantage of the people around them using their emotional feelings that people around them need to consider, as a weapon. They lack empathy that makes us feel and recognize the feelings of needs of others. These types of people also are the envy type ones and their behavior appears to us as haughty or arrogant.

A person with untreated Narcissistic Personality Disorder has a higher chance of substance abuse including drugs and alcohol, depression, problems with a relationship, difficulties at work or school and suicidal behaviors or thoughts.

Worst cases can turn a human being to someone who is very abusive both physically and sexually. Living with a narcissist can feel as if you're living a very confusing nightmare. It's like you are getting into jail with no exact way of escape. The spouse, co-workers, boss, and even the parent can sometimes get stuck in a relationship they find very hard to escape from. The emotional and physical damages caused by somebody with the disorder can be severe. Health care professionals aren't an exception to emotional exhaustion.

Narcissists feel superior with this wonderland that they made up in their heads without noticing the effects they are making to the people around them. They become involved in beauty, material things, and shallowly develop an interest in things that are not real such as soap operas, movies, games, and rock stars.

They fear their feelings. They cannot gain and keep a deep friendship or intimacy and cannot develop a mature love relationship. A fantasy world can be a sweet escape for a narcissist and can also become an attempt not to see what is really there in order to build up self-esteem. Narcissist people process information, emotions, and unresolved pain to make up for their hidden damaged childhood. They love achieving something with their own imaginations in their created world and they often place an unrealistic demand to someone else just to feel better. They are not one to tolerate negative emotional distress, as they are not very good at it. They usually push it to others and blame them instead of looking closer to see their own part of the problem. This is the defense of projection – when a certain person does not like him or herself, they get angry with those who have some of the likable traits.

The Self-image is distorted from a narcissistic point of view and the person believes that he is more superior than others. An over the top self-esteem is a defense to cover up the unforgettable shame deep within. Grandiosity is an insidious error in thinking that it is prevention and it stops them from blaming themselves and becoming depressed or disintegrated. Narcissist people like to hear the sound of their own voice. They are individuals that thrive on being the center of attraction and attention which tends to put down others whom they feel are inferior. At work, a narcissist is power hungry and will go to great lengths to gain power.

Learning if you are with a narcissist can be quite difficult and confusing in the sense that you also might be confused about what you feel towards the narcissist you are with. Narcissists prefer to work under their own set of rules. The narcissist only cares about themselves and therefore, when working with a narcissist, always remember that they will never be a great buddy to be with. They will befriend you to convert you into one of their victims or supply sources, will do favors expecting a big return and you will do the same thing as well to them. Unfortunately, in the workplace you can't just do anything that you want to this person and walk away without so much as an issue. So the best thing to do is to go along with him or her.

Getting in touch with a narcissist more often will keep them from thinking you don't like them. But be careful of getting too close with a narcissist because they think different and digest words from you differently. The narcissist does expect you to be immediately responsive the moment they demand attention just like a normal boss in your company who wants you to immediately follow him in everything he demands. Sharing your emotions to a narcissist is a big no because you are forcing them to prioritize your feelings. The next best thing that you can actually do is focus on solutions and not the problem. The narcissist likes to focus on the problem and turn it over, around, rearrange, and practically dissect it to pieces. They tend to make things very complicated. Stop looking at the glass as if it is half empty. The best thing that you can do is flip it and influence the narcissist to see the other side of truth.

It's actually a good choice to just present several solutions. The narcissist likes to be in control and they'd love you if you have this much-favored ability to offer them options. This is one of the several ways that you can make them feel as if you truly respect their opinion and that you are asking them to take control and show you what they are made of. If it still does not work out, your best last option is to make them feel good about themselves, unique, and special. Narcissists want to be praised and they like the feeling that they are higher than you. They get high off of being in power and they thrive in attention and admiration. If you want them to be happily productive for you, simply let them know how great they are. Praising them makes them feel at peace.

When a narcissist grows up, they harbor the irrational belief that the person they choose as a partner will give them perfect love and make up for all hurts and slights of their life.

This burning desire for getting unconditional love is an unresolved need from their damaged childhood. While most adults find the good thing about unconditional, understand also that it rarely happens. This is because the people we love usually holding us somehow responsible for our actions. Think carefully about imposing your neediness and bad behavior towards others. Being a narcissist is not an easy thing, people with this kind of disorder don't need to be rejected and taken for granted. They believe that everything is fine because that's the way they grew up with, which is a normal thing for them.

People with this kind of disorder need more attention and understanding, no one wishes to be born with this disorder.

Narcissism in Everyday Life

We have already defined narcissism, but how does it relate to normal everyday life? To have a better understanding of narcissism, let us look at a fictional character Tom. Tom is a regional cooperate manager. At first glance, he is a gem. He seems pleasant, charming, and endearing; all the traits you would expect from someone in his position. However, the moment you get to know Tom more, you start to realize some things that may not necessarily seem charming. Tom hates it when you contradict him in meetings, either at work or social settings. He is not as open to suggestions as you might believe. He thinks his opinions are of utmost importance, and for this reason, he expresses them freely without any consideration for anyone else. He may ask for your opinions but at this stage it is only a formality and not something he would devote his attention to.

He hates challenges, he is unsure of winning, and loathes criticism. He acts as if he is a demigod who deserves worship. He wants his words to be considered regarded as the Gospel and there is no argument beyond that. If he is kept waiting, or things do not go according to what he deems to be the correct way, in this case his way, he can blow things out of proportion.

Throwing tantrums or delving into an extremely unpleasant behavior is easy for such a person. He will hold grudges against people who stand up to him, regardless of whether they were right or not. This behavior is downright childish and is also not the only childish behavior he will exhibit. As a man who is used to getting his way, at restaurants, he is the person who must get the table he wants at the snap of a finger. When he does not get the table, or the service he wants, he is quick to throw an anger fit. For these reasons, Tom has no real friends. His self-inflated ego and sense of importance gradually throw him out of favor of almost all his acquaintances. Although he has a downright charming persona and a general gentlemanly attitude, all of it falls apart slowly as you get to know him more. Everyone who gets to know him eventually gets tired of him and his godlike, self-centered attitude. Due to his self-centeredness, he has difficulty connecting with people, as well as being sensitive to their needs or wants. Do not get me wrong, Tom helps a few people, but only when it casts him in a positive light or advances his own personal agenda. It is also debatable that Tom does not consider himself friends with anybody. As far as he is concerned, he owes a few people a few favors. He sees people as resources rather than friends. He uses them to get his will done.

For Tom, there is no separation from his self-righteousness. For this reason, his wife, children, and neighbors find it difficult to communicate with him as well as live with him because he expects everybody to agree with his opinions. Tom is a narcissist through and through.

And getting him to admit this will prove to be an uphill task. I am not saying Tom is a bad person. He might have a misplaced sense of self-righteousness that may seem absolutely right to him but is heavily flawed from another perspective. He may never realize this because the only perspective he is willing to consider is his own. If his wife is not a quiet woman, he is extremely likely to end up quarrelling with her often for petty reasons. Family life for such a person may be harder to maintain than for normal people. As a parent, his communication with the kids will be heavily one sided.

As I have said, narcissism, to some degree, is healthy. Confidence and solid faith in one's abilities is sometimes misinterpreted as narcissism. Confidence or over confidence can sometimes be considered arrogance but it is almost never a narcissistic trait. There are many confident people in the world; people who believe in themselves and their abilities. Absolute faith in one's abilities cannot be summarized as narcissism. The only difference between these people and a pathological narcissist is that unlike the narcissist, they do not consider themselves a cut above the rest (better than anyone) or demand that they are accorded special treatment. They do not insist that they stand above their peers and deserve special treatment. They are more devoted to the job or the task at hand. A confident and strong-willed individual is more likely to be successful than a narcissist. While a narcissist doles away admiring himself the confident person gets the job done.

This is not to mean that they do not consider themselves the best in their field of study; no, they simply are not envious or harbor any grudge against other accomplished people in the same field of study as for them. They are aware of their needs and feelings as well as those of people around them. They do not think that every opportunity to help someone else is an opportunity to advance their own agenda. They genuinely care about others. The narcissistic individual on the other hand is the opposite. He looks for loopholes and ways to divert every opportunity in his favor regardless of its impact on the people around him. Jealousy and peer rivalry might also induce him to drag down the people he envies.

A narcissist may even go so far as to refuse to help a colleague who works in the same field of study that he does. All out of hatred for that person!

Here are some of the main characteristics a pathological narcissist will display.

1. They always feel entitled, as if everything is their right.
2. They are constant attention-seekers who desire admiration most times.
3. They are exploitive. They will take advantage of a child if it advances their self-centered agenda.
4. If your suffering or distress will not advance his or her agenda, then it is of little concern to them. They are unable to identify with any feeling or emotion that is not helpful to the attainment of their agenda.
5. Jealousy is their middle name. When someone else gets the prize instead of him or her, he or she will be envious and feel like it should have been him or her.
6. They are extremely arrogant.
7. They are preoccupied with dreams of grandeur, unlimited success, beauty, ideal love, and marriage. They believe that their brilliance is comparable to Albert Einstein's.

Chapter 2: Narcissism Traits

Narcissistic Personality Disorder is diagnosed using DSM-5 (Diagnostic and Statistical Manual of Mental Disorders, 5th Edition) which is an improvement of the DSM-IV. Another point of dereferencing could be the ICD-10, F60.8 by the World Health Organization. Most professionals make use of the DSM-5 when making a diagnosis on narcissism, looking for a majority of similarity in the symptoms.

Obviously, diagnosis is made through a structured conversation, asking pointed questions with the person of interest. Other diagnostic methods such as blood tests and physical exams do not work in this case since narcissism has no physical symptoms. It is important to note that a large percentage of people with NPD rarely get treatment or seek professional help.

For diagnostic purposes, having two or three of the NPD symptoms is not sufficient to label someone as a narcissist. Ideally, you should have five or more of the signs before a confirmed diagnosis is made.

Identify the Common Traits of Narcissists Persons

However; there are extra indicators that can suggest to you that the person you know is suffering from NPD:

1. Low Self Esteem

This may seem surprising but people with NPD are often over the top to cover their own self esteem issues. In fact, it is this low self-esteem which is often the main driving force behind their lives. They spend the majority of their time striving to prove themselves; they want to believe in themselves and others to believe in them but they never feel their accomplishments are enough. The result is driving themselves onwards to achieve bigger and better things; at all costs.

Of course, people with NPD tend to be expert at portraying a high level of self-esteem and bravado. Perhaps the biggest clue to this issue is that they are constantly seeking compliments from others; if they are not forthcoming they will compliment themselves by bragging and boasting!

2. Self-Righteous and Defensive

The bigger their ego appears to be the more important it becomes to defend it from other people attacking. This means the trigger for their defense mechanism becomes shorter and shorter; resulting in even the slightest criticism or comment triggering it. At this point they will be certain they are right and that there path is the only one that can be chosen; they will also become exceptionally stubborn as they defend their actions; regardless of logic. They must cling to the knowledge that they are right to avoid destroying their fragile ego and exposing their low self esteem.

3. Quick to Anger

If those who are criticizing someone with an NPD do not back down or change their mind, then the person with the narcissistic personality disorder is likely to react with anger. This is the last, explosive defense mechanism of someone who feels their fears and insecurities are about to be exposed. Worse than this they are likely to be about to re-feeling their emotions and humiliation from the past and transferring this anger to the present day; thereby exploding and taking the current situation out of proportion. The response is likely to baffle the person who had been criticizing them and possibly even frighten them; it will probably end the discussion.

4. Projecting Traits

Someone with NPD sees themselves as right and perfect; others are beneath them. Should they discover personality traits in themselves that are not in keeping with this image they will transfer these flaws onto other people and then focus on those flaws; exposing them in others whether they exist or not! In fact this is a sign that they are unable to achieve any self-insight; a classic sign of a narcissist. Their defense mechanism is rigid and will not allow anything to come through it; not even themselves!

5. Interpersonal Boundaries

The issue that follows pushing your flaws onto others and failing to acknowledge their own personality traits is that it becomes very difficult to establish the boundaries of their own existence and those of others. This lack of boundaries is also prevalent in their attitude to others; they assume others are there to serve them and assist them in their aims. They cannot imagine that these people have their own lives, hopes and dreams!

An extension of this is their ability to share inappropriate items; such as how they berated someone. They will not be aware of how their words may shock or offend others; they will be too busy bragging about worrying about the response or whether they should be relating the facts.

Their lack of boundaries is also likely to see them asking questions that are too intimate for the situation or their knowledge of the other person. This can be very upsetting and damaging to any relationship. The lack of boundaries also extends to an inability to accept fault; they will borrow money, tools or promise you the earth and then blame you for not reminding them to return it to you.

6. Conversations

Someone suffering from NPD loves to hoard the conversation. In reality it is highly unlikely that you will get a word in edgeways. In fact, if you do manage to inject something into the conversation it should agree with their point of view; if it does not, your words will either be dismissed or they will take great pleasure in correcting you. Should you or anyone else manage to say a few words; or even have a separate conversation then it is highly likely that the narcissist will interrupt and quickly bring the conversation back to themselves. There will be little interest in any other topic of conversation. Conversations will generally revolve around them reciting a story; which you have probably heard before. It will be about an especially heroic incident; where they were the hero. Occasionally they may tell a story of when they failed at something; but even this will put them in a good light as they will be seen to be a victim of manipulation. Their other favorite topic will usually revolve around name dropping; even if they just saw a famous person it can be turned into a story about their best friend the celebrity.

7. Breaking the Rules

A person with NPD loves to show others how important they are by breaking the conventional rules. This may mean cutting into the front of a queue or creating and breaking multiple appointments. Any action which will make them feel they are above the generally accepted norm will enforce the idea in their head that they are special. They may even go out of their way to create situations where they can break the rules.

8. Image

The image which is projected by someone with NPD is essential; it must say successful, important and better than you. This will often be shown by driving expensive cars, indulging in cosmetic surgery or in their exaggerated stories of where they have been and what they have done. They are also keen to own the best items possible; they may purchase these items at incredible discounts but they will never pass this information on; they like you to feel that they are incredibly successful and money is not an issue.

9. Charming

Despite their lack of boundaries and their obsession with themselves, a person with NPD is very aware of the usefulness of others in achieving their aims. When they need to be they can be exceptionally charming, feeding you just the right amount of compliments to make you feel good about yourself and life.

In return you may find yourself doing what they want you to. Of course, once you have done their bidding they will lose interest in you straight away!

10. Negativity

Just as someone with an NPD will enjoy telling stories of their greatness they will also be happy to spread negative rumors and comments to both gain attention and leave others feeling insecure or unsure of their own sense of self-worth. This suits a sufferer as they look good and they are able to keep you close for when they need you again; it appeals to them on all sides of their personality disorder.

11. Social Media

Thus has been a gold mind for people who love to be adored. People are far enough away that they are rarely offended by the comments on any social media site. Someone with NPD can build a big following by posting perfect photos and comments; designed to attract a legion of fans that will all sing their praises and help them feel like the great leader they believe themselves to be.

12. Damage

As people with NPD do not have time for the feelings and thoughts of others they are quick to use someone and leave them behind. The result is a trail of carnage, people who have been taken in by them and had parts of their life destroyed.

The trail will become more visible the longer the behavior goes unchecked.

Thus damage is fuelled by the inability of someone with NPD to place other people's values, interests or well-being above their own. This combines with the slightest interest from another person, and the accompanying boost to their self-esteem; to make it very likely that someone with NPD will cheat on their current partner.

13. Awareness

Perhaps one of the biggest signs that someone is a narcissist is that they have no awareness of it. You can chat with them about narcissism and its various traits and they will be unable to relate that to their image of themselves.

This is why obtaining treatment can be so difficult; they do not know they need help! Of course if you realize the issue you may be able to choose to cut your losses and move on; however this may not be possible if they are a member of your family, a boss or if you really love them. At times, dealing with a narcissistic personality disorder requires you to flatter them to keep the peace. It is important to note that not everyone with NPD will have all these traits; they may have all of them or just a few of them. The critical point is that they are very self-obsessed and that they are not aware they have an issue. This disorder can be exceptionally destructive to the lives of those who suffer from it and the people who interact with them. Obtaining the right help is essential to ensure the cycle of self-destructive behavior can be ended and a sufferer can build lasting, meaningful relationships.

Early Signs of Narcissism

As unfortunate as it is, there is a certain point at which a relationship becomes too toxic. No matter how much you may love the person, it is time to end the relationship and move on so that you can find real happiness in your life. While milder forms of the narcissistic personality disorder have the potential to be dealt with and resolved; severe forms are often too far gone and the risk of staying with the person becomes too great.

Below are some warning signs that it may be time to get out of a toxic relationship with a narcissistic partner. If after all this, you are still unsure, you should consult a psychiatrist specializing in narcissistic personality disorder to discuss your relationship and seek his or her professional opinion about what you should do.

The Key Warning Signs

- Pathological lying: because narcissists often use manipulation in order to get the admiration they desire, they will often tell any lie they think will help them achieve that end goal. If your partner is lying consistently about important and trivial things, your relationship has no foundation in anything real. You cannot trust anything that they say, including when they tell you that they love you. If you cannot trust your partner, you have nothing to build on. This can approach dangerous extremes especially if your partner is having affairs. You will be at an increased risk for STDs if they sleep around and do not use protection.

- Fits of anger or rage: narcissists have a hair trigger. The slightest criticism or disagreement can spark an onslaught of abusive language and anger. When the fit of rage is over, your partner will act is if nothing had happened. He or she will show no sign of remorse and if they do apologize, it will not be genuine. It is unhealthy for you to endure such emotional abuse and it can have major consequences in the long term. In some cases the verbal abuse can even become physical.
Whether or not it has reached that point in your own relationship, it is time to get out if you are experiencing any form of abuse from your partner.

- Manipulative behavior: the person you love should not be doing anything to manipulate you. Period. Strong relationships are built on honesty and trust. You should be able to trust that the things your partner says and does for you are genuine and come from a place of love and not a place of narcissistic selfishness. This manipulative behavior can sometimes fool you into believing that your partner does genuinely care about and love you but you have to try to look past what you want to see and find out what really lies at the root of your partner's actions.

If you find yourself doing things you would not normally do or doing things that later make you feel guilty or unhappy just because your partner wants you to; this is manipulation. No matter how much your partner may say he or she loves you; people do not manipulate the people they love. You should never be forced into doing something you are not comfortable doing for a loved one.

- Feeling obligated: It is a bad sign if you are doing things (like staying in the relationship) simply because you feel obligated to or fear the consequences of not doing them. In a healthy relationship, partners do things for each other because they love each other and because they genuinely wish to see the other person happy. Of course, there are certain responsibilities and duties to uphold the maintenance of a relationship. But this is different than a sense of obligation.
If you are worried that your partner will abandon you or experience a fit of rage unless you do exactly what he or she wants; this is a sign that you are not doing it because you genuinely wish to see him or her happy but, rather, because you do not wish to see him or her unhappy.

- Feeling afraid: Just as you should not do things for your partner out of a sense of obligation, you should also not do things out of a sense of fear. Healthy relationships should provide a safe space for both your partner and you. Being with a person should make you feel secure and happy. Feelings of fear should not ever enter the equation. You should not have to fear the person you love.

- Becoming isolated from others: narcissists are often extremely jealous. Your partner will become more and more controlling of who you spend your time with and how much time you spend outside of his controlling reach. You will find yourself spending more and more time at home and growing distant from your friends and social circle. This isolation can make you feel unnecessarily dependent upon your partner; as if leaving him or her will mean being utterly alone. Becoming isolated from your social support is dangerous. If your partner does begin abusing, your friends and family may have no idea what is going on. So if you begin to notice that you have grown apart from your friends and family because of your partner, you need to leave. Your loved ones will be there for you. You will not be alone.

- Ignoring your own needs: if keeping your partner happy means neglecting or wholly ignoring your own needs, this is not healthy. A relationship should be about given and take with both partners providing emotional support for each other. Someone who loves you will not require you to put aside your own needs in order to appease them because they will have genuine concern for your needs just as you have for theirs. Never allow your own needs and desires to go unmet for the sake of your partner. This sort of relationship cannot end in happiness and will become extremely emotionally draining.

Type of Narcissism

While we talk about narcissism in general terms, there is more than one type. In the real world, when you meet a narcissist face to face, there may be signs that match the way a narcissist behaves because most of the time, they are a mix of the various types. As with typical mixes, there is always the dominant type mix with another. To help you to determine which one is what, here's a brief rundown of each different type and their specific characteristics or personality traits:

Cerebral

A cerebral narcissists believes that they are better than anyone and that their intelligence far exceeds that of anyone else.

They flaunt their intelligence and self-assumed superiority to be admired and envied by the rest. They know everything about, well, everything. They make it a point to have an opinion or suggestion for everything that you might throw at them. They will be happy to tell you stories that show off their sheer brilliance, whether the stories are real or just made up. They are happy to point out everyone else's failings and will look down on and sneer at anyone who is of lower intelligence. Such people are so obsessed with their grey matter that they will go out of their way to take alarmingly good care of it, sometimes to the extent that it reflects badly on their health and physical prowess.

Narcissism is very often associated with sexual stimulation. Cerebral narcissists rarely engage in sexual stimulation with others, as they prefer personal stimulation over the real deal. Therefore, it would not come as much of a surprise when I say that they prefer the anonymity and lack of intimacy that comes with pornography. For this reason they may choose porn over close real relationships. Besides maintaining a relationship with such people is a Herculean task in itself. As they will always insist on being the intellectually superior one in the relationship and assumes the right to control the other person's thoughts, emotions and actions. Even then, these relationships will be extremely short lived as they are constantly looking for more superior people to associate with. Cerebral narcissists should not be confused with somatic narcissists.

Somatic

Somatic narcissists are more closely in touch with the Greek legend of Narcissus. They are all consumed by how beautiful they believe they are. You will often find somatic narcissists at a gym or somewhere else where they are working on their appearance. For them it is all about their body and physique. They can be constantly seen flexing their muscles and bragging about their success in sporting events. They expect their body to be the source of their narcissistic supply and so they dress up immaculately and keep themselves well groomed.

Their narcissistic supply comes from how others react to how they look or from their sexual conquests – indeed, most somatic narcissists will have a long list of partners. They never cease to boast about their conquests in bed. Even though they may have bedded a lot of partners, most of the sex is bound to be cold and emotionless. Eventually, the word partner begins to lose meaning and they may be more aptly described as the victim. Cheating in marital life is something that you shouldn't put past a somatic narcissist. He is happiest when his narcissistic supply comes from multiple sources. They are quite dangerous as they know how to manipulate people both emotionally and through sexual intercourse. This tends to scar their spouse for life if they decide to be in a long term relationship with them.

Overt

This form of narcissism manifests grandiosity. They are preoccupied with having outstanding success in a lot of areas, like brilliance, attractiveness, sense of power, ideal love etc. Since they have a large sense of grandiosity, they believe that they can only be fully appreciated by other people on their level of grandiosity. The overt narcissist always has to be in control of any situation. They are never wrong and they will never be shy about making it clear that everything is about them and that everything has to be done the way they want it done.

Their egos are super-sized and they are not backwards in showing it to you either. The overt narcissist is able to cut you up, physically or verbally and will not show a single second of remorse or guilt. Such people are interpersonally very exploitative and will not think twice before using someone to achieve their own needs. Although very arrogant on the inside, they are experts at masking their egotism within a false humility. They envy other people to a great extent and get terribly jealous of their achievements, possessions and relationships. They seriously lack empathy and this makes them unfit to work in a group. They are usually loners. They may be seen as being overconfident and they are definitely extrovert in their behavior – in fact, it would easier to describe their personality as loud, obvious, larger than life, and somewhat oppressive.

Covert

The covert narcissist exhibits all the normal traits you would expect to find in a narcissist but with one difference – they want someone to take care of them. They are best described as the shy form of narcissism. He has grand fantasies similar to other types of narcissists but he lacks the drive to pull it off successfully. He is too timid to get what he wants and lacks self-confidence. He usually feels worthless at not being able to pull off exactly what he wanted. He faces large feelings of shame about the same thing. He rarely takes credit for his achievements.

He openly admires successful people and secretly envies them. He is unlikely to accumulate appropriate friends and prefers to surround himself with more inferior type of people. Such people are hyper vigilant to rejection and humiliation. They could be described as parasites, living off other people. They will normally exhibit some signs of an illness that needs taking care of and that is why they can never be what you want. They don't want to take responsibility for anything and will look for a partner who is strong, successful, and intelligent, one that can run their lives while they don't need to contribute anything. Covert narcissists will sometimes pair up with the overt narcissist.

Unprincipled

The unprincipled narcissist does not have a conscience and cannot seem to tell the difference between what's right and what's wrong. They care very little about laws, values and conventions and stay just within the boundaries of the law. They exploit others without the slightest bit of remorse because they consider other people as inferior to them anyway. This unprincipled lifestyle makes them more than willing to risk harm and they are remarkable fearless in the face of danger. Their malicious and diabolic tendencies are easily visible and they get them into trouble with the department of law. They achieve gratification by dominating and humiliating others.

These people never form an allegiance with anyone and so move from person to person with remarkable ease. They are alien to emotional attachments and do not feel the slightest remorse on ending a very promising relationship. The people they leave crumpled in their wake are very adversely affected, as the narcissist is usually very charming. These narcissists are exceptionally dangerous because for them, truth is only relative. They are masters of manipulation and deceit. They are very adept at scheming beneath a polite and civil veneer. Their plans are usually very cunning and worthy of admiration even though the means are hardly justified. They show no concern for other people's welfare, have no morals, scruples, and are highly deceptive when they deal with others. They will give off an air of arrogance and are driven by a need to get the better of everyone, just to prove that they are smarter. This kind of narcissist may be found in prisons or drug rehabilitation centers although there are an awful lot of unprincipled narcissists who never come up against the law. When in the vicinity of an unprincipled narcissist always be sure to keep your guard up. They smell insecurities a mile away and can easily turn you into a scapegoat for their next exploit.

Amorous

Amorous narcissists tend to be erotic or seductive in nature and they measure their entire self-worth around their, sometimes many, sexual conquests.

Their relationships are often pathological and, as soon as they seduce someone, they are likely to throw them to one side while they look for their next conquest. They are never looking for an emotional connect but rather seek to inflate their already bloated ego by sexually dominating other people who they consider as trophies. The victim has more or less no idea that they are being used and sometimes they sincerely fall in love with the narcissists. However, the narcissist sincerely lacks any empathy and will simply throw them away like paper towels. This makes them outrageous heartbreakers. Not only are they often known as heartbreakers, but they will also do some outrageous things, like pathological lying, conning their sexual partner out of money and other fraudulent acts. They use their sexual prowess to con unsuspecting people. The amorous narcissist is compensation for deep feelings of inadequacy. In most cases, they get away with it too because people hesitate to lodge a complaint against them.

Compensatory

Compensatory narcissists are constantly looking for a way to compensate for things that happened in the past, perhaps in their childhood and they do this by creating an illusion that they are superior. They tend to live in a fantasy world where they play the leading role in a theater that doesn't exist rather than living a real life. They imagine achievements in a bid to enhance their own self-esteem.

They need an audience filled with people who will believe their deceptions and they are extremely sensitive to how other people perceive them, looking for signs that they are being criticized. They literally try to compensate for everything that they feel they were deprived of. Their agenda is similar to the other narcissists except that they are more focused rather than being guilty of random acts of narcissism.

Elite

The elite narcissist is, in many ways, very similar to the compensatory narcissist in that they are obsessed with their own self-image. The sense of self they create rarely resembles the real person but they manage to convince themselves and others that they have unique abilities and talents. They will, more often than not, turn a relationship into a contest or a competition where the only goal is to win, to prove to others that they are truly superior. This will happen with any type of relationship, be it family, work, or love. The elite narcissist is a social climber and will be happy to step on anyone who gets in his or her way. In a way, he is the most dangerous of all the types as he hides in plain sight so effectively that even the ones closest to him perceive him as a good and honest person. An elite narcissist is usually a highly successful businessman or business woman who has a very reputable profile. They consider material wealth and assets as a primary objective over true emotion.

They are masters of deception and often use their talents to walk over other people. Being as cunning as they get, they usually have a legitimate and reputed business that they use as a front for all of their shady dealings. They are extremely protective of their personal space. If they get the slightest hint that you are a threat to everything that they have built up they will eliminate you without a second thought. They are ruthless and without remorse or empathy. They are concerned only with their well being and the achievement of their goals. They will go to any length to achieve what they want. Below are some of the narcissistic sub-types. These sub-types can be encountered from various people on a daily basis. Some can be annoying but tolerated, while some can cause emotional harm.

Conversational

Ever recall an instance where you are talking to a certain person, ranting or just randomly telling one of your everyday life stories to him?

What's unforgettable is how the conversation always manages to end up with him as the subject and the victor? Annoying, right? Not only is it sickening to hear stories with always the same triumphant result, but it is also annoying that they always make you forget what you are about to say due to their constant interruption. This kind of conversation can happen between normal people as well, but it is almost always the case with people suffering from narcissism.

There is even more aggressive conversational narcissist where they rudely cut you off while you were saying something, just so they can insist their own story whose lead character is always them. If, by reading this part of the book, you are reminded of that one person who never fails to do this each and every time you are having a conversation, try to observe. Check out his other mannerisms, habits, or the way he behaves with other people Chances are, you have a narcissist who is sneakily turning all his friends into his supply sources.

Group Narcissism

Whenever the topic is narcissism, we are always presented with the idea that it is all about a person who cares for nothing else but himself. This is true, but it does not necessarily rule out the possibility of narcissism that can occur in a group. In group narcissism, the narcissist individual is always a part of the group. Usually, the group is made up of narcissist people who mirror themselves and don't encounter any problem with having to co-exist with each other. They tend to become the narcissist supply source of each other and you will know that it is working out as the group acts as a narcissistic entity. You see, narcissists have the tendency to gather or join each other in groups because it brings them comfort. This is due to the fact that they are all, pretty much, similar and share the same behaviors or habits.

There's no questioning about why he behaves this way and she behaves that way, because they all know that they are trying to protect someone deep inside them. Now, this group becomes a protector of the hidden **real selves** of each member. While this looks nice and beneficial for a narcissist, this does not mean that they are already safe from the danger of self-destruction. It's always there, just below the surface.

Aggressive or Malignant Narcissism

This type of narcissism is your lesser type (like classic, cerebral, somatic, elite, and others) kicked up a notch because it becomes violent and psychopathic. Remember Adolf Hitler or Ted Bundy? They are categorized as aggressive types of narcissists. Not all narcissists prefer to physically harm their supply source or victims. Most of the time, they just torture or abuse you mentally. However, when a narcissist becomes a bit too physical and performs the murder, rape, or some other crimes with cold blood, that person can already be categorized as a malignant or aggressive narcissist.

Destructive Narcissism

So we have labels for, pretty much, every type of narcissist out there. Honestly, some psychiatrists do not exactly agree with these labels because identifying a narcissist is more than just knowing all the types and matching the several behaviors or signs dominant to that type. What is more, there are also narcissists who are too clever that they are able to compensate for some of the behaviors in order to cover them up. That way, lesser track means lesser disruption to the facade that took them years and so much lies to build and complete.

There are also some people who cannot be also classified as a narcissist, but confuses you because they really match some of a narcissist's description. Now, why am I saying all these? This is because of this type, the destructive narcissist, is one of those who do not technically fit the definition of a narcissist, but they also inflict plain on themselves and also shows general narcissist patterns.

Out of all the types, the destructive narcissist is the one that seems to be a bit irregular. It has some of the traits that can easily identify them within the various types of a narcissist and all the while lacks some narcissistic traits that will solidify their being categorized as a narcissist.

Destructive narcissists usually have the most intense characteristics that a narcissist can have. These characteristics are set to ruin and destruct people around the narcissist and because of this, you can easily associate them with a pathological narcissist. However, the mentioned characteristics are fewer.

Sexual Narcissism

While this may raise your eyebrows as we have come to know that narcissists aren't exactly crazy about having sex with someone else, let us take a quick look at who these sexual narcissists are. Sex, when blended with grandiose becomes sexual narcissism. A sexual narcissist boasts pleasurable sexual skills, has a sexual entitlement, and he also lacks sexual empathy.

The meaning? You get to have intercourse with a sexual narcissist, but as always, it is for his pleasure and not yours. You may feel satisfaction and this is no wonder because of the sexual skills of the narcissist. However, if the narcissist feels that he is already satisfied and you aren't yet, even if you are right in the middle of it and he wants to stop, he will stop.

He will only do it with you when he feels like it. So if a sexual narcissist doesn't feel like doing it, even if two weeks have passed already, you will never get one.

Another thing that you have to know about the sexual narcissist is that they have a big tendency to be an unfaithful partner. Big surprise! Since they feel like they have all the sexual skills, they also feel that they can do it with anyone as long as they are in the mood for it.

Acquired Situational Narcissism (ASN)

This narcissism sub-type is a lot different from the rest of the types, even the main ones, as ASN is acquired later on in life as an adult. All other narcissism types are acquired in the childhood phase of a person's life. ASN can't just happen to anyone. One needs to have the narcissistic tendency as a child for ASN to be successfully triggered. This type of narcissism is triggered when an adult with a narcissistic tendency suddenly comes across wealth, celebrity-status, or fame. Through this, the previous tendency suddenly blooms into a full-blown narcissistic personality disorder complete with signs, symptoms, behaviors and more harmful probabilities like the usual type of narcissism. The only difference is the age when the sufferer acquired it.

What feeds their narcissistic cravings are their fans, supporters, people around them, their fake friends, assistants, social media, and the traditional type of media.

Chapter 3: The Possible Causes of Narcissism

In this chapter, you will learn about some of the causes of narcissistic personality disorder. The specific causes differ for each individual. But, perhaps, by understanding some of the general factors that can contribute to the disorder; you will better be able to identify what might be the root cause of the disorder in your partner (if he or she does, indeed, have a narcissistic personality disorder).

While there is still comparatively little known about the exact causes of narcissistic personality disorder, a variety of potential contributing factors have been identified.

In 2006, Leonard Groopman and Arnold Cooper put together the following list:

- Hypersensitivity originating at birth: some people are just more sensitive than others from the day they are born. Hypersensitivity can lead to an inability to cope healthily with criticism or failure, leading to the need to overcompensate or set unrealistic standards for oneself in order to overcome feelings of inadequacy.

- Excessive praise during childhood: while it is, of course, important to praise your child for good behavior to encourage them to continue such behavior; too much praise can lead to an exaggerated sense of self worth. The popular parenting movement of the 1990s and early 2000s that sought to make every child feel special has led to an increase in cases of narcissistic personality disorder as those children who are now adults were raised to believe they were exceptional and superior to all others.

- Excessive criticism during childhood: Just as with excessive praise, excessive criticism can lead to the need for overcompensation in order to recover lost self esteem. Parents who are overly harsh with their children when they do something bad or fail at something risk raising a child that battles feelings of inferiority.

This can result in compensatory or fanatic narcissism or a variety of other personality disorders.

- Overindulgence by parents during childhood: That is, parents who spoil their children risk raising up a child who will later develop a narcissistic personality disorder.
This is because overindulging a child's every wish and desire will give them the inaccurate perception that they are entitled to everything they want.

- Severe emotional abuse in childhood: Emotional abuse is, unfortunately, an often overlooked factor by society. We take great pains as a society to prevent physical abuse but have few options for children who are being emotionally abused. However, emotional abuse takes a huge toll on the psyche and can lead to a wide variety of personality disorders later in life including narcissistic personality disorder.

- Unstable or unreliable care giving from parents: children of broken homes or of unreliable parents grow up without that feeling of security and safety that is necessary for a child to develop healthily and become a confident (but not too confident) adult capable of achieving real happiness in life.

- A narcissistic parent: This is a factor not necessarily because narcissism is hereditary but because the child grows up watching and learning from how its parents behave. If the child witnesses the manipulative and self-centered behaviors characteristic of a narcissist, it will learn to adopt those behaviors.

- Abnormality in the brain: recent research has suggested that there may be actual brain abnormalities associated with a narcissistic personality disorder. Specifically, those who have the disorder tend to have less gray matter in the left anterior insula.

  This region of the brain is thought to be responsible for empathy and compassion as well as for regulating our emotional responses. With this region underdeveloped, people have difficulties performing all of these important brain functions. The causes of this abnormality are still unknown.

Whatever the original origins of the disorder, narcissism is deeply rooted in the sense of shame and inferiority. These feelings are so deeply rooted, however, that someone with narcissistic personality disorder would never admit to feeling them— primarily because they are, themselves, completely unaware of these feelings.

At a subconscious level, every narcissist feels that they are fundamentally flawed in such a way that they are completely unacceptable or unsuited for normal society. This is why they deal so poorly with criticism, disagreements, or setbacks. Even if they are wonderfully ambitious and capable individuals, the slightest setback could throw them entirely off track; making it difficult for them to follow through or achieve long term goals.

The behaviors associated with a narcissistic personality disorder, then, are defense mechanisms the individual has developed to cope with these feelings of shame and inferiority. This is an important thing to understand as you attempt to help your partner deal with his or her narcissistic personality disorder.

Common Myths About Narcissism

We basically have an idea what narcissism is, however, not everything that we know about it is true. Just like any other illness or condition, there would be a bunch of people who would tell you what to do or what not to do whenever around this person, or what habits or mannerisms will tell you that this certain person is suffering from the sickness or disorder being currently talked about. It is good that we know how to identify the possible signs from someone who is suffering from narcissism, but not who frequently does the possible signs are already narcissist.

The problem with people is that whenever they do not know anything, they try to appear as they know it by piecing together a couple of signs, mannerisms, or attitude of a certain person and assume tons of things from there. You have to understand that not everything that we hear from our elders, those who have experienced firsthand a certain length of time with a narcissist, or have a narcissist for a family member are true and can be found in all narcissists. Your assumptions and the assumptions on the narcissism of people around you aren't always right, as well.

Is it making you confused? Let us proceed.

1. All narcissists have low self-esteem and are always insecure.

While looking at a list of the attitudes and behavior of a narcissist, you can almost agree to this myth without any hint of difficulty. It is not the case, however. Contrary to this popular belief, a narcissist does not adore themselves just because they are trying to protect their image, or they are badly wounded inside that they are trying to look very, very fine.

In fact, they do not need to defend themselves because, in truth, narcissist thinks they are the best at everything. If you're the best at everything that is the point of being insecure or even have low self-esteem? See, that is how serious narcissists are about adoring themselves.

They do not adore themselves for protection or just to cope. They adore themselves because they think they are supreme beings. It is that simple, no need for you to further understand why they do this and that. There is no use telling these people or suggesting having someone help them increase their self-esteem. The problem is, their self-esteem has already skyrocketed and seems like it won't be back even after a century.

2. Narcissism = Physical Vanity
Not really. Yes, narcissism is strongly connected to physical vanity, but it is not the only thing that makes these people live and breathe. Just because a person has the addiction or unbearable habit of looking in the mirror does not exactly mean they are already narcissistic.

One self-obsessive habit alone does not make a narcissistic. A narcissist's choice, wherever you look whether it is inside or out, will always be his or herself. They will simply choose themselves over anything and anyone and this choice will be made without even sweat or a twitch of the eyebrows from the difficulty of the decision.

There are so many things that complete a narcissistic like entitlement, antisocial behavior, relationship problems, materialism, and more. This disorder is more than skin deep, it is way beyond to the point of being unreasonably self-obsessed.

3. Deep down, they have a reason for being the narcissist that they are.
This is not true. Narcissists just love themselves like that. In fact, the term love itself is wrong to be used on them as the love that they practice or use on themselves is love that is not for their real selves.

Narcissists are like drunken people inside a bar who think they already love the person who is dancing in the dark right in front of them. However, as soon as they sober up or the light is shed on the face of the person they are facing, they realize that it was just a night that went uncontrollably fun and they lost control. They simply wake up realizing that there never has been that sort of love that bloomed the night before.

The good thing about the drunken party-goers is that they still get to wake up from this dream. Such is not the case with narcissist people. This is the problem, they cannot wake up from this drunken sort of love and annoyingly so, we simply have to endure their company or ignore them altogether.

There is simply no reason behind their narcissism. They simply think of themselves like Gods or legends and if you take the time to test their intelligence and beauty, almost always, they are average.

4. Narcissists do not have an idea that they are narcissists

When it comes to personality disorders, we usually have this notion that the sufferer of the disorder usually does not know that he is actually suffering from it. While this may apply to some like the multiple personality disorder this is not the case with narcissism.

Some narcissistic people cannot exactly pinpoint what is going on with them or if there is a disorder that they are suffering from. Yes, there are some who know exactly that they are narcissistic and would even think about it thoroughly. However, if there is one thing that all of them surely know, it is the fact that they lack something that every other human have and this lacking is something that they can use to their full advantage.

That missing part is, yes, empathy. They know this and they also know that this is should be a secret, a very deep and dark one that nobody else should ever know.

Now, comes denial in the picture and you should know that this comes hand-in-hand in being a narcissist. Every narcissist knows what they lack and they will not hesitate to go all out just to deny it.

5. Narcissism equates to high self-esteem

When the word narcissism is mentioned to us, we usually and unconsciously correlate it with skyrocketing self-esteem. This is not true as one can have very high self-esteem, but they are not necessarily narcissistic.

People with self-esteem, even those who have a skyrocketing one are still capable of having and maintaining a healthy relationship. That is exactly what our narcissistic ones are not capable of. Yes, they care about what you can do for them, but as soon as they have realized that you are of no use, you are officially out of the picture in a snap. Do not expect for even a drop of sweat coming out of a narcissist as they make this decision of burning bridges because they are like the master switch that really turns everything off as soon as you flip it. There is simply no feeling, whatsoever. For them, relationships are nothing but pure business for them and they do not care even somebody else gets hurt as long as that somebody isn't them.

Being narcissistic is necessary for success
Just because you see Donald Trump's face gracing your television screen from time to time, it does not mean that narcissism is necessary for one to be successful. Yes, he is undeniably successful, but narcissism nor high self-esteem isn't the key to success.

Very high self-esteem or narcissism, for that matter, is not correlated with success as there are different kinds of people who are very successful.

While it is true that to be successful one needs to be bold and daring, some of the traits that are very strong, high self-esteem cannot be treated as a trait that is a necessity for success. If a person has very high self-esteem but does not have the persistence, discipline, and creativity, success will most likely stay as a mere objective and nothing more.

Chapter 4: NPD (Narcissistic Personality Disorder)

This means that a person must exhibit this behavior both over time and in many different circumstances. They experienced it as a young adult and they grow older without much change in their behavior. They manifest the same behavior with their family, at work, and in the community. Their personality traits seem stable, no matter who they are with and what they are doing.

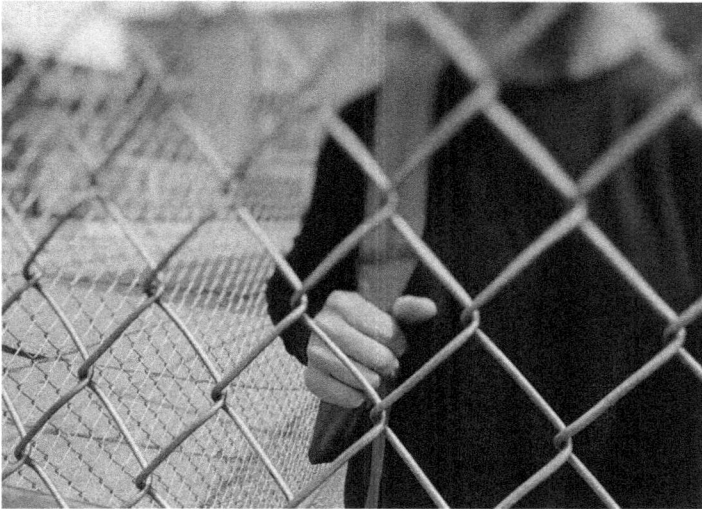

A person with NPD cannot have their behaviors explained based upon their age. For instance, many teenagers act like they are the center of the universe and may over-exaggerate their behaviors, but this can be seen as a normal stage in their psychological growth, which they will eventually mature out of.

Someone with NPD, however, does not outgrow it. It is not considered normal for the stage of life they are in. This is one of the reasons that personality disorders such as NPD may not be diagnosed until a person is older. Someone with NPD must act this way no matter their state of sobriety is. For example, someone who acts like a narcissist while drunk, but is a giving, loving person while sober, would not be diagnosed with NPD because their behaviors are based on the presence of alcohol in their system. Someone with NPD will act the same no matter what substance is in their system. Taken as a whole, when someone has Narcissistic Personality Disorder, they believe they are the center of the universe and act as such. They have no regard for the feelings of others around them, and compassion is a trait that they cannot develop. They will do whatever they can to be the center of attention and show others how worthwhile and valuable they are to the world, no matter who it hurts. They have shown these traits throughout their life, usually starting during adolescence, and it doesn't have anything to do with any substances they are taking.

It is estimated that up to 6.2% of the general population is a sufferer of narcissistic personality disorder. Men are more than twice as likely to be diagnosed as women.

How Narcissistic Personality Develops

As with any mental illness or personality disorder, there are a couple of different explanations for the disorder. These causes could show up independently or exist in conjunction with each other in someone's life, which will then encourage the growth and development of a personality disorder.

The first puzzle piece in the development of NPD is genetics. If a family member had NPD, it is quite likely that children and other relatives will also develop the disorder. This is because of psychobiology, the idea that the brain and behavior are connected. If the brain is genetically wired in one way because of the genes a person has inherited from parents and grandparents, then a person is likely to inherit the genes that caused the wiring to occur in such a way to cause NPD. People who have a genetic predisposition are more likely to suffer from NPD than those without it.

The other trigger for NPD is parenting issues. If a person lives with a parent or family situation where they are overly pampered, constantly treated as special, or given everything they ever ask for without any idea that there are limits, they are more likely to develop NPD. Children need limits and discipline, and without them, they will grow up with an unrealistic view of both themselves and how the world works. They incorporate the belief that they are special and perfect in their worldview.

On the other hand, people who grow up with parents who are especially harsh and never value anything the child does can also develop NPD. The child develops a defense mechanism to offset the negative and constant criticism that they receive. Think of it like a pendulum swinging the other way. If the parent is overly harsh to the child, the child will start to overcompensate by believing that they are entitled to everything, that they are special, and that they deserve the world, just to combat the negativity they are surrounded by every single day. This is generally thought to happen because the child may be overcompensating to try to prove their worth to their parent. They want to earn the parent's love and approval.

No matter which type of parent the person with NPD had, the parental behaviors began while the child was young, generally before the age of three.

A third factor that may be relevant to the development of NPD is society's ideas of who and what is important. For example, the idea that the most powerful, rich, and affluent are more important than "ordinary people" has become an ingrained belief thanks to mass media's preoccupation with these types of people. Even watching reality TV, where people who are self-centered, selfish, and rude to others are idealized, whereas people who are caring and compassionate are often marginalized or completely ignored. Second, people receive more approval from outside influence when they are smarter, richer, or have a higher status. This could cause people to work for this higher status so they can receive the same type of recognition.

Last, there is a weakening of the community in our society. Children are not often brought up to believe there is part of something bigger than themselves, which leads to kids having more difficulty identifying with others. Their ability to empathize is replaced with a grandiose self-image.

Usually, however, there is a mixture of both genetic factors and environmental factors, both personal and societal, at work with the development of any personality disorder. If a parent or other close family member has the disorder, it is likely that the child grows up both with a genetic link to get it and in an unstable home environment where the traits are more likely to develop. Because many of the traits have been showing to exist since childhood, it is easy to see why the disorder becomes so difficult to treat. However, that doesn't mean there are not treatments or options for a person suffering from NPD or their families. The next chapter will give some clues into the current treatments available through modern medicine and psychiatry to handle Narcissistic Personality Disorder.

Environmental factors play a very important role in the development of narcissistic personality disorder. In fact, one of the most common reasons why people suffer from this condition has something to do with how parents brought up their children. Below are scenarios related to environmental factors that can lead to the development of narcissistic personality disorder.

Narcissistic personality disorder can stem from oversensitive temperament which is inherent at birth.

- Children who grew up with excessive admiration from their parents without giving them realistic feedbacks also tend to develop this particular personality disorder.
- People who grew up with parents who give them excessive praise and criticisms for good and bad behaviors, respectively, also have tendencies to develop excessive narcissism.
- Giving overvaluation and overindulgence to children by parents, peers and other family members can inflate the self-entitlement of children thus causing narcissism.
- Being praised for exceptional abilities and looks can also lead to this disorder.
- Severe abuse – particularly emotionally abuse – in children can lead to narcissistic personality disorder.
- Children who grew up with manipulative parents are likely to become narcissistic.

The environmental factors play a vital role in influencing the development of narcissistic personality disorder. However, it is important to take note that environmental stimulus is just one facet that results in this disorder.

Genetics also plays an important role in the development of narcissistic personality disorder. Geneticists have correlated the existence of gene variations with personality disorders such as pathological narcissism.

In one study published in the Journal of Neuropsychopharmacology noted that the gene tryptophan hydroxylase-2 might be the cause of the development of narcissistic personality disorder. This particular gene regulates the production of serotonin which is an important chemical responsible for the effective regulation of mood.

People who suffer from narcissistic personality disorder often experience impairment in their relationships with other people. Since most pathological narcissists cannot form an empathic attachment with others including their family and peers, they often perceive themselves as unconnected to others. Thus, almost all people who suffer from narcissistic personality disorder experience a lot of complications that are mostly related to their relationships with other people. Below are complications of narcissistic personality disorder.

Relationship difficulties: Many narcissists are completely emotionally detached from other people including their parents and families. Since they are malignantly aware of their existence over other people, they are only capable of having shallow relationships. This is the reason why most pathological narcissists cannot last in serious relationships even for a short time.

Problems at school or work: Narcissists lack empathy and they are also poor when it comes to handling responsibilities and obligations. With this, many narcissists fail to perform well in school or at work. They are ambitious yet incapable of fulfilling their goals thus it makes them very difficult to work with.

Depression: People who have narcissistic personality disorder often feel dejected and threatened once criticized. This makes them very prone to depression. In order to protect themselves, they react with rage to any kind of criticisms thrown at them.

Drug or alcohol abuse: Narcissists have a deep sense of entitlement thus they are prone to abusing either alcohol or drugs. Their arrogance manner makes them less respectful to authorities and more adventurous thus they are willing to try things that will put them in the spotlight including drugs and alcohol.

The narcissistic personality disorder can cause a lot of problems not only to the people who are suffering from this disorder but also to those whom they associate themselves with.

Chapter 5: Narcissism in Relationship

When your relationship has not reached such a toxic point and you don't really see any severe warning signs, there may be hope for saving the relationship. There are treatments and techniques for managing narcissistic personality disorder. These will be discussed in more detail in the next chapter. Here we will discuss the strategy you yourself can use to live with a narcissist and help them overcome this personality disorder so that you can have a loving and nurturing relationship with each other.

So, if your relationship has not yet reached its critical breaking point, here are some things you can try in order to make life with your partner more enjoyable and satisfying for both of you.

- Identify the problem: if you are reading this book, you have already begun to work on this step. Look for the key traits that characterize a narcissist and decide if those apply to your partner. Then, read more about narcissistic personality disorder so that you understand not only the symptoms but the causes and treatment options. Learn as much as you can and then look for more to learn. Realize that this is a real problem that needs to be addressed.

- Do not be an enabler: once you know what the problem is and how the narcissistic personality disorder operates; you will be better prepared to deal with it. If you notice your partner acting in a narcissistic way (i.e.- acting arrogant, self-absorbed, or ignoring your needs and feelings), confront the problem rather than allowing it to continue or catering to it. Even if it seems easier at the time to just let it go; doing so will only allow the problem to become worse until it is too late and you have no option but to get out or suffer.

- Set firm boundaries: since narcissists tend to put their own needs before anyone else's, it is likely that your needs are beginning to fall by the wayside. You need to stop this process dead in its tracks. First, learn to distinguish between the legitimate needs and desires your partner has and the delusional or unrealistic ones. Then make it very clear for your partner what they can and cannot demand from you. Tread carefully here since narcissists are overly sensitive to criticism. Make sure to point out that you do love your partner and that you are willing to meet his or her needs. But only when those needs are genuine and realistic. You also need to make it clear that you expect the same in return from your partner.

- Avoid one-sided conversations: narcissists have difficulties with empathy and, if allowed, will steer every conversation into a discussion about themselves. They only want to talk about their needs and desires. While it is important to let your partner express his or her needs and desires, it is equally important that you have the space to express yours as well. If the conversation starts to become predominantly about your partner, balance it out and bring it back to yourself so that it becomes a two-sided conversation.

- Avoid blaming yourself: narcissists can be manipulative and may make you feel guilty for not allowing them to indulge in their narcissistic behaviors. Do not, on any account, allow yourself to feel guilty or blame yourself. Point out that your needs are also important. Explain that you respect his or her needs but that this relationship needs to be a give and take. If he or she really struggles with empathy, set out clear guidelines for how he or she can practice empathy. Do not play into their attempts at making you feel guilty.

- Avoid anger: in arguments, it is easy to become angry very quickly. This is particularly the case with narcissists who tend to fly off the handle quickly. When one person in an argument is angry, it makes the other one angry. Try to resist this and remain calm. Understand that this anger is coming from your partner's inability to healthily deal with conflict. If you also get angry, it will only make your partner angrier and less capable of rationally dealing with the issue. Maintain calm so that you can maintain control of the situation.
The more often your partner sees that you maintain calm even in these arguments; the more he or she will realize that you are not going to lose control of the situation or back down from your position no matter what they do.

- Get professional help: this is absolutely essential. Unless you are a trained therapist or psychiatrist yourself, you cannot deal with narcissistic personality disorder on your own. If your partner is unwilling to see a therapist—since doing so would mean acknowledging that he or she has a problem, something a narcissist cannot do—suggest couples therapy and frame the problem as a relationship issue rather than strictly an issue with your partner.

As you work through couples therapy, your partner will likely grow more and more willing to seek one-on-one therapy where he or she will be able to dig deeper down to the root of the problem. Furthermore, couples therapy can help provide you a safe space to address your issues with your partner. With a trained therapist in the room, it will be easier to keep control of the situation because the therapist will know how to handle your narcissistic partner.

It is important to talk to your partner and assess how much they want to change. Your partner may understand that his or her behavior is detrimental to your relationship. So it's either he or she would be willing to adjust or may not see it as a problem and refuse to alter his or her attitude. It is easier to change the dynamic of a narcissistic relationship if your partner realizes that there is a problem. Nevertheless, even if that person doesn't understand the need to change, you can do something about it.

741

Later, we will discuss things that your partner can do directly to facilitate the transformation, but first, we will tackle the things you can do to keep yourself safe and begin changing the dynamic of your relationship.

Stop Enabling the Narcissist's Behavior

This is quite essential. You need to be aware of how you manage your partner's behavior and how you will deal with it this time. For example, if your partner wants you to do something that is illegal, immoral, or something that you are uncomfortable with, you have the right to say "no". As long as you continue to play along with them and placate their caprices, they will not change at all. By making a single change and saying no to the things that you do not want to do, you will be able to modify the dynamic of your relationship. Your partner will have to assess his or her behavior precisely because of this and will eventually realize his or her mistake.

As mentioned earlier, it's important to keep in mind that your partner will probably be upset at first. He or she may do all the drama or even try to sweet-talk you into doing whatever it is they want from you. The most important thing you should do is not to pacify his or her wants. You do not have to defend yourself or your decisions.

Say no, tell them you love them, then walk away to cool things down. It is important to say that you still love them, even though you are saying no. As you do this, stay calm. Do not raise your voice, do not engage them, do not justify yourself. All of these steps are necessary. It is necessary to emphasize that you aren't rejecting them, you are only rejecting their request. Make sure they understand the difference.

Do Not Fight

As for refusing to engage with them, you need not get sucked into their anger. By getting mad, they will get the impression that they are succeeding trying to make you lose control of the situation. If you don't contain your emotions, your partner can get the upper hand of the situation. By reacting in a cool and composed manner, not engaging in their confrontation, you take that power away from them.

Your partner may become angrier at first when you react this way, but don't let this get into you. You need to calm down and be firm. After doing this a few times, their anger may subside. You will be forcing them to reevaluate how they act, which is precisely what is necessary for behavioral change. If their typical attitude does not get them what they want, they will have to change their behavior. You may have the desire to lash out at them. After all, you probably have great reasons to feel angry, both for the current situation and for all the past hurts you have suffered. However, by giving into your anger, you are only falling into their game.

You will need to find other ways to express your animosity in a healthy manner, but you cannot take it out on your partner, no matter how much you think you are justified in doing so.

If your partner is willing to talk about the situation in a calm, rational manner, the better. But never do it at the moment. Wait until both of you are calm and that your irritation and frustration have passed before engaging in this conversation. It is at this point that you can explain why you said no and that you will no longer allow them to take advantage of you. Reassure them that you still love them and want to be a part of their life, but that you cannot handle the difficult situation your partner puts you in anymore. At any point in this conversation, if your partner starts raising their voice, end the conversation and walk away to collect your thoughts. This is non-negotiable. As soon as you engage in conflict, you allow your partner to try and control you. Make sure they understand that only rational discourse will be allowed when dealing with these personal issues. Otherwise, you will need to shut down the conversation and walk away.

Do Not Allow One-Sided Conversations

If, during a conversation, your partner decides to talk only about themselves, you do not need to be a part of the conversation. You can try to interject another point of view in the conversation, but if they keep bringing it back to them, then you need to remove yourself.

Make sure your partner understands that you will not participate in a conversation if it's only about them. Remember, all communication has to be given and take, and if they cannot give you some part of the talk, then it is not true communication.

Do Not Allow Your Partner to Make You Feel Guilty

Because someone with a narcissistic personality doesn't generally understand that their behaviors are maladaptive, they will generally try to blame you for their behavior, especially as you try to back away from the things that are difficult. For example, your partner may try to tell you that the anger is your fault or say that you are the one who is yelling, not them. This behavior is to deflect the truth of their behavior onto someone else so they don't have to take responsibility for them. The key here is to stay strong and to not let them blame you, and not to blame yourself. Their behaviors are their responsibility, not yours.

Your partner may try to make you feel guilty for standing up for yourself by projecting their destructive feelings and behaviors onto you. You do not have to accept that guilt. You do not have to play along. This is another situation where you should walk away rather than mollifying them. Again, it may take a lot of strength to do this, but it is vital to get them to change.

If you choose to stand up to this tactic, your partner will need to reexamine how they get their own needs met in a more suitable way.

Do Not Apologize

Oftentimes, people who are codependent and in a narcissistic relationship apologize all the time, and oftentimes for no reason. This goes along very well with not taking responsibility for your partner's behavior. You should not be sorry for taking care of yourself and standing up for your own decision. You have every right to be an independent person and to stand up to someone who isn't treating you the way you want to be treated. So quit apologizing for this.

Many of the tips and ideas in this chapter are meant to force your partner to examine their behaviors. Because they will no longer be getting their needs met by manipulating you, they will be forced to examine how they do things. Your behaviors will make them reevaluate how they handle the world around them. And once they are able to note their own actions, they will be able to start the process of transformation. Unless your partner is challenged wherein there is a very high possibility that they won't change. It is up to you to start the process by modifying the dynamics of the relationship by using the techniques explained in this chapter.

How to End a Relationship with a Narcissist

If you can identify any or all of these warning signs in your own relationship, it is essential that you find the strength to cut ties and walk away. Your partner's happiness should never have to come at the expense of your own. Ending this toxic relationship as soon as possible allows you the freedom to heal and find someone with whom you can be genuinely happy and experience the full (and wonderful) benefits of a loving relationship.

Ending any relationship is difficult but ending a relationship with a narcissist comes with additional problems. So if you are having trouble figuring out how to approach this problem, here are few tips on how to get out of a toxic relationship with a narcissist:

- Go to therapy: as mentioned earlier, if you are feeling unsure or undecided about your relationship, you should consult a therapist to talk about the problems you are experiencing. They can advise you on how best to approach the problem. Additionally, they can provide an invaluable source of support and reinforcement as you work through the grueling process of escaping this unhealthy relationship with a narcissist. If you can't afford therapy sessions, find a support group. There are many out there and they can help you not only get professional advice but also find other people who have experienced many of the problems you are experiencing. Learning from other's experiences is a great way to figure out how to tackle your own problems.

- Do not be afraid to rely on your support system: whether it's your therapist, your support group, your family, your friends, or some combination of these; they are there to help you through this. You do not have to go through this difficult process alone.

These are people who love and care about you and want nothing more than to see you happy. Let them help you in this time of need. They know as well as you that when you are in a better place, you will be more than willing to do the same for them. If you feel that you do not really have a support system, make one. Reach out to old friends with whom you have lost touch. Reach out to your family. Find support groups for people who are in your situation. No matter how alone you may feel at this moment or how scared you are of a future without your narcissistic partner, you are not alone.

- Do not give in to manipulation or abuse: when you finally confront your partner and say that it is time to end the relationship, he or she will likely go to great lengths to discourage you. Your partner may try to manipulate you into staying or use fear to break down your courage. He or she might try to disrupt your everyday life as you are trying to heal from the break up. Instead of falling for these tricks; understand that each one is another sign that you have done the right thing and that all you need to do now is be vigilant and allow time and your social support system to heal you and build your strength back up. Each time you resist these attempts at tricking you, you will grow a little stronger and next time it will be a little easier. Reward yourself for each time that you make it through without giving in.

- Learn as much as you can about narcissistic personality disorder: knowledge is your most powerful weapon in this situation. The more you know about how a narcissist operates; the better prepared you are to deal with whatever he or she may throw your way. Also, the more you learn about the disorder; the more you will realize how much of your relationship was built on deceit and manipulation. Realizing that there was no actual love coming from your partner helps motivate you to stay away from him or her. It will also help you avoid falling for another narcissist in the future.

- Cut off all contact with your ex-partner: this is easier said than done as your former partner will likely seek you out and try to contact you. However, it is important that you do not initiate any contact and when he or she forces contact; keep it as short as possible and get out of there. If you are having trouble cutting contact, stay with someone who can help you. Let someone else answer your phone or the door. If you are at work, ask a trusted coworker to ask him to leave or call security.

If it begins to worsen to dangerous levels (such as threats or harassment), file for a restraining order.

- Start a journal: this tip may seem like its coming out of the left field but it is also important. You need to make sure to process your feelings during every step of the process. Write in this journal daily. Keeping a journal will help you to deal with what you are experiencing. It will also help you to track your progress. You can read through past entries and notice yourself becoming stronger and stronger even if it doesn't feel like it yet. It can also help to keep a journal about how the relationship was with your partner. Describe in as many details as possible how bad it was so that if you later find yourself tempted to go back to your partner, you can read these and remember just how unhappy and unfulfilled you were.

- Get rid of every reminder of your former partner: those little mementos around your home that remind you of him or her can make you feel nostalgic and start missing your partner. It will also cause you to think about your former partner on a near-constant basis. Removing these reminders from your home will also help solidify the feeling that he or she is really gone from your life and the healing process can begin to work faster.

- Start doing things for yourself again: all that time catering to every need and desire of your narcissistic partner likely left you with little time to pursue your own interests. This can make you lose your sense of self. Pick up an old hobby you used to enjoy or learn a new skill you have always wanted to learn. Did you dream of one day speaking French? Now's the time to do it. This will not only help you regain your sense of identity apart from your former narcissistic partner, but it will also help take your mind off of things. Most importantly, it will help you build up a sense of self-worth that is not connected to your former partner. Pursuing your own interests allows you to become the person you want to be. Not to mention, it will give you a chance to meet new people and begin the next chapter of your life.

- Allow yourself to grieve: do not spend all your time distracting yourself and avoiding your feelings. You need to let yourself grieve; to let your emotions out. If you are afraid of being alone during the grieving process; stay with a trusted friend or family member, someone with whom you will feel safe in expressing your emotions.

If you try to avoid feeling this grief now, the pressure will build and build until it explodes later in unhealthy ways. It is ok to feel upset, angry, guilty, or anything else you feel.

Just make sure you allow yourself to feel it and, more importantly, to feel it in a safe and nurturing space where you can work through your emotions and heal.

It is a difficult process. No one will tell you it is going to be easy. But you will become a stronger and happier person for it. So gather up all the strength you have and allow yourself to finally get out of this toxic relationship and find true love and happiness in your life.

Chapter 6: Narcissistic Abuse

Narcissists are emotional predators and they normally experience emotional emptiness. To deal with this, they have to carefully select their victims: who they seduce, charm and trap. The victim will then be providing what they lack. It is of the essence to note that narcissists are incapable of love, and most are characterized by the furious envy of those who have that ability. The moral qualities that normal people tend to have include life projects, goals, creativity, sensitivity, empathy and vitality. Narcissists are capable of switching their attitude from caring and charming to dismissive and ruthlessly critical, making their victims confused and full of self-doubt. If you are a victim of narcissist abuse it is paramount that you understand that it is not your fault by any form, way or shape. They target individuals for simply being human and therefore vulnerable to them. It is in targeting their victims' that narcissists observe and learn to identify whether they have favorable qualities. Therefore, you were selected by a narcissist because you have all or some of the following desirable traits.

A Person with a High Degree of Sentimentality

Narcissists are attracted to a person who loves deeply and is sentimental. It is easy for narcissists to appeal to such a person's needs and desires through the use of excessive praise and flattery, also termed as love-bombing. The narcissists tend to idealize their victims at the early stage of the relationship where they show a great deal of love towards them. At this stage the victim will see their partner as loving, caring and charming because they are doing all things in a perfect manner.

In other words, a narcissist is able to secure the victim's trust through appealing to their craving for love. Their actions are a deliberate intent to create pleasurable memories that a victim will romanticize and that will create confusion in their thoughts during future abusive periods.

Sadly, a narcissist gets pleasure by toying with another person's emotions. A person who is sentimental becomes an easy target because they love easily and deeply. They will be drawn to the actions that a narcissist does at the early stage of the relationship to create the sense of a soulmate and which makes the victim addicted and dependent on them. When it comes to sentimental people, all the narcissists have to do is manipulate their targets desire in having the most romantic relationship. A narcissist will carefully assess your personality and identify attributes that you value in yourself. They will then use these qualities against you because it is easy for them.

Resilience

People who have undergone difficult experiences in life serve as good targets for narcissists. It is of the essence to note that the quality of resilience means having the ability to withstand difficult situations with the hope of something better in the future. People who have had challenging experiences, such as abusive childhoods, are targeted because they are able to withstand enormous abuse without giving up. There are various aspects and understanding tied to this by psychologists where they state that when a person has been exposed to abuse for a long time, they grow into it such that they want it, argues Foster and Brunell (2018). There is another understanding of this whereby a person who has been under abuse will not give up easily and will take abuse from narcissists for a long period, also argues Foster and Brunell (2018).

They will make a good target because it means that the narcissist will have an unending supply of the benefits they seek. It is true that resilience is an invaluable quality when it comes to dealing with life's adversity but in an unhealthy abuse cycle, it becomes easy for them to be ensnared within the narcissist's web of deceit. Resilient people tend to have strong capability to detect threats in their environment. However, they still fall for narcissists and are subject to the same cycle of abuse that they encountered before. The reason for this is that they will opt to ignore their instinct and decide to fight for the relationship against all the odds. It is not surprising for a resilient person to compare love with the amount of faith one gets.

Low Self-Confidence and Low Self-Esteem

A person with these qualities could be highly vulnerable to a narcissist. One of the factors that make such a person vulnerable is that they crave acknowledgment from other people. They usually doubt their worth and capability to do certain things. Normally, a person with low self-esteem is not comfortable with the way they look, the way they do things and how they relate to other people. It is a quality that reduces a person's confidence such that they are not able to stand for themselves. Upon noticing this, the narcissist will take advantage of the situation in a way that during the idealized stage of the relationship they employ excessive flattery and praises. In return, the person will feel appreciated and valued. Naturally, a person will be attracted to someone who assures them that they are good looking, lovely and makes them happy. The praises and flattery will carry the victim to the point that they feel they have a purpose and that their partner cannot live without them.

Unfortunately, none of this was true and as time goes it, they will be subjected to abuse. The same qualities of low self-confidence and low self-esteem will make them more vulnerable to the abuse.

Integrity

A person with integrity is true to their words and has high morals. To some degree, narcissists can be told that they lack morals, yet they find people who have them highly attractive. Integrity can be termed as the basis of moral conduct because a person with it tends to have a wealth of attributes that a narcissist knows that they can exploit. Some of the aspects of a person with integrity are that they find that it is not within their moral code to lie, give up on a relationship defensively or cheat. It is desirable to have such a moral code, but when in a relationship with a narcissist only the narcissist benefits. They have no such moral qualities and will feel no remorse in hurting their victims. Subject to these moral codes the victims will be reluctant to betray the relationship by stepping back. Integrity is a vital quality when in a relationship with like-minded or empathic individuals. However, when with a narcissist it is more of a weapon to be used against the person to end their sense of self and their trust.

Empathy

Empathy is an important quality among human beings as it allows them to connect and consciously feel what others are going through. It is the basis for emotions and that is why narcissists fail to have emotions and feelings because they lack empathy. The reason why narcissists prefer empathic individuals is because of the emotional fuel that they provide is necessary for them to feel in control and in power. It is an aspect that makes them continue seeking empathic people due to their abundant supply. Empathy is an empowering human trait but when it comes to relationships with an abuser it serves to disempower (Wurst et al., 2017). The reason for this is that empathic people tend to see and try to identify with the narcissist's perspective when they are being abused by them. It is this aspect that the narcissists depend on to keep a continued cycle of abuse with their victims. A highly empathic person is an ideal and important choice of narcissists due to pity that they employ after abusive incidents. In most cases, an empathetic person's reaction to a given situation is easy to predict. It is a major advantage to a narcissist because they know how they can manipulate their victims to act in the manner they want or to control them. For instance, a narcissist knows that if they give a simple sob story or a faux apology their victims will be quick to forgive. An empathetic person is quick to rationalize a narcissist's behavior with the excuses they make for abuse. As such, they depend on their ability to sympathize and forgive them even after they have been subjected to a horrific incident. They appeal to the victim's empathy and in so doing they are not answerable for their actions. The challenge herein is that as an empathic person one always doubts their decisions in confronting their narcissist partner. They feel guilt and carry the burden as if they are the abuser in the relationship. Sadly, the narcissists take advantage of this as they count on an empathic person's compulsion to protect them instead of exposing who they are.

Conscientiousness or Dependability

The ability to be conscientious is an important quality and one that a narcissist will look for in a target. These are individuals who are concerned with the wellbeing of others. They are always ready and willing to help others in need. It is an important quality and makes a person more humane. However, narcissists look it as the way into a person and as a suitable aspect of exploiting in their victims. A person with this quality tends to make decisions with their conscience and projects a high degree of morality on the assumption that other people will depict the same. However, it is not the case when it comes to narcissists who take advantage of the quality of the notion that their victims worry about the needs of others. The bad thing with this is that for a conscientious person they will readily give a narcissist the benefit of the doubt; hence, granting them more chances. The care that they have in serving a narcissist's needs makes them sacrifice their own wellbeing.

Therefore, the analysis signifies that narcissists target individuals for their humane qualities. Normally, the noted qualities among others would play an essential role in enabling a person to properly relate with others and have a healthy and productive life. However, due to the lack of empathy in a narcissist, they tend to see the qualities as their enabling weapons to take control of their victims. They will manipulate and take advantage of their targets such that they forget their wellbeing and spend their time trying to make the relationship work.

The previously discussed qualities, and others such as intelligence, extreme perfectionism and personal accountability, will make a person take the blame on themselves as the reason why the relationship is not working.

Chapter 7: Who can help you?

Narcissists are known to crave love and respect for other people. When they enter relationships, they maintain their stand on how people should view them as individuals. Even though you may think that all relationships should be mutually beneficial, the love that other people extend to a narcissist is sometimes not enough to help him change.

A Romantic Relationship with a Narcissist

If you are in a relationship with a narcissist, then brace yourself – you are in for a roller coaster ride, and it is not likely a ride that you will enjoy. Narcissists tend to be amorous and passionate, but it does not mean that they are willing to give you the love that you expect – it is bound to be a one-way street where only you are in the giving lane. However, it becomes extremely difficult to get out of a situation, especially if you are the type who does not want to give up on love.

Narcissists are emotionally ranged, but all the emotions that they are willing to show are those that will provide them the avenue to take advantage of the situation and make them provide you their needs. They are willing to cajole you and tell you the things that you want to hear in order for you to stay by their side. At the same time, they are willing to cheat on you in order for them to feel good about themselves.

Why do narcissists do that? The reason is simple – they are not content that you are the only person that is willing to love them. They believe that if one person is willing to give unlimited love to them, they are likely to get affection from the entire world. It also works that these individuals are extremely charming – they seem to always find the right words and gestures to make people feel that they are worthy of their time.

When You Think You are About to Date a Narcissist

Some people want to date the bad ones, and they do it for the excitement, or for the challenge of seeing the good side of them. If you are out there, single and ready to mingle, you might encounter them. Scrap that – you are very likely to encounter them.

Narcissists are always on the prowl – they think that relationships are games that they are bound to win to prove to everyone that they are good-looking or extremely witty to make everyone fall for them. However, be careful when you get to be wined and dined by a narcissist – they prefer to place the rug under you and then pull it off. If you think that the person that you are dating a narcissist, you may end up breaking up with him after four months, the time where you would reach the emotional peak of constantly being with a person. It is also the time that people realize the true colors of a narcissist.

Narcissists and Addiction

You may notice that the most self-absorbed people that you know are very prone to addiction – they are the types that you would ofteñ find in casinos or in bars, whiling away time and money on vices. They are also very likely to get hooked up on drugs or become extremely workaholic. For psychologists, this behaviour is caused by a narcissist's desire to have a constant source of companion or activity. Some even believe that it is their way of self-medicating or coping with their deep-seated insecurity. Narcissists often find their "fix" of good feeling in addiction, because they also tend to have utter distrust in other people. They cannot believe that someone is capable of loving them as much as they love themselves, and for that reason, they rely on the temporary high of substances.

They also think that they have control over their addiction, and that because they have power over everything, they would be able to quit anytime. Deep inside, they know that they are making a mistake, but they convince themselves the next minute that they simply need the substance now.

Like most addicts, these people do not realize that self-medicating and finding a temporary source of happiness would make their pain harder to manage. Some realize that they are creating problems for their relationships and then try to take away their confusion by being drunk or high. They try to stop creating trouble by containing themselves, without thinking that addiction makes matters worse for them. Some narcissists also find the ability to be more powerful and louder when they are intoxicated, and then they take advantage of this when dealing with people. The reason is simple – they simply do not have the guts to expose their narcissistic side when they are sober.

Narcissism and Aging

What happens to narcissists when they age? They often feel the pain of being abandoned, or the fear that it will happen to them. Most narcissists, as they age, become extremely paranoid that people would not recognize the great things that they have done for others. They think that their children and the younger, more able people around them are ingrates, and they think that everyone is going to take advantage of their inability to perform as much as they did during their youth.

They deal with all these thoughts by doubling their efforts or simply saying that other people would not surpass their legacy. When this happens, they may sever any remaining relationships that they have and cause rifts because of the choices that they make. In the end, their fear of being alone becomes closer to becoming true.

You would also encounter narcissists that tend to be psychosomatic as they age, meaning that they are using illness, real or not, in order to manipulate people into giving their needs and getting attention. They become increasingly dependent on the people around them in order to escape some responsibilities that they are still perfectly capable of performing.

Why a Relationship with a Narcissist Hurts

All possible relationships with a narcissist become wounding because of the things that they make other people feel – they tend to make others feel extremely attached to them, then dissociate. This pattern of behaviour makes other people feel that they have made a mistake or that they are being hated. Children become most vulnerable to pain by this pattern of behaviour. Children often understand behaviour towards them as either an act of love or hate. Being praised and told good things are all love, while being punished and scolded can be regarded as hate. Some parents who care for what they think more than how their children may interpret their actions tend to not care about how their behaviour may register to the minds of young people.

They manipulate them into making actions that they think should be rewarded.

Romantic and professional relationships also go through a similar problem – people who want to benefit from the relationship feel that they are not doing anything enough, and then they are pulled into attaching themselves to a narcissist the moment they receive a reward. However, they do not realize that they are worthy of getting more out of the relationship. Because they tend to forget that they have a specific standard of what love and advancement should be, some people fall victim to always being compensated short for the effort that they shell out.

Now, there are situations wherein you would be required to deal with a narcissist and you have to fight to get what you want.

How to Communicate with a Narcissist

At this point, you already have an idea that talking to a narcissist and convincing him to give you what you want can be very hard to do. It may be difficult, but it is doable. Here are some things that you need to keep in mind.

1. In the mind of a narcissist, his interests come first.

How do you make a narcissist think that he should be on your side? The answer is simple: turn the situation as something beneficial for him to. All you need is to create the right deal to lay on the table. Think of it as dealing with a difficult customer – you need to know what his needs are first and then pattern your needs to them. If you want to convince a rather narcissistic company owner to give you a well-deserved raise, give him what he wants – he wants you to keep working for him, and that is what promotion or a raise will do for him. Place the situation as something beneficial for him, or an event that will make him look good.

2. Feed the ego carefully.

The best way to make a narcissist eager to listen to you is through praise. If you want to talk to a rock star that is not likely to give you the time and day to tour in your area because he thinks he is important, talk to him first about how great his art is and how you think it is important for the people in your town to hear his music. This way, you are telling him what you want him to do, and then meet his demand to be praised.

3. Be prepared to listen a lot.

Narcissists like to talk, and the topic is always himself and his interests. If you need this person for a particular project, then be prepared for long bouts of a listening session. The advantage is that you will figure out more about his interests and figure out what he needs to hear in order to seal a great deal. You also need to listen a lot because narcissists tend to pull strings and turn the table around when you are not watchful. Make sure that you observe his body language and verbal shifts. Stand your ground and be prepared to maneuver back to the topic.

4. Make him think that it is his idea.

A narcissist is a person who thinks that his ideas are the best, and if they came from him, then they are worth hearing. If you want to make a narcissist agree with you, make him think that you think that the idea is great because it is what a person like him would think. That might give you an instant audience too.

5. Be specific about your needs.

Get straight to the point when you are asking a narcissist favour. While it would always be a good idea in any conversation, it pays to be direct in asking narcissists for anything. It allows you to engage with them less and be able to make sure that you can redirect them back to the topic. It also helps you to set up boundaries with them as well. At this point, you may think that narcissists are extremely difficult to deal with, but do not get it wrong – they are not bad. They are still people that are worthy of being loved, and they are capable of changing. The next chapter will tell you how you can help a narcissist out and enable him to build healthy relationships again.

Loving and Helping a Narcissist

Let's go back to an earlier point discussed in this book – everyone can be a narcissist, and in fact, everyone you know is possibly a narcissist at a certain point in their lives. It is easy to judge them because they are difficult to understand. However, people who have lived most of their lives minding their own business and those who seemingly not care for others all have reasons why they act that way.

The Right Love

If you have a loved one who you think is a narcissist, then you probably have the ability to help this person out. You may think that this person does not have the ability to love others, but it is because he was not able to realize that people around him love him enough to want him to improve. With your love and support, you would be able to end this person's dependency and distrust on the affection of others.

Now, do narcissists think the same way you do about them? No, they don't. They may think that their needs are more important than yours, but they do not realize that giving pain to others was unnecessary. They may also have simply accepted the idea that they are inherently bad people and that people expect them to be cruel. However, it does not mean that they like the way they are.

What can you do to help a narcissistic loved one? Here are some tips that you could use:

1. Remember that narcissists were not born that way.

No one is born selfish or arrogant – experience taught people how to acquire these traits. Your understanding of their situation allows you to have the leverage of having a better knowledge of how they should be behaving and how to deal with them.

The acknowledgement that narcissists have learned to deny, coerce, or project behaviour makes you aware that they can learn to undo it.

People like you would be able to guide them back to self-acceptance and change.

2. Think that it is not your job to change them.

Again, you may empathize, but you cannot force them to change. They are the only ones who can do that for themselves. What you can do instead is to inform them of how they affect you, without judgment or criticism. Take note that narcissists cannot behave the way they do when they are within a vacuum – they need other people to effectively hide their flaws and make sure that they are going to put on a better show.

3. Break that vicious cycle gently.

What prompts a narcissist to act the way that they do is the shame they feel when they are uncertain and when they are sure that they have made a mistake. For that reason, make them feel that it is okay to make a mistake and that they are worthy of being loved, warts and all. That makes them realize that it is futile to deny their vulnerability, and that they are going to be loved without trying too hard.

4. Make them feel that you are not their fan.

Narcissists tend to love people who are not adoring fans – like everybody else, they long to shed their make-up and reveal who they really are.

Their fear is that the best people around them may soon deem them unworthy. What you need to do is to make them feel that their flaws are okay, and that you are willing to grow up and become better people with them. Show them that you are not working out towards perfection, but towards harmony.

5. Keep your sense of fun and humor.

If you are able to show them that you are capable of laughing at your own mistakes, they would realize that there are people out there that can be okay with imperfection. Show them that you are able to live a healthier and happier life by just being who you are and holding on to your values. Show them how it is to be happy to not hurt people just to get your ways, and still feel that you are on the top of the world.

6. Show him that he is independent.

The most crippling fear of a narcissist exists on his own because nobody wants him. However, should he really care about what other people think? Show him how happy some people have become because they are able to live their lives without the fear of judgment and having to fend for their own. He would realize that there are values that he stands for, and that he does not really live for the personal standards that he has been upholding and has been hurting him in the process.

Tell this person that you have appreciated him for his humanity, and that you think that his beauty shines the most during the moments that he has been hiding. Show him that you can see him through, and that you are fine with what you have seen. He would realize how loved he is, without the fake adoration that he has preferred in the past. The moment he realizes that he is loved to the point that you are willing to help him change is the start of his better path. If you are wondering how it is to make a narcissist want to change and acknowledge his behaviour, then show this person how fine it is to be human. The things that you dislike in him are also some things that you may exhibit in a particular situation. Have the knowledge that you are not a better person because you do not judge, condemn, or avoid error as much as the other person does. He would realize that it is okay to value one's self without having to seek another person's approval, and that there is no one measure to tell a person's value. Once he realizes that there is no such thing as a perfect life to envy, he would be empowered to become the person that he really is.

Chapter 8: The Steps to Take Back Control

When survivors of emotional abuse leave the harmful relationship, they have just begun on their journey of healing. In fact, it becomes a lifestyle in which you have to practice so as not to back-peddle to the position that you were in the first place when the interaction between you and the narcissist ended. Victims of psychological abuse continuously have symptoms of trauma such as nightmares, recurring flashbacks, and anxiety. They also have depression and feelings of low self-esteem. They could even have an urge to check or even connect with their abuser because of the intense trauma bonds which are there during the abuse cycle. Gradual practices of self-care to supplement the therapy that you should get after detachment are some of the powerful ways to tend to the mind, body,and spirit after being abused.

Eat healthily and keep a healthy mental status

In this busy world, people often do not have time to have a proper meal and sometimes does it while doing work or watching television. In so doing, they deny themselves the pure experience of a meal that is nourishing and well thought out.

You need to treat yourself with the same respect that you would give the first date and so indulge yourself to a meal without having a lot of distractions as well. That means having the right proportion for each food group in your meal such as protein, vegetables, and starch. When your diet is right then, you will have the right energy levels and be more likely to be as mentally strong. During the times when the brain is traumatized, the areas of the brain that relate to executive functioning, emotion and focus become disrupted. Meditation has actually been proven from a scientific basis to benefit similar parts of the brain which have also been affected by trauma like the amygdala, the hippocampus and the prefrontal part of the cortex. That is because meditation entails clearing your mind completely of things that burden you and allowing you to process things that have burdened your subconscious for a long time. In so doing, you will find you are no longer guided by your emotions, but you are placed back in the driving seat of your psyche. It enables the survivor, so they are able to claim their reality and act from an area of empowerment as opposed to a place designed by the trauma.

Therefore, meditation allows you to be in better control of the way that you would respond to trauma triggers. Meditation apparently also enables one to be aware of your cravings so that you do not cave in and start to contact the narcissist who will take this as a sign they will be able to continue with their abuse. It would allow you the space to consider the potential alternatives before deciding to act impulsively on urges to go back to the interaction.

Exercise

This is not only for the physical benefits that translate into mental health; it is also for the advantage of discipline. Exercising on a regular basis can make you better able to handle your emotions because the act itself instills discipline in your psyche. A daily exercise regimen can save your life after being abused.

It could be running on the treadmill or even going to aerobics classes or long walks. If you do not have the motivation, then you just have to set yourself up with something that you enjoy. This could even be thirty minutes of walking each day or an hour if you feel that it is necessary. The reason is exercise tends to release endorphins and lowers the levels of cortisol which then replaces the biochemical addiction that is developed with the abusers with a healthier outlet.

Exercise may allow the individual to embody increasing resilience and strength after getting free from a narcissist. It combats the biochemical addiction that the body developed during the abuse. This addiction is created through the release of chemicals such as adrenaline, cortisol serotonin and dopamine which exaggerate the bond that one has with their abusers through the highs and the lows that are there during the abuse cycle. The benefit of exercise is that it can counter the physical side effects which are there with the abuse such as gaining weight, prematurely aging and illness which is all caused by an immune system that is being overwhelmed by stress from trauma.

Stress does limit the ability of the immune system to counter diseases, and narcissistic abuse can cause the immune system to be weak to the point of exaggerating illness or allowing infections to take hold.

Taking care of your inner child

Even though you may have been traumatized, there could have been other instances that were brought to the surface because of the abusive relationship. Your id may be wounded and thus would need to be soothed by your adult self when you are feeling emotional. The unmet needs during childhood were probably compounded by the experience which means self-compassion is needed during this time.

Survivors tend to struggle a lot with blame and shame after their abuse. Even though they are aware, the abuse was not their fault. It has the power to bring up old issues that were not addressed. It may also point out to a larger pattern of not being good enough. Changing the course of your negativity is crucial when one is healing as it assists in tackling narratives that were mostly cemented because of the new trauma. At the time that these deep-seated emotions arrive, you have to be gentle with yourself as if you were actually speaking to someone that you love. You can proceed to write down positive words of affirmation whenever you feel overwhelmed by the feelings of grief.

Remember when you are blaming or judging yourself, you have a higher likelihood of engaging in self-sabotage because you do not feel that you are worthy of peace and stability. When you finally accept and show love for yourself, you will remind yourself that you are worthy of your own care and kindness.

Reality check anchoring

This allows for the habit of reconnection with reality to take place as it is something that the abuser had eroded at first. It validates the survivor, and it reduces dissonance concerning the identity of the narcissist. Survivors may be very vulnerable after leaving the abusers, and the latter usually try and manipulate them into going back to their routine. That is why it is necessary to not only block texts and calls from your abuser but also remove connections between them and other enablers that are on social media. That would remove temptation and information on the narcissists from the healing journey. It would also provide a clean slate where one can reconnect with what really happened and the way that it made you feel or how the narcissist will try to manipulate the situation going forward.

How To Break Free From A Narcissist

When you decide that enough is enough and you need to free yourself from the narcissistic abuse you have been suffering, it's helpful to have some guidelines to follow. This is not going to be easy; it is not like breaking apart a "normal" relationship and you will go through some tough times. Besides splitting away from a control freak is not an easy task. As if it is not hard enough already the narcissistic individual will only make it living hell for you. You may find that you have no energy. You will feel as though you are alone, that you are worthless and you will feel an intense rejection but, believe me, sticking to your guns will pull you through this and you can come out the other side in one piece. Without further ado, let's get started.

Step 1 – Say Goodbye

When it finally hits home that you are in a narcissistic relationship, you must get away from the situation as quickly as possible. You will never ever change the person you are with and you can never make the situation better so cut your losses before you get to hurt. The only person that you have the ability to change is you and you do that by not allowing yourself to be abused by this person. You are entitled to be treated with dignity and respect. Occasionally, you have to demand it.

If you are with a person who is forever putting you down and undermining you, then look at it this way

– they do not deserve you. If you can't make the break, the situation is only going to get worse. Yes, sure, you will have times when everything is fine but that won't last and things will just get progressively worse. Telling yourself it will change means you are living in a land of make believe; you need to snap out of it and get back to reality.

Narcissists are generally unhappy people deep down and he or she will continue to push that unhappiness on to you if you stay around. The sooner you can walk away the better; the sooner you can begin to recover and move on with your life while he or she gets on with theirs. Don't be surprised to see them turn to someone else immediately; that's what they do. They need to have someone on whom to project their inadequacies and if it can't be you, quite simply it will be someone else.

Do not fall into the trap of missing the good times or envying the new partner those good times. They don't last, as you well know and, if you really think about it, they weren't all that good because of what followed. All of the negativity inside him or her has been dumped on you and, in their eyes; they can start again with a clean slate. It won't take long for that negativity to appear again though, especially if you are seen to purge him or her from your life completely. The new partner will then become the target for the negative emotions. Look at it this way – the more you grab back the energy you lost, the more you begin to rebuild your self-worth, the less energy he or she has and that's why the new partner becomes the next target.

You see, he or she took your energy from you so they could seduce the next target. If you take that energy back, what will they use then? Their new partners, that's what.

Don't be tempted to sit around and pity yourself. Just because he or she may have a younger, perhaps better-looking model now doesn't mean that you need to continue feeding their energy. If you do, you will never recover fully. It's time to turn your love on yourself. Yes, you may have had some good times and you may have loved him or her once but not anymore. Trust your intuition – it's what told you to leave in the first place and it's what is telling you now that you need a loving relationship, a stable and healthy one. You opened the door to let them go, now shut it behind them and don't let them in again.

Step 2 – Break All Contact

The only way to break away from a narcissist is to break of all contact with them and that has been proven by many different studies. This means NO contact whatsoever. Delete their phone numbers; change yours if necessary. Delete their email addresses and have a system in place so that any emails they send you are blocked. If any letters arrive from them, bin them straight away, burn them if necessary but do not read them and do not respond. Curiosity is a dangerous thing and if you fall foul of it, you are allowing them to control the situation again, which is exactly what they want.

Whatever he or she has to say to you is going to be some form of manipulation or anger at you shutting them out.

You are going to ask yourself if they ever really loved you and the truth of the matter is that NO, they did not. Narcissists are not capable of projecting that love on to anyone else. The simple reason for that is that they do not love themselves, not deep down. He or she is spending their entire life hiding from himself or herself and from everyone else and this is why they live in a world of make believe. However, that does not mean that you are an unlovable person because you are. You do need to work on your own self of self-worth and self-love first because a lack of these is what drew you to the narcissist. When the time comes to cut all contact with the narcissist in your life, you should do it as if it is a matter of life and death. If he or she knows that there is a chink in your armor, that is their way back in. You have to act as though you do not exist in his life, as if you are dead to all intents and purposes. He or she cannot be made aware that you are still there. He or she must be made to feel that you do not care, you never did, and that you are totally indifferent to them. Indifference is absolutely the worst thing to do to a narcissist but in a good way. If you are still pining for him or her, they have a way in. If you are angry, they have a way in but if you are indifferent, that will hurt them. Because indifference means that you are totally detached, have no emotions whatsoever where they are concerned. And emotion is the food that a narcissist needs to survive.

It doesn't matter if your pain is the worst kind, he or she does not need to know. That pain is between you and your support circle, no one else. If you happen to run across him or her anywhere, push the indifference to the fore. Ignore them; you do not see them. A little trick here to get you started – wear a pair of dark sunglasses on your head.

If you see your ex-narcissist, simply put the glasses on and walk on by. If they can't see your eyes, they can't see you and they have no way in.

When the time comes to make that break, write one letter – the last one you will ever write to them. This is your chance for closure so write everything in that letter. Write about how they spend all their time dumping their negative energy on you so now it's time to turn the tables. Send that negative energy right back. Dump on them the way they dumped on you and make sure you say everything you want to say, no matter how mean or nasty. This is the last thing you are going to do and, once the letter is sent, you are going to shut that door forever.

This final part is important –make sure that the door is shut and you have removed all avenues of contact. The first thing he or she is going to do is attempt to contact you. Block your emails, block your phone calls, and send mail back unread. This is not your problem anymore; don't let it become one again.

Step 3 – Get Angry

When you have suffered through long periods of abuse, you should be angry although you may not realize it at the time. You must allow that anger to come out – keeping it locked away will just damage you further and will stop you from healing. And, to deny yourself the right to be angry, well, you are acting in much the same way as your narcissist did.

It is difficult because, when you are in your relationship with your narcissist, you have taught yourself not to show your anger. If you did get angry over anything, you were "out of control" or you were the one that was being abusive and you were told that you needed to calm down.

You could have been voicing your opinion of their treatment of you but it would turn around to put the fault squarely on your shoulders. The subject of their abuse would be neatly sidestepped, a highly typical manipulation of a narcissist.

Victims of abuse from a narcissist do not believe they can have a voice simply because they spent so much time under the control of him or her. The only voice you were allowed to have was to positively praise them; anything about them that was negative would be shut out immediately.

The end result of being kept quiet and not being allowed to show your feelings is one of the worst kinds of depression. This is what your anger will do if you have an outlet for it; it eats away at you and makes you bitter. You cannot allow that to happen because then they have won; not you.

Allow your anger free reign. Express how you feel. That is what the last letter to them is all about – getting angry. If you have already shut down all contact then right your anger down in a letter and then burn it – do not send it because that is opening up the doorway again and that can never be allowed to happen.

Do be careful whom you take your anger out on – it won't do you any good hurting those who are close to you. Go and see a therapist if necessary, that's what they are there for. Use a punching bag, punch your pillow, scream, and throw things. Whatever you do, get all that anger out of your system. You will feel an innate sense of calm afterwards and you will start to feel your energy returning to you.

I must add a word of caution here – if you have been in a long relationship with a narcissist or a particularly intense one, you may be emotionally unstable for a time.

You must NOT do anything stupid. Do not let your anger get the better off you and start stalking the narcissist; don't break into his or her house or damage their possessions or, even worse, them! Nothing is worth falling foul of the law for.

Properly expressed, anger is healthy. Work it off in a positive way and get back your sense of self-worth without doing any harm to anyone, least of all yourself.

Step 4 - Grieve for What You Have Lost

Once you have expressed your anger, allow your grief to come out. You will feel grief, whether it is because you have lost someone you thought was special or because your love has been used and thrown back in your face. It doesn't matter whether they are worth your grief; you are.

Think of it as experiencing a death. The death of your relationship and of the illusion as to what the relationship was. That's right, it was just an illusion, not real, and this is possibly the most painful part you will have to deal with.

Crying is healthy, it helps you to release tension and emotion, and I guarantee that you will feel better after having a good cry. It may not last and you will have to do it again but it will get better. You will be purging yourself from deep inside. There are several stages to grief:

- Denial – the first stage, the disbelief that this is actually happening to you
- Anger – the second stage, where you start to ask, why you, what did you do to deserve this?
- Bargaining – the third stage where you make deals with yourself to get through it
- Depression – the fourth stage where you just can't be bothered with anything
- Acceptance – the fifth stage where everything is going to be just fine and you tell yourself that

787

It is not as straightforward as working through the stages one at a time. Most people bounce around and will feel some stages two or three times. You may not even experience the in that order. The important thing is that you do go through all five stages in order to heal and come to terms with what has happened, so you can move on.

However you choose to grieve, do not let it go on for too long. You must start getting on with your life again and interacting with new people even if you really do not feel like it. Once you make that first outing, you will start to feel much better about life and about yourself.

One thing that you can do to make yourself feel better is gathering up everything that reminds you of your ex-narcissist and burns it – all letters, mementoes, everything that reminds you of the life you had together.

Do whatever it takes to show your grief, it is an important part of the healing process. It shows that you are human and that you are capable of feeling.

Step 5 – Remove the Psychic Bonds That Hold You Together

Whether you believe it or not, there is an energy web that holds us all together. You can't see it, but it is there. And that energy bond runs between you and the narcissist.

More than that, your energy fields have bonded together, they are interwoven and they must be broken otherwise he or she still has access to your energy and to you. In fact, just by thinking about a person you are letting them in and giving them access to your energy. You must cut the bonds between you and the narcissist in your life. This is important, to stop him or her from feeding on your energy, from using you any further even though there is no longer a physical relationship there.

There is a process you can do to cut those chords. It is simple and you won't see it happening but you will feel it. Before you start, get yourself in the mindset that this is a ceremony of sorts. Light a candle or two burns some incense or some sage and make yourself comfortable, so you are relaxed. Lying down is the best way for this. Close your eyes and imagine that there is a chord coming from your solar plexus, just above the navel, and it is stretching all the way to the narcissist. You can see it. Now, you have to imagine yourself cutting that chord. Imagine that you have a large pair of golden scissors or a sword. Now cut it at a level with your navel. Take hold of the cut end and direct it upwards towards the sun or down towards the ground. You must do something positive with it so it cannot reattach itself to you. Now, because you imagine all of this you can let your imagination take over and run riot here; do what you need to do to end this once and for all. Visualize those ties being cut, See the energy in that chord splitting; yours is coming back to you and theirs to them.

Ask him to return to you all that he has taken from you – the pieces of your soul, your heart, and your very being and give back anything that you have taken from him. Now imagine a brilliant white light is surrounding you. It is providing you with protections and sheltering you from any bad energy that may come your way. Once the chord cutting ceremony is complete, run yourself a warm bath with sea salt in it. Sea salt is known for its properties in removing negative energies. Just pour half a cup into a hot bath and lay in it for at least 20 minutes.

Remember one thing – it is very easy for those negative chords to attach themselves back to you if you let the narcissist in, no matter how you do it. You only have to think of him or her and it will happen so you may need to perform this ceremony a few times to be certain the chords are cut forever.

Step 6 – Look after Yourself

When you feel down and a little depressed, it is hard to even think about looking after yourself but this is the very time when you should be. You need to eat properly, get plenty of rest and fresh air, exercise is important as well. A narcissist will take great joy in watching the people he hates to suffer. He will goad every second that he sees you in a miserable state. Do not give him that pleasure. It will only fuel his already inflated ego. Take good care of yourself and enjoy every minute of your life without him in it. Watching you enjoy yourself could tear apart the narcissist and that could be the sweetest revenge you could ever have.

If you get lucky, he might miraculously make an effort to change himself for your benefit. Now is the time to pay attention to you, read the books that you want to read, listen to music, relax in long hot baths and treat yourself – all of the things you couldn't do in the relationship with the narcissist.

One of the most important things is what you eat. Most of the food available to us today is poor quality, full of sugar and the wrong kinds of fat, not to mention chemicals and toxins. These all affect how the chemical balance in your body works, as well as your health and a poor diet has been shown to adversely affect moods as well.

Just making a few changes in your diet can have a significant impact on your wellbeing and on how you feel about yourself. The very first thing to do is remove all forms of processed food from your diet. Anything that has white sugar, table salt, white flour, anything fried or boxed, in a bag or a can. Cut out all convenience foods and fast foods. If you are used to living on a diet like this, it's going to be tough at first but I promise you will start to feel the benefits very quickly. Plus, an added bonus – having to eat more healthily means preparing more meals from scratch and choosing your ingredients carefully which leads to another place to focus your energy. That leaves you less energy to think about the narcissist you left, thus shutting him or her even further out. When you switch to a whole food organic diet, your body will start reacting straight away. Your body has been crying out for these nutrients for so long and it will repay you in spades for giving it what it needed.

791

Eat plenty of fruits and vegetables, nuts, seeds, whole grains and drink plenty of purified water and herbal teas. Your body will react by balancing out the chemicals that affect your moods – you won't have the sugar highs and lows and you will feel so much better, both in yourself and about yourself. You will have more positive energy to focus on a new lifestyle, one that does not include being bullied by a narcissist. Exercise is an excellent way of looking after yourself. Take up yoga, go for long walks, even go to a gym, or join a trampoline club. Not only are you getting fitter you are also releasing negative energy through exercise and replacing it with positive.

Meditating is an excellent form of exercise for someone who has been depressed, or is down and out. Your mind needs time out sometimes and meditation is a good way of clearing your mind of all the negative thoughts. Combine this with deep breathing and your mind, body and spirit will benefit immensely. Do this twice a day to start with until you start to feel better and then you can do it when you feel the need to.

Relaxing in hot sea salt baths is also an excellent way to release negative energy and boost the positive energy. You can also combine this with candles and meditation for the ultimate relaxation experience.Believe it or not, one of the best ways to look after yourself is to write, on a daily basis, in a journal. It can help you to touch base with your feelings and your emotions. It can also help you to see yourself on an objective basis and see where you need to change things.

Getting out about in nature can be of tremendous help. Nature is one of the biggest healers; along with time, and the more you are in it, the more you will feel its power healing you. Walk in meadows, in the woods, by a river or stream. Just sit and watch the stream, listen to the birds and the other sounds and signs of nature and you will begin to feel an inner peace you thought you had lost, forever. The most important thing is, no matter how you do it, to take time out for you. Everything I have talked about here needs commitment from you and now is the best time to start looking after you for a change.

Put yourself above everything for a time. Buy yourself treats, go for a massage, eat well, and be happy. Go back to college or night school and learn a new subject. Give your life a meaning again, a new direction. In short, when life gives you lemons do not turn your nose up at them – use them to make lemonade with and enjoy what you have.

Step 7 – Go Out Into the World Again

Hibernating at home, shut away from the world will only serve a purpose for a short time. The longer you stay like that, the harder it will be to face the world again so the sooner you do it, the better. This time, you will step out with your head held high. You must reconnect with positive people and you can do this in a number of ways. Go to a spiritual growth class to start with; it will help you to bring back that positive energy.

Volunteer at a place that needs you, a cause that needs your help, and one that you believe in. Doing something for others can help you to feel better about yourself and it's a great way to get out and meet new people. Your compassion for other people will show through and you will benefit from the way that makes you feel.

If you find that you cannot do it, you can't take that first step then you may need to consider seeking help in the form of therapy of some kind. Do be sure to find a counselor who specializes in or at least has some knowledge of narcissism and the way it affects victims. They are the only ones who can possibly understand what you are going through and how you feel. You could look on the internet for support groups for victims of narcissistic abuse; these are people who have been through it or are going through it now and they can be of tremendous help to you. Fill up your spare time with positive things, go out, see people, and generally get back into the land of the living. Take yourself off to the movies, to a restaurant for a nice meal. Go to places where you can meet new people. You could even go on a short vacation to a retreat somewhere. Whatever you, you need to get out from inside your head, especially while you are in the healing phases.

Make a list of all the things you have ever wanted to do. Put them in order of those that are easily achievable down to those that may be more difficult. Now write down what is stopping you from doing these things. Find a way around what is stopping you and do it.

Live your life in ways you have never been able to do before. Get out and be seen. Be heard and take up your rightful place on this earth. Live your life the way you want to and be positive above all else. Life really is only what you make of it. Forgive yourself for everything that you have done in the past and that includes letting yourself be badly treated and abused. Let go of the past and embrace the future and remember this – it is not your fault. It never was. You cannot win in a relationship with a narcissist; all you can do is break free and walk on.

Conclusion

Narcissism has been around for a long time,but it is only recently being given the attention that it deserves as concerns recovery from such abuse. Narcissus was the first indication in the history of a person that was in love with themselves to the extent they wanted to have a romantic relationship with their reflection. This book considers the history and theories of narcissism before elaborating on narcissistic abuse and the means that a person can use to recover from such treatment. There are different approaches as to why narcissism starts in individuals from the time of childhood. These would be the object relations and social learning constructs. In the former case, the individual is nurtured in an environment where the caregivers are quite harsh on everything that they do. The person has no choice but to develop perfectionist tendencies that end up being used for relationships. They also develop a disparaging attitude towards others and measure human value according to their standards. The theory appears to be counter-intuitive,but it results in the same thing which is someone that only considers relationships as a means to an end. The social learning theory considers the entitlement side of narcissists whereby caregivers allow the narcissist to do anything they please during the formative years. In this way, they feel they can get away with anything,and this translates into their worldview as they grow up.

It is no wonder that during relationships they feel a certain sense of entitlement and take advantage of people that have a low self-perception. The book also dispels some myths about narcissists such as the one that they are internally hurting and think very lowly of themselves which is why they manipulate to get what they want. It is not hard to see why this theory is furthered. After all, they have tendencies such as envy and manipulation which are both traits that you would expect to see in a person that has low self-esteem. They are not insecure about their status or appearance. Quite the opposite in fact, as they have high self-esteem and think the world revolves around what they do and what they think. Some narcissists would be described as introverts. This group of narcissists also displays the same tendencies of entitlement and self-regard that the aggressive narcissists have.The net part of the book deals with the types of approaches that narcissists use to be prepared for their advances and avoid the abuse that will follow thereafter. This includes the phases of an interaction with a narcissist. At first, there is a feeling of euphoria that they bring to the interaction. It is like they are too good to be true and they are. They make it very easy to trust them and to make them the center of your world. Because the façade takes a lot of energy to keep up, it can only last for a short time such as weeks or months at most before they snap. This is the beginning of the cycle of abuse that you would be subjected to. The abuse has a cyclical nature.

At one time, it would seem the person is emotionally feeding on your fears, shame and ambition and the next thing is you are suddenly uplifted and become important again. By this time, they will have broken your psyche down so that you are a slave to what they think and say about you. In fact, there are cases where the person's emotional health is so damaged they feel to see any abuse going on,but it is evident in the rest of the world. The narcissist is also intelligent to the point they start to isolate you from others because they know that for the abuse to work uninterrupted, you should not be affirmed by the likes of friends and family that would reinforce your mental and emotional strengths. That also lends to the reason why it is so hard to get over narcissistic abuse. The first thing is you have to accept there is a problem and a problem is a particular person. The second thing is to admit that you have a problem and that is the reason that you are still in a relationship with that particular person. Going forward the book considers different approaches that you can take to sever the connection with the narcissist and then make sure the connection is cut because narcissists keep trying to contact their prey even after they have fallen out. The recovery process seems a bit counter-intuitive,but it is necessary if it is to work. During a relationship with a narcissist, they make sure to break down your patterns of thought to fit what they feel is suitable and they make it so that they want what is best for you. In the end, it becomes baffling as to how they were able to do so much to your emotional health and the harder question is what motivated them to do such a thing to someone.

That is why recovery entails breaking away from the person and steering clear of that person rather than trying to figure out what went wrong. Detachment is better than obsessing and falling back into a cycle that is comparable to addiction. As such, the best way to consider the narcissist is the same way that one would look at cocaine or a predator. The only way forward is to avoid them. Narcissist's relationships operate in such a manner there is a predator and a victim. This is applicable regardless of the interaction between the individuals which can be work-related, social, romantic or transactional. The narcissist views others as potential prey or insignificant in the grand scheme of things. The recovery methods used for narcissistic abuse would be said to be similar to the ones that are used for recovery from post-traumatic stress. It is that bad. As the victim, you are prone to having anxiety attacks or breakdowns once you think about the past interactions. Some of these recovery approaches include EFT which is a way to reduce levels of cortisol, adrenaline and other PTSD symptoms. It also assists in helping with physical manifestations of pain related to narcissistic abuse.

During the time that you had been in the relationship with this person, they separated you from friends and family or tried to limit the connections that you had with the outside forces. It is quite daunting,but after breaking up or severing connection with such a person, it would be advisable to recreate the bonds that you had with particular people in your life that you had lost touch with. This will help with any feelings of obsession or loneliness when you detach from the abuse.

There is a void that is left over after the breakup,and this needs to be filled with something constructive. Otherwise you may fall back to destructive behaviors.

That being said you also need to grieve for your sake. Many are of the perception that if the relationship was a fraud, then it would be pointless to grieve as if the act is giving something to the perpetrator,but this is not the case at all. The purpose of grieving is for you because you would be grieving your feelings which were taken advantage of. The grief is for your mind and emotional health and from there; you can take part in some self-healing approaches which will take you further along the path of recovery. Some of these approaches include exercising and keeping a healthy mental status. Exercising allows your mind to keep fit as well as your physical state. The purpose of working out is also to create a sense of mental discipline that will then instruct your thought process and make you less vulnerable to narcissistic abuse in the future. There is also self-soothing and anchoring which is similar as they tie you down to reality. These activities are meant to give you a sense of security in your thought process and the relationships that you have with other people. Self-reassurance acts as an optimal guidance system.

It makes you sure of yourself and assists in the overall healing process. Recovery from narcissistic abuse takes time and ought to be adopted as a lifestyle because it is meant to rewire the way that you perceive relationships and yourself.

CPSIA information can be obtained
at www.ICGtesting.com
Printed in the USA
BVHW041354121020
590816BV00012B/636

9 781914 028151